Living in Bible Times

Living in Bible Times

F. F. Bosworth and the
Pentecostal Pursuit
of the Supernatural

Christopher J. Richmann

◥PICKWICK *Publications* · Eugene, Oregon

LIVING IN BIBLE TIMES
F. F. Bosworth and the Pentecostal Pursuit of the Supernatural

Copyright © 2020 Christopher J. Richmann. All rights reserved. Except for brief quotations in critical publications or reviews, no part of this book may be reproduced in any manner without prior written permission from the publisher. Write: Permissions, Wipf and Stock Publishers, 199 W. 8th Ave., Suite 3, Eugene, OR 97401.

Pickwick Publications
An Imprint of Wipf and Stock Publishers
199 W. 8th Ave., Suite 3
Eugene, OR 97401

www.wipfandstock.com

PAPERBACK ISBN: 978-1-5326-9404-2
HARDCOVER ISBN: 978-1-5326-9405-9
EBOOK ISBN: 978-1-5326-9406-6

Cataloguing-in-Publication data:

Names: Richmann, Christopher J., author.

Title: Living in Bible times : F. F. Bosworth and the Pentecostal pursuit of the supernatural / Christopher J. Richmann.

Description: Eugene, OR: Pickwick Publications, 2020. | **Includes bibliographical references and index.**

Identifiers: ISBN 978-1-5326-9404-2 (paperback). | ISBN 978-1-5326-9405-9 (hardcover). | ISBN 978-1-5326-9406-6 (ebook).

Subjects: LCSH: Bosworth, F. F.—(Fred Francis)—1877–1958. | Pentecostalism. | Spiritual healing—Christianity. | Evangelist—United States—Biography.

Classification: BV3785 B63 R55 2020 (print). | BV3785 (ebook).

Manufactured in the U.S.A.   JANUARY 7, 2020

Contents

Abbreviations | vi

Introduction | 1
1. The Gospel of the Supernatural | 10
2. A Pentecostal Leader-in-the-Making | 39
3. Emboldened and Empowered to Preach, 1907–1913 | 67
4. Organizations and Orthodoxy, 1914–1918 | 92
5. The Healing Evangelist, 1919–1932 | 132
6. The Lost Years, 1933–1947 | 170
7. The Voice of Healing Years, 1948–1958 | 193
8. Theologian of the Supernatural Gospel | 221

Conclusion | 243

Bibliography | 247
Index | 289

Abbreviations

C&MA	Christian and Missionary Alliance
FGBMFI	Full Gospel Business Men's Fellowship International
MEC	Methodist Episcopal Church
NHA	National Holiness Association

Introduction

> For, after all the facts and functions of religion are reduced to a second-hand character—a reported history, a contrived and reasoned dogma, a drill of observances, where no fire burns, and no glimpses into eternity are opened by visions and revelations of the Lord, or where no God appears to be found, who is nigh enough to support expectation in His worshippers—then, at length, even the outer people of unbelief begin to ache in the sense of vacuity, and there, not unlikely, the pain is first felt. Their religious and supernatural instincts have been so long defrauded, that it would be a kind of satisfaction to get the silence broken, if only by some vision of a ghost—anything to show or set open the world unknown ... But the Church also, or Christian discipleship, after some way out of the dullness of a second-hand faith, and the dryness of a merely reasoned gospel, and many of the most longing, expectant souls, are seen waiting for some livelier, more apostolic demonstrations. They are tired, beyond bearing, of the mere school forms and defined notions; they want some kind of faith that shows God in living commerce with men, such as He vouchsafed them in the former times.
>
> —Horace Bushnell, *Nature and the Supernatural* (1858)[1]

---

1. Bushnell, *Nature and the Supernatural*, 321.

IN APRIL OF 1928, an "old church member" in Rochelle, Illinois, came to the family home of four deaf children, announcing that "if they had faith," God would cure them. She told them to go to Chicago, where an independent pentecostal evangelist named F. F. Bosworth was holding services at Paul Rader's Gospel Tabernacle, an independent full gospel church whose pastor had formerly been president of the Christian and Missionary Alliance. Bosworth had already healed thousands, she claimed. The four children, whose ages spanned fifteen to twenty-three, were sent to Chicago, along with two others who were their classmates at a school for the deaf. At the service, the six came to the platform when Bosworth asked "if any sick or infirm wished to be prayed for." All six testified to instantaneous healing and could be heard later at a local Baptist church repeating "over and over the simplest words as their teacher encouraged them." "Soon they will know the whole alphabet," brimmed their teacher Gertrude Virgin in a newspaper interview, "and will be able to talk."[2] Recalling the scene thirty years later, David du Plessis, a pentecostal minister and well-known ecumenist, claimed that the school for these six children had to be closed since they no longer had any deaf students to teach.[3] The scene was not completely jubilant, however. After reading the newspaper story of the healings, an incredulous South Dakota rancher challenged Bosworth through the offices of the *Chicago Daily News* to a $25,000 wager. The rancher was certain Bosworth could furnish no proof that the children had been cured. The family doctor for four of the children agreed that about a week after the supposed healing "the children tested just as they always have." For his part, Bosworth responded that the rancher was "totally ignorant of what the gospel has to offer" and stuck by the healings, as did the children's parents.[4]

F. F. Bosworth (1877–1958) was a high profile and influential leader in American pentecostalism. The pentecostalism he proffered centered on experience of the supernatural—like the healing of six deaf children—rather than doctrinal purity or denominational loyalty. Bosworth conducted his healing ministry with full confidence that God was continually active in the world—a position that illumined his theology of healing and spirit-baptism as well as his understanding of biblical prophecy. Despite his lack of long-term affiliation with any of the pentecostal denominations, Bosworth was one of the most celebrated pentecostal figures of the 1910s and 1920s, as

2. "Six Able to Speak and Hear," sec. 1, 7.
3. *World-wide Revival*, April 1958, 10.
4. "Ranchman Offers $25,000 Wager," 7.

seen in the fact that none other than David du Plessis—"Mr. Pentecost" to the second and third generations of pentecostals worldwide—reflected with awe on Bosworth's work and legacy. Furthermore, Bosworth's work brought pentecostalism to the attention of the wider public: secular newspapers like the *Los Angeles Times* quoted above and the *Chicago Daily News* reported on the healing. Such attention highlighted the key themes of pentecostalism's cultural importance: celebrated supernatural activity, controversy with an unbelieving public, and tension with the medical community. Yet except for his role in an early doctrinal controversy over speaking in tongues and his support of the new generation of healing evangelists in the 1940s and 1950s, scholars have generally placed Bosworth on the periphery of the American pentecostal story. The sources, however, indicate that Bosworth is a central figure, because of his interactions with the major figures and institutions of pentecostalism, his remarkable success in pentecostal ministry, and his continuing impact on pentecostal identity through his writings and the work of those he influenced.

In many ways, Bosworth's story is typical of those who generally sit at the center of the pentecostal narrative. Like most early pentecostals, Bosworth participated in the late-nineteenth-century holiness and divine healing movements, experiencing his own healing of tuberculosis by the itinerant faith healer Mattie Perry. Like several other leaders, Bosworth was closely associated with the flamboyant healer John Alexander Dowie, who at the turn of the century established a utopian mecca of healing at Zion City, Illinois, just north of Chicago. In 1906, Bosworth experienced spirit-baptism and tongues under Charles Parham, famed (or notorious) as the doctrinal innovator of the early pentecostal movement. Bosworth affiliated occasionally with the Christian and Missionary Alliance (C&MA), the interdenominational holiness group that produced many important pentecostal leaders. Finally, Bosworth was a founding delegate and early presbyter of the Assemblies of God, which in 1914 became the main organizational force for pentecostalism in the Midwest and grew to become the largest pentecostal denomination in the United States.

In other ways, however, Bosworth's story is atypical. He left the Assemblies of God in 1918 over its teaching on tongues as the initial physical sign of spirit-baptism. Many criticized his "confession" doctrine—a claim that faith, particularly when spoken, can seize earthly blessings. Bosworth embraced the maligned British-Israel theory, a type of premillennial eschatology that contradicted the dispensationalism of most pentecostals. Late in his life, Bosworth assisted the controversial postwar healer William Branham. Bosworth's similarities to other early pentecostals place him firmly in the pentecostal story. His differences challenge and complexify the traditional narrative.

The dominant interpretations of pentecostalism rely either on the doctrine of tongues as initial evidence of baptism of the Holy Spirit formulated by Charles Parham in 1901 or historical connections to the Azusa Street revival (1906–1909) to distinguish pentecostalism from other religious traditions.[5] Such interpretations reinforce (intentionally or not) a denominationally-centered understanding of pentecostalism. Bosworth had no strong ties to Azusa Street, he openly disagreed with the initial evidence teaching, and he had no durable connection to any pentecostal denomination. And Bosworth's is not the only story that challenges traditional categories. Even the key early leaders Charles Parham and William Seymour were never part of the so-called classical pentecostal denominations. Other important early pentecostal leaders—like John G. Lake, Maria Woodworth-Etter and Carrie Judd Montgomery—worked from beyond the bounds of the pentecostal denominations, and until recently, have been largely overlooked by historians. Along with these others, Bosworth's story forces us to look beyond the traditional markers of identity for the distinguishing feature of pentecostalism. As the six deaf children who attended the Chicago meeting in 1928 knew, Bosworth's work centered on the ministry of supernatural healing. A recurring theme in this book, therefore, is that pentecostalism's distinctive core, driving impulse, and cultural significance is found not in the doctrine of initial evidence or the legacy of Azusa Street, but in the quest for the supernatural that was inherited from the radical holiness movement of the late nineteenth century.

Identifying the pursuit of the supernatural as the heart of pentecostalism draws attention to the continuity of the pentecostal story. The "Apostolic Faith" movement that would become known as pentecostalism was not some "sacred meteor"[6] untouched by terrestrial forces and later necessitating protection by denominational Kaabas, but a tree in the garden of the intense supernaturalism of the holiness and divine healing movements that thrived at the margins of American Protestantism in the late nineteenth century. Likewise, the mid-century waves of heightened supernaturalism that flowed beyond the pentecostal denominations—such as the Latter Rain movement, the postwar healing revival, and the charismatic movement—are not historical peculiarities,[7] but the natural flow of the pentecostal impulse. In this

---

5. A thorough case is made for the Parham-tongues thesis by Goff, *Fields White Unto Harvest*. For the Azusa thesis, see Robeck, *Azusa Street Mission and Revival*, and, more recently, Espinosa, *William J. Seymour*.

6. See Wacker, "Are the Golden Oldies Still Worth Playing?," 86.

7. The postwar healing movement is often described with words like "explosion."

light, Bosworth stands as a quintessential pentecostal especially deserving of study—for only Bosworth was a living and influential link between the nineteenth century divine healing movement, the pentecostal revival of the early 1900s, and the postwar healing revival. It should come as no surprise, then, that the pursuit of the supernatural is a useful guiding theme for understanding Bosworth's thought and impact on American religious history.

This book seeks to continue the work of scholars who have seen beyond traditional categories. Fruitful approaches focus on the relationship between early pentecostalism and American culture, deemphasize or reassess tongues in the explanation of pentecostalism's emergence, emphasize divine healing as pentecostalism's chief contribution in the twentieth century, and stress the symbolic rather than direct institutional impact of the Azusa Street revival.[8] The charismatic movement of the 1960s and 1970s forced a widening of traditional categories by revealing that believers outside the pentecostal denominations could adopt pentecostal beliefs and practices. But still left out of this discussion of pentecostal identity are earlier figures—like Bosworth—who carried on the pentecostal quest for the supernatural from outside pentecostal denominations. In fact, in major studies of pentecostalism, Bosworth has received little attention, with most writers focusing narrowly on Bosworth's struggle with Assemblies of God leadership over the initial evidence doctrine[9] and a few analyzing Bosworth's thought more closely but lacking adequate historical context.[10]

In this book, "supernatural" refers to perceptible manifestations of divine activity.[11] In part, this means that such occurrences require no sophisticated theological interpretation, as necessitated, for instance, in recognizing suffering as God's will. A corollary to "perceptible" is "immediate"; while believers did not always insist that God's work should be instantaneous, they tended to stress the present, as opposed to future dimension of blessing. As pentecostal evangelist Aimee Semple McPherson

---

See, for example, Synan, *Holiness-Pentecostal Tradition*, 213.

8. Wacker, *Heaven Below*; Dayton, *Theological Roots of Pentecostalism*; Friesen, *Norming the Abnormal*; Robinson, *Divine Healing*; Creech, "Visions of Glory," 405–24.

9. Brumback, *Suddenly . . . from Heaven*, 216–25; Menzies, *Anointed to Serve*, 124–30; Synan, *Holiness-Pentecostal Tradition*, 164; Blumhofer, *Restoring the Faith*, 135–37; Robeck, "An Emerging Magisterium?," 164–215: McGee, ed., *Initial Evidence*, 104, 109, 110, 118, 119, 124, 126, 130, 132, 187.

10. Jacobsen, *Thinking in the Spirit*, 287–313; Barnes, *F. F. Bosworth*; Hejzlar, *Two Paradigms for Divine Healing*.

11. This definition bears some resemblance and owes some debt to the concept of "primal spirituality" as used by Cox, *Fire from Heaven*, 81, and to the notion of "primitivism" in Wacker, *Heaven Below*, 12.

preached repeatedly, "God's time is now."[12] Supernatural works in this context are generally attributed to God and for the benefit of believers or the spread of their message. This definition also encompasses works of God that demonstrated God's wrath or the fulfillment of prophecy in tragedy. From Frank Bartlemann's tracts on the San Francisco earthquake of 1906 to Pat Robertson's televised pontifications on the 2010 earthquake in Haiti, pentecostals have been quicker than most Christians confidently to identify God's direct intervention, even in calamity. Furthermore, the pentecostal impulse also drives toward identification of demonic activity as a correlate to divine activity.

Supernaturalism includes foremost the spiritual gifts as listed in 2 Corinthians 12:8–11 and miracles like those performed by Jesus and the apostles in the New Testament. But the concept also encompasses a wider range of phenomena that is less biblically-grounded, suggesting that the subjective experience of the supernatural is more important than objective definitions. For instance, falling "under the power" (in the words of holiness-turned-pentecostal evangelist Maria Woodworth-Etter) and the ability to discern illness through a vibrating left hand (as postwar healing evangelist William Branham claimed), as well as relying on God miraculously to provide finances or instantaneous words for a sermon are just as much part of pentecostal supernaturalism as prophecy or speaking in tongues. While pentecostals sought to justify their experience of the supernatural in biblical terms, such apologetics were secondary to the experience itself; a range of mystical experiences and miracles classify as supernaturalism.[13] Broadly speaking, mystical experiences were a protest against the "formalism" of the churches, while miracles were a protest against an overly scientific approach to epistemology. But these distinctions were not always so clear to the holiness and pentecostal adherents who centered their religion on experience of the supernatural.

Supernaturalism is a contested category, and this is no less true in the study of the holiness and pentecostal movements. Some commentators deny the label to those forms of divine healing, such as that which prevailed in the 1870s, that stressed healing as a natural consequence of atonement and faith, rather than a dramatic act of divine intervention.[14] But this is to read forward into Victorian religion a particular Enlightenment definition of miracles—a definition that made "promise" and "miracle" incompatible:

12. McPherson, *This Is That*, 416, 432, 446.

13. For an insightful history of Protestant mystical experience and its apologists and adversaries in the English-speaking world, see Taves, *Fits, Trances, & Visions*. For debates on miracles, see Mullin, *Miracles and the Modern Religious Imagination*.

14. Opp, *Lord for the Body*.

since God's promise was a type of law, maintaining that God promised a miracle would be like maintaining that God established a law to violate his law. But as Robert Bruce Mullin notes, beginning in the mid-nineteenth century, the traditional Enlightenment definition had been losing ground.[15] As a result, the relationship between law and the supernatural was ambiguous and sometimes contradictory. A. J. Gordon, one of the most ardent proponents of healing in the atonement, subtitled his apologetic for divine healing "*Miracles* of Cure in All Ages" and argued that miracles were "supernatural" but not "contranatural."[16]

Divine healing was not the only late Victorian theology of healing that struggled with the categories of natural and supernatural. Mary Baker Eddy, the founder of Christian Science and proponent of the most law-centered theological exposition of healing, described her own healing: "I could not explain the *modus* of my relief. I could only assure [the homeopathic physician in attendance] that the divine Spirit had wrought a miracle—a miracle which I later found to be in perfect scientific accord with divine law."[17] Divine actions like healing were supernatural because of their spectacular character, notwithstanding fine philosophical points about whether they violated natural laws. Our understanding of disease, disabilities, and medical care has changed significantly in the years since the experiences of those recorded in this book. For instance, many today would no longer view deafness as an infirmity in need of "healing." But rather than pour their experiences through the sieve of modern science, I have chosen to let both healer and healed speak on their own terms. For the purposes of this study, what matters is less what medically happened and more what the experiences meant for the holiness and pentecostal saints involved. In short, these experiences meant what Horace Bushnell prophetically described: a "faith that shows God in living commerce with men such as He vouchsafed them in the former times." The pursuit of such a faith developed from holiness perfectionism and became essential to pentecostalism. In framing the discussion this way, we can maintain the continuity between nineteenth century and later pentecostal understandings of supernaturalism, without neglecting important shifts.

Bosworth's life provides the structure of this book. Chapter one will review the holiness movement, divine healing, premillennialism, and early pentecostalism. This chapter will argue that the unifying theme of these

15. Mullin, *Miracles and the Modern Religious Imagination*, 192.

16. Gordon, *Ministry of Healing*, 22, 44; emphasis added. See also Baer, "Perfectly Empowered Bodies," 145.

17. Eddy, *Retrospection and Introspection*, 38–39; Gill, *Mary Baker Eddy*, 163.

movements was a quest for the supernatural. This chapter will also provide the broader historical context for Bosworth's religious development.

Chapter two will treat Bosworth's life from birth to 1906—the year of his spirit-baptism under Charles Parham's ministry. Through his interactions with holiness Methodism and divine healing, Bosworth emerges as a typical pentecostal leader-in-the-making. His experience mirrors that of other important early pentecostals—like Marie Burgess and John G. Lake—who, like Bosworth, had no substantial ties to Azusa Street. Consequently, links to Azusa Street are more limited in their historical importance than most historians acknowledge.

Chapter three will cover 1906 to 1914, showing Bosworth to be one of the most influential pentecostals in the pre-denominational phase. The 1912 revival in Dallas that Bosworth facilitated with the help of Maria Woodworth-Etter contributed to many crucial developments in early pentecostalism and importantly refocused the pentecostal movement on experience of the supernatural during a time of doctrinal controversy. This revival also raised Bosworth's stature in the movement and cast him as an expert in revivalism.

Chapter four will treat 1914 to 1918—the year Bosworth resigned from the Assemblies of God. In addition to outlining Bosworth's pastoral, evangelistic and denominational work during this period, this chapter will cover Bosworth's role in the initial evidence controversy, arguing that early pentecostals held a range of views on speaking in tongues and that many resisted the initial evidence teaching. Accordingly, tongues alone is not an adequate identifier of the pentecostal impulse, and the definitions of classical pentecostalism that are built on the initial evidence teaching are historically suspect. Finally, I will argue that while speaking in tongues was a key component of pentecostal supernaturalism, the initial evidence doctrine reflected social, rather than spiritual concerns.

Chapter five covers 1919 to 1932—the year of Bosworth's last widely-publicized campaign before World War II. Even though he did not belong to a pentecostal denomination, Bosworth continued to bear all the marks of pentecostal spirituality. Noting Bosworth's role in the healing revival of the 1920s, this chapter will use Bosworth as a lens for investigating the culture of divine healing, the developing relationship between divine healing and medicine, and the role of pentecostal supernaturalism in the modernist-fundamentalist debates. A thorough investigation of the context for the appearance of Bosworth's *Christ the Healer* (1924) will shed light on the interactions between full gospel adherents and fundamentalists.

Chapter six will cover 1933 to 1944. In Bosworth scholarship, these are essentially "lost years," as no direct sources for Bosworth's activities have yet been uncovered. Other scholars have referred only obliquely to this period, during which Bosworth adopted the controversial British-Israel theory. Through a recovery of three writings from Bosworth dated to this period and numerous references to his activities in a British-Israel periodical and in secular newspapers, I will show that Bosworth remained active, though on a much smaller scale. Furthermore, an investigation of British-Israelism will reveal that although censured by other pentecostals, the doctrine is not contradictory to pentecostalism but served as a non-dispensationalist argument for scriptural authority and premillennialism.

Chapter seven will cover the last decade of Bosworth's life (1948–1958). Bosworth's work with the emerging celebrities of the postwar healing revival demonstrates his continued ability to reflect and shape the main impulses of pentecostalism. I will argue that Bosworth was the major stream through which extra-denominational, supernaturalist pentecostalism flowed into the healing revivals and the charismatic movement.

Chapter eight will treat Bosworth's thought. I argue that Bosworth's thought is unified by a belief in the continuity of God's activity. Therefore, he criticized cessationism (relegating miracles to the past) and futurism (relegating fulfillment of prophecy to the future). His British-Israelism parallels his belief that Christ heals in the present as in the past. I will identify the theological pillars of Bosworth's doctrine of healing and argue that it was a scriptural response to emerging modernism and fundamentalism. This chapter will also offer a historical analysis of Bosworth's healing doctrine, arguing that he popularized much of the thought of metaphysically-tinged Baptist E. W. Kenyon and that his work in the postwar healing revival marks him as an architect of the prosperity gospel.

Identifying three themes from Bosworth's story, the conclusion will summarize the study and contend that he embodied and helped shape pentecostal identity. First, Bosworth's career provides the most direct and identifiable bridge between the two paramount moments of pentecostal history: the revivals of the early twentieth century and the postwar healing campaigns. Second, Bosworth's unpopular theological positions highlight the theme of independent thinking that characterizes pentecostalism. Finally, Bosworth's success was due to his healing ministry more so than his reputation as a preacher, his theological acumen, or his denominational loyalty. This suggests what the six deaf children on the platform in Bosworth's healing service in 1928 knew well—that pentecostalism's driving impulse and cultural impact is centered on experience of the supernatural, with healing as its common expression.

1

The Gospel of the Supernatural

> The characterizing feature, and that wherein we differ from evangelical churches of the present day, is in the belief that Pentecost can be repeated the same as recorded in the Acts of the Apostles, with all the accompanying signs, manifestations, operations and gifts of the Spirit. It is this supernatural, divine element in the Movement that has attracted attention and held spellbound such a multitude of people.
>
> —R. E. McAlister, *The Pentecostal Movement* (ca. 1916)[1]

THE HOLINESS MOVEMENT

JOHN WESLEY EMPHASIZED A decidedly this-worldly element in soteriology that he called Christian perfection. Influenced by Anglican divine William Law, Moravians in England and on the continent, and his reading of the church fathers, Wesley's stress on sanctification was not new, but his confidence that it could be fully attained in the present life was. He challenged the traditional Reformation teaching on total depravity with its correlate that the Christian remains a sinner in life while also justified by faith. Wesley believed that with the grace of God, Christians could attain a state in which one no longer sinned. This perfection is not

---

1. McAlister, *Pentecostal Movement*.

freedom from ignorance or mistake, as Wesley carefully defined sin as "a voluntary transgression of a known law."[2] According to Wesley, few had experienced this salvation from sin, and "some who once enjoyed full salvation have now totally lost it."[3] In other words, sanctification was a rare gift, and vigilance was required to maintain it. Wesley believed that in most cases sanctification happened at death or very near to it. But he also allowed that it may happen soon after conversion. And while the cessation of sin was by definition a moment—or instant—in time, Wesley frequently spoke of the process of gradual progress as well as continuing growth after the moment of sanctification.[4]

Wesley called Christian perfection the "grand depositum" of the Methodists, their distinctive witness to the world. But by the 1830s, some Methodists in America worried that the teaching and experience was beginning to disappear. This was coupled with rising concerns over the wealth and worldliness of Methodist congregations, especially those in the cities. A push for a renewed emphasis on holiness came from three main sources.

Timothy Merritt began publication of *Guide to Christian Perfection* in Boston in 1839. The magazine was a product of Merritt's desire to fulfill Wesley's dream that "sanctifications would be as common as conversions," but it was also a response to growing interest in Christian perfection among a scattering of New England churches beginning in 1837.[5] The *Guide* quickly became the main promoter and vehicle for the early American holiness movement.

Phoebe Palmer testified to the experience of entire sanctification in 1835. Her sister, Sarah Lankford, had also experienced the blessing earlier that year and had quickly organized in her New York home "Tuesday Meetings for the Promotion of Holiness." Although Lankford had the crucial organizational instinct, Palmer's struggle to attain and her determination to articulate the experience of sanctification were essential to the formulation of holiness doctrine that stirred believers across the country.

Palmer modified Wesley's teaching on sanctification by stressing its instantaneous nature, insisting that it should happen early in the Christian life, and systematizing the process whereby it is attained.[6] According to

2. Wesley, *Works of John Wesley*, VI: 2–3, 417.
3. Wesley, *Works of John Wesley*, VI: 419.
4. Dayton, *Theological Roots of Pentecostalism*, 48; Walters, "Concept of Attainment," 12–29; Wood, "Origin, Development, and Consistency," 33–55 (49).
5. Dieter, *Holiness Revival of the Nineteenth Century*, 1–3.
6. White, "Beauty of Holiness," 24–27; Peters, *Christian Perfection and American Methodism*, 190; Lowery, "Fork in the Wesleyan Road," 187–222.

Palmer's reading of a hodgepodge of biblical texts, those who consecrate themselves fully to God, have faith for the blessing of sanctification, and testify to its reality were guaranteed the experience. "All that remains," she said, "is for you to come complying with the conditions and claim it . . . it is already yours. If you do not now receive it, the delay will not be on the part of God, but wholly with yourself."[7] In Palmer's holiness theology, the ambivalence and apprehension of Wesley were gone. As Methodist elder and editor of the *Christian Advocate* Nathan Bangs pointed out, Palmer's "altar terminology" threatened to erode Wesley's focus on the witness of the Spirit in favor of potentially self-deluding "naked faith."[8] Nevertheless, Palmer's theology set the tone for the holiness revival as she took lead of the Tuesday meetings in 1837 (and opened the meetings to men in 1839), published a number of treatises on holiness, and evangelized for the holiness cause.

The third impetus of the holiness revival came from the Reformed wing of American evangelicalism. Since the 1730s, Calvinist doctrines had suffered permutations on American soil to reconcile them with the reality of revivalism. The trajectory set by Jonathan Edwards was extended by the New Divinity men and culminated in the New Haven theology of Nathaniel Taylor. Taylor argued that "sin is in the sinning," and that humans, despite being thoroughly sinful, have "power to the contrary." Charles Finney combined the New Haven theology openness to the power of human will with an intense interest in Christian perfection. As a pastor in New York in 1833, Finney came into contact with the ideas of the New Haven Perfectionists, a group formed around the teachings of Taylor's student John Humphrey Noyes that would eventually settle in a utopian community in Oneida. Finney was intrigued by their teachings, but also discerned their errors. In the meantime, Finney's colleague at Oberlin College Asa Mahan had been unsettled by a student who asked "what degree of sanctification we may expect from [Christ]."[9] The two formulated what would be known as Oberlin Perfectionism in *Lectures to Professing Christians* in the winter of 1836–1837.

In 1838, the *Oberlin Evangelist* began publication to explain and spread the Oberlin style of Christian perfection. Finney and Mahan had read Wesley's *Plain Account of Christian Perfection*. But the Oberlin leaders differed from Wesleyan perfectionism in the central role they gave to the intellect, human will, and natural ability and their practical ethical focus on

---

7. Dieter, *Holiness Revival of the Nineteenth Century*, 24.
8. Dieter, *Holiness Revival of the Nineteenth Century*, 24–26.
9. Mahan, *Scripture Doctrine of Christian Perfection*, 232.

"disinterested benevolence"—emphases they inherited from New Divinity theology.[10]

The Oberlin theology created controversy in Calvinist circles and influenced Methodist theologies of sanctification, but as a distinct thread of the holiness revival, it was short lived. The importance of Oberlin perfectionism lies in its demonstration that Methodists would not have a monopoly on Christian perfection. Thomas Upham, a Congregationalist minister, was converted to Palmer's teachings in 1839 and combined Wesleyan sanctification with a love for Catholic mysticism. A. B. Earle, a Baptist evangelist, experienced sanctification in 1859. He preferred to speak of the second blessing as the "rest of faith." William Boardman read the writings of Finney and Mahan, professed the second blessing, and entered Lane Seminary in 1843 to prepare for the Presbyterian ministry. Prizing the experience over theory, Boardman popularized holiness by adopting more neutral language. His *Higher Christian Life* (1858) was published at the height of the "Businessmen's Revival," which also benefited from the evangelistic work of Palmer, Finney, and Earle. All this cemented a relationship between evangelical religion and sanctification that would last the next four decades.

While entire sanctification began to permeate evangelicalism, Methodists continued to view it as their special privilege and responsibility. Some tension among Methodists over the teaching was apparent in an address to the 1852 General Conference that warned against "new theories, new expressions, and new measures" in the doctrine of sanctification.[11] Such disagreements also played a role in the formation of the Free Methodists in 1860. A new phase began with the 1867 General Camp Meeting for the Promotion of Holiness at Vineland, New Jersey, which spawned the National Holiness Association (NHA). The chief organizer was John Inskip, a disciple of Palmer. Many of the leaders kept cordial ties with the Methodist Episcopal Church (MEC), but the threat of divisiveness appeared occasionally. Most often the friction was not doctrinal, but ecclesial. Within a few years of the 1867 camp meeting, regional holiness associations began to appear. Beginning in the 1880s, some associations began to operate as denominations by forming churches, ordaining ministers, and issuing literature.[12] This is partly explained by the fact that many holiness adherents were also recent converts who had less patience than longtime Methodists for reforming the

---

10. Guelzo, "Oberlin Perfectionism and Its Edwardsian Origins," 159–74.

11. Cited in Smith, *Revivalism and Social Reform*, 128.

12. See Jones, *Perfectionist Persuasion*, 58; Dieter, *Holiness Revival of the Nineteenth Century*, 223.

church from within.[13] In search of order and unity, General Holiness Conventions were held at Cincinnati and New York in 1877. The MEC did not participate, indicating a growing rift.

While American Methodists were in a state of dilemma, the holiness seed flowered in England. The Quaker Hannah Whitall Smith had been converted during the revival of 1858. She publicized a less-crisis-oriented brand of holiness in her wildly popular *The Christian's Secret of a Happy Life* (1875). The Smiths began to minister in England in 1873. Along with Asa Mahan and William Boardman, they were central to the Oxford Union Meeting for the Promotion of Holiness of 1874. The holiness movement in England was denominationally broader than its American counterpart, and theologically expressed itself more along the lines of "higher life" popularized by Boardman, who spent the last decade of his life in England engaged in the ministry of divine healing. While Wesleyan holiness advocates tended to speak of sanctification in terms of the eradication of inbred sin, higher life adherents envisioned sanctification as suppression of sin and spiritual empowerment. The success of the Oxford meeting led to the most important development in the British movement: the Keswick Convention of 1875.

Animated in large part by American higher life advocates, the Keswick movement, with its annual meeting for the "promotion of scriptural holiness," stimulated a new phase of the American holiness movement. D. L. Moody, who had been central to the evangelical and higher life consensus that produced the first Keswick convention, returned to the United States in 1875 and inaugurated his own Keswick-style convention at Northfield, Massachusetts, in 1880. Moody also worked closely with the British higher life Baptist F. B. Meyer, who evangelized widely in the United States in the 1890s.

One of the most important leaders of the higher life movement was A. B. Simpson, a Presbyterian minister who experienced the second blessing upon reading Boardman's *The Higher Christian Life* in 1873. Simpson also experienced a miraculous healing in 1881 and subsequently resigned from his New York pastorate. An indefatigable organizer, Simpson founded two organizations in 1887, the Christian Alliance for domestic work, and the Missionary Alliance for overseas evangelism. In 1897, these organizations united to become the Christian and Missionary Alliance (C&MA), which by the 1910s had become functionally a denomination.

By the 1890s, the trickles of Methodists leaving their denomination in the name of holiness became a river. Twenty-three new holiness

---

13. Jones, *Perfectionist Persuasion*, 57, 90.

denominations were formed during the decade.[14] Much of the rationale for this "come-outism" came from Daniel S. Warner, who was stripped of his ministerial license in the Winebrennarian Church of God in 1878 for preaching holiness. He began to see denominations as the enemy:

> the Lord showed me that holiness could never prosper upon sectarian soil encumbered by human creeds and party names, and he gave me a new commission to join holiness and all truth together and build up the apostolic church of the living God. Praise His name! I will obey him.[15]

Warner "sought to apply the logic of Christian perfection . . . to the church question."[16] His 1880 *Bible Proofs of the Second Work of Grace* expressed his wish that "the blood of Christ may reach and wash away every vestige of denominational distinction . . ."[17] By equating denominations with sin, Warner supplied the theological justification for the holiness exodus from the denominations. Ironically, the Church of God Reformation Movement sparked by Warner's work went on to become one of the largest holiness denominations. In 1891, John P. Brooks wrote *The Divine Church*, considered by some scholars "the textbook" of come-outism.[18] Brooks was a leader in the movement of independent holiness churches arising from the Southwest Association for the Promotion of Holiness in 1883. "Holiness," Brooks wrote, "can no more be subjugated to sectarian domination."[19] Like Warner, Brooks considered denominationalism not just a hindrance to holiness, but its chief enemy.

Animosities heightened in 1894 when the MEC revised the *Discipline* to give local pastors more control over their territories and curtail the activities of itinerant evangelists. This action took aim at holiness preachers, who thrived on a traveling ministry. The differences between holiness adherents and other Methodists had become blatantly clear to one writer in the *Wesleyan Christian Advocate*: "They preach a different doctrine . . . ; they sing different songs, they patronize and circulate different literature; they have adopted radically different forms of worship."[20] Furthermore, as many holiness adherents had adopted premillennialism and divine healing, their

---

14. Robinson, *Divine Healing: The Holiness-Pentecostal Transition Years*, xiii.
15. Cited in Dieter, *Holiness Revival of the Nineteenth Century*, 209.
16. Dieter, *Holiness Revival of the Nineteenth Century*, 208.
17. Ware, *Restorationism in the Holiness Movement*, 43.
18. Ware, *Restorationism in the Holiness Movement*, 43.
19. Cited in Ware, *Restorationism in the Holiness Movement*, 51.
20. Cited in Stephens, *Fire Spreads*, 141.

decision to leave institutional Methodism was eased by the denominational resistance to these teachings. James Buckley became editor of the flagship Methodist periodical the *Christian Advocate* in 1880 and came out strongly against divine healing, calling it an "absurdity."[21] In 1897, the NHA banned discussion of these and other "side-track" issues.[22]

Facing such resistance, holiness advocates like A. B. Crumpler argued that new groups were needed for "those who had been saved and sanctified, many of whom belonged to no church, and many of whom had been turned out of their churches for professing holiness."[23] The Cincinnati minister Martin Wells Knapp formed the International Holiness Union and Prayer League in Cincinnati in 1897 and finally left the MEC in 1901, clashing with his denomination over his commitment to premillennialism and his interracial services. The Pilgrim Holiness Church traces its lineage to Knapp's work, as does the Metropolitan Christian Association, or "Burning Bush Movement." In 1894, California holiness preacher Phineas Bresee left the MEC to found the Pentecostal Church of the Nazarene (they dropped "Pentecostal" from their name in 1919), which became one of the largest holiness denominations in the world.

Holiness concerns were not limited to white churches; in addition to interracial ministries like those conducted by Knapp, many predominantly black churches began to gather under the holiness banner. Amanda Berry Smith, a black holiness evangelist with ties to John Inskip, published her influential autobiography in 1893. William E. Fuller worked with B. H. Irwin's Midwest-based Fire-Baptized Holiness Church and eventually formed a separate black version of Irwin's denomination. Charles Mason and Charles Jones came from a Baptist background, and became leaders in the southern black holiness movement, consolidating their work in the Church of God in Christ. The United Holy Church of America formed out of revival meetings of black holiness adherents in North Carolina in the mid-1880s and became one of the earliest holiness denominations to embrace the pentecostal message.[24]

---

21. Cited in Robinson, *Divine Healing: The Holiness-Pentecostal Transition Years*, 185.

22. Brown, *Inskip, McDonald, Fowler*, 250–51. Brown here reproduces a large portion of the 1897 resolutions.

23. Cited in Brown, *Inskip, McDonald, Fowler*, 141.

24. Lovett, "Black Holiness Pentecostalism," 419–28.

SUPERNATURALISM IN THE HOLINESS MOVEMENT

The holiness movement was concerned about more than holiness. Especially in its more radical elements, holiness adherents became some of the chief champions of two new doctrines: premillennialism and divine healing. When combined with sanctification and the deeply-rooted commitment to conversion, this constellation of beliefs became, in A. B. Simpson's words, *The Four Fold Gospel* (1890). The supernaturalism of holiness adherents was not limited to the fourfold gospel, but it received its fullest explication along these *foci*. The fourfold gospel was conceptually held together and made distinct in American religion by its pursuit of the supernatural. Holiness saints were not the only nineteenth-century believers concerned with supernaturalism, but other supernaturally-centered groups, like Adventists and Mormons, had by mid-century routinized and institutionalized their supernatural impulse in a limited prophetic office.[25]

Holiness supernaturalism was rooted in Wesley's stress on sanctification as a present possibility. Influenced by the Enlightenment demand for empirical verification, Wesley raised experience to an unprecedented role in theology.[26] "Whatsoever else it imply," he wrote, sanctification "is a present salvation. It is something attainable, yea, actually attained on earth."[27] This was a divergence from Reformation thought. According to Luther's *simul iustus et peccator*, to be justified by faith is to remain a sinner, trusting in Christ's righteousness rather than evidences of personal righteousness:

> that righteousness is not essentially in us, as the Papists reason out of Aristotle, but without us in the grace of God only and in his imputation; and that there is no essential substance of righteousness in us besides that weak faith or firstfruits of faith, whereby we have begun to apprehend Christ, and yet sin in the meantime remaineth verily in us.[28]

Calvin balanced Luther's hard emphasis on external righteousness by teaching also that the indwelling Christ, through the Holy Spirit, regenerates sinners so that progressively "our will is rendered conformable to God's will." But Calvin also insisted that "until we slough off this mortal body, there remains always in us much imperfection and infirmity, so that we

---

25. Alexander, "Wilford Woodruff and the Changing Nature of Mormon Religious Experience," 56–69. For Adventist concentration of prophecy in the person of Ellen G. White, see Taves, *Fits, Trances, & Visions*, 153–65.

26. Guelzo, "Oberlin Perfectionism and Its Edwardsian Origins," 160.

27. Dayton, *Theological Roots of Pentecostalism*, 47.

28. Luther, "Commentary on Galatians," 131–32.

always remain poor and wretched sinners in the presence of God."[29] For Wesley, on the other hand, a purely imputed righteousness and full sanctification deferred to death were insufficient. Rather, salvation "is not a blessing which lies on the other side of death . . . It is not something at a distance. It is a present thing, a blessing which through the free mercy of God ye are now in possession of."[30] With Wesley began the quest for a perceptible experience of the supernatural.

In America, Wesley's Methodists had enjoyed intense religious experience since the Chesapeake-area revivals of the 1770s. Methodists joined with Presbyterians and Baptists in enjoying physical manifestations of divine activity during the interdenominational frontier camp meetings of the early 1800s. The "jerks," trances, shouting, falling and other displays were recognized as authentic, but not necessary signs that "the power of God came down" for conversion or sanctification. By 1804, Baptists and Presbyterians largely abandoned the camp meeting format that fostered such exercises, while Methodists combined their camp meeting fervor with African spirituality in the shout tradition—an interactive, performative complex that placed ecstatic experiences at the center of the conversion process. Much of the shout tradition ethos was renewed in radical holiness circles of the late nineteenth century.[31]

In reaction to the perceived decline in sanctification experiences in the 1820s and 1830s, Phoebe Palmer and the early holiness movement emphasized the instantaneous and immediate nature of sanctification. That sanctification was expected to happen immediately signaled that holiness was not simply a matter of discipline and obedience. A dramatic infusion of grace became the *sine qua non* of full salvation. Along with the stress on the instantaneous nature of sanctification, the holiness movement expanded on Wesley's teaching by more closely identifying sanctification with baptism in the Holy Spirit and other pentecostal language. Wesley did not stress the Holy Spirit in sanctification,[32] but Wesley's associate John Fletcher made this connection explicit. In the mid-nineteenth century, this spirit-filled language took on a life of its own. Finney was probably the first among American holiness advocates to revive this terminology.[33] He was followed by many holiness adherents, both Methodist and Reformed. The fate of holiness phraseology was sealed when Palmer embraced the pentecostal

---

29. Spitz, ed., "Geneva Confession," 116–17.
30. Cited in Dayton, *Theological Roots of Pentecostalism*, 47.
31. Taves, *Fits, Trances, & Visions*, 76–117; quote from 94.
32. Wood, "Origin, Development, and Consistency," 45–49.
33. Smith, "Doctrine of the Sanctifying Spirit," 92–113, especially 106.

model with *Promise of the Father* (1859). The title of Asa Mahan's *Baptism of the Holy Ghost* (1870) provides a pointed example of this development, as his earlier systematic work on holiness bore the didactic title *The Scripture Doctrine of Christian Perfection* (1839). By the end of the century, holiness periodicals went by the name of *Pentecostal Herald* and *Guide to Holiness and Pentecostal Life,* and holiness books ran under titles like Martin Wells Knapp's *Lightning Bolts from Pentecostal Skies* (1898) and Charles J. Fowler's *Back to Pentecost* (1900).

The linguistic shift from "Christian perfection" to "baptism of the Holy Spirit" has been charted well by Donald Dayton and need not be retraced here.[34] But it should be stressed that the shift was almost total, and this "Pentecostal hermeneutic" reveals a remarkable shift in Protestant approach to scripture from a preference for the didactic Pauline corpus to the narrative Luke-Acts texts.[35] Undoubtedly holiness advocates who were convinced of the doctrine of instantaneous sanctification found a helpful biblical precedent in the Acts 2 narrative, even though "[a] study of the biblical doctrine of 'perfection' does not naturally lead to the account of Pentecost, and vice versa."[36]

The switch to pentecostal language was more than semantics. Rather, "[t]he Pentecostal formulation had its own power that pulled in new directions."[37] All these directions incorporated a heightened expectation of the supernatural. Believers saw sanctification as "an instantaneous bestowal of divine power," and "a more tangible event" than it had been for Wesley.[38] They mused on what manifestations might accompany spirit-baptism, since it came with supernatural effects for the apostles. Additionally, the pentecostal paradigm sharpened eschatological hopes, first of an imminent earthly millennium, and later of an imminent return of Christ. Finally, divine healing emerged as a pillar of the holiness creed in this atmosphere of heightened expectation of the miraculous and focus on Holy Spirit power.

---

34. Dayton, "From Christian Perfection to the 'Baptism of the Holy Ghost,'" 39–54.

35. Dayton, *Theological Roots of Pentecostalism,* 23.

36. Dayton, "Asa Mahan and the Development of American Holiness Theology," 65. As Dayton notes elsewhere, a tension between the Wesleyan cleansing theme and the pentecostal power motif existed throughout the latter half of the nineteenth century, prompting various solutions from the mainstream holiness movement's equating purity to power, to the radical holiness (and later pentecostal) theology of a third blessing, to the higher life/Keswick movement's emphasis of power at the expense of purity. This tension finally helps to explain the pentecostal movement's de-emphasis of sanctification. Dayton, *Theological Roots of Pentecostalism,* 90–106.

37. Dayton, *Theological Roots of Pentecostalism,* 92.

38. Lowery, "Fork in the Wesleyan Road," 191, 192.

Sanctification and Manifestations

Palmer's "shorter way"—which relied on "naked faith" and the "naked word"—was meant to do away with the need for manifestations or evidences of the second blessing, as well as Wesley's ambiguous "witness of the Spirit." But paradoxically, Palmer was not hesitant to relate the spiritual sensations that immediately followed sanctification. "My spirit returned consciously to its source, and rested in the embrace of God," she wrote. "I felt that I was but a drop in the ocean of infinite LOVE, and Christ was all in all."[39] This ambivalence explains why Palmer's method can be seen as both mystical and as a "radical doctrine of *sola scriptura*."[40]

Recourse to pentecostal language only heightened the expectation of a dramatic supernatural experience at the time of sanctification, as seen in Finney's account of his spirit-baptism:

> [T]he Holy Spirit descended upon me in a manner that seemed to go through me, body and soul. I could feel the impression, like a wave of electricity, going through and through me. Indeed it seemed to come in waves and waves of liquid love for I could not express it in any other way. It seemed like the very breath of God. I can recollect distinctly that it seemed to fan me, like immense wings.[41]

Furthermore, since spirit-baptism was "power from on high" for the apostles, the theme of power became more central as the century wore on. As Simpson wrote of sanctification as the indwelling Christ, "[i]t is the only secret of power in your life, and mine, beloved . . . it is true, that God will come to dwell within us, and be the power, and the purity, and the victory, and the joy of your life."[42] Spirit-baptism resulted in supernatural power to live the faithful Christian life.

Claims about the nature and evidence of this power became more specific among the most radical holiness adherents. B. H. Irwin, a key rabble-rouser in the midwestern holiness movement wrote vividly that he was "literally on fire," but felt only "unutterable ecstatic bliss."[43] Competing claims about the meaning and relative merit of such manifestations troubled some. As Charles Parham bemoaned,

39. Cited in White, "What the Holy Spirit Can and Cannot Do," 114; emphasis in original.

40. Heath, *Naked Faith*; Bassett, "Theological Identity of the North American Holiness Movement," 85. Cited in Lowery, "Fork in the Wesleyan Road," 204.

41. Finney, *Memoirs of Rev. Charles G. Finney*, 20.

42. Simpson, *Days of Heaven Upon Earth*, 143.

43. Robins, *A. J. Tomlinson*, 43.

[E]ach have their private interpretations as to [the Spirit's] visible manifestations; some claim shouting, leaping, jumping, and falling in trances, while other inspirations, unction and divine revelation.[44]

Parham was probably familiar with the Christian Metropolitan Association, which for a time determined that jumping was the evidence of spirit-baptism.[45] This group had been inspired in part by Martin Wells Knapp, who after being arrested in 1901 for the excessive noise of his worship services, claimed that "Baptism of the Holy Ghost moves to vocal demonstration."[46] For Knapp, manifestations were not optional or dispensable. He warned that "[i]t is far safer to play with lightning rods in a thunder storm than to oppose this baptism or any of its manifestations."[47]

Regardless of how holiness adherents described sanctification, they understood it as a supernatural experience. The yearning to make the spiritual tangible was heightened by the new pentecostal model that taught believers to expect manifestations. This yearning was also magnified by and evident in the newly surging doctrine of the premillennial return of Christ.

Premillennialism

In the mid-nineteenth century, premillennialism had a bad reputation. The doctrine, which teaches that Christ will physically return to earth prior to his millennial reign of peace and righteousness, was blighted by William Miller's failed predictions of Christ's return in 1844. Most Protestants adhered to a vague but generally agreed-upon doctrine of postmillennialism, which taught that Christ would return to earth following the righteous earthly millennium (whether figurative or a literal thousand years) and that the advent of the millennium was partly dependent on human righteousness and achievement. The theological notion that human society was on the cusp of a period of peace and righteousness complemented the general sense of progress shared by all as well as the American crusade to civilize the West. Lyman Beecher's famous *Plea for the West* (1835) summarized the tenor of the times:

> It was the opinion of Edwards, that the millenium [sic] would commence in America. When I first encountered this opinion, I thought it chimerical; but all providential developments since,

---

44. Parham, *Sermons of Charles F. Parham*, 27–28.
45. Kostlevy, *Holy Jumpers*, 84–85.
46. Kostlevy, *Holy Jumpers*, 33.
47. Knapp, *Lightning Bolts from Pentecostal Skies*, 25.

and all existing signs of the times, lend corroboration to it. But if it is by the march of revolution and civil liberty, that the way of the Lord is to be prepared, where shall the central energy be found, and from what nation shall the renovating power go forth? What nation is blessed with such experimental knowledge of free institutions, with such facilities and resources of communication, obstructed by so few obstacles, as our own?[48]

Despite the moral challenges connected to immigration, slavery, and the frontier, most Protestants in the first half of the nineteenth century felt assured that they were approaching a period of unprecedented societal righteousness.

The only serious contender to the dominant postmillennialism emerged from John N. Darby, a priest in the Church of Ireland who helped found the Plymouth Brethren. Although Darby began articulating his version of premillennialism with its historical dispensations and pretribulational rapture of the church in the early 1830s, his teachings did not receive significant acceptance in America until about 1875, when a group of premillennialists began yearly meetings of what came to be known as the Niagara Bible Conference.[49] At the same time, premillennialism made inroads into the Keswick movement in England. Through contacts with Keswick and the Niagara conferences, several high-profile American ministers adopted premillennialism, including D. L. Moody and A. B. Simpson. Moody in particular was influential in the spread of the new eschatology through his Northfield conferences beginning in 1880. Many of these new premillennialists were "inconsistent dispensationalists," embracing only parts of Darby's grander system.[50] But like Darby they all combined the message of the soon return of Christ with an aversion to eschatological date-setting.

Before the Civil War, holiness advocates of all stripes endorsed the postmillennial vision. Henry Cowles was Oberlin's most avid millenarian. Based on "some deep pervading action in the social and moral atmosphere," he declared that "THE MILLENNIUM IS AT HAND."[51] The postmillennial creed fit well with the Arminian soteriology of the holiness movement. Both teachings emphasized the need for human cooperation with God and magnified the potential of human activity.

---

48. Beecher, *Plea for the West*, 9–10.

49. Sandeen, *Roots of Fundamentalism*, 132–61. The most complete and recent treatment of premillennialism in America is Weber, *Living in the Shadow of the Second Coming*.

50. Van De Walle, *Heart of the Gospel*, 191.

51. Cited in Dayton, *Theological Roots of Pentecostalism*, 156, 157.

Given this resonance, the holiness embrace of premillennialism by the end of the century requires some explanation. Perhaps the triumphant postmillennialism of Oberlin and other holiness advocates simply raised hopes too high.[52] With the expectation of the millennium reaching a fever pitch in theologians like Cowles, the social and moral disappointments of the second half of the century—the Civil War, growth of cities and their vices, loss of Anglo dominance, and financial panics—were especially devastating. Coupled with these social factors was the intellectual challenge posed by biblical higher criticism. As Ernest Sandeen pointed out, the premillennial approach to scripture found reinforcement in the Princeton doctrine of biblical inerrancy.[53] And biblical inerrancy was inseparable from supernaturalism: for Princeton-style fundamentalists, it meant affirming the miracles of scripture; for holiness premillennialists, it meant affirming present-day miracles. The premillennial script also called for end-time apostasy, which premillennialists found in the modernist threat.

The postmillennial optimism of Beecher and Cowles seemed misplaced by the end of the century. But the millennial impulse was too deeply imbedded to be discarded. As Dayton writes, "The only way to sustain the hope of the millennium was to radically rearrange the chronology along the lines of premillennialism."[54] And this is what thousands of believers—both holiness and non-holiness—did in the last years of the nineteenth century. This suggests that the millennial fervor of the antebellum era was driven by supernaturalism, rather than a specific theological or biblical commitment. Both postmillennialists and premillennialists were focused on testifying to evidence of God's intervention in the world; they only disagreed on the order of its details.

A more specific reason for holiness acceptance of premillennialism was its power to make sense of holiness adherents' experience. As more and more holiness folk—especially in the South—encountered hostility from their denominations, they turned to an apocalyptic eschatology that confirmed their elect status while condemning their adversaries. Being shunned by their denominations seemed to confirm their belief in the imminent end. Holiness adherents never tired of quoting Jesus' words in John 16:2: "They shall put you out of the synagogues." Such resistance only pushed holiness folk further into pentecostal language and imagery, which in turn intensified their apocalypticism. Since the denominations had abused their

---

52. Dayton, *Theological Roots of Pentecostalism*, 158.

53. Sandeen, *Roots of Fundamentalism*. Sandeen missed the importance of holiness (and later pentecostal) adherence to premillennialism (177), a problem partly rectified by Marsden, *Fundamentalism*, 72–101.

54. Dayton, *Theological Roots of Pentecostalism*, 158.

authority, true power rested only in those who had the fullness of the Holy Spirit, and the biblical scene of Pentecost affirmed a close connection between the work of the Holy Spirit and the eschaton. As the church on earth seemed to be rejecting the key holiness doctrine, holiness people could no longer affirm the postmillennial vision of the progress of righteousness.[55]

Premillennialism also complemented the holiness conviction that sanctification was a restoration of apostolic Christianity. As Stephen Ware argues, the restorationist ethos led many to the conclusion that the rediscovery of apostolic teaching begun with Luther had reached its zenith in the holiness movement; the only thing left was Christ's return. In support of this belief, holiness folk developed the "evening light" doctrine, which claimed on the basis of Zechariah 14:6–7 that the restoration of lost doctrines directly preceded the end of time.[56] Early pentecostals embraced a related doctrine of "latter rain," which argued from Peter's Pentecost sermon and Palestinian rainfall that a special spiritual outpouring would occur just before Christ's return.[57]

Divine Healing

Almost without exception, those who embraced divine healing had already adopted some form of holiness teaching. Divine healing appealed to late-nineteenth century Christians for many reasons. To some degree, the doctrine of divine healing was an extension of the logic of sanctification. As Randall Stephens puts it, holiness adherents concluded that "[t]he body . . . was perfectible much like the soul."[58] In other words, the supernaturalist drive for evidence of present divine activity was at work in both teachings. The move to divine healing was surprisingly simple for radical holiness leaders like Charles Parham, who "realized the mighty power of God in sanctifying the body from disease as He had from inbred sin."[59] Leaders like R. Kelso Carter increased expectations of supernaturalism by arguing that healing was "in the atonement." This teaching was also polemical; as liberal theology denied the supernaturalism of the biblical and the present world, it threatened to disenchant the earthly realm and make the atonement more "subjective." As Raymond Cunningham suggests, divine healing

---

55. Stephens, *Fire Spreads*, 136–85; quote on 170.
56. Ware, *Restorationism in the Holiness Movement*, 101.
57. Myland, *Latter Rain Covenant and Pentecostal Power*.
58. Stephens, *Fire Spreads*, 175.
59. Parham, *Sermons of Charles F. Parham*, 16.

may have been an effort by proto-fundamentalists to bolster the doctrine of the atonement.[60]

Divine healing was also for some holiness folk the logical conclusion of their premillennialism. If a special outpouring of the Holy Spirit was to presage Christ's return, then all sorts of miraculous occurrences like healing could be expected. For some, divine healing was also a practical necessity of the last days—God needed fit laborers for the end-time harvest. As A. B. Simpson put it, "The blessed gospel of physical healing in the name of Jesus will prove an invaluable handmaid to the cause of missions."[61]

Social factors also contributed to the rise of divine healing. The steady erosion of Calvinism opened the possibility that affliction may not be providential and that miraculous intervention could be God's will for all times.[62] Others felt that miracles were the perfect antidote to an overreliance on science. "It may be," wrote Smith Platt, an early and prolific Methodist holiness advocate,

> now that the modern era of science has begun to shape the thoughts of men by only scientific methods, that a special occasion has arisen for a fresh display of signs and wonders to keep the church and the world alive and open to the realities of God's immediate visitation.[63]

In the rapidly-changing intellectual climate of post-bellum America, old questions—like human agency and the place of the miraculous—received new answers.

Seldom appreciated in discussions of divine healing is the underdeveloped state of professional medicine in the nineteenth century. The heroic approach of revolutionary-era physician Benjamin Rush (1746–1813) dominated medical thought in the early republic. Rush believed that an excess of nervous energy, or "capillary tension," was at the heart of all disease; cure came in the form of tension-release through purgation, often induced by dangerous levels of toxins such as calomel and arsenic.[64] Samuel Thomson (1769–1843) offered a different philosophy, believing lack of heat to be the taproot of sickness. Thomsonians treated their patients by restoring vital

---

60. Cunningham, "From Holiness to Healing," 512.

61. Cited in Curtis, *Faith in the Great Physician*, 78–79.

62. In reaction to the abuses of Catholicism, reformers like John Calvin had argued that miracles were needed in early Christianity to help establish the truth of the gospel. But since there was no new gospel to be established, miracles were no longer needed. Calvin, *Institutes of the Christian Religion*, xxiv.

63. Cited in Cunningham, "From Holiness to Healing," 512.

64. Curtis, *Faith in the Great Physician*, 28–31.

heat to the body, either through baths or a carefully prescribed herbal diet. For twenty dollars, Thomson's followers could purchase his plan in his *New Guide to Health* (1822), reflecting the Jacksonian ideal by stressing the accessibility of medicine to all.[65] Another alternative was homeopathy, a coined term meaning "similar to the disease." Homeopathy centered on two philosophical positions: (1) like cures like; a treatment that causes symptoms in a healthy patient can cure those same symptoms in a sick patient; and (2) the law of infinitesimals; the smaller the dose, the more potent it is. Homeopaths believed that the illness created by their diluted drugs displaced the original disease and awakened the body's vital force to overcome it. Throughout the nineteenth century, irregular healers (homeopaths, heroic, Thomsonians, and others) constituted roughly twenty percent of practicing physicians.[66] Despite disagreements, irregular physicians all crossed easily back and forth between physic and metaphysic.[67]

Regular physicians struggled to distinguish themselves in the midst of these competing philosophies. Tracing its impulse from Paris, regular medicine took a stricter empirical approach, making advances in anatomy and physiology but offering few therapeutic alternatives to heroic medicine or Thomsonianism; they were known primarily for their fondness for heavy drugging, as seen in a mid-century ditty:

> Whate'er the patient may complain
> Of head, or heart or nerve, or brain
> Of Fever high, or parts that swell—
> The remedy is calomel[68]

Not only were regulars' drug therapies undiscerning and dangerous, their understanding of pathology was severely limited. Germ theory was just coming to public attention in the 1860s and 1870s. The most immediate application was Joseph Lister's antiseptics, which made surgery safer but also increased the number of unnecessary surgeries.[69]

Another indicator of the precarious state of late-nineteenth century medicine was the development of functional disease theories.[70] Distinguished from organic diseases, functional diseases were those ailments that

---

65. Starr, *Social Transformation of American Medicine*, 51–52, quote on 52.
66. Starr, *Social Transformation of American Medicine*, 99.
67. Albanese, "Physic and Metaphysic in 19th-century America," 489–502; Whorton, *Nature Cures*, xii.
68. Cited in Whorton, *Nature Cures*, 1.
69. Whorton, *Nature Cures*, 156.
70. Trimble, "Functional Diseases," 1768–70.

produced real symptoms without discernible organ or tissue damage. The most notorious functional disease of the period was neurasthenia. Confronted by a web of symptoms including headache, fatigue, anxiety, partial paralysis and depression, doctors, following Charles Beard, began pronouncing the vague diagnosis, especially for women. But treatment for this "Americanitis" was haphazard and taxing, ranging from rest cure to electrotherapy. To understand why so many would turn to unscientific methods of healing (whether unorthodox physicians, mind-cure, or divine healing) is to note how crude medical science was in the late nineteenth century. Gender issues were also at play, as many female neurasthenics, chaffing under ineffective male care, turned to female divine healers.[71]

Through most of the nineteenth century, regular medicine was hampered by its lack of regulation. For instance, students could claim an MD with as little as eight months of study at proprietary schools. But toward the end of the century, regular medicine engaged in a painful self-evaluation, which opened it to further critique but ultimately strengthened the profession. *Dent v. West Virginia* (1888) essentially ruled that doctors needed degrees from reputable schools. The John Hopkins University medical school, established in 1893, set a standard for science-based medical education. The 1906 Pure Food and Drug Act took aim at so-called patent medicines. In 1910, Abraham Flexner, in a report funded by the Carnegie Foundation, evaluated the quality of every medical school in the nation. John Alexander Dowie, the divine healer who instigated a riot in Chicago with his attacks on the medical profession, probably would have agreed with Flexner's assessment of Chicago's medical education as "the plague spot of the country."[72] But rather than denouncing medicine like Dowie, Flexner sought to improve it with lower enrollment, stricter standards, and a research-based approach.[73]

The regular physicians' growth of authority rested partly in their willingness to cooperate with moderate homeopaths and other irregular physicians. Consequently, these alternative medicines became less philosophically-driven. And as they did, a new, purely philosophical approach filled the void. In 1862, Mary Baker Eddy began to be treated for chronic digestive and spinal problems by Phineas Quimby, who taught that healing comes through the positive alignment of spirit and body. Weeks after Quimby's death in 1866, Eddy suffered a fall on ice. She had to be carried

71. Robinson, *Divine Healing: The Holiness-Pentecostal Transition Years*, 136–46.

72. Flexner, *Medical Education in the United States and Canada*, 216.

73. For an overview of the rise of regular medicine see Starr, *Social Transformation of American Medicine*, 79–144.

home, but in three days she was walking again, claiming further insight into healing through her study of the scriptures. Eddy institutionalized her philosophy with the 1875 publication of *Science and Health* and the formation of the Church of Christ, Scientist, in 1879. Her fame grew quickly as testimonies of healing under her care multiplied, spread by her *Christian Science Journal*. She became the object of wide fascination, generating lengthy investigations from Mark Twain and the future novelist Willa Cather. Eddy claimed to have taught four thousand students between 1881 and 1889 at her Massachusetts Metaphysical College—an institution that was, tellingly, chartered by the state for medical instruction.[74]

The extent of Eddy's debt to Quimby is a matter of debate.[75] Regardless, Eddy's system distinguished itself with an explicitly Christian worldview and by totally denying the reality of the material. Health came from realizing that disease was an illusion; sufferers were to deny the reality of their symptoms as well as the underlying sickness. Similar versions of this "counterfactual confession" appeared in later New Thought doctrine and divine healing.[76] Eddy's teachings pushed supernaturalism to the extreme, so that "natural" and "supernatural" took on completely new meanings. She claimed to teach the "Principle, before which sin and disease lose their reality." As a "principle," her approach to healing was "scientific," and she claimed that "these mighty works are not supernatural, but supremely natural."[77] Here it can be seen that naturalism and supernaturalism are ends of a circular spectrum: supernaturalism becomes most important to those who are most concerned about the problems of the natural world; and those who argue most for supernaturalism wish to raise it to the level of scientific predictability associated with nature.[78] Nevertheless, for the average adherent, what was important was not the philosophy, but the results. As Willa Cather put it, Eddy's teaching appealed to those who "had a great need to believe in miracles."[79]

---

74. Eddy, *Science and Health*, xi–xii.
75. Gill, *Mary Baker Eddy*, 122–68.
76. Bowler, *Blessed*, 13–14.
77. Both quotes from Eddy, *Science and Health*, xi.
78. Finney was dealing with similar issues on the relation between the natural and the supernatural when he defined religious revivals as not miraculous but "the purely philosophical result of the right use of constituted means." Although Finney was more beholden to the Enlightenment definition of miracles than Eddy or many later divine healing advocates, he clearly expressed a similar concern for reconciling spiritual experience with rational categories of causation. Finney, *Lectures on Revivals of Religion*, 12.
79. Cather, *Life of Mary Baker G. Eddy*, 313.

Divine healing emerged in this milieu of science, scientific incompetence, pseudoscience, and metaphysical rejection of the material. Most leaders of the divine healing movement did not categorically condemn medical intervention like healer John Alexander Dowie, who lumped "Doctors, Drugs, and Devils" together as foes of Christ.[80] But they all considered divine healing the "better way,"[81] noting the infighting among physicians as a sign of impotence. As Daniel Bryant, an overseer in Dowie's organization and one-time cooperator with pentecostals in Zion City, argued as late as 1907,

> It is inexplicable that anything with so unbroken a history of change as the so-called Science of Medicine could live a day in a civilization characterized by the commonest intelligence. Look at the practice of medicine today. It is split up into scores of factions, each asserting itself to be right and the others wrong . . . After nineteen centuries of study and research, as a result of which the world blazes with the light of scientific research along many lines, the so-called Science of Medicine is in the greatest confusion, and continues to be one of the greatest humbugs on the earth today. The Bible teaches that God is the Healer of His people. Nothing else can succeed.[82]

Those who took God as their healer had often exhausted the expertise of physicians. By 1890, Jennie Paddock of Chicago suffered from a tumor that was "so enlarged she could not fasten her dresses by about six inches." She had sought treatment at numerous hospitals and from many specialists, but no one would operate on her. One doctor only exacerbated her suffering through an "electric treatment." Her last doctor told her she was near death. Paddock's friend brought a prayer request to Dowie, who prayed for her at a mass gathering at nearby Western Springs. The next morning, Paddock declared she was healed, and within a few days was "doing a hard days [sic] work." Paddock's hard-won trust in divine healing was passed on to the next generation when her daughter fell ill and wanted a doctor. Paddock assured her that "God cured mamma, and He will cure you." After a prayer and laying on of hands, Paddock's daughter was healed.[83]

Paddock's healer John Alexander Dowie stood in a line of earlier pioneers of faith healing. Before a discernable movement had begun, several scattered ministries from 1830 to 1860 focused on divine healing. Edward

80. Dowie, *Doctors, Drugs and Devils*.
81. Opp, *Lord for the Body*, 51.
82. Bryant, "Baptism of Holy Spirit," 1.
83. "Miracle of Healing," 220–22.

Irving endorsed healing as well as other spiritual gifts in his London ministry beginning in 1831.[84] The German Johann Christoph Blumhardt developed a theology and ministry of healing after a lengthy pastoral struggle with a demon-possessed girl in his parish at Möttlingen. After the girl's recovery in 1843, Blumhardt established the internationally known healing facilities at Bad Boll. Dorothea Trudel of Männerdorf, Switzerland, healed four of her co-workers in 1840 with her prayers, and by the mid-1850s, she operated a series of healing homes.[85] Trudel's work in particular inspired later faith healers in the English-speaking world.[86]

Ethan O. Allen (grandson of the Revolutionary War hero) was probably the first American to devote himself to a ministry of divine healing. He was healed of a liver ailment in 1846 and afterwards began a healing ministry. Allen's work was that of an itinerant, and he never institutionalized his ministry through a base or a periodical. Of more lasting importance was Sarah Anne Freeman Mix (known as Mrs. Edward Mix), who was healed by Allen of tuberculosis in 1877. Mix's ministry was short (she died in 1884), but her fame grew quickly, aided by her periodical *Victory Through Faith* and her influence on one of the most famous early divine healers, Carrie Judd (1858–1946).

After a painful fall on an icy sidewalk in 1876 (not unlike Mary Baker Eddy's experience), Judd's health devolved quickly. Doctors despaired of treating her chronic pain, and Judd resolved herself to a life of sanctified suffering. This did not stop Judd from reaching out to Mrs. Edward Mix in 1879, however. Mix replied to Judd, telling her that she would pray for Judd at an appointed time according to James 5, encouraging the invalid to "claim that promise," and assuring her that "[i]t makes no difference how you feel, but get right out of bed and begin to walk by faith."[87] This counsel for counterfactual confession reveals the surface similarity between divine healing and Christian Science. Mix's advice also shows how the divine healing

---

84. Robinson, *Divine Healing: The Formative Years*, chap. 1.

85. Healing homes were the dominant form of divine healing practice until about 1900. The environment of healing homes was thoroughly domestic and sacred, as participants stayed sometimes many weeks or months in devotional pursuit of healing. The main purpose of the domestic setting was insulation from the unbelieving world, providing time and encouragement for the believer to build up faith for healing. Healing homes corresponded well to the Victorian notion that home (rather than hospital) was the site of both sickness and convalescence—that health was a personal rather than clinical matter; they also provided opportunities for women to serve in high profile positions of leadership under the cover of domesticity. See Curtis, *Faith in the Great Physician*, chap. 5.

86. For Blumhardt and Trudel, see Curtis, *Faith in the Great Physician*, chap. 2.

87. Cited in Hardesty, *Faith Cure*, 8.

movement had imbibed the logic of Palmer's "shorter way" to sanctification and applied it to physical restoration—the seeker did not wait for confirmation in the form of immediate evidence, but rather "stood on the promise." But like Palmer, divine healing advocates gave a mixed message on the role of experience; more than one sufferer described the "warm wave" or other sensations that accompanied or anticipated the moment of restoration.[88]

Gradually, Judd regained her strength and health, and she set out to spread the blessing of divine healing to others. She embarked on a fifty-year ministry, moving from the holiness movement to pentecostalism without breaking stride. Judd's *The Prayer of Faith* (1880) was probably the first theological treatment of divine healing published in America. As this title suggests, early practitioners of divine healing grounded their beliefs in the straightforward words of James 5:14–15:

> Is any sick among you? let him call for the elders of the church; and let them pray over him, anointing him with oil in the name of the Lord: And the prayer of faith shall save the sick, and the Lord shall raise him up; and if he have committed sins, they shall be forgiven him.

Judd's writing brought her to the attention of others in the holiness and growing divine healing movement. One contact was Charles Cullis (1833–1892), a homeopathic physician and Episcopal layman who after a visit to Trudel's Männerdorf (now run by Samuel Zeller) in 1873 incorporated faith healing into his practice. Cullis was a major shaper of the healing movement through his healing homes, promotion of healing and holiness literature through the Willard Tract Society and personal publications such as *Faith Cures* (1879), and connections to other healing and holiness leaders.

A. B. Simpson was healed of chronic heart problems at a camp meeting in 1881 led by Cullis at Old Orchard, Maine. Simpson's greatest contribution, as has already been noted, was his "fourfold gospel," a synthesis of the themes of justification, sanctification, healing, and premillennialism bubbling to the surface of the holiness movement. He also was one of the first to place divine healing on a more comprehensive theological basis:

> [R]edemption finds its center in the Cross of our Lord Jesus Christ, and there we must look for the fundamental principle of Divine healing, which rests on the atoning Sacrifice. This necessarily follows from the first principle we have stated [that the causes of disease and suffering are traced to the Fall]. If sickness

---

88. Opp, *Lord for the Body*, 58.

be the result of the Fall, it must be included in the atonement of Christ, which reaches "as far as the curse is found."[89]

This "healing in the atonement" forms one third of what James Robinson calls the "radical triad" of the healing movement. While many early adherents of divine healing, such as Methodist Daniel Steele, argued that healing was only given to some in special circumstances, during the 1880s, leaders like Simpson argued that it was secured for all by Christ's sacrifice.[90] Another element of the radical stance was the belief that faith obligates God to heal, which was implicit in the stress on James 5. The third component was the rejection (or at least implicit denigration) of medicine.[91]

The healing movement reached its transatlantic apex in 1885 at the International Conference on Divine Healing and True Holiness in London, led by Simpson and Boardman. At that time, the little-known holiness and healing minister Dowie wrote to the conference from Australia, regretting his inability to attend. For Dowie, the healing movement indicated that "primitive lines of spiritual power" were being restored, specifically in the "perpetuity of the gifts of Healing by the Holy Spirit."[92] It was clear from this early date that Dowie had a different approach to healing than his colleagues.

Dowie rose to fame and scorn at the turn of the century for his healing ministry in Chicago and nearby Zion City, Illinois. In his denunciation of medicine, understanding of healing as an apostolic gift, and identification of Satan as the cause of sickness, Dowie moved beyond other faith healers. As Robinson argues, Dowie's ministry marks a turning point in the divine healing movement. Earlier leaders—like Cullis, Simpson, and Boardman—practiced healing in intimate settings, oriented healing around holiness and perpetual dependence on God, deemphasized their personal role, and attributed healing to faith and the atonement. In contrast, later healers, following in Dowie's train, healed in mass meetings, functionally separated holiness from healing, emphasized their own role and sometimes attributed healing to the spiritual gifts.[93] The distinction is not precise, though. Earlier healers like Maria Woodworth-Etter (who, like Carrie Judd, took her ministry into the pentecostal movement) and Daniel S. Warner displayed some

---

89. Simpson, *Gospel of Healing*, 34.

90. Baer, "Perfectly Empowered Bodies," 162–63.

91. Robinson, *Divine Healing: The Holiness-Pentecostal Transition Years*, 2–3.

92. Boardman, *Record of the International Conference on Divine Healing and True Holiness*, 171; Robinson, *Divine Healing: The Holiness-Pentecostal Transition Years*, 55–56.

93. Robinson, *Divine Healing: The Holiness-Pentecostal Transition Years*, 83, 169.

of these radical tendencies before Dowie came to wide public notice. Still, Dowie stands as a crossroads in divine healing for at least two reasons. First, Dowie had a phenomenal impact on early pentecostalism. As will be seen in the next chapter, dozens of first generation pentecostals had spent time at Zion City, including F. F. Bosworth, who arrived there in 1902. Second, Dowie attracted opposition even from other supporters of divine healing. Dowie's divisive nature revealed that the movement was not monolithic and that many, when confronted with the options of softening their beliefs or being identified as radicals, would happily choose the latter.

The teachings of spirit-baptism, premillennialism and divine healing were mutually reinforcing, but they presented no syllogism. Believers could easily accept some points without accepting all. But the elements of the fourfold gospel complemented one another and spoke to common supernaturalist concerns. The higher life evangelist R. A. Torrey, who increasingly distanced himself from divine healing after the turn of the century, nonetheless addressed a conference of premillennialists in 1914 arguing that "The Lord's Second Coming [is] a Motive for Personal Holiness."[94] Martin Wells Knapp said much the same thing: "[He] [w]ho constantly expects the coming of the Bridegroom will see that no stains be found on bridal robes, and that slumbering souls be awakened and prepared."[95] Furthermore, the logic of sanctification (attainable by faith, instantaneous, visible to the senses) applied easily to theologies of healing.

EMERGENCE OF PENTECOSTALISM AND THE HOLINESS RETREAT

The ardent embrace of the fourfold gospel among the radical holiness constituency was short-lived, due mostly to a division in the ranks that was permanent by the 1910s. A significant number of holiness adherents who became pentecostals embraced a new expression of supernaturalism that claimed speaking in tongues as evidence of spirit-baptism. This teaching appeared first with Charles Parham in 1901 in his work with Bible students in Topeka, Kansas, and garnered wide attention in 1906 as the teaching became the focal point of the Azusa Street revival in Los Angeles. Those who rejected this teaching at first cautiously critiqued, and then dramatically denounced pentecostals.[96] In their effort to distance themselves from the "tongues movement," non-pentecostal holiness believers also distanced

---

94. Cited in Sandeen, *Roots of Fundamentalism*, 226.
95. Knapp, *Lightning Bolts from Pentecostal Skies*, 137.
96. Wacker, "Travail of a Broken Family," 23–49.

themselves from other elements of extreme supernaturalism that pentecostals embraced. The removal of "pentecostal" from many holiness denominational names and publications indicated not only that these groups wanted to remain separate from the new tongues movement, but that they were willing to sacrifice to a remarkable degree the supernaturalism that pentecostal language and imagery had brought into the holiness movement.[97]

Aside from speaking in tongues, the most obvious reaction against supernaturalism among holiness adherents was their response to divine healing. The holiness movement had already challenged divine healing before pentecostalism emerged, and this controversy may have been already sketching the boundaries of religious alignments that would become permanent with the advent of pentecostalism.[98] James M. Buckley exemplified the opposition, aligning the MEC against faith healing through his editorship of the *Christian Advocate*.[99] In 1897, the NHA forbade discussion of the "side-track" issues of divine healing and premillennialism.

Moderate supporters of divine healing also turned against the doctrine. The Salvation Army maintained an open but non-dogmatic stance in 1891: "That God should heal the sick after this fashion is in perfect harmony with the views and experience of The Salvation Army from the beginning."[100] As the Army consolidated its work in the 1890s, and William Booth faced the sad fact of his wife's breast cancer, tolerance eroded. A final break came in 1902, when Booth's daughter, Kate, and son-in-law, Arthur Booth-Clibborn, left the Salvation Army. Arthur had become enamored of Dowie's teachings when Dowie had preached in London in 1901. The departure of the Booth-Clibborns scarred William Booth, who banned faith healing and railed against it as "false, misleading, and ruinous ... dangerous and productive of evil."[101]

Some holiness leaders who earlier embraced divine healing came to temper their views. Concerned with the extreme views of radical healers like Dowie, A. B. Simpson began in the 1890s to downplay the teaching as "very subordinate."[102] In 1884, R. Kelso Carter's *The Atonement for Sin and Sickness* was one of the strongest theological arguments for divine healing. But when his health began to decline and he failed to receive healing under Cullis, Dowie, or Simpson, he drastically reevaluated his theology,

---

97. Jones, *Perfectionist Persuasion*, 173.
98. Cunningham, "From Holiness to Healing," 499.
99. Robinson, *Divine Healing: The Holiness-Pentecostal Transition Years*, 185–86.
100. Salvation Army, *Orders and Regulations*, 52; Opp, *Lord for the Body*, 85.
101. Opp, *Lord for the Body*, 82–89. William Booth quote on 88.
102. Baer, "Perfectly Empowered Bodies," 95–96.

as seen in his *"Faith Healing" Reviewed After Twenty Years* (1897).[103] R. A. Torrey, Dwight Moody's colleague in Chicago, also backpedaled on his initial support for divine healing. Torrey had sought Dowie's prayers for his daughter in 1898, around the same time that Moody and Dowie (also still in Chicago at the time) were sparring over the teaching. Torrey was forced to disavow Dowie's teachings as a face-saving measure for Moody.[104] By the 1920s, Torrey had become an outspoken critic of divine healing, especially as practiced by pentecostals. Radical supporters of divine healing, like holiness evangelist Seth Rees, saw the writing on the wall: "[H]oliness preachers and camps which oppose Divine healing are losing their fire and juice."[105]

But even among its radical supporters, divine healing suffered a decline around the turn of the century. Martin Wells Knapp showed caution: "that Jesus 'bore our infirmities and carried our sickness' will be known in its fullness only when clad in resurrection robes at His appearing, though scintillations of it reach us here." Neither did Knapp take Dowie's hard line on medical means.[106] The Pilgrim Holiness Church remained committed to supernaturalism, but they too allowed for deviance from the hard line on divine healing, refusing to "pass judgment upon those who use other providential means for the restoration of health."[107] Daniel S. Warner's Church of God reformation movement abandoned its strict commitment to the doctrine in the mid-1920s.[108] As a result of complex negotiations, the Pentecostal Church of the Nazarene adopted an intentionally vague statement on divine healing in its 1908 *Manual*.[109]

Many holiness groups also softened on premillennialism. As noted above, the NHA stifled preaching on premillennialism in 1897. Although their constituency leaned toward premillennialism by the 1920s,[110] the Pen-

---

103. Dieter, *Holiness Revival of the Nineteenth Century*, 253; Robinson, *Divine Healing: The Holiness-Pentecostal Transition Years*, 189, 194–95.

104. Robinson, *Divine Healing: The Holiness-Pentecostal Transition Years*, 78–80.

105. Cited in Baer, "Perfectly Empowered Bodies," 187.

106. Robinson, *Divine Healing: The Holiness-Pentecostal Transition Years*, 205; Knapp, *Lightning Bolts from Pentecostal Skies*, 127–28. Knapp's work spawned several groups. The Metropolitan Christian Association, known more colloquially as the Burning Bush movement after its muckraking periodical, carried all the elements of the fourfold gospel into the twentieth century, but had a very small appeal due to their rejection of personal possessions. Kostlevy, *Holy Jumpers*.

107. *Manual of the Pilgrim Holiness Church*, 19.

108. Stephens, "'Who Healeth All Thy Diseases.'"

109. Pentecostal Church of the Nazarene General Assembly et al., *Manual of the Pentecostal Church of the Nazarene, [1908]*, 35.

110. Dieter, *Holiness Revival of the Nineteenth Century*, 263; Smith, *Called Unto Holiness*, 316–17.

tecostal Church of the Nazarene officially gave "full liberty of belief among the members" on this doctrine.[111] Daniel S. Warner's Church of God reformation movement adopted a type of amillennialism.[112]

The experience of sanctification was also toned down in many of these holiness groups. J. G. Morrison of the Church of the Nazarene argued that they had no need for "boisterous praying, great bodily exercise," or "vociferous and constant shouting" and urged adherents to distance themselves from those who taught that visions, dreams, or speaking in tongues authenticated the experience.[113] The Pilgrim Holiness Church likewise repudiated "any teaching . . . that holds to any particular manifestation, as by the Gift of Tongues, so-called, as proof of this Baptism."[114] A. B. Simpson's C&MA gradually underwent a "modification of original objectives" with regard to supernaturalism as well, due in part to its increasing attacks on pentecostalism.[115]

Some holiness believers began to reconcile spiritual experience with psychological notions in what Heather Curtis has called "a sane gospel." Urban higher life leaders like A. B. Simpson and Carrie Judd felt that an appeal to the subliminal mind and temperament could explain spiritual experience while maintaining personal volition and judgment. But the use of psychological categories to describe supernatural experience undercut the supernaturalist impulse. For radical holiness believers like Woodworth and for later pentecostals, Simpson's plea that "God does not ask us to give up our sanity" sounded like a betrayal of the original holiness call for complete consecration. Psychological categories also tended to pull the specific theological meaning out of religious experience, as seen in the theories of William James. Finally, this approach seemed to anchor the validity of supernaturalism to recent scientific theory rather than the self-evident power of the divine. And as the subliminal conscious theories receded behind developmental psychology, this alliance between supernaturalism and psychology ceased to benefit the supernaturalist cause.[116]

In the early twentieth century, while holiness and higher life groups equivocated on divine healing, produced vague statements on eschatology, denounced manifestations associated with spirit-baptism, and yielded

111. Pentecostal Church of the Nazarene General Assembly et al., *Manual of the Pentecostal Church of the Nazarene*, [1908], 26.

112. Ware, *Restorationism in the Holiness Movement*, 67–75.

113. Smith, *Called Unto Holiness*, 316.

114. *Manual of the Pilgrim Holiness Church*, 17.

115. Wilson, "Christian and Missionary Alliance."

116. Curtis, "Sane Gospel," 195–226, Simpson quote on 204; Mullin, *Miracles and the Modern Religious Imagination*, 184–85.

spiritual experience to the judgment of science, the new pentecostal churches clung to their supernaturalist inheritance.[117] Pentecostal beliefs and practices were not simply a carbon copy of earlier holiness trends. For many reasons, divine healing and spirit-baptism looked different in pentecostal hands.[118] Pentecostal supernaturalism also had limits. If practices were too easily confused with counterfeits and had no clear biblical justification, they could be judged as "fanaticism."[119] But by the 1910s, supernaturalism stood, in the words of R. E. McAlister quoted at the opening of this chapter, as pentecostalism's "characterizing feature." McAlister's tract did not even specifically mention tongues. Canadian pentecostal A. H. Argue urged in 1921 that pentecostals focus on "essential things," which meant preaching Christ as "the One who heals the sick, as the One who baptizes with the Holy Ghost as at Pentecost, as the One who is coming again very soon."[120] Pentecostal superstar Aimee Semple McPherson made the "foursquare gospel" the doctrinal foundation of her work in 1922.[121] Pentecostal spirit-baptism was attested by the supernatural sign of tongues and also frequently accompanied by intense physical sensations. In William Durham's experience, "my body was worked in sections, a section at a time."[122] Commitment to divine healing found expression in pentecostal doctrinal statements, the healing ministries of McPherson, John G. Lake, and F. F. Bosworth, and in the 1920 controversy in the International Pentecostal Holiness Church, which insisted that faith in the Great Physician precludes trust in doctors.[123]

---

117. The story of holiness retreat from supernaturalism could also be explored as a function of the improved socio-economic status of its adherents by the third decade of the twentieth century, as well as its development from sect to church. The literature on the holiness movement in relation to these sociological factors is mainly speculative, providing nothing comparable to Anderson's well-researched thesis on early pentecostalism in *Vision of the Disinherited*. See Wacker, "Travail of a Broken Family," 30; Dieter, "Wesleyan/Holiness and Pentecostal Movements," 11; Jones, *Perfectionist Persuasion*, 142.

118. Opp, *Lord for the Body*; Robinson, *Divine Healing: The Holiness-Pentecostal Transition Years*.

119. This was the case with "writing in unknown languages," which had been encouraged in the early months of the Azusa Street revival. But when a local Spiritualist began performing this feat for crowds, the pentecostals backed away from the practice, claiming "we do not read anything in the Word" about it. Robeck, *Azusa Street Mission and Revival*, 111–14; *Apostolic Faith (Los Angeles)* 1.10 (September 1907) 2.

120. Cited in Opp, *Lord for the Body*, 140.

121. Blumhofer, *Aimee Semple Mcpherson*, 191.

122. "Personal Testimony of Pastor Durham," *Pentecostal Testimony* (March 1909) 7.

123. Williams, *Spirit Cure*, 37.

With the new pentecostal movement emphasizing all the traditional holiness elements of supernaturalism, and non-pentecostal holiness denominations vacillating, pentecostalism emerged as the favored son of the nineteenth-century gospel of the supernatural. Speaking in tongues added a point of doctrinal and social cohesion and validation for believers who felt beset by the culture around them. But the core impulse remained the simple quest for perceptible divine action, and those who were nurtured in holiness supernaturalism and continued to promote it after the turn of the century, like F. F. Bosworth, became the key leaders of the early pentecostal movement.

2

A Pentecostal Leader-in-the-Making

> I did rise and say these few words, but in a quiet voice, "Praise God, praise God, I believe Pentecost is for me tonight" and sat down . . . I was definitely conscious of two things—the very near presence of the Devil on one hand and the dear Lord Jesus standing very close by.
>
> —BERNICE C. LEE, "A HOLY JUBILEE"[1]

WHEN FRED FRANCIS BOSWORTH rehearsed his life story for an audience gathered at the Toronto Christian and Missionary Alliance Tabernacle in 1923, several details were conspicuously lacking.[2] Two of the most important figures in Bosworth's early professional and spiritual development—John Alexander Dowie and Charles Parham—went unmentioned as Bosworth recalled his providential tale. Dowie's utopian community Zion City, Illinois, became a haven for divine healing advocates of the turn of the century, including Bosworth, who lived there, served as a

---

1. Lee, "Holy Jubilee," 9.
2. Bosworth, *Bosworth's Life Story*. Although undated, this Toronto address was most likely delivered in 1923. Bosworth held meetings in Toronto in the spring of 1921 and the first week of May 1922, but the "Alliance Tabernacle" in which he delivered this account was not opened until May 14, 1922. See Reynolds, *Rebirth*, 67–69. The 1923 date is corroborated by the fact that the earliest advertisement I have found for this publication is in *Alliance Weekly* October 20, 1923, 552.

deacon, and worked in Dowie's employ for years. Parham, who had visited Dowie's work in Chicago in 1900, came to Zion City in the fall of 1906 and introduced to Bosworth and a host of other Dowieites the doctrine of baptism with the Holy Spirit evidenced by speaking in tongues. Dowie made Bosworth a spiritual leader; Parham made him a pentecostal.

Spiritual autobiography is a meaning-making endeavor laden with theological and personal agendas. As D. Bruce Hindmarsh explains, it "is always apologetic of the individual."[3] This is especially true of holiness and pentecostal leaders, whose "testimonies" are often central to their ministries. The holiness-turned-pentecostal evangelist Maria Woodworth-Etter left out of her lengthy personal story her part in the failed prophecies of a tidal wave to hit the California Bay Area in April of 1890.[4] Aimee Semple McPherson's numerous autobiographical writings are, according to Edith Blumhofer, "an intentional and selective presentation of the parts of her experience that she chose to disclose because such disclosure suited her purpose."[5] The subjectivity of spiritual autobiography must be considered when weighing Bosworth's own retelling of his life, as well as the biography written by his early admirer Eunice Perkins.[6] While frustrating to the historian looking for hard facts, it is helpful for understanding the deeper truths of motivation and the construction of meaning within communities.

Bosworth had good reason in the early 1920s to leave Dowie and Parham out of his account. Neither leader, each who showed so much promise in the early years of the century, claimed many disciples by the end of the first decade. In September of 1905, Dowie had suffered a debilitating stroke and increasingly came under suspicion of sexual misconduct and misappropriation of funds. His progressively grandiose claims about himself—first as Messenger of the Covenant, then Elijah the Restorer, then First Apostle of the Lord Jesus Christ—began to create tensions and further alienate him from others in the holiness and divine healing movement. Dowie's death in 1907 simply capped his steady decline in authority. And Parham, although beginning from a position of strength in the early 1900s as he propagated his view of spirit-baptism, quickly fell from grace in the pentecostal movement he helped create. He began to lose control when he decided not to go immediately to Azusa Street when his student William Seymour reported a

---

3. Hindmarsh, *Evangelical Conversion Narrative*, 5.
4. Warner, *Woman Evangelist*, 99.
5. Blumhofer, *Aimee Semple McPherson*, 396–97.
6. Similarities in phraseology between Bosworth's autobiography and Perkin's work abound. Compare, for instance, Bosworth, *Bosworth's Life Story*, 2–3; and Perkins, *Joybringer Bosworth*, 21.

new Pentecost at this outpost of Parham's Apostolic Faith network. When Parham finally did come to Los Angeles at the end of 1906, he lambasted the worship and preaching he encountered, making many more enemies than friends. By mid-1907 he was also effectively disowned by his supporters in the Midwest and South after the national press aired allegations of sexual misconduct and connected Parham's ministry to the manslaughter of an invalid woman exorcised by pentecostals. Of particular concern to Bosworth, Parham was the originator of the tongues evidence teaching, which by 1918 Bosworth viewed as an unscriptural innovation. Bosworth, being effectively disowned by pentecostal denominations who embraced this teaching and finding his support in broader evangelical circles, gained nothing by advertising his earlier connections to Parham.

Bosworth's own self-conscious editing notwithstanding, no discussion of his life is complete without Dowie and Parham. In part, this chapter will attempt to do what Bosworth avoided, that is, place Bosworth firmly in the stream of the radical holiness and early pentecostal movements developed by Dowie, Parham, and others who carried into the new century the radical holiness quest for the supernatural. Like Bernice Lee, who witnessed Bosworth's pentecostal baptism and experienced her own eleven days later at Dowie's Zion City, these believers had a penchant for sensing both God and the devil at work in the world. Coming to spiritual maturity in this milieu, Bosworth emerges as the typical pentecostal leader-in-the-making, but one who, like others who are often marginalized in pentecostal history, had no lasting connection to the pentecostal denominations and no significant ties to the famed Azusa Street revival.

CHILDHOOD, CONVERSION, AND HEALING

Fred Francis Bosworth, the second son of Burton and Amelia Bosworth, was born on January 17, 1877, on a farm near what would be Utica, Nebraska.[7] He was an adventurous yet sensitive youngster, showing an early interest in turning a profit and entertaining through music. Bosworth carefully taught himself how to play the cornet during down time while working in his father's feed store. His passion for music would prove to be a decisive factor in his later development as a religious leader. Although his parents were "devout Methodists," Bosworth never indicated that his family had any decisive spiritual influence on him. Instead, his spiritual journey—as he saw

---

7. Unless otherwise noted, biographical information on Bosworth's life before 1902 comes from Perkins, *Joybringer Bosworth*, 19–38; and Bosworth, *Life Story of Evangelist F. F. Bosworth*. This booklet appeared with slight variations as Bosworth, "From Farm to Pulpit," 5–6, 8, 11.

it—began when at age seventeen he joined his friend Maude Greene at a Methodist meeting in Omaha. To please his friend, he came forward when a call for salvation was offered. Once there, however, he felt that he must make a definite decision. At the altar, he said "yes" to God in typical Methodist and revivalist fashion.

While his altar experience was for Bosworth an authentic and joyous occasion, Bosworth was—by his own admission—without direction after his conversion. As his early biographer put it, sensitive believers are often "restless and wholly unsatisfied," until finding "the very center of God's will."[8] Bosworth's late teenager years provide ample evidence of what historian Robert M. Anderson called the "job-hopping tendency" that typified the transitory economic experience of the early pentecostal leaders.[9] In the 1890s, Bosworth worked in turn as an engineer in a windmill factory, grocery clerk, cook, butcher, railroad worker, cross-cut saw operator, and house painter. Upon later reflection, Bosworth said what was missing was baptism with the Holy Spirit. Along with many early pentecostals, Bosworth felt that spirit-baptism could remedy a myriad of problems converted Christians experienced—lack of power over sin, ineffectiveness in ministry, vocational indecision, and assurance of salvation, among other issues.[10]

Bosworth's family had moved to University Place, a suburb of Lincoln, sometime in the early 1890s. Around this time, Bosworth developed a lung ailment that he attributed to exposure to the winter air. Bosworth's condition did not improve with "lung builder and food tonic," and a physician pronounced him incurable. After a brief bed-ridden visit with extended family in Prophetstown, Illinois, Bosworth traveled to the newly-incorporated city of Fitzgerald, Georgia, where his parents had moved.[11] Bosworth expected this to be his last chance to see his family before he died. While his health improved slightly in the Georgia air, he continued to suffer a painful cough.

In Fitzgerald, Bosworth's life took many turns for the better. He operated a barber shop, became assistant post master and later city clerk. His music blossomed, as he took charge of the Empire State Band. Bosworth

---

8. Perkins, *Joybringer Bosworth*, 38.

9. Anderson, *Vision of the Disinherited*, 107.

10. An excellent example of early pentecostals' view of spirit-baptism as a panacea is seen in the testimony of Antoinette Moomau: "To sum it up, the baptism of the Spirit means to me what I never dreamed it could this side of Heaven: victory, glory in my soul, perfect peace, rest, liberty, nearness to Christ, deadness to this old world, and power in witnessing." Moomau, "China Missionary Receives Pentecost," 3. Cited in Land, *Pentecostal Spirituality*, 153.

11. Fitzgerald was incorporated in 1896 as a haven for Union veterans. Barnes, "Why F. F. Bosworth and His Family Moved."

met Estella—like him, a Nebraska transplant—whom he married in late 1900. This series of improvements began with the most important event in Bosworth's early life: the healing of his lung problems under the ministry of holiness evangelist Mattie Perry sometime between 1896 and 1898.[12]

Mattie Perry (1868–1957) of South Carolina was the daughter of a traveling Methodist evangelist who, as she put it, "trusted God for healing."[13] Perry was converted at age twelve and sanctified in July 1887.[14] While she claimed the blessing by faith, she testified to an immediate experience of assurance. "He most graciously heard my cry," she gloried, "cleansed my heart, and flooded my soul with His Spirit. I knew that the work was done."[15] Her sanctification theology evinced the Wesleyan cleansing theme as well as the newer pentecostal imagery. "[W]e can't live [a pure, virtuous life]," she declared, "until we are cleansed, and filled with the Holy Spirit."[16]

At Williamston Female College, Perry's lifelong health problems first surfaced: recurring eye problems, heart and lungs diseases, and neuralgia. Like most others who testified to divine healing, she complained of growing worse under physicians and of being discouraged "by some that the day of miracles was past." But she could not square this with her simple reading of Hebrews 13:8: "Jesus Christ the same yesterday, today, and forever." At one point her illness forced her to leave school for a year, during which she claimed to be healed through the prayers of one "who taught divine healing."[17]

With her health renewed, Perry returned to school, finishing her studies in June 1892. Around this time, she began independent city mission work in Spartanburg.[18] In 1893 she applied to the Methodist Church for official commission in city mission work. She was discouraged when all they would

---

12. Pavel Hejzlar dates Bosworth's healing to 1900. Hejzlar, *Two Paradigms for Divine Healing*, 19. Roscoe Barnes puts the healing around 1899. Barnes, *F. F. Bosworth*, 77. Bosworth nowhere gives the exact date of his healing but indicated that *after his healing* he worked as a barber for an unspecified time, two years as assistant post master, and two more as city clerk—a position he lost in December 1900. Bosworth, *Life Story of Evangelist F. F. Bosworth*, 6. In his *Life Story* published in 1923, Bosworth stated that he would have been dead "twenty-five years now" had he not been healed. This would place his healing in 1898 at the latest. Finally, placing Bosworth's healing between 1896 and 1898 also better corresponds with Mattie Perry's itinerancy, as she began a more settled ministry in 1898 when she founded Elhanan Institute.

13. Perry, *Christ and Answered Prayer*, 22.

14. Perry, *Christ and Answered Prayer*, 28, 35.

15. Perry, *Christ and Answered Prayer*, 36.

16. Perry, *Christ and Answered Prayer*, 37.

17. Perry, *Christ and Answered Prayer*, 40–42, 69.

18. Perry, *Christ and Answered Prayer*, 46–47.

offer her was work as a sales agent of *Way of Faith*, an influential southern holiness periodical that would later be a chief promoter of pentecostalism to southern holiness circles. Another setback occurred in 1894 when the Methodist Episcopal Church Board of Missions denied her application for work in China.[19] But Perry was soon tapped to work interdenominational tent meetings in connection with her *Way of Faith* work. She worked alongside evangelists J. A. Williams and H. H. Merritt, her brothers Sam and Jim, her sister Lillie, as well as her father. Perry claimed to have traveled to twelve states, with their work centered on the Carolinas and Georgia.[20] After attending a Christian and Missionary Alliance (C&MA) convention in New York in 1895, Perry trained at the C&MA's New York Missionary Institute.[21] She left the Missionary Institute in May of 1896, serving as the C&MA superintendent for a number of southern states in conjunction with her tent evangelism.[22]

Feeling convicted that she had not testified publicly to her healing, Perry began to devote one service in each revival to healing. "Sinners wanted a perfect Savior," she beamed, "one who can save to the uttermost, both body and soul."[23] She soon began to see results, praying successfully for the healing of an Atlanta woman who had broken her leg and hip. In South Carolina, a "poor crippled negro boy" claimed salvation and healing the same night under Perry's ministrations. In Fitzgerald, Georgia, where Perry prayed for Bosworth, a woman was healed of chronic scrofula, which affected the lymph nodes and often resulted in drainage from the neck. Perry emphasized the instantaneous nature of divine healing. In North Carolina, a woman suffering from dropsy asked for prayer. Perry asked her: "If [God] is willing and able to heal you [as you have confessed], when does He want to heal you?" The woman gave the only acceptable response: "Now." She was healed "the moment her faith took it," according to Perry.[24]

Perry is remembered most for her Elhanan Bible and Training School in Marion, North Carolina. The school opened in 1898, added an orphanage in 1901, and had some 1,200 students pass through before fire crippled the institution in 1926 and it was closed the following year.[25] For Perry, evangelism worked hand in hand with social service. She aimed to "bless suffering

---

19. Perry, *Christ and Answered Prayer*, 53.
20. Perry, *Christ and Answered Prayer*, 55–57.
21. Perry, *Christ and Answered Prayer*, A. B. Simpson's introduction, 42–43.
22. Perry, *Christ and Answered Prayer*, 145.
23. Perry, *Christ and Answered Prayer*, 59.
24. Perry, *Christ and Answered Prayer*, 72–76.
25. Perry, *Christ and Answered Prayer*, 158.

humanity, rob hell of her victims, make earth better, and heaven richer and sweeter."[26] Her theology of healing flowed from this recognition that "the whole man is included in redemption."[27]

Through much of the first two decades of the twentieth century, Perry had severe health problems and was often confined to a wheelchair. But Perry resumed itinerant ministry in the 1920s and 30s. In fact, she assisted in Bosworth's Pittsburg campaign in 1920.[28] She also held meetings at Bosworth's Dallas church in March of 1921.[29] In 1928 and 1929 she undertook a year-long trip to the Holy Land. Inspired by the sacred geography, she began producing Bible harmonies to use as correspondence courses, and in this connection, Perry joined the faculty of God's Bible School in Cincinnati in 1937, which was founded by holiness legend Martin Wells Knapp.[30]

Like many holiness leaders, Perry had a complex relationship with the pentecostal movement. Perry's brother Samuel received his spirit-baptism in August of 1907, and by the end of the year, he had led pentecostal meetings in Marion in conjunction with Elhanan Institute.[31] In 1909 he joined the Church of God (Cleveland, Tennessee) and continued to spread Pentecost throughout the South. Mattie probably received her pentecostal baptism at the 1907 meetings, and she accompanied Samuel on his pioneer pentecostal mission to Cuba in 1910.[32] Mattie nowhere detailed her understanding of pentecostal baptism and never mentioned speaking in tongues. At different times, both Samuel and Mattie were on the ministerial roster of the Assemblies of God.[33]

Although Perry's precise pentecostal theology is difficult to ascertain, she clearly shared the pentecostal supernaturalist worldview. While at school in New York, she testified constantly to miraculous answers to prayer. The money for her trip was provided when she did not even have enough to mail a letter to the school. "In one day in answer to prayer," she beamed, "a hat, money, fruit and tracts were given me by my loving heavenly

---

26. Perry, *Christ and Answered Prayer*, 123.
27. Perry, *Christ and Answered Prayer*, 228.
28. Perry, *Christ and Answered Prayer*, 229.
29. Perry, *Christ and Answered Prayer*, 237.
30. Perry, *Christ and Answered Prayer*, 266.
31. "Good Tidings from Marion, N. C.," 1. See also "Report of Meeting: Newton, N. C.," 4.
32. Perry, *Christ and Answered Prayer*, 65.
33. For Samuel's and Mattie's affiliation with the Assemblies of God, see *Constitution and By-Laws of the General Council . . . 1929*, 116; *Official List of Ministers and Missionaries . . . 1930*, 28. A handwritten note in the 1930 roster states that Mattie Perry's ordination lapsed November 18, 1931.

Father." Perry saw God's supernatural benevolence everywhere she looked. The smallest incidents in life took on epic spiritual meaning, and even the unexpected gift of fifty cents was a cause to rejoice that "faith takes hold of promises."[34] Yet Perry's interpretation of life events was more nuanced than later healing advocates would often have it. She did not believe that healing was always God's will, and she recognized that suffering was often given by God as a test.[35] Being "proved" through her suffering, Perry testified to renewed health at the time of her pentecostal spirit-baptism.[36] After she was healed again in 1919, she embarked on an evangelistic trip in the West.[37] As reporters recognized, "the big attraction was divine healing" in many of Perry's meetings.[38]

For Bosworth, the most important development in Perry's life was her dedication to faith healing in the mid-1890s. While attending Perry's service in Fitzgerald, Bosworth "coughed painfully" and "went to the front to be prayed for." As Perkins explained it,

> Miss Perry told him how lovingly ready God was to make him well, in the name of Jesus, and laying her hands on him she prayed that he might be healed. From that self-same hour Fred began to mend, until, ere many days, his lung trouble was entirely a thing of the past.[39]

As Bosworth told the Toronto audience, "Miss Perry told me that I did not need to die, that it was God's will to heal me. Then she prayed for me and I was healed."[40]

Bosworth's aimlessness following his conversion disappeared after his healing. Now he had, according to Perkins, both the ambition and physical ability to work.[41] After a short stint as owner of a barber shop, Bosworth was encouraged to serve as Fitzgerald's assistant post master. He leveraged this experience into a successful bid for City Clerk. His support for Prohibition hobbled his reelection campaign in 1900, but his political—and presumably fiscal—experience fitted him well for subsequent jobs as a bookkeeper and

---

34. Perry, *Christ and Answered Prayer*, 44.
35. Perry, *Christ and Answered Prayer*, 68.
36. Perry, *Christ and Answered Prayer*, 72.
37. Perry, "Call to Prayer," 8–9; Perry, *Christ and Answered Prayer*, 204.
38. Perry, *Christ and Answered Prayer*, 239.
39. Perkins, *Joybringer Bosworth*, 28.
40. Bosworth, *Life Story of Evangelist F. F. Bosworth*, 6.
41. Perkins, *Joybringer Bosworth*, 31.

bank teller. All the while, Bosworth developed his musical talents as leader for two local bands that merged under his direction.

THE CITY OF GOD

While Bosworth was basking in the after-effects of his divine healing, he grew frustrated with the ungodly associations into which he was led by his musical interests. He discovered these two concerns could merge when in Fitzgerald he came across an issue of *Leaves of Healing*, the periodical published by John Alexander Dowie from Zion City, Illinois. Dowie had dedicated Zion City on the shores of Lake Michigan in 1900, opened its gates to residents in 1901, and formally incorporated the city in March of 1902. That same year, Bosworth and his family moved to the midwestern utopia. Thoroughly bearing the stamp of its enigmatic leader, Zion City was an exhaustively supernaturalist experiment, founded on "primitive order and primitive power."[42]

John Alexander Dowie (1847–1907) was born in Scotland, grew up in Australia, and returned to Scotland for his university education.[43] He began his ministry with the Congregational Church in 1872 in the Sydney area. In 1876, Dowie's ministry expanded to include divine healing when, in the course of a plague that had him conducting some forty funerals, he prayed for a woman who quickly recovered. He left the Congregationalist ministry in 1878 and established his Free Christian Church in Melbourne in 1883. Shortly after this, he also organized the Divine Healing Association and began making a name for himself by denouncing liquor. Inspired by a vision, Dowie took his ministry to the United States in 1888, establishing a base in San Francisco and itinerating along the West Coast. He moved into the Midwest in 1890, launching evangelistic campaigns from his base in the Chicago area. His fame exploded during the Chicago World's Fair in 1893 when he set up a wood hut tabernacle across from the Wild West Show of Buffalo Bill Cody and even healed Cody's relative Sadie Cody.[44]

Dowie began to run afoul of medical law in 1895; he claimed he was arrested almost one hundred times and spent $20,000 in legal defense. These altercations gave him a platform from which to preach the gospel,

---

42. Cook, *Zion City*, 172.

43. Unless otherwise noted, this outline of Dowie's ministry is based on Wacker, "Marching to Zion," 496–511; and Wacker, Armstrong, and Blossom, "John Alexander Dowie," 3–19. More detail can be found in Rolvix Harlan, "John Alexander Dowie"; and Cook, *Zion City*. A sympathetic, but sober and straightforward account of Dowie's life can be found in Lindsay, *Life of John Alexander Dowie*.

44. For the Sadie Cody healing, see Cook, *Zion City*, 12.

denounce sin, denominations, and medicine and make declarations about his own unique role as God's end-time servant. That year, he created the Christian Catholic Church. From this point forward, he viewed his own organization as the only true church. He declared that his mission was to "smash every other church in existence."[45]

Dowie envisioned Zion City to be a place where his "full gospel" of salvation, healing, and holy living could thrive. Dowie ran Zion City as a theocracy—a label he proudly claimed. From June of 1901, acceptance of Dowie as Elijah was required for residence in Zion City.[46] The population during its utopian era probably topped around 7,500, bringing residents from across the nation and the globe (they claimed thirty-seven nationalities) to the approximately ten square miles that hugged Lake Michigan's shoreline between Milwaukee and Chicago—or "Beer and Babel," as Dowie referred to the cities. As Philip Cook puts it, Dowie's followers yearned for "a community where it would be easy to do right and hard to do wrong."[47] Residents were prohibited from smoking, dancing, drinking, gambling, swearing, and even spitting.

The nearly self-contained society enjoyed a small boom in its early years, and many residents were drawn to the community for financial security during one of the bleakest times for the American working class. A profit-sharing system persuaded residents that Zion's slogan was true: "Where God Rules Man Prospers." With a lace factory as the backbone, a bank, building society, publishing company, general store, hotel, daily newspaper, and manufacturing of candy, furniture, and soap rounded out the economy. Homes for orphans, wayward women, and the elderly attested to its commitment to benevolence. A school system provided education for all ages through college. And of course, religion was at the center of life, just as the 5,200-seat Shiloh Tabernacle sat at the center of the city. Residents leased their property for 1,100 years, signaling the belief that Christ would return within a hundred years to establish the millennium. The lease also signaled residents' complete submission to Dowie's leadership, since leases could be revoked for infractions of Zion policy.

Dowie's vision was grand and ever-expanding. In the fall of 1903, Dowie led a group of three thousand Zionites on a crusade to New York City. The visitation was an object of fascination for the press, as it was covered daily in the *New York Times* and received national attention. From October

---

45. Harlan, "John Alexander Dowie," 1.

46. Wacker, Armstrong, and Blossom, "John Alexander Dowie," 8. For the "restoration vow," see Cook, *Zion City*, 145–46.

47. Cook, *Zion City*, x.

18 to November 1, Dowie held meetings at Madison Square Garden, mostly to mediocre results: only eighty baptisms and one hundred twenty-five new members.[48] Still, Dowie declared the trip a success because his workers had canvassed one million homes with Zion's gospel and he was confident that "what God would do would be seen in due time."[49] But heavenly jewels do not pay the rent. The New York work cost at least $250,000 and coincided with financial difficulties in general.[50] Dowie's extended absence during a world tour in 1904 strained finances and confidence, as did his increasing obsession with pouring scarce resources into a new Zion settlement in Mexico. In January of 1905, a couple of high-profile deaths cast a pall over the community that viewed health as signs of divine pleasure. To make matters worse, Zion's General Financial Manager and Dowie's secretary resigned around the same time.[51]

Through these trials, Dowie was usually able to restore confidence by sheer force of charisma. It did not hurt that his return from his world tour in 1904 seemed to trigger much-needed rain during a summer drought. His followers believed Dowie—by this time recognized as First Apostle—had the stamp of God upon his work. But neither Dowie nor Zion could recover when the Apostle suffered a stroke in September of 1905 and again in December. The Apostle left for Jamaica to recover, leaving Zion in the hands of Wilbur Glenn Voliva, the Overseer of the Australian branch. Voliva became Dowie's chief adversary, accusing him of financial and sexual misconduct. In September Voliva was elected leader of a hobbled Zion. Dowie died the next year deserted by all but a few devotees who sat at the Prophet's bedside to listen to his sermons.

How much Bosworth knew of the battles in 1906 is not known. As a deacon and leader of the City Band, Bosworth could not have been ignorant of the disputes. With more than a decade of distance from the tumultuous months in Zion in mid-1906, Bosworth's biographer exonerated Bosworth for his participation in the failed utopia:

> There are sane, spiritual, trusted men of God, in this country today, who will agree with the writer that when 'Mr. Dowie' first came to the public notice he was a true Christian man, most certainly used of God.[52]

---

48. Cook, *Zion City*, 146–50.
49. "New York Visitation of Elijah the Restorer," 146.
50. Cook, *Zion City*, 154–58.
51. Cook, *Zion City*, 177–79.
52. Perkins, *Joybringer Bosworth*, 35.

This half-excuse was the normal defense of those who came from Zion. As early as 1906, in the midst of Voliva's upheaval, Harlan noted that those who left Zion or repudiated Dowie disagreed with his leadership style, his morals, or his misguided claims about his own spiritual role, but never disavowed his ability to heal.[53] In other words, Dowie's followers would not disown their own experience of the supernatural at his hands.

Arriving in 1902, Bosworth was baptized on August 10 at Shiloh Tabernacle. Dowie's particular understanding of baptism required believers to be rebaptized. Dowie argued that the biblical pattern for baptism was triune immersion, and all other forms were "useless." Dowie went so far as to say that "all who believe in single immersion are lost forever."[54] In submitting to baptism, Bosworth joined more than thirteen thousand who had been baptized in Dowie's church since the opening of Chicago's Central Zion Tabernacle in 1897. How long Bosworth had been in Zion City is unknown, but by the time of his baptism, he considered the Illinois utopia his home.[55] Bosworth, along with thirty-four others, was ordained a deacon in Zion on July 21, 1903, and at this time (if not earlier), he likely assented to Dowie's claim to be Elijah.[56] Over the next year or so, Bosworth's immediate family—father, mother, and brother Burton—joined him in Zion City and were baptized.[57] His children Vivian and Vernon were consecrated in 1904.[58]

Turn-of-the-century Americans like the Bosworths were attracted to Zion City for several reasons. Divine healing, financial prosperity, protection from worldliness, a progressive political policy, and Dowie's publicity skills all contributed to the remarkable growth of Zion City.[59] By the time the Bosworths arrived, at least two thousand residents called it home. Bosworth's early biographer claimed that Bosworth was attracted to the city as a place where his musical talents could flourish in a wholesome environment.[60] Economic reasons may have played a role, since Bosworth's parents

53. Harlan, "John Alexander Dowie," 79.

54. "Dowie Rails at Churches," 2.

55. "Obeying God in Baptism," (August 16, 1902) 576.

56. "Closing Service of the Feast," 576; "Close of Third Feast," 155; "Some Figures of the Feast," 158.

57. "Obeying God in Baptism," (August 30, 1902) 644; "Obeying God in Baptism," (November 1, 1902) 60.

58. Vivian's name was sometimes spelled Vivien. For Amelia Bosworth's arrival in Zion City, see "Personal Mention," 370. For her baptism, see "Obeying God in Baptism," (September 26, 1903) 742. For the consecrations of Vivian and Vernon, see "Obeying God in Baptism," (July 30, 1904) 490, 491.

59. Wacker, Armstrong, and Blossom, "John Alexander Dowie," 10–15.

60. Perkins, *Joybringer Bosworth*, 36. As Perkins admits, this may have been only a

also came to the city. Another possibility is that Bosworth's lung problems continued to bother him, and he looked for healing in the community.[61]

Regardless of what brought him to Zion, Bosworth soon found his place and began playing cornet with the band on Sunday morning services while working as bookkeeper for the Fresh Food Supply. By February of 1903, Bosworth was the leader of the Zion City brass band, making his large-scale debut at the Seventh Anniversary of the Christian Catholic Church before an audience of four thousand at Shiloh Tabernacle.[62] On March 1, the position became full-time with a salary, allowing Bosworth to leave his work at the Zion City Credit Department.[63] The band leader position entailed selecting music, writing arrangements, conducting the band, and training amateur musicians in private lessons. The Zion City community was thrilled with Bosworth's musical and leadership talents, calling him a "born musician," and a "director of unusual ability."[64]

In his capacity as band leader, Bosworth played an indispensable role in one pillar of Dowie's organizational success. Dowie had a knack for public spectacle and celebration, creating Zion holidays out of the anniversary of the Church's founding, the dedication of the site for the Temple (which was never erected), and an annual Feast of Tabernacles. The band was prominent at all these celebrations. The band also played the role of ambassador for Zion City to neighboring communities, performing well-received public concerts for nearby Kenosha, Waukegan, Racine, and Chicago.[65] The joy of Bosworth's musical career came later in 1903 when he accompanied Dowie and three thousand Dowieites to New York City, where the thirty-eight-member band played for ten days at Madison Square Garden.[66] Dowie was proud of not only the musical quality, but also the moral integrity of the band. "Those young men in the band love God," beamed Dowie, "and there is no beer or tobacco in them, but the Spirit of God, and that makes the

---

"subconscious" motivation.

61. Bosworth, *Life Story of Evangelist F. F. Bosworth*, 7.

62. "Seventh Anniversary," 593. For other references to Bosworth's musical work, see "Zion Musical Organizations," 178; "Third Anniversary," 426; "All Night with God," 372; and "Citizens' Mid-Week Rally," 701.

63. "Zion City Brass Band."

64. "Splendid Music," 145. "Zion Musical Organizations," 178. See also the praise for Bosworth in "Early Morning Sacrifice," (August 6, 1904) 515.

65. "Zion City Band to Give Concerts," 289; "Gave a Fine Concert," 7; "Zion City Band Concert," 246. This article quotes the Racine *Daily Journal* of April 19, 1905.

66. "Dowie and His Host," 3.

music sweet."[67] Dowie was so impressed with Bosworth's abilities that on the way home from New York, he requested that the band increase tenfold.[68]

Bosworth's work with the band put him in contact with other Dowieites who had a similar commitment to clean living and divine healing. J. Roswell Flower, who went on to be a high-profile denominational leader in the Assemblies of God, played cornet in Bosworth's band in Zion City.[69] D. Norton, a former Salvation Army worker, came to Zion City in September of 1905 after Zion work in England and South Africa, and he joined the band immediately.[70] Gilbert Gay, a fourteen year-old member of the Zion Band, testified to healings of numerous ailments, including colds, toothaches, and a dog bite. His most dramatic supernatural recovery occurred in August of 1902, when he tripped over a stick that cut clean through his pants, tearing his scrotum. After receiving prayer from his mother and three neighbors, the profuse bleeding and intense pain ceased.[71] Bosworth was well-liked by his bandmates, who helped him celebrate his fifth wedding anniversary and the birth of his son, Vernon.[72] Bosworth's leadership brought him to the attention of more than his fellow bandmates, as the *Zion Banner* felt compelled to make know that the band leader of fair features and slight frame was indeed married.[73]

Three weeks before the 1903 New York crusade, Bosworth's spiritual service in the Zion community expanded briefly and dramatically. Mary Louise Shepard, a Zion City lace worker who as part of the Restoration Host was also scheduled to depart for New York, came down with a severe fever. She was at the time living with the family of Deacon O. L. Sprecher, and Mrs. Sprecher brought Bosworth in to pray with Shepard. Feeling intense pain as well, Shepard testified that after Bosworth prayed for her, her pain was gone. But she did not regain health immediately; her fever persisted, and Bosworth was called in to pray again a few days later. This time, she testified that before Bosworth removed his hands, the fever had left her. Her healing allowed her to participate in the New York canvasing and return to factory work without interruption.[74] Bosworth may have demonstrated

67. "Notes from Zion's Harvest Field," (March 26, 1904) 693.
68. "Zion City Bands for Next Visitation," 10.
69. Gardiner, *Out of Zion*, 31. For Flower's baptism in Zion City, see, "Obeying God in Baptism," (August 1, 1903) 487.
70. "More Musicians for Zion City Band," 411.
71. "God's Witnesses to Divine Healing," 745–47.
72. "Bandmaster Bosworth Surprised," 58; "Zion's Birth Record for 1903," 122.
73. "Splendid Music by Zion Band," 145.
74. "Healed of Fever," 709.

his budding interest in spiritual leadership by hosting cottage meetings in his home. According to John G. Lake, Charles Parham's sister-in-law Lilian Thistlethwaite preached in Bosworth's home in Zion before 1905. At this time, according to Lake, he and Bosworth experienced sanctification in preparation for spirit-baptism.[75]

PENTECOST IN ZION

When Dowie's empire began to crumble in early 1906, everyone in Zion City was affected. Bosworth felt the financial strain on his beloved band, which reorganized musical training in January of 1906. Whereas previously music lessons were provided free of charge to those interested in joining the band, from this point forward, aspiring musicians were required to pay for instruction. This possibly indicates that Bosworth's salary was eliminated or severely cut, as Bosworth immediately began advertising for private students.[76] For pentecostal history, the most important aspect of Dowie's decline began when a group of Dowieites in Zion City invited Charles Parham to the city.

On New Year's Day, 1901, Charles Parham (1873–1929) and his students at the short-lived Bethel Bible school in Topeka, Kansas, had come to the conclusion that the "indisputable proof" of baptism with the Holy Spirit (which Parham taught was a third blessing following sanctification) was speaking in tongues, by which Parham meant foreign human languages that were unknown to the speaker. For Parham, tongues were a way to acquire languages for foreign missions without lengthy study. But Parham also believed tongues signaled the nearness of Christ's return as a definite indicator of the "latter rain" and designated that the recipient was "sealed" for the coming rapture. Parham referred to tongues as the "Bible evidence" of spirit-baptism, and within two days more than a dozen had the experience, including Parham and his sister-in-law, Lilian Thistlethwaite. The surge of excitement for the pentecostal experience in early 1901 was followed by a series of evangelistic disappointments. Parham's ministry

---

75. Lake, *John G. Lake*, 164–65, 458–59. "Before 1905" is deduced from Lake's account. After describing Thistlethwaite's meeting in Zion City, Lake wrote that "Later, Brother Parham was preaching in Texas." According to Parham's wife and Parham's modern-day biographer, Parham was not in Texas before 1905. See Parham, *Life of Charles F. Parham*, 107; and Goff, *Fields White Unto Harvest*, 94. Lake's account, however, is problematic because Thistlethwaite is not mentioned in any other account of the only instance of Parham representatives in Zion City prior to 1906. See Gardiner, *Out of Zion*, 2; Carl Brumback, *Suddenly . . . from Heaven*, 72.

76. "Musicians Meet at Shiloh Tabernacle," 129. For Bosworth's private lessons, see *Zion Banner*, January 17, 1907, 136; January 24, 1906, 144; January 31, 1906, 151.

focus shifted to divine healing while he continued to spread his views on tongues and spirit-baptism among close followers. After notable campaigns in Galena, Kansas, and Joplin, Missouri, in 1903 and 1904, Parham was invited to Texas, opening a short-term school in Houston at the start of 1906. One of Parham's students at the Houston school was William Seymour, a black holiness preacher who had earlier contact with Martin Wells Knapp's work in Cincinnati. In February of 1906, Seymour accepted an invitation to spread Parham's doctrine of spirit-baptism at a holiness congregation in Los Angeles. Although the congregation dismissed his views and locked him from the church, Seymour found a small group of supporters who became the nucleus of the Azusa Street revival.[77]

While Seymour was overseeing the rapidly-expanding work in Los Angeles, Parham answered the call to Zion City, arriving around September 20 and intentionally postponing a visit to Azusa Street in the process. This was not Parham's first contact with Dowie's ministry. In 1900, Parham made a trip across the United States observing the ministries of a number of high-profile holiness ministers who emphasized the restoration of the New Testament experience, including Dowie's work in Chicago and A. B. Simpson's work in New York.[78] Parham also had indirect contact with Zion City through a Mrs. Waldron, who had received spirit-baptism under Parham in Kansas and moved to Zion City around 1904.[79] Waldron attempted to spread Parham's teaching in Zion City, believing Parham's message to be compatible with Dowie's. Dowie and his officers did not agree, and Waldron, along with a handful of others, was pressured to leave the city.[80] In March of 1906, D. C. O. Opperman, Zion's director of education, came into contact with Parham in Houston. Opperman became convinced of Parham's teaching and wrote to leaders in Zion City, urging them to consider the

---

77. For this period in Parham's ministry, see Goff, *Fields White unto Harvest*, chap. 3–5.

78. Parham, *Life of Charles F. Parham*, 48.

79. One may speculate that Waldron's presence in Zion City in 1904 corresponded with the meetings conducted in Zion City by Lilian Thistlethwaite. See Burpeau, *God's Showman*, 42.

80. Gardiner, *Out of Zion*, 2; Brumback, *Suddenly . . . from Heaven*, 72. Waldron was baptized in Zion City on May 1, 1904. "Obeying God in Baptism," (May 14, 1904) 111. Another who accepted the pentecostal message in 1904 was Louise Albach, whose address (2819 Emmaus Ave.) was very near the Bosworths, who lived at 2807 Emmaus Ave. and 2810 Elisha Ave. (These houses shared a back yard.) See "Directory of The Ordained Officers," 618. This perhaps supports the contention that Bosworth was somehow involved in this 1904 visit of Parhamites in Zion. See Burpeau, *God's Showman*, 42.

matter. Opperman's correspondence and later brief visit probably paved the way for Parham's arrival.[81]

When Parham came to Zion City with a handful of helpers, he found a small, but eager reception. Leading meetings in Elijah Hospice, the main hotel of Zion City, Parham steadily increased his audience, and within a week's time, had won hundreds of sympathizers. When Voliva became wise to Parham's work, he banned him from the hotel, driving Parham's meetings into private homes. One of the homes that opened its doors to Parham was F. F. Bosworth's. As Parham's wife Sarah remarked, Bosworth's home was "literally converted into a meeting house."[82] Initially, Parham did not emphasize tongues. But on October 17, the pentecostal experience erupted, as twenty-four Zionites reportedly spoke in German, Italian, Russian, Spanish, and Norwegian.[83]

This incident opened the floodgates of pentecostal expectation. The next day, one of Parham's assistants, Jessie Brown, was encouraging a group of seekers at the home of a Mrs. Ames. Echoing Phoebe Palmer, Brown instructed seekers "of the need to praise for what we believed we were to receive"—in this case, the baptism of the Holy Spirit. Zion member Bernice Lee sat next to Bosworth at the meeting, and she later described how the experience began to spread. Responding to Brown's encouragement, a man on the other side of Lee suddenly "rose to his feet while [Brown] was speaking, and with face uplifted, his eyes shining, he padded back and forth in the room, singing in tongues." Then, as if emboldened by what he saw, Bosworth "leaped to his feet, burst out in tongues, and sat down."[84] When the blessing came, it was immediate, according to Bosworth.[85] But it was not without preparation. "I knew these people had something I did not have and I wanted it," he later recalled. To prove to himself and to God that he was ready for the blessing, he spent a few days doing "personal work" in Zion City. According to his later pentecostal coworker Cyrus Fockler, Bosworth believed that "God had sanctified and purified his heart" during these weeks. Incensed that Bosworth had opened his home to Parham's party, Voliva "gave him a chance to prove" his sanctification by calling Bosworth into his office for an abusive reprimand. Bosworth was undeterred and endured

---

81. Gardiner, *Out of Zion*, 142–43.
82. Parham, *Life of Charles F. Parham*, 156–57.
83. Goff, *Fields White unto Harvest*, 125.
84. Gardiner, *Out of Zion*, 334, 341.
85. Bosworth, *Life Story of Evangelist F. F. Bosworth*, 7.

the scolding with grace.[86] The following Sunday, Bosworth was publicly "read out" of fellowship with the Christian Catholic Apostolic Church.[87]

Though Bosworth later came to disagree with the teaching that tongues always accompanied spirit-baptism, he never doubted his pentecostal experience or the supernatural power it gave to his life and ministry. Throughout his life, Bosworth identified his spirit-baptism as the moment of "being divinely equipped for unlimited service to God."[88] In fact, so great was the supernatural power of his spirit-baptism, that Bosworth claimed a simultaneous healing from a lingering spot on his lungs.[89] He continued to host meetings in his home and actively encouraged others to make the necessary surrender to God. "I put the last thing on the altar coming up the hill," he told Campbell when she was struggling with the requisite consecration.[90] Phoebe Palmer's altar theology had been claimed for the pentecostal cause in Zion City.

Like Dowie, Charles Parham knew how to cultivate publicity, even if he could not always ensure that it was favorable. Local newspapers viewed him as a serious challenge to Voliva's leadership, and even the *New York Times* took an interest, declaring Parham "a new leader in Zion."[91] Confident that he had begun a good work, and with about fifty who had testified to speaking in tongues, Parham left Zion City on October 23, leaving the work in the charge of W. F. Carothers, Parham's right-hand-man in Texas. While Parham made his overdue trip to Los Angeles, the pentecostal movement in Zion City continued to grow among hundreds of rank-and-file Zionites and leaders. Notable among Zion leaders who became pentecostals were George A. Rogers, manager of the Elijah Hospice, A. F. Lee, the general ecclesiastical secretary of the Christian Catholic Apostolic Church, Hubert Grant, Dowie's personal secretary, and J. G. Speicher, who had baptized Bosworth.[92] Elder William H. Piper sympathized with the dissidents but did

86. Fockler, *Overcomers*, 20–21.
87. "Voliva Drives Out Deacons."
88. Perkins, *Joybringer Bosworth*, 49.
89. Bosworth, *Life Story of Evangelist F. F. Bosworth*, 7.

90. Gardiner, *Out of Zion*, 7. Dowie did not stress a second definite crisis experience for sanctification; rather he preached multiple "consecrations" necessary for growth in holiness and spiritual power. Parham at this time was content with conflating (or at least not pressing the differences between) Dowieite "consecration" and the sanctification experience. See Gardiner, *Out of Zion*, 332, 339; Bosworth, *Life Story of Evangelist F. F. Bosworth*, 7; Perkins, *Joybringer Bosworth*, 48; Blumhofer, "Pentecostal Branch," 136–37; Lake, *John G. Lake*, 164–65, 458–59.

91. "New Leader in Zion City," 7.

92. Goff, *Fields White unto Harvest*, 124; Gardiner, *Out of Zion*, 37–47; Blumhofer, "Christian Catholic Apostolic Church," 137. Speicher later credited his openness to the

not identify with the movement until 1907. Piper's Stone Church in Chicago became a major organizing force for early pentecostalism. With nearly forty former Dowieites later becoming leaders in the Assemblies of God and many converts also going into independent pentecostal work, Zion was clearly a flashpoint of early pentecostalism that operated largely independently of the contemporary Azusa Street revival.[93]

Many factors converged to bless Parham's work at Zion City. As Edith Blumhofer argues, Dowie's "essential message inclined many of his followers towards Parham's ministry."[94] Parham himself assured Zionites and curious onlookers that he presented "no new gospel" in Zion.[95] That was not exactly true, but many in Zion found it easy, as Kemp Burpeau puts it, to accept the "overlay of Pentecostalism" brought by Parham.[96] Future pentecostals were particularly influenced by Dowie's intense restorationist message and practice of spiritual gifts. Dowieites were trained to expect a "latter rain" Holy Spirit outpouring—terminology that was decisive for pentecostal self-understanding.[97] As J. R. Flower, the Assemblies of God statesman who lived in Zion City as a teenager, would later remark, Dowie's ministry "awakened in many a desire for the supernatural and a longing for spiritual reality, which went a long ways toward preparing the way for the rise of the Pentecostal Movement in the twentieth century."[98]

Dowieites saw supernatural forces at work all around them. As an early scholar of Dowieism put it, "What seems to them mysterious and even miraculous is regarded by those who have made a scientific study of human nature as liable to occur at any time."[99] In short, Dowie's supernaturalism stirred a hunger that Zion was ultimately unable to feed, so many latched on to the pentecostal movement as a reasonable replacement or extension of their Dowieite beliefs. In fact, pentecostalism may have spiritually saved

---

pentecostal message to the upright character of Bosworth and other pentecostal converts. See "Is It the Latter Rain?"

93. Anderson, *Vision of the Disinherited*, 270, n. 50. The Zion Faith Homes carried on pentecostal work in Zion that had loose ties to other denominations. See Gardiner, *Out of Zion*, 285–322.

94. Blumhofer, "Christian Catholic Apostolic Church," 140.

95. Parham, *Life of Charles F. Parham*, 182.

96. Burpeau, *God's Showman*, 36.

97. For an example of Dowieite discourse on the "latter rain," see Excell, "Notes of Thanksgiving," 827. For the importance of the latter rain model for early pentecostalism, see Faupel, "Function of 'Models,'" 54–57.

98. J. R. Flower, "History of the Assemblies of God," unpublished notes for course at Central Bible College, 1949, cited in Blumhofer, "Christian Catholic Apostolic Church," 144, n. 45.

99. Harlan, "John Alexander Dowie," 182.

those experiencing the disaster of Zion in 1906–1907. Pentecostalism certainly had some different emphases than Dowieism. While Dowie closely tied spiritual gifts to the apostolic office,[100] later pentecostals determined the gifts were available to every believer. And while Dowie bred an expectation of the miraculous, he had little use for mystical spirituality that would become prominent in the lives of many pentecostals. Nonetheless, decades later, Gordon Lindsay, who worked with F. F. Bosworth in the postwar healing campaigns and whose parents had been residents of Zion City during Dowie's rule, remarked that one major lesson "vividly taught in the life of John Alexander Dowie is the all-importance and power of a supernatural ministry."[101] But without the troubles in Zion in early 1906, it is unlikely that the pentecostal message would have been able to penetrate Zion's walls. Furthermore, the instability of Zion in 1906, combined with Parham's insistence that the spirit-baptized believers go out and preach, encouraged many of the new pentecostals to leave the city, zealously proclaiming their new message as they went.[102]

FROM DOWIEITES TO PENTECOSTALS

Bosworth was one who was not long for Zion after his personal Pentecost. With Zion in turmoil and Bosworth identifying with the pentecostals, Bosworth quickly lost or forfeited his position as band leader.[103] Either way, after his pentecostal experience, he turned to selling pens to make money.[104] But he combined this work with a new call to evangelism. As discussed in subsequent chapters, he set out on evangelistic work in Indiana and Ohio, later pastored a pentecostal church in Dallas, and then embarked on a high-profile divine healing ministry across the United States and Canada. In all these ways, he was influential in the spread of a pentecostalism that was connected to, but not reliant upon Azusa Street. And in this task he was not alone. Other Dowietes-turned-pentecostals were, like Bosworth, major carriers of turn-of-the century holiness supernaturalism into the new pentecostal movement.

John G. Lake (1870–1935) first came into contact with Dowie's work around 1894 in Chicago.[105] Lake visited Dowie's healing home and claimed

100. "Second Special Conference of Ordained Officers," 740.
101. Lindsay, *Life of John Alexander Dowie*, 273.
102. Parham, *Life of Charles F. Parham*, 173.
103. "Zion City Band," 2.
104. Gardiner, *Out of Zion*, 334.
105. Unless otherwise indicated, biographical information on Lake comes from Burpeau, *God's Showman*, 23–73. For Lake's own accounts of healings under Dowie,

to be healed of rheumatism and chronic constipation. Lake's brother and two sisters also experienced healing under Dowie. Most dear of all to Lake was the healing of his wife, whose many healings were featured in the June 15, 1901 *Leaves of Healing*. Through the prayers of Dowie, Jennie Lake was healed of heart disease and tuberculosis in April of 1898. Jennie's healing was the main spur for Lake and his wife to join Dowie's church.[106] Jennie was also healed dramatically of a gunshot wound in August of 1900. John Lake, who had trained for the Methodist ministry, was a natural fit for leadership in Dowie's organization. By 1900 he was conducting meetings in Sault Sainte Marie and was soon ordained deacon.[107] Lake was a faithful Zionite, distributing copies of *Leaves of Healing* in Sault Sainte Marie[108] and dutifully preaching on familiar Zion themes like "Doctors, Drugs and Devils," and "Elijah the Restorer."[109] The Lake family moved to Zion City in 1901, and John Lake began working with the Zion City building department while continuing to serve as a minister.[110] By 1905, Lake was no longer working in Zion City, but continued to preach while conducting a purportedly lucrative insurance business.[111]

Through contacts in Chicago, Lake became aware of the developing pentecostal movement, particularly the revival at Azusa Street. But then the revival came closer to home, as Parham stirred pentecostal enthusiasm at Zion City beginning in September. When Parham led a watch-night service on New Year's Eve, Lake was there, hoping to experience what some of his Zion friends had claimed. From this point forward, Lake threw in his lot with the pentecostals. Lake had an arduous journey to his pentecostal experience. He reportedly spoke in tongues at Zion City's New Year's Eve meeting, but he did not recognize this as a full spirit-baptism. He spoke in tongues a few months later, when he received a word from God to go to Indianapolis, where he was to convince Tom Hezmalhalch, who had received spirit-baptism at Azusa Street, to come to Zion City.[112] At a series of

---

see Lindsay, *John G. Lake, Apostle to Africa*, 10–15; and Lindsay, *Sketches from the Life and Ministry of John G. Lake*, 24–29.

106. "God's Witness to Divine Healing," (June 15, 1901) 226.

107. "Notes from Zion's Harvest Field," (July 21, 1900) 410.

108. "Notes from Zion's Harvest Field," (December 29, 1900) 314.

109. "Notes from Zion's Harvest Field," (April 4, 1903) 760.

110. For conflicting evidence on Lake's professional status, see Morton, "'Devil Who Heals,'" 103; "God Uses Diaconate," 1; "Gift of the Holy Spirit," 3.

111. Lake claimed to leave Zion City in 1904. Lake's residence is listed in March 5, 1904, as the intersection of Gabriel Avenue and Thirtieth Street, Zion City. "Directory of the Ordained Officers." See Morton, "'Devil Who Heals,'" 103.

112. Lake and Morgan, *John G. Lake's Life & Diary*, 45.

meetings beginning in May in Zion City, Lake and Hazmelhalch led dozens of seekers into the pentecostal experience. But Lake had not yet arrived. Apparently, Lake struggled with the spiritual consecration he felt was necessary. In his diary, Lake recorded encouragement he received from F. F. Bosworth as he struggled for his spirit-baptism:

> [S]ome months later as [Tom Hezmalhalch] visited our town again one day, I joined Bro. Tom and Bro Fred Bosworth on the sidewalk as we walked down the street; I stepped between them taking each by the arm. Bro. Bosworth turned to me saying Lake when are you going to surrender to Jesus. I said anytime Fred. Tom turned to me saying do you mean it? I replied, I do Tom. We all three fell on our knees on the sidewalk and right there I surrendered to my Lord. Then I sought God for sanctification and my Baptism in the Holy Ghost.[113]

Finally, in October of 1907, Lake's search was over. When called to pray alongside Hezmalhalch for an invalid, Lake felt in turns a calm quiet, followed by a "warm tropical rain," then "currents of power." Praying in tongues, he laid his hands on the sick woman, and at that moment he felt he was given the enduring gift of healing, and the woman was healed.[114] This was his spirit-baptism, but this was not the end of his dramatic experiences with God. In late 1907 or early 1908, Lake received confirmation from God that he was now endowed with the ability to cast out demons—a gift he quickly put into action for the sake of an Indianapolis man whose insanity Lake attributed to demon possession.[115] Throughout his ministry, Lake would confront demons and devils.[116]

Sensing that he was now equipped for full ministry, Lake, along with Hezmalhalch and J. O. Lehman, traveled to South Africa in early April 1908. There Lake ministered for five years, building upon the work of earlier Dowie missionaries—like Daniel Bryant, who would also later cause much stir in Zion City by supporting the pentecostal cause. South Africa proved extremely welcoming to Lake's pentecostal message, and he formed the Apostolic Faith Mission of South Africa to organize their work.[117] Lake's

---

113. Lake and Morgan, *John G. Lake's Life & Diary*, 33; emphasis in original.

114. Lake gave at least three varying accounts of this incident. See Lake and Morgan, *John G. Lake's Life & Diary*, 23; Lindsay, *John G. Lake, Apostle to Africa*, 18–19; Lindsay, *Sketches from the Life and Ministry of John G. Lake*, 15–16.

115. Lake and Morgan, *John G. Lake's Life & Diary*, 49. See also Morton, "'Devil Who Heals,'" 106–7.

116. See, for example, Lake and Morgan, *John G. Lake's Life & Diary*, 73.

117. For Lake's South Africa work, see Burpeau, *God's Showman*, 63–150.

South Africa mission was well-publicized in pentecostal publications in the United States and England. His reports of healings and conversions quickly achieved legendary status in a movement that had no shortage of missionary exploits.[118]

Lake permanently returned to the United States in 1913 and carried on an independent healing ministry that eventually settled in Spokane and Portland. In America, Lake continued to wield considerable influence in pentecostal circles, joining forces for a time with Cyrus Fockler, a former Dowieite elder with whom Bosworth would conduct itinerant ministry in 1907 and 1908.[119] Lake led a revival with Charles Parham in 1924 that led to the conversion of Gordon Lindsay, who became a major organizing force for the post-World War II pentecostal healing revival.[120] Generally suspicious of denominations, Lake did not join the Assemblies of God when it formed in 1914, although he attended its inaugural meeting. Lake preferred spiritual fervor over doctrinal rigor and maintained contact with pentecostals on all sides of the sanctification issue and the trinitarian controversy of 1916. Lake's approach to divine healing—particularly his use of healing rooms following the early Dowie model—continued to inspire pentecostal healing ministries in the late twentieth century.[121]

Lake thoroughly imbibed Dowie's teachings that miracles had not ceased and that Satan was the cause of sickness, and he combined this with the pentecostal emphasis on the immediacy of mystical experience, or what he called an "intense longing for an intimacy and a consciousness of God."[122] Like Bernice Lee, Lake saw supernatural forces—benevolent and malevolent—active in the most dramatic ways at key moments in his spiritual journey. As Lake described his own spirit-baptism,

> My tongue and throat began to move in a manner I could not control presently I realized I was speaking in another tongue, a language I had never learned. Oh the sense of Power, the mighty moving of the Spirit in me. The consciousness it was God who had come. Then Satan came and suggested it is not real power it is only imagination. These are not currents of real power it is

---

118. For reports of Lake's South Africa work in the British pentecostal press, see Lake, "South Africa," 185; "Has Pentecost Come to Johannesburg?," 27–31; and "Extracts from a Very Important Letter," 74–75. For reports in the American pentecostal papers, see "Missionaries to Johannesburg," 4; and "From Africa," 1.

119. For Lake's post–South Africa career, see Burpeau, *God's Showman*, 151–98. For Lake's work with Fockler, see 152.

120. Burpeau, *God's Showman*, 177; Lindsay, *John G. Lake, Apostle to Africa*, 4–7.

121. Poloma, "Old Wine, New Wineskins," 59–71.

122. Lindsay, *John G. Lake, Apostle to Africa*, 16.

only psychic phenomena. I said, "it's power." I know it and God in His loving mercy proved it to me.[123]

Despite Lake's animosity toward Christian Science, his tug-of-war with how science related to divine healing sounded like Mary Baker Eddy's. "[I]n the Spirit of God there is a science far beyond physical or psychological science," taught Lake, "and the man or woman who enters into the spirit relation with God and exercises His power is most scientific . . ."[124] Lake's pentecostal supernaturalism tended toward the language of law and science to explain miraculous benevolence.[125]

While Bosworth and Lake flourished in independent pentecostal ministry, other Zion alumni became loyal pentecostal denominationalists. Marie Burgess (1880–1971) received her pentecostal baptism in Zion City the same night as Bosworth, October 18, 1906. Years before she encountered Dowie, Brown showed a predilection toward supernaturalism. As a teenager in Eau Claire, Wisconsin, and before she was a devoted Christian, she experienced a vivid vision of Jesus that led to her conversion and dedication to Christian service as well as paving the way for her miraculous healing of tuberculosis. For Burgess, this event marked more than the simple cessation of illness, but the beginning of "new life, the divine touch manifested in my body."[126]

Burgess's contact with Dowie began when her sister Ella showed signs of tuberculosis a few years later. While in Colorado, the Burgess sisters got word of Dowie's healing work in Zion City. They visited Zion City for some time probably in October of 1903.[127] Burgess officially became a member of the Christian Catholic Apostolic Church on July 17, 1904, by which time she had become a resident of Zion City.[128] Marie was a faithful devotee to the First Apostle, defending his ability to heal when some followers had begun to claim that his power had ceased.[129]

123. Lake and Morgan, *John G. Lake's Life & Diary*, 25.

124. Lindsay, *John G. Lake, Apostle to Africa*, 57.

125. The resonance of New Thought in Lake's teaching deserves further study. From 1914, Lake maintained close and cordial relations with the Spokane New Thought teacher Albert C. Grier and even named his son in honor of Grier (Livingston Grier "Jack" Lake, born August 1914). Lake's initial Spokane congregation consisted of followers of Grier. See Burpeau, *God's Showman*, 152–54, 190. In the 1920s, Lake was also in contact with E. W. Kenyon, a Baptist evangelist with clear New Thought leanings. See Lake, *John G. Lake*, 474.

126. Argue, "Chosen of God," 12; Gardiner, "Herald of Glad Tidings: Part One," 4, 8.

127. "Obeying God in Baptism," (October 24, 1903) 29.

128. "Given the Right Hand of Fellowship," 523.

129. Gardiner, "Apostle of Divine Healing," 14.

Like many in Zion City, Burgess was curious about the pentecostal message spreading in the fall of 1906. As Dowie had trained Zionites to see enemies of his church as inspired by Satan, the polemic against Parham's meetings that Burgess overheard was that "people were filled with the devil."[130] Burgess began attending house meetings of pentecostal seekers, and she quickly recognized "that the devil was not at work, but that this thing was of God." Although losing her retail position in a Zion City business in Chicago for identifying with the pentecostals, Burgess continued to attend meetings. Believing that spirit-baptism was divinely promised (like salvation and healing), she was disappointed that even after three days of fasting and non-stop seeking, she had not received the experience. Only when she felt God tell her to "take it and thank him for it," did the real experience begin. Phoebe Palmer's theology of "naked faith" clearly governed the categories of attaining pentecostal experience. But Burgess also believed her experience was real because of three signs: shaking in the Spirit, speaking in tongues, and a vision of the mission fields. Burgess claimed that her experience was so visibly genuine that it helped F. F. Bosworth, who witnessed it, to press on to his own personal Pentecost that same night.[131]

Burgess seamlessly carried the supernaturalism of her spiritual journey up to 1906 into the new pentecostal sphere. When Parham asked Burgess to go to New York as a pentecostal messenger, she determined that if God wanted her to go, he would supply her fare from an outside source. When a man "who knew nothing of the matter" placed fifty dollars in her hands, she could no longer resist her call.[132] Early in her New York ministry, she vowed if God did not supernaturally provide for her, she would take it as a sign that she was no longer to continue in ministry.[133] Burgess saw God supernaturally involved in supplying needs for life and ministry and directing the saints' paths.

With ongoing assistance from her Zion contacts, Burgess was influential in the new pentecostal movement. Her New York work was boosted by Jessie Brown, who had led the meeting where she and Bosworth received spirit-baptism. Parham visited in 1907 and helped Burgess open a pentecostal mission, drawing support from Zion alumni Bernice Lee and Edith Baugh.[134] Burgess was active in early pentecostal conventions, such as those held at Stone Church in Chicago, which was pastored by former Zion elder

---

130. Gardiner, "Herald of Glad Tidings: Part One," 8.
131. Gardiner, "Herald of Glad Tidings: Part One," 9–10.
132. Gardiner, "Herald of Glad Tidings: Part One," 10.
133. Gardiner, "Herald of Glad Tidings: Part Two," 6.
134. For Parham's time in New York, see Parham, *Life of Charles F. Parham*, 194–95.

William H. Piper. Burgess returned to Zion in 1909 to wed Robert Brown.[135] Their ministry was marked by exorcism, healing, and numerous spirit-baptisms, and Marie was renowned for speaking many foreign languages under the power of the Holy Spirit.[136] The Browns affiliated with the Assemblies of God in 1915, with Robert elected to the executive presbytery.[137] The missionary support from her Glad Tidings church was unparalleled in the denomination.[138] In the 1950s, Marie supported David Wilkerson's inner-city efforts, which would blossom into Teen Challenge.[139]

DOWIEITE PENTECOSTALISM: PENTECOSTAL IDENTITY AND ORIGINS

Comparing Bosworth's journey from Dowieism to pentecostalism with that of John G. Lake and Marie Burgess Brown demonstrates that Bosworth was part of an important subgroup of influential first-generation pentecostals. These pentecostals distinguished themselves by carrying a Dowie-inflected supernaturalism into the new movement. While they largely accepted Parham's tongues evidence doctrine, the gospel they preached was more broadly a continuation and adaptation of the supernatural gospel in which they had been reared by the holiness and divine healing movements, and particularly Dowieism. Marie Burgess Brown credited Dowie's Zion City: "That's where I got my foundation. And if it hadn't been for the truths of the Word of God as I learned them there I would not be here today."[140] John G. Lake too showed—and admitted—the patent influence of Dowie throughout his pentecostal career. Like Dowie, Lake called himself "Apostle" and "Doctor" and used many of the "showman" techniques that had been Dowie's trade.[141] A pentecostal-friendly Zion City newspaper put it well:

> The preaching of the "full gospel" by John Alexander Dowie in which healing and holy living were added to the gospel of salvation hitherto preached was in itself a great stride towards what

---

135. For details of Burgess's early work in New York, see Gardiner, "Herald of Glad Tidings: Part Two."
136. Gardiner, "Herald of Glad Tidings: Part Three," 9–10.
137. *Minutes of the General Council of the Assemblies of God . . . 1915*, 9.
138. Curtis, "'God Is Not Affected by the Depression,'" 588.
139. *In Loving Memory, Marie Estelle Brown*, 10.
140. Gardiner, "Herald of Glad Tidings: Part One," 8.
141. For Lake's debt to Dowie, see Burpeau, *God's Showman*, 34–36.

now seems to be the full gospel of salvation, healing, holy living and the Baptism in the Holy Spirit.[142]

The stories of these Dowieites-turned-pentecostals also counterbalance the traditional importance of Azusa Street. This distinction is not merely discerned by later historians; the participants were themselves aware of this important issue of pentecostal self-understanding. John G. Lake was adamant that the pentecostal movement owed its origin to Parham and Topeka, rather than Seymour and Los Angeles. Despite his contacts with Azusa Street and his respect for William Seymour,[143] Lake told Parham in 1924,

> One thing I observe [,] however, is that the truth of the origin of the Pentecostal movement and its origin in your school at Topeka and the fact that you formulated the first Pentecostal message to the world is growing and is daily becoming a better known fact. So that now, even the prejudices of the Assemblies of God cannot submerge that truth and neither can Florence Crawford of Portland, Oregon, get the world to believe any longer that she was the first white woman baptized in the Holy Ghost after Pentecost came. And the people of Los Angeles cannot use it much further for a Los Angeles advertising stunt.[144]

Parham's importance could not be doubted or ignored for pentecostals like Lake whose spirit-baptisms were not connected to Azusa Street.[145]

In reality, Lake's ministry illustrated the more complex truth of pentecostal origins—that various centers of pentecostalism inspired, interacted, and influenced one another from the beginning of the movement. Shortly after Lake, Bosworth, Hezmalhalch, and Fockler visited Azusa Street in 1907, Seymour came to Zion City. So impressed was Seymour with the revival there that he said, "it reminds me of old Azusa ten months ago."[146] Another telling example is that of Lucy Leatherman. As Parham was proud to report,

142. "Epoch in History of Zion," 1.

143. Burpeau, *God's Showman*, 118–20. Lake spoke of Seymour in glowing terms: "I do not believe that any other man in modern times had a more wonderful deluge of God in his life than God gave to that dear fellow." Lake, *John G. Lake*, 459–60.

144. Lake, *John G. Lake*, 479.

145. Tom Hezmalhalch, who was a participant at Azusa Street, was present at Lake's pentecostal baptism, but only as a witness. Not surprisingly, the independently-minded Lake received his spirit-baptism without the ministrations of a fellow believer. See Lake and Morgan, *John G. Lake's Life & Diary*, 19.

146. "'Latter Rain' in Zion City," 1. Seymour's co-worker and later wife Jennie Moore also visited Zion City in the spring of 1908. *Zion City News*, March 27, 1908, 1. Zion Historical Society.

Leatherman received her own spirit-baptism at Azusa Street, but only after witnessing the first pentecostal experiences with tongues at Parham's Bible school in Topeka, Kansas. She was also in Zion City, where she was accused of teaching that "speaking in tongues was the greatest of the nine gifts."[147] On her way to Palestine, Leatherman spent time in New York City and implored Parham to send pentecostal workers there—a call that was answered by Marie Burgess.[148] Other early pentecostals were content to recognize—as many scholars do today—that the early twentieth-century outpouring of the Holy Spirit sprang up in numerous locations with little connection between them.[149] As Alfred G. Garr, the first overseas missionary from Azusa Street and one who believed that tongues were never given to those who were not spirit-baptized, wrote in early 1907, "Reports are coming in from all over the world about how people are speaking in tongues, *even before they heard of the Los Angeles meeting.*"[150] The important thing for early pentecostals like Garr was not the historical lineage of the message, but the dramatic revival of specifically apostolic supernatural phenomenon.

In the decade after Parham brought the pentecostal message to Zion City in 1906, former Dowieites who joined the movement—like F. F. Bosworth, John G. Lake, and Marie Burgess Brown—became key to pentecostalism's propagation and formation.[151] In many ways, their lives narrated the development of the turn-of-the-century gospel of the supernatural. As Bosworth moved through the experiences of a Methodist conversion, holiness-inspired divine healing, leadership and tutelage under John Alexander Dowie, and finally spirit-baptism under Charles Parham, he was nicely equipped to become a leader in the emerging pentecostal movement. And in all these experiences, he was in good company with others who became leading lights of early pentecostalism.

147. "Questions Lovingly Addressed," 3.

148. "Our Trip East," 7; Anderson, *Vision of the Disinherited*, 130.

149. Even some early North American pentecostal centers functioned quite independently of other major centers, such as the Hebden Mission in Toronto. See Stewart, "Canadian Azusa?," 17–37.

150. Garr, "Tongues," 2–6. Cited in McGee, *Miracles, Missions, and American Pentecostalism*, 93; emphasis added.

151. Numerous other examples of figures who came into pentecostalism after experiences with Dowie's ministry could be related. Others will be addressed as they are encountered in subsequent chapters. One particularly interesting case is that of Lilian B. Yeomans (1861–1942), who trained as a regular physician and was healed of morphine and chloral hydrate addiction in Dowie's healing home in 1898 and baptized into Dowie's church the same year. Yeomans experienced spirit-baptism in Calgary in 1907 and led a largely independent healing ministry. Gardiner, *Out of Zion*, 125–38; Opp, "Balm of Gilead"; Opp, *Lord for the Body*, 91–92, 196–202.

3

Emboldened and Empowered to Preach, 1907–1913

> One result of the precious baptism ... [is that] God has brought one into the sphere of the supernatural, the sphere of the Holy Ghost who can now work in and through one's being much more effectively.
>
> —Max Wood Moorhead, "A Personal Testimony" (1907)[1]

IN ZION CITY, F. F. Bosworth had matured as a leader in the radical holiness and divine healing movement, but his work centered on his musical gifts and had provided him with a comfortable salary. Although he readily sought the experience of spirit-baptism when Parham brought the pentecostal message to Zion City in 1906, Bosworth was initially worried that the blessing would require him "to give up all to God [and] that he would ask me to preach the gospel." With a wife and two children to provide for, the prospect of living on faith had little appeal. But the pentecostal experience rearranged his priorities. "After I had been Baptized with the Holy Ghost," he later testified, "I was afraid God would *not* call

---

1. Moorhead, "Personal Testimony," 38. Cited in McGee, *Miracles, Missions, and American Pentecostalism*, 103.

me to preach."[2] Bosworth found that spirit-baptism not only seemed to require a new commitment to evangelization, but it also emboldened him to do so. Bosworth set out on evangelistic work across the Midwest and South. Eventually he planted a pentecostal church in Dallas that he pastored for almost a decade and from which he launched a wildly successful revival with Maria Woodworth-Etter. This revival solidified Bosworth's reputation among pentecostals, situating him to attract adherents to the new message and strengthen the churches and institutions that would help turn pentecostalism into a major American denominational family.

As Bosworth's testimony demonstrates, pentecostals believed in a direct link between spirit-baptism and evangelism. J. G. Speicher, a Zion City leader who knew personally Bosworth's pentecostal transformation, said "the one great feature of this work is the wonderful missionary spirit that it inspires in the hearts of whose who come under its influence."[3] The expectation of supernatural empowerment, millennial fervor, and the wider mission movement of late-nineteenth century Protestantism formed a potent evangelistic cocktail in the new pentecostal movement. Charles Parham's view of divinely-endowed tongues as missionary languages nicely represents early pentecostals' evangelistic passion as it combined with holiness supernaturalism. Although most pentecostals by 1909 no longer limited tongues speech to foreign languages, the evangelistic zeal implied in Parham's teaching remained.[4] Pentecostals were self-consciously missionary people, believing that they continued the work neglected since the end of the first century. As the *Missionary Manual of General Council of the Assemblies of God* stated in 1931, "In the year 1901 the latter rain began to fall in different parts of the world. Again, waiting, hungry-hearted people were baptized in the Holy Spirit. The Lord's Pentecostal missionary movement was resumed."[5]

Pentecostals believed that tongues generally accompanied spirit-baptism, and this belief alienated them from all other Christians. Yet every pentecostal would say that spirit-baptism was more than tongues. Articulations differed, but pentecostals agreed that the experience imparted supernatural power and divine intimacy that could be obtained no other way. As early

---

2. All quotes in this paragraph are from Bosworth, *Bosworth's Life Story*, 7–8; emphasis added.

3. "Is It the Latter Rain?"

4. Goff, *Fields White Unto Harvest*, 15; McGee, *Miracles, Missions, and American Pentecostalism*, 102.

5. The prologue of the *Missionary Manual* is reprinted in McGee, "'The Lord's Pentecostal Missionary Movement,'" 63–65; quote on 64.

pentecostal missionary to India Max Wood Moorhead explained in this chapter's epigraph, spirit-baptism's essential import was that it brings one "into the sphere of the supernatural." The experience was both a tangible demonstration of supernatural activity and a gateway for deeper supernatural power. In the words of Bosworth's coworker Bernice Lee, spirit-baptism was only "the merest beginning; the first glimpse into the Glory as the great, beautiful door of Pentecost swings open!"[6]

By detailing Bosworth's first seven years of ministry and placing his work within the early pentecostal milieu, the character of Bosworth's ministry and the reasons for his success come into focus. In his evangelistic zeal and commitment to the empowerment of spirit-baptism, Bosworth was a typical pentecostal. In his success in itinerant ministry and church-planting, Bosworth was a remarkable and influential early leader. Both of these dimensions were grounded in Bosworth's devotion to a dynamic, non-dogmatic supernaturalism that was at the heart of the pentecostal movement.

EARLY ITINERANCY, 1907–1910

Bosworth was a significant part of the controversial pentecostal movement in Zion City that contributed to the chaos in the months after Dowie's fall; and pentecostals with close ties to Bosworth continued to threaten the old guard for years after Parham left in early 1907. Those who embraced or entertained pentecostalism saw in the movement a much-needed dose of spiritual renewal. The Holy Spirit, said Speicher,

> is taking little children and young people and simple hearted people and is speaking through them more powerfully than He has ever spoken through the great Overseers and Elders and hundreds of officers of Zion. The ministry of Zion has been unfruitful for years. No one can deny it. We have been set aside and God is allowing us to pass through a new course of training for His glory.[7]

But many categorically rejected pentecostalism. In the summer of 1907, the *Zion Herald*—Voliva's megaphone of righteous indignation disguised as a newspaper—railed against the new movement, finding particular delight in the allegations against Parham of "sodomy with a Jew boy." From the beginning describing the contest against pentecostalism as a "war," Voliva called upon Zion City residents to set "Zion City free from this Terrible Curse brought here by the Devil, through this Miserable Degenerate,

6. Lee, "I Will Be Within Thee a Well of Water," 20.
7. "As Dr. Speicher Sees It," 2.

Parham." In a cavalcade of smear, Voliva called out Dowieites-turned-pentecostals Cyrus Fockler, John G. Lake, John Spiecher, A. F. Lee, William H. Piper, and their leader Tom Hezmalhalch, branding them thieves, drunks, adulterers and lovers of indecency.[8]

Zion's faithful also had religious and theological reasons for condemning Parham's teaching as "the mildew of Hell."[9] While pentecostalism was "emotionalism, spiritualism, fanaticism and other nervous manifestations," Zion appealed to the intellect.[10] Behind the bombast was hurt: "How is it," asked one harried Zion City resident, "that overseers, elders, evangelists, and deacons, who have taken such a strong stand for Zion in past years, will now throw the teachings to the wind?" The answer? They were either predators or unstable.[11] Zion stalwarts described pentecostalism in terms of sexual deviance, uncontrolled emotionalism, moral permissiveness, and stubborn rejection of human organization.[12] The pentecostals' anti-authoritarianism was mentioned often, as this appealed to disillusioned Zionites while greatly offending those who remained loyal to Zion and Voliva. The religious battle was tangled in civic life, as Parhamites battled Voliva's party for control of the Zion City school board.[13]

The most scandalous episode for pentecostalism in Zion City occurred September 18, 1907. A 64-year-old Zion resident and invalid named Letitia Greenhalgh died after three Parhamites, rebuking the spirits of illness, roughly straightened and broke her impotent limbs. Although Lake and Hezmalhalch were not involved, Zion leaders held them responsible and demanded that "Tom and his stripe of religious derelicts must be curbed in their practices and made to walk soberly."[14] Although Zionites had been accused of similar abuse and Parham was not in Zion City at the time, the national press sided with Zion City, laying the blame at Parham's feet.[15] The incident spurred investigations into other deaths.[16] While not mentioned

---

8. "Relentless War Against Iniquity of Every Kind!!!"
9. "Warning to Zion," 1.
10. Hess, "Frenzied Religion," 3.
11. Hess, "Frenzied Religion," 3.
12. "Invasion of the Barbarians," 1, 4.
13. "Warning to Zion," 4; "Zion vs. Parhamism," 2.
14. "Fruits of Parhamism," 1; "Tragedy," 1. The rival newspaper *Zion City News* did not completely absolve the pentecostal leadership. "Horror in Zion City," 2.
15. "Mother Tortured in Religion's Name," 7. See also "As Dr. Speicher Sees It," 2.
16. "Other Cases of Torture," C5.

in pentecostal histories, this incident was another contributor to Parham's decline.[17]

Lake and Hezmalhalch left Zion City shortly after the Greenhalgh incident, but loyal Zionites continued to express concern about pentecostalism through the next few years.[18] William H. Piper, who had been a high-ranking officer under Dowie, formed his Stone Church in Chicago in December of 1906 and identified with the pentecostals the following summer. Rumors about the growth of his church and the circulation of his *Later Rain Evangel* worried Zion leaders, who derided these pentecostals for talking incessantly about visions and other supernatural experiences.[19] Clearly the pentecostal movement was growing: the Ohio pentecostal periodical *Household of God* had nearly 300 subscribers in Zion at the end of 1908.[20] Dowie's famous disciple, Sadie Cody, attended the Stone Church, embraced pentecostalism, and would even record a number of Bosworth's sermons in 1914 and 1915.[21] Zion was freshly disrupted by pentecostalism in early June 1908 by the arrival of Daniel Bryant, a missionary for Dowie's church in South Africa.[22] Although Bryant had doubts about the doctrine of tongues as evidence of spirit-baptism, for a time, he identified with the pentecostals, rallying their forces in Zion City.[23] Through 1908, Bryant, Piper, and Marie Burgess continued to lead pentecostal meetings in Zion City, periodically raising the ire of Zion's faithful.[24]

---

17. Parham's fall from leadership is usually credited to his inability to work with other leaders (demonstrated most damagingly in his criticism of Seymour's work at Azusa Street), his sexual scandal, and his botched attempt to travel to Palestine to recover the Ark of the Covenant. See, for example, Blumhofer, *Assemblies of God*, 91–92. The Zion pentecostals changed their name from Apostolic Faith to Christian Assembly of Zion City in October of 1907 (less than a month after the death of Greenhalgh). Voliva's party interpreted this as an attempt to distance themselves from Parham. "Rominger a Parhamite!!!," 2.

18. Morton, "'Devil Who Heals,'" 108.

19. "Evil Men Wax Worse," 1; "Poor Piper," 2.

20. "Zion City Subscribers," 8.

21. Cody, "Miracle of Healing," 19–22. For Cody as reporter for Bosworth's sermons, see Bosworth, "Power in the Holy Ghost," 244–47; Bosworth, "Living Faith in the Power of God," 29–33; Bosworth, "Healing in the Atonement," 226–31; Bosworth, "Clay in the Hands of the Potter," 254–59.

22. *Zion Herald*, June 24, 1908, 2.

23. Burpeau misses Bryant's close association with Zion City pentecostals. Burpeau, *God's Showman*, 68. For Bryant's flirtation with pentecostalism, see "Smallpox?," 1; "Questions Lovingly Addressed," 3; "Is It Not Awful?," 3; and "Dirtiest and Biggest Lie," 3.

24. "Is It Not Awful?," 3.

Following Bosworth's pentecostal experience, he was only an occasional presence in Zion City. But Zion pentecostals followed his work through the pages of their local newspapers, and his influence on others in the city was considerable. In July of 1907, John Speicher, formerly Zion's Commissioner of Health, pointed to the example of Bosworth and Lake (as well as his experience at Azusa Street) as decisive on his journey into pentecostalism.[25] Between meetings in Plymouth, Indiana, in September of 1908, Bosworth returned to Zion City to lead services at the pentecostal Christian Assembly.[26] A report noted that Bosworth spoke "in his usual quiet and unassuming, though earnest way," on the need for caution against "extravagant manifestations." Bosworth pleaded that the pentecostal experience should "make people more like Jesus."[27] On a brief stay in the city in January of 1909, Bosworth preached on "The Consecrated Mind."[28]

Bosworth's first major evangelistic work occurred in April of 1907 in Milwaukee alongside Cyrus Fockler (1863–1933), who had been an elder in the Christian Catholic Church. As a representative of Zion, Fockler had been in charge of the Zion work in Mansfield, Ohio. He also ministered frequently at Zion Home in Chicago and, like most of Dowie's leaders, had more than one healing attributed to his prayers.[29] Fockler made a name for himself by suffering for Dowie's gospel. In 1899, Fockler was arrested in Mansfield for interfering with the duties of a public officer (Fockler advised a family not to use medicine). Fockler was cleared, but when the child of a Zion member died a few months later, Fockler was blamed. On July 21, the disgruntled Mansfieldians formed a mob, stripping and beating Fockler.[30] Dowie reassigned him—along with William Piper—to Chicago's South Side Zion Tabernacle in May of 1901.[31] In 1903, Fockler cut ties with Dowie but reemerged in Zion City during the commotion of 1906.[32]

Like his friend John G. Lake, Fockler had an intense spiritual struggle leading up to his personal Pentecost, even coming to doubt his salvation.[33] But he received his spirit-baptism with tongues in March of 1907, guided

25. "Is It the Latter Rain?" For Speicher's experience at Azusa Street, see "As Dr. Speicher Sees It," 1, 2.
26. *Zion City News*, September 11, 1908; "Crowded with Blessing," 1, 3.
27. "Sensible Talk."
28. "Fred Bosworth in City," 4.
29. "Voices of Children Praising God," 80.
30. "Mansfield, Ohio," 371; "Kingdom of God Is Come," 427–35.
31. *Leaves of Healing* 9.3 (May 11, 1901) 73.
32. The last mention of Fockler in *Leaves of Healing* is "Obeying God in Baptism," (August 1, 1903) 486.
33. Fockler, "Message to Seekers," 16–17.

by Lake and Tom Hezmalhalch in a Chicago meeting.[34] His wife knew the importance of this experience, telling Fockler, "I suppose you are now ready to answer any call that comes."[35] He was, and he demonstrated this by joining Lake and Bosworth in Milwaukee, beginning services on April 7, 1907. They successfully planted pentecostalism in Milwaukee with the healing of Alice Baumbach, who for years had been bedridden with spinal tuberculosis.[36]

Thus began a nearly two-year ministry partnership between Bosworth and Fockler. After Milwaukee, the two "went south," with Fockler possibly accompanying Bosworth on his evangelistic work in Texas from late April to early June in 1907.[37] It was perhaps after the Texas work that Bosworth, Fockler, Lake, and Hezmalhalch visited Azusa Street. By March of 1908, Bosworth and Fockler—along with B. F. Lawrence—were doing extended work in South Bend, Indiana.[38] They then went to Plymouth, Indiana, where Bosworth conducted meetings from June until the end of the year.[39] Bosworth's ministry at this stage reflects the strength of the early ex-Zion network: in Plymouth, Fockler was with Bosworth for about five weeks; then Jean Campbell and Bernice Lee came from New York, where they had been working with Marie Burgess.[40]

Bosworth's report in the August 21 issue of *Zion City News* of the Plymouth meetings is the first account of his itinerant work from his hand. He was deeply concerned with supernatural guidance and confirmation of his work. "While in prayer," Bosworth testified, alluding Ephesians 6:12, "God made it so plain to me that we wrestled not against flesh and blood but

34. As with many Zion City believers who became pentecostals, the circumstances of Fockler's spirit-baptism are not precisely clear. For conflicting accounts, see Gardiner, *Out of Zion*, 12; and Fockler, "Message to Seekers," 16.

35. Fockler, "Message to Seekers," 16.

36. Gardiner, *Out of Zion*, 12–13; Fockler, "Church at Milwaukee," 11; Fockler, *Tuning in with the Infinite*, 73–75.

37. *Zion City News*, April 26, 1907, 1; *Zion City News*, June 14, 1907, 2. "Went south" could have meant that the two returned to Zion City. Fockler was still assisting in pentecostal meetings in Zion City in the summer of 1907. Hess, "Frenzied Religion," 3.

38. *Zion City News*, March 27, 1908, 1; *Zion City News*, May 8, 1908, 1; *Zion City News*, June 19, 1908, 1. Bosworth's permanent departure from Zion may have been in 1908. "God Approved Man Condemned," 3.

39. Lee was expected to "assume charge of the work" in Plymouth beginning December 28, 1908, which may indicate Bosworth was no longer there. Bosworth returned to Zion City shortly after the New Year. See "Christian Assembly," 4; "Fred Bosworth in City," 4. The February issue of *Latter Rain Evangel* has Plymouth as Lee's residence, but her article is unfortunately not dated. Lee, "Be Not Anxious," 8.

40. Bosworth, "Confirming the Word," 7.

against the rulers and of the power of this darkness." Bosworth recognized that resistance came from "wicked spirits" and prayed that "[God] would send a stream of power upon the city which would penetrate through the darkness and drive back the foe."[41] He had good reason to suspect demonic activity, as in Plymouth he was intimately involved with the exorcism of a woman who was housed in a jail next door to Bosworth. She had gone insane and was threatening to kill her children.[42] Around this time, Bosworth experienced a vision in which he saw a light emerging from a single point in the heavens and widening over the city as it came down. Within the light were angelic forces traversing to and fro, while a "most intense darkness" surrounded the light. Taking this vision as assurance of divine assistance for the work, Bosworth concluded that "thus far we have had little opposition."[43]

Speaking in tongues was one part of the diverse supernatural confirmation of Bosworth's ministry. At a meeting in nearby La Paz, a woman came under conviction after hearing the tongues speech and returned to the next meeting testifying to a mystical experience and an interpretation of the tongues message. "We praise Him for giving this sign in the very first meeting," wrote Bosworth. He also reported that some saw fire "with the natural eye" come upon them during their spirit-baptisms. Bosworth had also fully come to terms with ministry on the faith principle: "We are taking no collections and it is beautiful to see God supply us day by day out of an unseen storehouse."[44] Bosworth's supernaturalism covered the range from the fantastic to the mundane.

His travels continued. In February of 1909, Bosworth went to his old hometown of Fitzgerald, Georgia, conducting meetings there that summer. In Fitzgerald he led the Baptist preacher S. J. Parrish into the pentecostal experience. Parrish went on to work with G. B. Cashwell, known to many as the "apostle of Pentecost to the South."[45] That same year, Bosworth attended the annual Texas camp meeting in Austin, where he met Elias G. Birdsall, who would become his partner in ministry for the next decade. Birdsall was ordained as a missionary by Charles Parham and Warren F. Carothers in May of 1906 and was ordained as an evangelist by D. C. O

41. "Letter from F. F. Bosworth," 1, 2; quote on 2.
42. Bosworth, "Enthronement of Self," 3.
43. Bosworth, "Confirming the Word," 7.
44. All quotes in this paragraph are from Bosworth, "Confirming the Word," 8.
45. For Bosworth's move to Fitzgerald, where his wife and child had preceded him, see *Zion City News*, February 12, 1909, 1. For the revival services, see "Notice," 2. Bosworth may have been assisted by Jean Campbell, who returned to Zion City from Fitzgerald in August of 1909. *Zion City News*, August 20, 1909, 1.

Opperman and Carothers a few months before he met Bosworth.⁴⁶ At the Texas meeting, Bosworth was asked to preach on the atonement and, in the course of his sermon, explained that "the bread [of communion] stood for our healing just as definitely as the blood stood for our salvation." This was a message the sickly Birdsall needed to hear, and he was healed the next day during a communion service.⁴⁷ This Texas meeting was likely the setting of Bosworth's first ordination in the pentecostal movement, which occurred on August 2.⁴⁸ Bosworth made other stops in Texas at Alvin, Waco, and Fort Worth and also traveled to Conway, South Carolina,⁴⁹ expanding his network beyond the circle of ex-Zionites.⁵⁰

DALLAS, TEXAS: BOSWORTH THE RISING STAR

Upon receiving a telegram invitation, Bosworth came to Dallas in October of 1910.⁵¹ Soon his wife and daughter Vivian joined him (his son Vernon had died in June 1907). Bosworth's friends in Zion City read reports of his Dallas work as early as November 4, learning that some "old-time Zion healings" were occurring under his ministry.⁵² However, with no other pentecostals in the city,⁵³ the work started slowly and faced much opposition, testing Bosworth's reliance on God. "I have seen my wife set the table without anything to put on it to eat," Bosworth later said of his early days in Texas, "and often we came down to our last crust." Yet he continued to trust in God's supernatural providence, taking turns with his wife and daughter shouting "Glory" into their empty lard tin. He demonstrated his faith by his frequent giving away his last dollars, acts which were vindicated when a stranger handed him a load of groceries.⁵⁴

---

46. Birdsall, "Application Blank for Ordination Certificate."

47. Bosworth, "Discerning the Lord's Body," 3. See also Bosworth, "Healing in the Atonement," 228.

48. Executive Presbytery, "Certificate of Ordination, Fred F. Bosworth."

49. Perkins, *Fred Francis Bosworth*, 69. Bosworth was with Cyrus Fockler in Alvin, Texas. See Fockler, *Tuning in with the Infinite*, 61–62.

50. A number of camp meetings line up with Bosworth's general route during this period. "Conway, S. C.," 2; "Camp Meeting Notes," 3; "Campmeetings," (June 1910) 9.

51. "Great Revival in Dallas, Texas," 14.

52. "God Approved Man Condemned," 3. See also *Zion City News,* November 25, 1910, 4.

53. Bosworth, *Life Story of Evangelist F. F. Bosworth*, 8.

54. Bosworth, *Life Story of Evangelist F. F. Bosworth*, 8–10. Quotes are on p. 9.

Their work turned a corner on February 2 the following year. Bosworth credited the success to their persistent prayers for revival.[55] Their first convert—labeled by one historian as "the first known person in Dallas, Texas, to 'speak with other tongues'"—was Harriet Wasson (or Watson), followed by a few others, including an "old baseball player" named Jimmy Hutton, who served for a time as song leader for their meetings.[56] Bosworth particularly boasted of successes among "the colored saints" in the Queen City neighborhood of south Dallas, with thirty experiencing spirit-baptism in the spring of 1911.[57] By June, Bosworth claimed that 185 people had been baptized in the Spirit with tongues. At the end of August, he put that figure at 225, exulting that a number of ministers would be spreading the pentecostal message.[58]

Building on this growth, Bosworth took charge of the sixth annual Apostolic Faith Interstate Camp Meeting for Texas and the Southwest in Dallas July 7–2 3, 1911, which he hoped Chicago pentecostal leader William Durham would attend.[59] Although Bosworth's professional focus had shifted from music to preaching, he still brought his cornet to meetings and used music to draw a crowd.[60] Working with Birdsall and conducting initial meetings in his home and later under a tent, Bosworth described the first semi-permanent facilities as "a big shed," where his services sometimes had 1,000 to 1,500 participants. In one remarkable service, he related that a number of people testified to hearing divine voices, feeling a heavenly breeze, and seeing a multitude of angels "filling the rafters of the building." To Bosworth, this demonstrated the pentecostal truth dearest to his heart: "[God] confirms his word with signs and wonders."[61]

Despite success, Bosworth encountered one of his most traumatic experiences during this early period in Texas. In the summer of 1911, black pentecostals were holding their annual state encampment at Hearne,

---

55. "Great Revival in Dallas, Texas"; Bosworth, "Pentecostal Outpouring in Dallas, Texas," 10; Bosworth, *Life Story of Evangelist F. F. Bosworth*, 9.

56. Loftis, *History of First Assembly of God*, 7; "F. F. Bosworth to His Mother."

57. Bosworth, "Beating in Texas," 14; Opperman, "Our Lord Is Giving the Victory," 3.

58. "Great Revival in Dallas, Texas"; Bosworth, "Pentecostal Outpouring in Dallas, Texas," 10; Bosworth, "Beating in Texas," 14.

59. "Campmeetings," (June 11, 1911) 12. Previous camp meetings of the Apostolic Faith Movement in Texas were led by Bosworth's fellow ex-Zionite, D. C. O. Opperman. "Campmeetings," (June 1910). For Bosworth's invitation to Durham, see "Great Revival in Dallas, Texas."

60. Loftis, *History of First Assembly of God*, 7; Perkins, *Joybringer Bosworth*, 98.

61. All quotes in this paragraph are from "Not I But Christ," 4–5.

Texas, about 150 miles southeast of Dallas. The meetings attracted many white onlookers, who requested a white preacher for the meetings. They summoned Bosworth, who arrived on a Saturday evening in early August and straightaway preached to an audience of blacks and whites.[62] While Bosworth was on his way to spend the night with a fellow minister in the area, "several roughs" approached them. Cursing and complaining that the preachers aimed to put them "on a level with the d- niggers," the attackers brandished a revolver. Bosworth explained that he was invited by the white believers, and that he had "no thought or desire of pushing them on a level with anyone." The ruffians relented but ordered Bosworth and his companion to head straight for the train and leave town. Bosworth consented, and while he was alone for a moment, he was set upon by a group of twenty-five who were uninterested in talking. They knocked Bosworth down, punching him and hitting him with wooden clubs. Satisfied that he got the message, they demanded that Bosworth leave by foot, forcing the wounded preacher to walk nine miles to the next train station in Calvert.[63]

Bosworth may have learned something about finding solace in suffering for the gospel from Cyrus Fockler, whose encounter with a mob in Mansfield had become legendary among Zionites. Bosworth's beating was a seminal experience for him, as he recounted it in some detail in his brief life story in the early 1920s. In a letter to his mother a few weeks after the incident, Bosworth claimed that his left wrist was broken and that "my flesh was mashed to the bone on my back nearly to my knees." But he also said that God had spared him from suffering in the aftermath. Furthermore, he claimed to meet the whole experience with equanimity and love. Although he was ambivalent on the racial issues involved,[64] Bosworth was certain that in this case, God had called him to preach "to every creature." Considering himself blessed "to know something of the fellowship of [Christ's] sufferings," and content that the suffering brought his experience closer to

---

62. Although Hejzlar claims that Bosworth preached to the black and white audiences separately, Bosworth related that he "stood on the platform between the tent and the arbor" while he preached. From Bosworth's letter to his mother, we learn that the black congregants were in front of the tent and the white congregants were in the adjacent arbor. Bosworth, *Life Story of Evangelist F. F. Bosworth*, 12; Hejzlar, *Two Paradigms for Divine Healing*: 241. That Bosworth preached to a single segregated audience is corroborated by the account in the *Zion City Independent*, which stated that Bosworth "was conducting meetings . . . at which both blacks and whites were present, although seated on opposite sides of the house." "Victim of Race Prejudice," 4.

63. Details of this incident are recorded in Bosworth, "Beating in Texas"; Bosworth, *Life Story of Evangelist F. F. Bosworth*, 12–14; "Victim of Race Prejudice," 4; "Mob Victim Improving," 3; and "F. F. Bosworth Fully Recovered," 4.

64. Wacker, *Heaven Below*, 233; Hejzlar, *Two Paradigms for Divine Healing*, 242.

that of the first Christians', Bosworth interpreted the incident as worldly resistance to the gospel. As the *Latter Rain Evangel* reported, Bosworth did not retaliate or seek justice. The periodical advised pentecostals to leave vengeance in God's hands.[65]

Bosworth continued his outreach in Dallas with meetings on the street, under tents, and speaking to gatherings like the Business Men's Christian League.[66] A dramatic change in his ministry occurred in May of 1912, when Bosworth attended the annual Stone Church Convention in Chicago. Before returning home to Dallas, he spent three days with Maria Woodworth-Etter in Indianapolis, where she was conducting an eight-month campaign.[67] For years, Bosworth had admired Woodworth-Etter's ministry as detailed in her numerous popular autobiographies. He was impressed by the miracles in Woodworth-Etter's meeting, such as the healing of two deaf people and one child born blind. To promote their joint work, Bosworth procured three hundred copies of her most recent (1904) autobiography. "It is doubtful there is any record written since the 'Acts of the Apostles' that is so wonderful," exclaimed Bosworth. "'[Christ] was manifested to destroy the works of the devil' as much in Dallas and Chicago as in Jerusalem," he wrote with expectation of Woodworth-Etter's arrival. "If Jesus and His apostles could not convince unbelievers without miracles of healing does He expect more from us?"[68] This endorsement of Woodworth-Etter's ministry reveals the leitmotif of Bosworth's ministry: the continuity of God's supernatural activity throughout history. Bosworth's work in Dallas gained momentum through the summer of 1912, and he was already referring to his work as a "pentecostal outpouring" before Woodworth-Etter arrived on July 25.

Maria Woodworth-Etter (1844–1924) began her ministry in the early 1880s in Ohio and Indiana after the death of five of her children.[69] In 1880,

---

65. "Miracles of Healing in Dallas," 14. See also "Wonderful Works of God," (September 13, 1912) 1; and Bosworth, "Wonderful Revival," 1.

66. "Local Notes," 11.

67. For slightly different chronology, see Barnes, "F. F. Bosworth," 171; and Woodworth-Etter, *Signs and Wonders*, 173. May is deduced here from the fact that Bosworth wrote that he visited Woodworth-Etter after the Stone Church Convention, which began May 12 and lasted for about two weeks. Bosworth, "Pentecostal Outpouring in Dallas, Texas," 11. For Bosworth's participation in the convention, see "Not I But Christ," 2, 4–5. For Woodworth-Etter's description of the Indianapolis meetings, see Woodworth-Etter, *Acts of the Holy Ghost*, 343.

68. Bosworth, "Pentecostal Outpouring in Dallas, Texas," 11.

69. Maria Beulah Underwood married P. H. Woodworth during the Civil War. She divorced Woodworth in 1891. In 1902 she married Samuel Etter. For convenience I will use the name Woodworth-Etter throughout. Unless otherwise noted, biographical information on Woodworth-Etter comes from Warner, *Woman Evangelist*.

after a number of visions had impelled her to the work of ministry, she experienced an "anointing power" (which she later labeled her baptism with the Holy Ghost) and decided she could no longer resist her calling. Within a few years, she earned a reputation for reviving flagging congregations, and she moved freely between many evangelical denominations. In 1885, her ministry gained national attention, not least because she and her converts experienced trances during the meetings. These trances were intense supernatural experiences that often brought a vision and resulted in writhings, convulsions, and uncontrolled vocalizations or left the person prostrate, "as if dead." The press dubbed her the "trance evangelist," and around this time she also gave began to emphasize divine healing. Intensely focused on the supernatural, Woodworth-Etter attracted those with the same predilections. As the *New York Times* described her audiences in 1885, "all, without exception, of those affected are very impressionable in their natures, quite excitable in their dispositions, and ready believers in the wonderful, mysterious, and supernatural."[70]

Contemporaries were both repelled and drawn by the trance phenomenon, and those who commented on it used a range of explanations from mesmerism to hysteria to true holiness to diabolical counterfeit.[71] Those who recognized it as valid religion admitted that while such experiences were not new, the centrality Woodworth-Etter gave to them was.[72] "Manifestations are the way of the power," proclaimed Woodworth-Etter.[73] She spoke of the trance experience as being "under the power" and explained it in terms of Peter's vision in Acts 10 and a vision she herself had of "falling sheaves."[74] As Joshua McMullen argues, the overt supernaturalism of Woodworth-Etter's meetings is the central historical significance of the woman evangelist:

> With many individuals lamenting the supposed decline of evangelical zeal, Woodworth's distinctiveness does not lie in her emphasis on enthusiasm but rather her focus on physical manifestations—trances, visions, dreams and healings—as the most accurate markers of renewal. Whereas earlier preachers may have seen religious manifestations as signs of God's presence,

---

70. "Said to Be Religion," 1. Cited in Kline-Walczak, *Testimonies of Signs and Wonders*, xi.

71. Taves, *Fits, Trances, & Visions*, 242. Taves does not include diabolical counterfeit, which was central to other holiness adherents' rejection of Woodworth-Etter's ministry.

72. Warner, *Woman Evangelist*, 49.

73. Warner, *Woman Evangelist*, 77.

74. Woodworth-Etter, *Acts of the Holy Ghost*, 32, 42–43.

Woodworth viewed these phenomena as essential aspects of her revivals.[75]

Some who experienced being "under the power" in Woodworth-Etter's meetings later testified that they also spoke in tongues, and with the hindsight of pentecostal theology, declared that they had been baptized with the Holy Spirit.[76] Woodworth-Etter's theology of the supernatural was not systematized, but she generally regarded manifestations as inspired by the Holy Spirit and indicators of God's deeper work. She saw no reason to limit God's miraculous power to a bygone era, saying, "Instead of looking back to Pentecost, let us always be expecting it to come, especially in these last days."[77]

In 1889 Woodworth-Etter began a series of meetings in Oakland, California, where she came into contact with John Alexander Dowie. The relationship between the two powerhouses of divine healing would portend the friction between Dowieism and pentecostalism sixteen years later. Dowie called into question the healings Woodworth-Etter claimed under her ministry and mocked her "continuous, croaking cry for 'power.'" According to Dowie, Woodworth-Etter's trances were "diabolical delusions" and the woman evangelist herself could only be compared to Jezebel.[78] Woodworth-Etter responded by saying that the people "would see [Dowie] go down in disgrace."[79] Woodworth-Etter also met Carrie Judd Montgomery in her Oakland meetings. Montgomery, who was at that time a highly respected pioneer of divine healing, gave Woodworth-Etter a solid but cautious endorsement. Woodworth-Etter's time in Oakland was sullied by her prophecy in January 1890 that the Oakland area would be devastated by an earthquake and tidal wave in eighty days. This prediction incited further wild prophecies from her supporters and scathing critique from ministers and the press on a whole new scale.[80] The prophetic failure was perhaps "the worst scare since the Millerites experienced their 'Great Disappointment' during 1843–44."[81]

---

75. McMullen, "Maria B Woodworth-Etter," 187.
76. Warner, *Woman Evangelist*, 145.
77. Cited in Warner, *Woman Evangelist*, 147.
78. "Trance Evangelism," 99–100.
79. Cited in Warner, *Woman Evangelist*, 81.
80. Warner, *Woman Evangelist*, 83; Judd, "Work and the Workers," (January 1890) 21–22. Carrie Judd retracted her initial endorsement of Woodworth-Etter after the prophecy scandal. See Judd, "Work and the Workers," (September 1890) 213.
81. Warner, *Woman Evangelist*, 122.

Despite the failed prophecy, a well-publicized legal battle in St. Louis in 1890, and her divorce in 1891, Woodworth-Etter had much success throughout the 1890s and early 1900s. Having encountered tongues speech in her earlier meetings, she was not offended by the new pentecostal movement. In her later accounts, she reported frequent tongues speech in her meetings beginning in 1904, no doubt reflecting the spread of Parham's teaching. But as pentecostalism rose, Woodworth-Etter seems to have opted for the quiet life. The period from 1905 until her Indianapolis meeting that Bosworth attended in the spring of 1912 constitute a "slow-down" of Woodworth-Etter's career.[82] As of 1908, a fellow holiness minister who worked with Woodworth-Etter and who was seeking his Pentecost indicated that she had also not yet had the pentecostal experience.[83] At what point Woodworth-Etter embraced pentecostalism is unknown.

While Bosworth bore the stamp of Dowieite supernaturalism, Woodworth-Etter's more dramatic brand was capturing his imagination. Quickly recognizing the potential of Woodworth-Etter's work for the young pentecostal movement, Bosworth took on the role of promoter, publishing accounts for pentecostal periodicals and preparing statements for the secular press.[84] While conversions and spirit-baptisms also occurred at these meetings, the bulk of Bosworth's coverage went to the miraculous healings.

The meetings started strong, with eight hundred in attendance on the first night.[85] Bosworth's detailed account described numerous healings and announced that Woodworth-Etter would remain in Dallas for a few months. One participant reporting to Zion City proclaimed that "The work in many ways is a repetition of Dr. Dowie's; and I think it is not too much to say—at Dowie's best."[86] But Bosworth also demonstrated the particularly pentecostal take on divine healing, relating that many who were healed experienced spirit-baptism at the same time.[87] Bosworth also wrote a letter to his brother Burt in the early weeks of the Dallas revival that appeared in a

---

82. Warner, *Woman Evangelist*, 163.

83. Warner, *For Such a Time As This*, 153–54. See also Kline-Walczak, *Testimonies of Signs and Wonders*, 154–63.

84. Probably from Bosworth's hand was the report from the *Dallas Daily Times-Herald* of September 7 included in "Miracles of Healing in Dallas," 13. See Warner, *Woman Evangelist*, 165.

85. "Tent Revival Has Begun," 4.

86. "Latest from Dallas, Tex.," 2. Another update on the Dallas work appeared in "Latest Word from Dallas," 1.

87. Pinson, "Trip to the Southwest," 1; Bosworth, "Wonders of God in Dallas," 3. On the shift in approach to divine healing under pentecostal influence, see Opp, *Lord for the Body*, 121–45.

number of periodicals and in Woodworth-Etter's later account.[88] Demonstrating the influence of Woodworth-Etter on his understanding of healing and other post-conversion experiences, Bosworth stressed the "power of God" in connection to a range of supernatural experiences from salvation to healing to visions to spirit-baptism. Adopting Woodworth-Etter's terminology, Bosworth exulted in the "slaying power," which facilitated "visions and revelations, throwing light on the coming of the Lord."[89] According to Bosworth, some received spirit-baptism when they were slain under the power. While some who "received the Holy Spirit" spoke in tongues, this was not central in Bosworth's reports.[90]

While hundreds reportedly received healing during Woodworth-Etter's stay in Dallas, a few testimonies received particular publicity. One, a young "newsboy" and orphan from Dallas named Emmett Martin, came to the meetings with one arm paralyzed since the age of one and the other arm recently broken from a fall off a street car. Woodworth-Etter laid hands on him and he was instantly healed. Another case that received considerable press was the healing of Mrs. Clay E. Martin (no relation to Emmett), also of Dallas. Born deaf, Martin testified that Woodworth-Etter "put her finger in my mouth at the root of my tongue and then in my ears, commanding the 'deaf and dumb spirit' to come out." Mrs. Martin was one of the few whose testimony of spirit-baptism was given in detail. At the time of her healing, she also received her pentecostal baptism and tongues—both English and "other tongues."[91]

This incident shows the spectrum of meaning early pentecostals attached to tongues. For Mrs. Martin, who had never spoken before in any language, tongues were not only the sign of her spirit-baptism, but a further confirmation of her healing and ratification of its divine source. Tongues were also for her and other healed deaf-mutes a type of empowerment in a culture that devalued the disabled, a very literal giving of voice to the "voiceless."[92] Tongues were not treated by Bosworth and Woodworth-Etter

88. Bosworth, "Miracles in Texas," 202–205; Bosworth, "Wonderful Revival," 1; "Wonderful Works of God," (September 13, 1912) 1, 3; Woodworth-Etter, *Acts of the Holy Ghost*, 354–57. The *Zion City Independent* also had such demand for news of Bosworth's Dallas work that they reprinted the letter in September 27, 1912. 3.

89. Woodworth-Etter, *Acts of the Holy Ghost*, 369.

90. Bosworth, "Miracles in Texas." Bosworth referred to God's power no less than nine times in the letter.

91. The stories of Emmett Martin and Mrs. Clay E. Martin can be found in "Miracles of Healing in Dallas," 13–14; Bosworth, "Wonders of God in Dallas," 3 Quote from "Miracles of Healing in Dallas," 13.

92. Anderson, *Vision of the Disinherited*, 233–35. The Dallas workers also emphasized that deaf-mutes spoke in tongues upon receiving spirit-baptism in Barth, "Dallas

as clinical evidence of a particular spiritual experience, but as a potent supernatural manifestation capable of taking on many meanings in the pentecostal context.

Not only were tongues multifaceted, but other supernatural occurrences could serve to verify spirit-baptism in the Dallas meetings, as in the case of H. C. Mears, a "dear old minister" who was "a great student of the Scriptures." Rather than tongues, what was emphasized as accompanying his spirit-baptism was a series of revelations and visions, centering on the nearness of Christ's return. The account clearly contrasts the minister's intellectual knowledge of the scriptures with the supernatural visions he received at the time of spirit-baptism. As with the deaf-mute who received tongues, the minister supernaturally received what he had been conspicuously lacking—in this case, vital experiential knowledge of God's word.[93] For Bosworth, all of the supernatural experiences confirmed God's message. After describing a "cloud of glory" that was visible to a number of the faithful in one meeting, Bosworth stated, "[these] things, together with healing, speaking in tongues and interpreting, etc., convince the people, and the long altar is filled with seekers every night."[94] As corporate confirmation, tongues did not receive pride of place.

Originally planned to last just a week, the meetings continued under Woodworth-Etter's leadership from late July until the end of the year.[95] What remained constant was Woodworth-Etter's intense supernaturalism, which pitted the forces of good against the forces of evil in a dramatic battle played out in the bodies of the faithful. As Stanley Frodsham remarked, "In almost every case Sister Etter dealt with the disease as if she was dealing with the devil himself."[96] In December Carrie Judd Montgomery visited the revival and smoothed over her criticisms of Woodworth-Etter in favor of the wonders she witnessed.[97] Woodworth-Etter conducted her last service in Dallas on December 29. But Bosworth and Birdsall, with the help

---

Revival," 1.

93. Delaney, "More About the Revival," 2. See also Woodworth-Etter, *Acts of the Holy Ghost*, 362–65; and Delaney, "God's Mighty Power," 3. Faupel incorrectly identifies this account as from Bosworth. Faupel, *Everlasting Gospel*, 275 n. 182.

94. Bosworth, "Revival at Dallas, Tex.," 2.

95. Frodsham, "Glorious Victories of God," 1. For the original announcement of one week, see "Will Conduct Meeting Here," 14. In mid-August, M. M. Pinson indicated that Woodworth-Etter was planning on staying in Dallas "a month or six weeks." Pinson, "Trip to the Southwest," 1.

96. Frodsham, "Glorious Victories of God."

97. Montgomery, "Mighty Power of God," 267–70.

of others like A. W. Smith, continued the work, planning to move out to an unreached part of the city with a tent come spring.[98]

The Dallas meetings were a turning point for Bosworth's career, providing him with the means to construct a tabernacle for his Dallas congregation[99] and bringing him admiration in pentecostal circles internationally. The meetings also revitalized Woodworth-Etter's ministry. Whatever Woodworth-Etter's relation to the pentecostal movement was before arriving in Dallas, by the end of 1912, she was convinced that "[t]he Lord has clearly showed [sic] me that my great work is to blow the trumpet, to gather the Elect, the Household of Faith, together, that they may be baptized with the Pentecostal baptism and sealed with the seal of the Living God."[100] Upon selling out of her 1904 book in October, Woodworth-Etter updated and released a new version to include the marvels of the Dallas work.[101] Perhaps influenced by Bosworth's repeated comparison of her ministry to the biblical book of Acts, she titled the new installment *Acts of the Holy Ghost*. From Dallas, Woodworth-Etter took her recharged ministry to San Antonio, Los Angeles, Massachusetts, and Arkansas—and that all just in 1913. She was now also connected to the pentecostal work through deep personal ties, particularly with Bosworth and Birdsall, whom she referred to as her "two dear boys."[102]

For several reasons, the Dallas meetings were also a turning point for American pentecostalism. First, its scope and drama were unparalleled. According to Robert M. Anderson, the Dallas work was the only true revival between Azusa Street and Aimee Semple McPherson's national tour beginning in 1918.[103] Nightly attendance regularly exceeded five thousand, and people came from across the country. About twelve hundred people received spirit-baptism, and hundreds were converted and healed. No extended campaign had attracted as many pentecostal heavyweights since Azusa Street. In addition to M. M. Pinson and Carrie Judd Montgomery, Bosworth entertained numerous pentecostal leaders: Frank J. Ewart, successor of William Durham; Andrew D. Urshan, the leader of the Persian pentecostal mission in Chicago; A. P. Collins, minister in Fort Worth and later general chairman of the Assemblies of God; and Stanley Frodsham, a

---

98. Frodsham, "Glorious Victories of God," 1.

99. The first service in the tabernacle was held on November 1, 1912. Bosworth, "Miracles in Texas," 204; Loftis, *History of First Assembly of God*, 8.

100. Woodworth-Etter, *Acts of the Holy Ghost*, 580.

101. Bosworth, "Brother F. F. Bosworth About the Dallas Revival," 1.

102. Frodsham, "Glorious Victories of God," 1.

103. Anderson, *Vision of the Disinherited*, 137.

leading British pentecostal. The Dallas revival had become a model to which other pentecostal centers aspired.[104] S. A. Jamieson, previously a successful Presbyterian minister who would go on to join Bosworth in the organizing meeting of the Assemblies of God in 1914, experienced his spirit-baptism at the Christmas Eve service in Dallas.[105]

Second, the Dallas revival came at a crucial moment in pentecostal history. While most pentecostal histories imply that the waning of the initial pentecostal revival (1906–1909) made space for doctrinal crisis, none credit the renewed revival under Bosworth and Woodworth-Etter with refocusing the pentecostal movement.[106] By mid-1912, pentecostals had been engaged in a sometimes vicious debate over sanctification for about two years. Some maintained that sanctification was a second distinct crisis experience that followed conversion and prepared one for spirit-baptism. An increasing number of others were attracted to Chicago leader William Durham's teaching that sanctification was part of the "finished work" of Calvary and so required no crisis experience beyond conversion. In 1910, Durham, along with A. S. Copley of Kansas City, began publicizing their non-holiness theology of sanctification. Through Durham's itinerant preaching and distribution of over half a million copies of his periodical and tracts, the finished work position quickly won adherents in the Midwest and along the Pacific coast. Persuading Howard Goss, who had largely taken control of Parham's work in the South and lower Midwest, was an especial boon to the finished work camp.[107] While controversy may have been "the very life and breath" of early pentecostalism, controversy also had the potential to hobble a movement barely a decade old.[108] The threat to unity loomed large, and many thought the issue was a distraction.[109]

In this context, Bosworth's Dallas revival reminded pentecostals of what was attractive about pentecostalism in the first place—not rigorous doctrine but focus on supernatural experiences that bless the faithful and

---

104. Bosworth, "God of All the Earth," 1; Frodsham, "Glorious Victories of God," 1. The figure of twelve hundred is from Frodsham. Frodsham also wrote about the Dallas revival in Frodsham, *"With Signs Following,"* 34. Presumably because Bosworth had left the Assemblies of God at the time of this book's publication, Frodsham left Bosworth's name out of the account.

105. Jamieson, "God Still in Dallas," 2; Jamieson, "How a Presbyterian Preacher Received the Baptism," 2–3.

106. Reed's assessment is typical: "Revival Wanes and Schism is Born." Reed, *In Jesus' Name*, 83.

107. For Copley's underappreciated role in crafting the early finished work theology, see Richmann, "William H. Durham and Early Pentecostalism," 224–43.

108. Anderson, *Vision of the Disinherited*, 193.

109. "History of Pentecost," 14.

confirm their eschatological message and select status. Although William Durham claimed Bosworth for the finished work teaching,[110] accounts of the Dallas revival indicate that Woodworth-Etter and Bosworth aimed to unify pentecostals in the wake of the divisions created by Durham's teaching. Bosworth himself reported that "controverted points of doctrine [are] not mentioned."[111]

Third, the success in Dallas heightened expectations that God was preparing the ground for Christ's soon coming or for some new revelation.[112] This expectation bore fruit in the "World Wide Pentecostal Camp Meeting" held in Los Angeles in April of 1913. R. J. Scott, a Los Angeles businessman who attended the Dallas meetings, was so impressed with the work that he spearheaded the Los Angeles gathering, advertising Woodworth-Etter and Bosworth as headliners.[113] Woodworth-Etter's success in Dallas had the inadvertent result of creating the atmosphere where a new, divisive doctrine could begin to take shape. Pentecostal historians know this meeting as the setting in which the controversial new doctrine of baptism in Jesus' name only was first publicly aired. This gave rise to further investigation of the question of the Trinity, ultimately leading to the Oneness teaching, a type of modalist theology that identifies God's revealed name with his essential nature, the divine name in the present dispensation being "Jesus." By 1916, those who sided with the new teaching were forced out of the infant Assemblies of God, and a third major doctrinal strand of pentecostalism was born—in many ways owing its origin to the atmosphere of expectancy of the Dallas revival.[114]

Finally, the Dallas revival and the trail of publicity that now followed Woodworth-Etter encouraged pentecostals to work for greater cooperation and organization. The Los Angeles meeting was, in Faupel's words, "a

---

110. "Great Revival in Dallas, Texas."

111. Bosworth, "God of All the Earth," 1; Montgomery, "Mighty Power of God," 268; "Great Revival in Dallas, Texas," 14; Faupel, *Everlasting Gospel*, 274–75. S. A. Jamieson's testimony anecdotally corroborates the fact that the second work theory was not preached at the Dallas revival. After unsuccessfully seeking sanctification in preparation for spirit-baptism in Portland, Oregon, at Florence Crawford's mission, Jamieson went to the Dallas revival and received spirit-baptism with no mention of a sanctification experience. Jamieson, "How a Presbyterian Preacher Received the Baptism," 2–3 .

112. Montgomery, "Mighty Power of God," 270; "Miracles of Healing in Dallas," 13; Delaney, "More About the Revival in Dallas, Texas," 2. At least one date for Christ's return was given. See "Woodworth-Etter Meetings in Dallas (Texas)," 259.

113. "Apostolic Faith World-Wide Camp Meeting," (February 1913) 45–46.

114. A full account of the history and theology of Oneness pentecostalism can be found in Reed, *In Jesus' Name*. See pp. 147–66 for details of the controversy during this period.

qualified success": while it fueled further theological confusion and division, it also demonstrated the strength of pentecostal numbers and their willingness to gather in furtherance of God's work.[115] Following the Dallas and Los Angeles work, Woodworth-Etter continued to make headlines in Chicago; Framingham, Massachusetts; and Hot Springs, Arkansas. In Framingham, Woodworth-Etter's stand for divine healing became a particular *cause célèbre* for pentecostals.[116] Along with Earl W. Clark and Bosworth's former co-worker Cyrus Fockler, Woodworth-Etter was arrested in mid-August of 1913 on the charge of obtaining money through fraud. In Arkansas, an influential group of pentecostals closely followed the Framingham saga. They invited Woodworth-Etter to headline their annual state encampment in Malvern and then continue on with a campaign in nearby Hot Springs. She arrived in September for what would be a three month stay. While Howard Goss and E. N. Bell had nurtured a thriving pentecostal community in Malvern, Woodworth-Etter's work in Hot Springs bolstered the pentecostal presence there and may have given Goss and Bell the nerve to call for an organizing of their work beyond the periodicals, short-term Bible schools, camp meetings, loose nominal affiliations, and network of traveling evangelists.[117] Woodworth-Etter left Hot Springs in November, and in December, the famous call for a "General Convention of Pentecostal Saints and Churches of God in Christ" that gave birth to the Assemblies of God was first issued.

STONE CHURCH REVIVAL:
BOSWORTH THE REVERED LEADER

When the call for the organizing meeting of the Assemblies of God was still a year away, Bosworth found himself extremely busy. After Woodworth-Etter's departure from Dallas, Bosworth continued to facilitate a revival in Dallas while also periodically embarking on evangelistic trips. He planned to attend the Los Angeles meeting but after participating in meetings in Chicago in March he extended his stay in the Windy City. He went on to take charge of a special convention at the Stone Church that spring (William H. Piper died in 1911), preaching a number of sermons that were published in the *Latter Rain Evangel* and later printed as tracts. Like the Los Angeles

---

115. Faupel, *Everlasting Gospel*, 277.

116. "Montwait Meeting," 4; "Testimonies Under Oath," 1. According to the *Word and Witness* article, the pentecostal testimonies in Woodworth-Etter's case were also published as a tract.

117. For reports of the Hot Springs meetings, see Opperman, "God Stretching Out His Hand," 1; and Goss, "Jehovah Still Working," 1.

meeting that was happening at the same time, the Chicago convention was designed to foster unity among pentecostals.[118] And these pentecostals believed that unity was achieved not through doctrinal agreement but through revival and experience of the supernatural. "God gave us in Chicago," wrote one participant, "an object lesson for the whole Pentecostal Movement of what He can do when doctrinal differences and prejudices are kept in the background and Christ is lifted up."[119] Bosworth became their spokesperson. His sermons on "revival wrought through prayer" and "how to receive the faith of God" show that Bosworth was an authority who could divulge the "secret" of revivals. The success of the Dallas meetings and the experience he gained working alongside Woodworth-Etter brought Bosworth into his own as a pentecostal leader.

The nearly month-long Stone Church Convention bled into an even longer period of revival in Chicago, incorporating also its annual May convention, with Bosworth taking the leading role. Reports revealed how eager midwestern pentecostals were for Bosworth's gospel of the supernatural. "Pentecostal saints who have seen the power of God wane where it once shone forth with great effulgency, and felt the dearth in different places, have reason to be encouraged," reported the *Latter Rain Evangel*. "The outpouring He is now giving at the Stone Church is greater than at the beginning of the Pentecostal work in our midst."[120]

An important development for Bosworth's career came when Woodworth-Etter rejoined Bosworth at the Chicago revival in July. In the earlier Dallas meetings, Woodworth-Etter was the one praying and laying hands on the sick, with Bosworth taking on a promotional role while praying over handkerchiefs and tracts.[121] But in the Chicago meetings, Bosworth assumed a large portion of the public ministry of healing. In one case, while a deaf and dumb boy waited for prayer from Woodworth-Etter, Bosworth approached him and "commanded the deaf spirit to depart," resulting in his healing. Another elderly lady was seeking healing from deafness. When Bosworth offered to pray with her, she at first refused, wanting prayers from Woodworth-Etter. But Bosworth took her aside, rebuked her ailment, and her hearing was restored.[122] That he took such initiative while sharing the

---

118. "Campmeetings and Conventions," 16; "Apostolic Faith World-Wide Camp Meeting," (March 15, 1913) 2; "Stone Church Meetings," 12; "Chicago Convention," 5.

119. "Cloud of His Glory Upon Us," 2.

120. "Cloud of His Glory Upon Us," 2. The convention included such ex-Dowieites as L. C. Hall and Bernice Lee.

121. *Latter Rain Evangel* 5.8 (May 1913) 13–14.

122. Reiff, "Day of Chicago's Visitation," 6–7.

stage with the best-known pentecostal healing evangelist of his era suggests that Bosworth was charting a new course in his career.

Like the Dallas meetings, the Chicago revival was marked for its supernaturalism. Participants at the Chicago meetings described being "carried . . . into the supernatural."[123] Anna C. Reif, who took over publication of the *Latter Rain Evangel* after William Piper's death, described the revival that followed the Chicago convention as "the mightiest visitation of the supernatural [Chicago] has ever known."[124] For her part, Woodworth-Etter did not miss a step in bringing her message to a pentecostal audience. As she told a gathering at Chicago in 1913, "If you . . . show the people a supernatural God, and give them light on what is coming in the millennial age—that they will be kings and priests—they will realize that the King is in our midst in power and might and glory."[125]

Bosworth returned to Dallas in late July. He moved their tent to a new location in north Dallas before returning to the tabernacle in the winter.[126] Bosworth was also performing the normal functions of more settled ministry, like weddings.[127] The Dallas church, which was going by the name Church of the Apostolic Faith, was now sending out workers to nearby towns, like Grand Prairie, which were experiencing their own miracles.[128] In the spring of 1914, Elizabeth Sisson, longtime co-worker of Woodworth-Etter, visited Bosworth's church and reported three mission off-shoots in Dallas and a tabernacle holding nine hundred worshippers that was usually full on Sundays.[129]

Bosworth's Early Theology of Healing

Later in his career, Bosworth indicated that a turning point in his ministry came in 1920 during meetings at Lima, Ohio. Prior to this point, Bosworth said, he believed that it was God's will "only to heal some." He claimed that at this time God revealed to him that just as the fear of a sinner not heeding the message of repentance is not an excuse to refrain from preaching salvation, so fear of a sick person not receiving healing is no excuse to refrain from

---

123. Reiff, "Day of Chicago's Visitation," 3.
124. Reiff, "Day of Chicago's Visitation," 2.
125. Woodworth-Etter, "Neglect Not the Gift," 16.
126. Birdsall, "Revival News in Home Land," 1; "Our Summer Meetings," 13; Bosworth, "Revival News in Home Land," 3.
127. "Jacobs-Wasson Marriage," 16.
128. "Church Notes," 4; Bosworth, "Revival News in Home Land," 3.
129. Sisson, "Healing a Man Born Blind," 2.

preaching healing.[130] Yet Bosworth's record of ministry and writings challenges the portrayal of this as a watershed moment in Bosworth's thought. Divine healing was always central to Bosworth's ministry, beginning with his healing of Mary Shepherd in Zion City, through his work alongside Cyrus Fockler in Milwaukee, the Dallas meetings with Woodworth-Etter, and into the work in Chicago in 1913.

Furthermore, divine healing in Bosworth's early sermons was overwhelmingly a message of certainty and inclusiveness. In May of 1913, he delivered an early version of his sermon "Discerning the Lord's Body," which he would preach a year later and which would be published as a tract. Here he already determined that "everyone who meets [God's] conditions can be healed." And God's condition for healing was faith.[131] His stress on faith took on a particularly cognitive shade, much like New Thought. "We partake of the divine nature as our thoughts dwell on God and the attributes that belong to him."[132] Like Mary Baker Eddy and John G. Lake, Bosworth searched for the assurance of scientific language to describe divine healing, likening it to the laws of gravity.[133] He also used the legal language that E. W. Kenyon would become especially known for. "We can do nothing in our own name," Bosworth declared, "but in the name of Jesus we can do everything God wants done. Not merely using the words 'In Jesus' name,' but acting, as it were, by His power of attorney."[134] As early as 1914 he even mentioned the specific conclusion that he claimed he had only in 1920: that healing was as certain as salvation, and the fact that some are not healed does not reflect God's will, but the failure of believers to meet God's conditions for healing. "I maintain," he wrote, "that God's law for healing of the body is just as absolutely dependable as for the soul."[135]

As Bosworth developed his ideas, he was never concerned about forming dogma. His project was persuasion rather than coercion, because he believed his insights could help those who struggled to receive God's blessings.[136] One may speculate that Bosworth later obscured these early

130. Bosworth, *Life Story of Evangelist F. F. Bosworth*, 11–12.

131. "Cloud of His Glory Upon Us," 3; Bosworth, "Discerning the Lord's Body," 2, 5.

132. Bosworth, "Practice of the Presence of God," 8. This sermon was delivered in the Stone Church on June 30, 1913. For New Thought's affinity with and influence on the development of pentecostal healing, see Williams, *Spirit Cure*, 21.

133. Bosworth, "Discerning the Lord's Body," 4.

134. Bosworth, "Wonders of Faith," 6. Bosworth's relation to Kenyon is explored in chapter eight.

135. Bosworth, "Discerning the Lord's Body," 4.

136. The imploring and non-dogmatic character of Bosworth's message can be seen in Bosworth, "Discerning the Lord's Body," 3.

insights on divine healing in order to distance himself from the pentecostal movement (since he left the Assemblies of God in 1918) or to provide a fresh impetus for re-launching his itinerant ministry in 1920. Nevertheless, the record shows that by 1913, the main themes of his mature thought on the subject were already present.

CONCLUSION

As it did for all early pentecostals, Bosworth's spirit-baptism changed the course of his life. No longer was he only a believer in the gospel of the supernatural; following his spirit-baptism, he felt emboldened and empowered to become its herald as well. After being nurtured in the pentecostal community in Zion City, he itinerated for a number of years, expanding his pentecostal network while maintaining ties to the ex-Zionite pentecostals. When Bosworth established his mission in Dallas, he was firmly planted in pentecostal ministry. He shrewdly partnered with Maria Woodworth-Etter, a high-profile leader of the late-nineteenth century gospel of the supernatural. The Dallas revival was propitious for Bosworth, Woodworth-Etter, and pentecostalism. The meetings were Bosworth's apprenticeship in mass revivalism, leaving an enduring stamp on his ministry. But the meetings also gave Bosworth the recognition to venture out as an authority on revivalism and divine healing in his own right. As the only extended pentecostal revival receiving international acclaim in the decade after Azusa Street, the Dallas meeting is hard to over-esteem. For both Bosworth and pentecostalism, supernatural healing was the most important aspect of the Dallas revival, for it demonstrated that pentecostalism's power rested in the pursuit of the supernatural.

Bosworth's supernaturalism propelled him to the center of the early pentecostal stage. This was a supernaturalism in which tongues played a supportive role. During her visit in 1914, Elizabeth Sisson credited the blessings in Dallas to unceasing prayer, relating that Bosworth once prayed for nine days straight.[137] These were the stories that demonstrated the movement's admiration for the young minister, situating Bosworth to join the call for a new pentecostal organization and become one of its primary leaders.

---

137. Sisson, "Healing a Man Born Blind," 4.

4

Organizations and Orthodoxy, 1914–1918

> I believe that, to a great many Christians, the evident supernatural element in the [pentecostal] movement is a great stumbling-block. It is very strange to say the least that believers who accept freely and fully all the supernatural or miraculous which appears in the Holy Scriptures should be stumbled by the same to-day, and seek diligently to find either natural explanations of the phenomena, or worse still, in their stubborn and unreasoning disbelief, attribute the work to Satan.
>
> —W. Bernard, "The Gift of Tongues and the Pentecostal Movement" (1916)[1]

Pentecostals could not live on revivals alone, as important as revivals were to their message and self-identity. F. F. Bosworth was among the many pentecostals who agreed that as long as human organizations did not overstep their scriptural bounds and become conscience-binding usurpers, they could provide much-needed stability for the young movement. But the development of pentecostal denominations introduced tensions, particularly in doctrinal matters. The debate over sanctification drew a dividing line that largely had pentecostals already belonging to a denomination on one side and independent pentecostals on the other.

---

1. Bernard, "Gift of Tongues and the Pentecostal Movement," 5.

The independent pentecostals created a new organization, the Assemblies of God. Soon the Assemblies of God was embroiled in controversy over the Trinity. This battle changed the nature of the organization, providing justification to take up the legislative role it had decried two short years earlier. One of the many doctrines that the Assemblies of God subsequently outlined as "a basis of unity for the ministry" concerned the exact relationship of tongues with spirit-baptism.

As a result of these developments, tongues as the "Bible evidence" of spirit-baptism developed into the more tightly-defined "initial physical sign," as construed by the Assemblies of God.[2] An early ambiguity and room for diversity on the relationship of tongues to spirit-baptism evaporated. Bosworth initially supported the tongues evidence doctrine, though he often showed uneasiness with an overemphasis on tongues and attempted to focus pentecostals' attention to the lasting effects of spirit-baptism rather than its evidence. Finally in 1917, Bosworth openly rejected the doctrine, citing a lack of scriptural and historical foundation as well as his own pastoral struggles surrounding its implementation. As a result of this critique, he left the pentecostal denomination, but this did not mean he ceased being pentecostal. An investigation of Bosworth's pentecostal contemporaries reveals a wide range of positions on tongues comfortably sheltered under the pentecostal umbrella. Furthermore, the crystallization of the initial evidence teaching is more a reflection of external factors and second-decade developments than the inherent or original impulse of pentecostalism. Bosworth recognized, as W. Bernard did in 1916, that the central element of pentecostalism—the point that rallied its followers and repelled its foes—was supernaturalism, of which tongues was but a part.

FORMATION OF THE ASSEMBLIES OF GOD

Many early pentecostals staunchly opposed the formation of pentecostal denominations. Some, like A. A. Boddy in England, felt that the pentecostal movement should be a pan-evangelical revival within the established denominations. Others, like Chicago leader William Durham, took the old holiness stand against all denominations. In some cases, such as Piper's Stone Church in Chicago, a strong congregation could provide for wider fellowship and organization.

---

2. The most common shorthand for the doctrine is "initial evidence," which was first used in 1908 by the Pentecostal Holiness Church. Synan, "Role of Tongues," 71. I will usually refer to the "tongues evidence" doctrine, which reflects something of the ambiguity before 1918 and Bosworth's own usage.

Yet pentecostal ministers were eager to be recognized by some official body—if for no other reason than the discounted railroad passes that came with ordination. Holiness denominations in the South that adopted pentecostalism, like the Church of God in Christ and the Church of God (Cleveland, TN), did not have the same anti-institutional qualms. Although Parham vocally denounced human organizations, his Apostolic Faith network ordained ministers and tended more towards a denominational structure after Parham resigned in 1907. Howard Goss and E. N. Bell largely took charge of this work, which was strong in Texas and Arkansas. In Alabama, a group centered on H. G. Rodgers was issuing credentials under the name Church of God. But by 1911 both groups had adopted the name Church of God in Christ and merged soon after.[3] In 1912 and 1913, Bosworth and Birdsall were both listed as ordained ministers with the Church of God in Christ in connection with Goss and Bell.[4] This association was loose and provided no real discipline or oversight, such that Goss called it only a "gentleman's agreement."[5]

By 1913, even the most independent pentecostals were growing concerned over the proper methods and channels of sending and approving workers. A. H. Argue came to Bosworth's and Woodworth-Etter's work in Chicago after attending the Arroyo Seco meeting that had introduced the issue of baptism in Jesus' name. According to the editor of the *Latter Rain Evangel*, Argue pleaded with fellow pentecostals to understand that "ministers who were about to be prayed for with the laying on of hands were not being sent out by Sister Etter or to claim any authority from her or the Stone Church." The problem was that "some had not exercised wisdom and had gone out claiming authority from certain missions because hands were laid on them in that place."[6] Further organization was also on the minds of Goss and Bell, who produced their official lists of ministers in 1912 and in 1913 began calling for names of ministers to add to their roster. In October of 1913, they established a Bureau of Information, which had several pentecostals who were close to Bosworth, such as Lydia Piper and Marie

---

3. For this group's relationship to Charles Mason's organization and the possible racial issues involved, see Rodgers, "Assemblies of God and the Long Journey toward Racial Reconciliation," 50–61.

4. "Ordained Ministers of the Churches of God in Christ with Their Locations," August 1, 1912; "Ordained Ministers of the Churches of God in Christ with Their Locations (revised)," February 1, 1913; "Ordained Elders, Pastors, Ministers, Evangelists and Missionaries," 4.

5. Goss, *Winds of God*, 163.

6. Woodworth-Etter, "Neglect Not the Gift," 13.

Burgess Brown's husband Robert.[7] As many started to realize, having no organization meant having very little accountability. Goss was inclined toward a more organized system of gospel work in part because of his experiences cleaning up after unnamed ministerial vagabonds he called "the cleverest of confidence men, posing as our preachers." And yet the widespread resistance to human organizations was such that Goss and Bell thought it best to discuss their initial plans for organization secretly.[8]

Nevertheless, support for a General Council increased, especially among non- or loosely-affiliated pentecostals who identified with William Durham's theology of the finished work of Calvary. The original call in December of 1913 had only five signatories, but a month later the number had doubled and included Bosworth and Birdsall. By March, over thirty ministers committed.[9] The stated purpose of the council was to advance the work of ministers, missionaries, publishing, and education—issues with which many pentecostals were increasingly concerned. When the Council assembled on April 2, over a hundred delegates from about twenty states were present.[10]

The representatives were certain that organization would not hamper spiritual blessings: "Scriptural co-operation and fellowship . . . go far to guarantee the presence and power of God."[11] But they were also ambivalent on the human role in such organization. "We recognize ourselves as members of said GENERAL ASSEMBLY OF GOD, (which is God's organism)," they resolved, and made it clear that the Council had no intent or authority to legislate laws or articles of faith or have "unscriptural jurisdiction over its members." To make matters muddier, the General Council reserved the right to "recognize Scriptural methods and order for worship, unity, fellowship, work and business for God, and to disapprove of all unscriptural methods, doctrines and conduct."[12] This ambivalence would be a thorn in the side of the Assemblies of God when it dealt with the "New Issue" of baptism in Jesus' name and with Bosworth's doctrinal challenge in 1918.

---

7. "To Preachers," 4; "Bureau of Information," 1.

8. Goss, *Winds of God*, 163–74. Quote on p. 168. For examples of resistance to the General Council, see Brumback, *Suddenly . . . from Heaven*, 156–58. For Bell's defense of organizing, see Bell, "Bible Order Versus Fanaticism," 2–3.

9. "General Convention of Pentecostal Saints," (January 20, 1914) 4; "General Convention of Pentecostal Saints," (March 20, 1914) 1.

10. A definite count of the delegates has not been possible. For the conflicting evidence, see Blumhofer, *Assemblies of God*, 417, n 34.

11. *Combined Minutes of the General Council*, 2.

12. *Combined Minutes of the General Council*, 4.

And even after the General Council met in April, the old way of organizing through informal conventions flourished.

Bosworth was involved in the Council but did not take a leading role. He had a hand in the discussion that led to the creation of an executive presbytery.[13] Bosworth and his wife joined the ministerial roster of the new body in 1914, although at that time the exact nature of the organization was unclear. It was obviously growing, however, and within months, over five hundred workers held Assemblies of God credentials. This growth necessitated another General Council, which convened in November at the Stone Church in Chicago. Here the number of executive presbyters was expanded, and Bosworth was one of the sixteen men who were selected to serve.[14] Presbyters were "only servants," charged with conducting the business of the General Council between meetings, calling meetings, and establishing official fellowship with ministers and assemblies.[15] In the executive presbyter meeting following the General Council, Bosworth was appointed to serve on a song book committee.[16]

DALLAS AND BEYOND: BOSWORTH AS PASTOR, EVANGELIST, AND DENOMINATIONAL STATESMAN

Between the General Council meetings of April and November, Bosworth continued his work in Dallas. He reported to the *Christian Evangel* that his ministry was especially blessed in conversions and baptisms.[17] In an essay from this period, he explained that sin is a larger concept than "stealing, cursing, adultery, [or] getting drunk." For "[t]he best thing a sinner might do in the place of wholly yielding to God, even if it is dropping all his bad habits, is only a new and more subtile [sic] form of resistance, and leaves him still guilty of the terrible sin of rebellion." In line with his Dowieite training, Bosworth saw human activity as the battle ground between God and Satan. "To defer repentance is to resist God and co-operate with the Devil." Only a yielding of one's will to God is sufficient to bring the sinner to God's favor. Because true repentance "secures a man's consent, in advance, to every future revelation of the will of God," it is the key not only to conversion but to the spirit-filled and supernatural life. "This yielding to the truth,"

13. *Combined Minutes of the General Council*, 5.
14. *Combined Minutes of the General Council*, 9.
15. "Hot Springs Assembly," 1; *Combined Minutes of the General Council*, 11.
16. "Minutes of the Executive Presbytery." Apparently, this intended song book never materialized. The Assemblies of God did not compile a general song book until 1924, when *Songs of Pentecostal Fellowship* was published.
17. Bosworth, "Tide Still Rising in Dallas, Texas," 6.

argued Bosworth, "takes away every obstacle so that the mighty gushings of faith break forth and God cleanses the heart and fills it with the Holy Ghost. Such people receive the Baptism in the Spirit the first time they know their privilege." In the concept of faith—understood as perfect yielding to the gospel—Bosworth found an organizing principle for his entire theology of the supernatural.[18]

Bosworth also traveled again to the Stone Church for its annual May Convention, bringing with him a man named Walter Martin, who had been healed of complete blindness and became a living emblem of the supernatural ministry Bosworth promoted.[19] Bosworth's words were taking on a supernatural role, as one woman testified to healing while reading Bosworth's sermon on healing through Christ's body.[20] Revealing the role faith was taking in his preaching and theology, Bosworth told the conventioners that "[a]ny person can have the baptism in the Holy Spirit before he leaves this place, even though he is the worst sinner in the world, if he will yield to God." Such preaching stirred those who had expected a long period of tarrying, resulting in numerous spirit-baptisms.[21]

Bosworth was also a key leader at a Los Angeles pentecostal convention in October of 1914, and again Walter Martin was there to share his story of healing.[22] Under the leadership of A. G. Garr, well-known pentecostal missionary, the convention also boasted leadership from the British Smith Wigglesworth and Bosworth's longtime acquaintance through Woodworth-Etter, Elizabeth Sisson.[23] In Los Angeles, Bosworth spoke on one of his favorite subjects, revival. Like all his preaching, this too was now subsumed under faith. "The way to have a revival is not only to ask for a revival, but to believe for it," said Bosworth.[24] "Just as far as we can have a living faith,"

18. All quotes in this and the previous paragraph are from Bosworth, "Sin and Repentance," 2. This work bears much resemblance to Bosworth, "Sinfulness of Procrastination," which was originally preached in Dallas on March 15, 1914.

19. R. L. Erickson, now the pastor of the Stone Church, had spent a few weeks with Bosworth in Dallas. Sisson, "Series of Baptisms," 10–11. Sisson, "Healing a Man Born Blind," 2–4; *Latter Rain Evangel* 6.8 (May 1914) 12–13; "Man Born Blind Now Sees," 19–21; Bosworth, "Letter from Dallas, Texas." Sisson's article was later published in tract form. See "New Tracts," 11.

20. "Notes," 12.

21. *Latter Rain Evangel* 6.9 (June 1914) 10; Bosworth, "Enthronement of Self the Great Sin," 2. This sermon was delivered in the Stone Church on May 24, 1914.

22. In the spring of 1915, investigations proved that Martin's case was full of errors. Bosworth and others publicly refuted Martin's claims. "Refutation," 14–15.

23. *Triumphs of Faith* 34.10 (October 1914) 240; Cody, "Report from Los Angeles Convention," 263.

24. Bosworth, "Power in the Holy Ghost," 245.

he told the audience at Los Angeles, "it will bring to pass the things God wants done."[25] In another sermon at Los Angeles, Bosworth told those who felt their faith to be small or ineffectual that the first step in living faith is to "purpose with all your heart":

> Let us take hold of God with our whole hearts. God does not want us to simply CHOOSE to have a thing which is according to His will, but to PURPOSE WITH ALL OUR HEART to have it. God looks at what we have; we may not have faith at first, but we have a will, and if we will with God that is all he wants of us. If we will with God, faith then will spring up with perfect naturalness.[26]

A tension existed in Bosworth's thought, a tension inherited from the mixed Calvinist and Arminian roots of the holiness and divine healing movements. While elsewhere Bosworth maintained that faith was purely God's gift given by hearing the preached word, he also often stated that the believer must show obedience or "purpose of heart" before living faith will come.[27] He was consistent, however, on "the omnipotence of faith": if a believer could be certain of God's will in a matter, faith materialized the blessing.[28]

Bosworth's leadership in the Assemblies of God did not slow his pastoral and evangelistic work. In March, he reported that the Dallas work was in "excellent shape," with thirty cottage meetings across the city.[29] During this time, Bosworth conducted a three-week campaign in Bridgeport, Texas, where a man was converted after hearing Bosworth's tongues speech in German.[30] In April, Elizabeth Sisson described the Dallas work as an "unbroken revival" of four years, owing its success to unity in prayer.[31] That spring, Bosworth was a key speaker at a pentecostal convention in Newark, New Jersey.[32] Bosworth spent a short time in St. Louis in June, working alongside Woodworth-Etter.[33] Later that month he re-joined Cyrus Fockler, assist-

---

25. Bosworth, "Power in the Holy Ghost," 246.
26. Bosworth, "Living Faith in the Power of God," 31.
27. For a typical statement on "faith comes by hearing," see Bosworth, "Discerning the Lord's Body," 5. For a typical statement on "obedience will produce faith," see Bosworth, "Wonders of Faith," 7.
28. Bosworth, "Wonders of Faith," 11.
29. Bosworth, "Dallas and Bridgeport, Texas," 1.
30. Hines, "Tongues Are for a Sign," 2.
31. Sisson, "Four Years' Continuous Revival," 69, 71–72.
32. Armstrong, "Newark Convention," 4; "Fifteen Days with God," 13.
33. "Sister Etter Now in St. Louis," 1; Woodworth-Etter, *Signs and Wonders God*

ing with Fockler's "six week campaign against sin, sorrow, and sickness" in Milwaukee.[34] The Milwaukee campaign met Fockler's expectations, as seen in the testimony of one female alcoholic who also suffered paralysis and consumption. On her way to drown herself, she heard the joyous singing from the meetings, and "[i]nstead of going to the river she came to the meeting at the Hall and plunged into the life-giving current that never runs dry."[35]

The Milwaukee work was also assisted by E. N. Richey, who like Bosworth and Fockler, was a Zion City veteran.[36] From this point forward in Bosworth's itinerant work, his brother Burt and Charles O. Benham from Chicago were frequent helpers, and music regained a central place in his ministry. In September and October, the Bosworth brothers were leading services in Oakland, where they received the enthusiastic support of Carrie Judd Montgomery.[37] From there, Bosworth traveled to Los Angeles, where he teamed up with A. G. Garr and Woodworth-Etter for a series of meetings. In November, Bosworth was back at the Stone Church, leading meetings that were marked by "soul travail for the lost," visions of Christ, and numerous healings. Again, Bosworth was tapped to preach on revival and the relation of faith to God's promise of the Holy Spirit.[38]

Early in 1916, Bosworth spent a month headlining a pentecostal convention in Osborne, Kansas.[39] That summer, he was assisted in Dallas by William Black of Los Angeles. Bosworth reported that they were "having the best results in the history of our work," particularly in number of conversions.[40] When the *Weekly Evangel* editorialized that "the power of God [was] again falling in Dallas," Bosworth felt compelled to correct the publication, insisting "there has never been a time in the history of the work here when sinners were not flocking to the altar for salvation." This was not simply a matter of personal pride. As a recognized authority on revival he wanted to make clear that he practiced what he preached and that his

---

Wrought, 425–27.

34. Fockler, "Big Meeting in Milwaukee, Wis.," 2.

35. "Signs Following in Milwaukee," 15.

36. Mitchell, "Milwaukee, Wis.," *Weekly Evangel*, 1.

37. *Triumphs of Faith* 35.9 (September 1915) 213; Montgomery, "Special Meetings in Oakland," 216. For Bosworth's sermons in Oakland, see Bosworth, "Healing in the Atonement," 226–31; Bosworth, "Clay in the Hands of the Potter," 254–59.

38. *Latter Rain Evangel* 8.3 (December 1915) 12; Bosworth, "Nothing Can Hinder a Revival," 6–8; Bosworth, "Promise of the Father," 2–7.

39. "Convention at Osborne, Kans.," 14.

40. Jamieson, "Revival on at Dallas, Texas," 14. Quote from Bosworth, "Greatest Revival in Dallas," 7.

principles bore fruit. As he told the *Evangel*, "I have always maintained that the revival would continue as long as the preacher and the saints stayed full of the Spirit, for then He will never fail to do His office work of convicting of sin, and righteousness and judgment."[41]

No longer an executive presbyter, Bosworth nonetheless attended the 1916 General Council of the Assemblies of God at St. Louis in October, giving a sermon on evangelism and serving on the enrollment committee.[42] During this General Council, the Assemblies of God passed a Statement of Fundamental Truths, largely in response to the Oneness controversy. Although Bosworth was not involved in the controversy, as part of the executive presbytery in May of 1915, he was attached to a statement that said, in part, "we cannot accept a doctrine merely because some one claims to have a modern revelation to that effect."[43] As the issue came to a head at the 1916 General Council, the Council emphasized that the new Statement was not a creed but a "basis of unity for the ministry alone" and empowered the Credential Committee to refuse credentials "to those who seriously disagree" with the Statement. Aside from affirming the Trinity in a lengthy and detailed article, the Statement described the baptism in the Holy Ghost as primarily an "enduement of power for life and service," the full consummation of which "is indicated by the initial sign of speaking in tongues, as the Spirit of God gives utterance." A vague statement on sanctification was crafted to make room for holiness pentecostals in the predominantly finished work organization.[44] In the aftermath of the divisive meeting, the General Council recalled prior ministerial credentials and began the process of reissuing new certificates. Bosworth was one of the hundreds of ministers who received new credential certificates in the months after the 1916 General Council.[45]

Bosworth continued his itinerant evangelism. He and his brother conducted a midwinter convention in Pawhuska, Oklahoma, which was both an evangelistic outreach and a meeting for the Assemblies of God district council in that state.[46] Later in the spring of 1917, Bosworth was in Winnipeg, contributing to a revival that had been in process since October.

41. Bosworth, "Continuous Revival in Dallas, Texas," 8.

42. *Minutes of the General Council of the Assemblies of God . . . 1916*, 4, 5; "Messages of the Moment," 8.

43. "Preliminary Statement," 1.

44. For the above quotes from the Council, see *Minutes of the General Council of the Assemblies of God . . . 1916*, 10–11.

45. "F. F. Bosworth Ordination Certificate."

46. "Midwinter Pentecostal Convention," 11; Pope, "Great Times of Refreshing," 16; Welch, "Visit Among the Saints," 8.

Bosworth left Winnipeg on March 26, his time being "a continuous victory," according to G. D. Lockhart's report.[47] Bosworth was back in Dallas in April, and a new feature of the work was emerging. The Bosworth evangelistic party sought the cooperation of other churches in their soul-winning efforts, enlisting the preaching of Presbyterian William M. Holderby and the use of the Cole Avenue Methodist Church facilities and choir.[48] This interdenominational character was a point of pride for Bosworth.[49] During August, Bosworth was in Houston, holding meetings that received much attention in the local press and focused on the message of salvation.[50] A deadly uprising of black soldiers on August 23 forced Bosworth to close a meeting early, as bullets pierced the top of his tent. He later recalled that he felt divinely led to preach that night that some in the audience would not have another chance to repent—a leading that was confirmed when Bosworth learned that some in that audience were later killed in the mutiny.[51] In September, he was at the General Council meeting—again in St. Louis—preaching on the centrality of love to the Christian faith. At this meeting, Bosworth was also elected to the General Presbytery, a more widely representative body of consultative presbyters that was created the year before.[52] After the General Council, Bosworth returned to work in Dallas, assisted by Assemblies of God evangelist William Gaston.[53]

Also at the September Council was Raymond T. Richey, son of Zion City's former mayor E. N. Richey. Raymond urged evangelism among soldiers. The Council agreed that pentecostals must "become all things to all men that by all means we may save some"—an implied support for

---

47. Lockhart, *Weekly Evangel* no. 185 (April 14, 1917) 11; Bosworth, "B. B. Bosworth to J. W. Welch."

48. *Weekly Evangel* no. 204 (August 25, 1917) 16. As this account states, Holderby apparently experienced spirit-baptism that summer.

49. Sisson, "Council and Missionary Conference," 4.

50. "Bro. Bosworth at Houston, Tex.," 11. The campaign in Houston began on August 5 and closed September 2, 1917. Reports on the meetings in secular press appeared almost daily. For a sample of the coverage, see "Large Audience Greets Evangelist Bosworth," 3; "Hell Is a Reality and Full of Sorrows," 8; "West End Revival Campaign Closes," 6. For coverage in pentecostal papers, see Bosworth, "Will of God Boiled Down into Five Words," 1; "Overflowing Audience Hears Rev. Mr. Bosworth," 8; Bosworth, "Holy Spirit," 1. For an advertisement of Richey's collection of clippings from the Houston work, see "Bosworth Revival Campaign in Houston, Texas," 14.

51. "F. F. Bosworth, Raymond T. Richey, and B. B. Bosworth," 8. For the Houston race riot of 1917, see Smith, "Houston Riot of 1917, Revisited," 85–102.

52. Bosworth, "Call to Love," 2; *Minutes of the General Council of the Assemblies of God . . . 1917*, 11.

53. "Mt. Auburn Revival Campaign, 10"; "Gospel Tabernacle Revival," 3.

interdenominational work.⁵⁴ In December Richey invited the Bosworth brothers back to Houston to work with soldiers who were preparing to enter combat in Europe. Like Bosworth's Dallas ministry, the Houston work was interdenominational, under the auspices of Richey's United Prayer and Workers' League and with frequent preaching by Holderby.⁵⁵ After Houston, the Bosworth brothers were in Oklahoma, conducting a revival meeting that preceded the state council in April.⁵⁶

THE TONGUES EVIDENCE CONTROVERSY

On July 24, 1918, Bosworth, at the height of his influence and prestige in the young denomination, resigned from the ministry of the Assemblies of God. In his letter to chairman J. W. Welch, Bosworth indicated the reason for his resignation: "I do not believe, nor can I ever teach, that all will speak in tongues when baptized in the Spirit." With his views spreading through the ranks, Bosworth received letters telling him he "had no right to hold credentials," and he recognized that Welch would be blamed if Bosworth were allowed to retain them. Bosworth also accused A. G. Garr and William Black of intentionally splitting Bosworth's Dallas congregation and spreading "false and misleading" information that, as Bosworth claimed, "put me in a bad light with thousands of those dearest to me over the land." By the time Bosworth resigned, Garr and Black had taken over Bosworth's original tabernacle in Dallas.⁵⁷ Bosworth was distraught over the slander, but he was more focused on the doctrinal issues, telling Welch that "if I had a thousand souls, I would not be afraid to risk them all on the truth of my position . . ."⁵⁸

Bosworth had probably been voicing his doubts about the doctrine since the General Council of 1917, and he told Welch that he hoped the issue would be "lovingly considered from the Scriptures" at the next General Council.⁵⁹ When the Council met in September, Bosworth got his wish.

54. Richey, "Work Amongst the Soldiers," 10; *General Council of the Assemblies of God . . . 1917*, 16.

55. Richey, "Work Amongst the Soldiers," 10; Richey, "Telegram from Houston, Texas," 3; "Bosworth Brothers Here to Assist," 8; "Tabernacle Warmed for Night Service," 9. For details on the 1917–1918 campaign see Foxworth, "Raymond T. Richey," 70–75.

56. O'Neal, "Announcement," 15.

57. Loftis claims that Bosworth and Birdsall resigned their pastorate of the Dallas pentecostal church in April. Loftis, *History of First Assembly of God*, 10.

58. For Bosworth's resignation letter and all of the quotations in this paragraph, see Bosworth, "F. F. Bosworth to J. W. Welch."

59. According to Frodsham's report on the 1918 Council, the doctrine had been "challenged during the past twelve months." Frodsham, "1918 General Council," 3.

Bosworth was allowed the courtesy of presenting his views. Yet the Council held fast to language that had been part of the Statement of Fundamental Truths since 1917: "[t]he full consummation of the baptism of believers in the Holy Ghost is indicated by the initial physical sign of speaking with other tongues as the Spirit of God gives utterance."[60] In fact, the 1918 Council made their stance on the issue more explicit, referring to the initial evidence doctrine as the "distinctive testimony" of the pentecostal movement, and unofficially suggesting that tongues "invariably accompanies" spirit-baptism. The Council resolved that no minister should hold Assemblies of God credentials who "attacks as error our distinctive testimony"—a problem Bosworth, for his part, had already solved with his resignation.[61]

Bosworth's Early Ambivalence

Although Bosworth later recalled that during his early years in pentecostal ministry he "tenaciously contended" for the tongues evidence doctrine, he admitted that he had ceased preaching the doctrine some years before he publicly came out against it.[62] In fact, his written record prior to 1917 does not show him as an enthusiastic supporter of the teaching. In a sermon in 1915, Bosworth associated tongues with spirit-baptism, but in a descriptive rather than prescriptive way. "If there is one thing above another that you can know for sure, it is when you are filled with the Holy Ghost," he proclaimed. "On the day of Pentecost it was the same, the Spirit was poured out, fell upon them, they spake in tongues, received the Holy Ghost, and it was called a baptism."[63] Bosworth was unnerved by the emphasis on tongues in pentecostal circles. As he said at the Stone Church in 1913, his discomfort with the tongues doctrine was rooted in his pastoral concerns:

> I tell you, dear ones, there is something more to this baptism than the speaking in tongues, wonderful as that is. Let not

---

When the General Council voted on inserting the qualifier "physical" (which they claimed was an oversight of the 1916 council) in the article of the Statement of Fundamental Truths on "initial physical sign" in 1917, Bosworth's was probably one of the "three or four dissenting votes" recorded in the minutes. *Minutes of the General Council of the Assemblies of God . . . 1917*, 21. Brumback claims that Bosworth had been voicing his position before the Council of 1917, which responded with a resolution requiring missionaries to sign the Statement of Fundamental Truths. Brumback, *Suddenly . . . from Heaven*, 220; *Minutes of the General Council of the Assemblies of God . . . 1917*, 22.

60. *Minutes of the General Council of the Assemblies of God . . . 1917*, 21.
61. *Minutes of the General Council of the Assemblies of God . . . 1917*, 7–8.
62. Perkins, *Joybringer Bosworth*, 57, 74.
63. Bosworth, "Promise of the Father," 4.

anyone be satisfied with his experience until he has a burden for souls. The same Holy Ghost who at the time of our baptism gave us utterance in other languages is He who "Himself maketh intercession with groanings that cannot be uttered." And the groanings that cannot be uttered may be a better evidence that we have retained the experience than speaking in tongues, for after the first warmth of love has died away the tongues may continue, but the spirit of prayer will not continue without the love of God moving in our hearts.[64]

For Bosworth, the chief result of spirit-baptism was that it aligned the seeker with God's will in the salvation of others, a burden he often referred to as "soul travail."[65] In this context, Bosworth even challenged the later important marker of "initial," saying, "As the Spirit falls upon some, they are given soul travail even before speaking in tongues." He fully endorsed this order of events. "I am always glad," Bosworth said, "when this operation of the Spirit [soul travail] precedes speaking in tongues, otherwise the seeker may be so overjoyed at receiving the Comforter that he ceases to wait upon God and misses being taken into the wonderful experiences of soul travail."[66] While at this time, Bosworth was not aware that later pentecostals would identify Paul's remark about "groanings that cannot be uttered" as tongues speech or the distinction the Assemblies of God Statement of Fundamentals would make about tongues as the initial *physical* sign, he was clearly challenging the prominence tongues was given in the interpretation of spirit-baptism. He emphasized that tongues are one of the results of "living faith."[67] At a Los Angeles gathering in 1914, Bosworth wrestled with the problem of seekers who went a long time without the sign of tongues. His advice was to put faith into action:

> When people ask God to baptize them with the Holy Spirit, many times the Spirit falls upon them and His power gets into their tongues, and they wait for the Spirit to utter the words through them; but the Spirit gives them utterance . . . The reason why some people have asked for the baptism for so many years is because they have (when God put the power on them) shut

---

64. Bosworth, "Ministry of Intercession," 2.
65. For the language of "soul travail" in the nineteenth-century holiness movement, see Weaver, "Baptists and Holiness," 169.
66. Bosworth, "Ministry of Intercession," 2.
67. Bosworth, "Wonders of Faith," 10.

their mouths and waited for the Spirit to do what they should do . . . He is already in His temple.⁶⁸

While before 1917 Bosworth was not directly attacking the link between spirit-baptism and tongues, his comments showed apprehension about the tongues teaching. He asserted that the baptism may be complete ("He is already in His temple") before tongues occur. A believer could go days, weeks, or longer having spirit-baptism, but not yet speaking in tongues. According to Bosworth, while tongues naturally followed spirit-baptism, they may be deferred. In 1915, Bosworth also challenged the uniqueness of a singular spirit-baptism experience and therefore the need for a unique proof of that experience.⁶⁹

Context: Early Pentecostal Fluidity on the Tongues Evidence Teaching

The tongues evidence doctrine underwent significant changes in the eighteen years between Parham's first articulation of "Bible evidence" and the Assemblies of God's 1918 Statement of Fundamental Truths. Major pentecostal leaders disagreed about what the doctrine meant and how strictly to enforce it.⁷⁰ The most important development was the gradual rejection of Parham's view that tongues were always unlearned foreign languages. Led by Parham's associate Warren F. Carothers, as early as 1906 pentecostals claimed that "there is abundant use for the tongue whether any man understands him or not . . . [and] it is not primarily intended that any man should understand the tongues."⁷¹ While this eased the burden of determining what language a person was speaking when glossolalizing and seemed to conform more to the way tongues were actually practiced, it created new problems. If tongues were not identifiable foreign languages, then they were often gibberish—at least to those listening. While it could be assumed that an identified foreign language was inspired by the Holy Spirit, non-linguistic utterances seemed to be more open to the suspicion of being inspired by

---

68. Bosworth, "Power in the Holy Ghost," 246.
69. Bosworth, "Promise of the Father," 6.
70. Friesen, *Norming the Abnormal*, chap. 2–3.
71. Carothers' distinction between tongues missionary languages and non-human languages is connected to, but not synonymous with, his distinction between tongues as evidence and tongues as ongoing gift—a distinction also pioneered by Carothers. Carothers, *Baptism with the Holy Ghost*, 21. Cf. Robeck, "Emerging Magisterium?," 174. A. G. Garr also publicized his views—based on his own inability to speak Bengali while in India—that tongues did not primarily operate as missionary languages. Garr, "Tongues," 3. See also "Value of Speaking in Tongues," 4.

the flesh or demonic powers.[72] Furthermore, since Parham had felt that the gift of tongues endowed in spirit-baptism had a definite utilitarian function as power to witness, he felt that the evidence of tongues did not need to be corroborated by other gifts or spiritual fruits.[73] Once tongues were divorced from Parham's missionary orientation, pentecostals became concerned that tongues *alone* were not sufficient evidence of spirit-baptism. This all led to deeper reflection on what pentecostals meant by tongues as evidence of spirit-baptism. Many began to define more tightly their doctrine of tongues evidence, insisting that only those spoken "as the spirit gives utterance" and "accompanied with the fruit of the Spirit" were valid.[74] In addition, they added qualifiers to the evidence doctrine: by labeling tongues the "initial" evidence, they suggested that other evidences would follow. Thus, when Bosworth began criticizing the tongues evidence position, he was not rejecting a monolithic doctrinal heritage. Rather, he was operating within the flux in pentecostalism surrounding the relationship of tongues to spirit-baptism.

Even more important, Bosworth was not alone in his rejection of a rigid tongues evidence teaching. Just after Parham relinquished his title as Projector of the Apostolic Faith, his network of churches and ministers began dealing with divergent views of the role of tongues. At a February 1907 convention in Waco, Texas, the issue was openly aired. According to Howard Goss, an early Parham convert, those who held the "orthodox" (by which he meant non-Parhamite) position argued that any of the nine spiritual gifts could serve as evidence of spirit-baptism. But Warren F. Carothers, Parham's right-hand-man in Texas, argued that according to Acts 10:45–46, "tongues *alone* finally convinced the Jews that the Gentiles as well as themselves had actually received the Holy Ghost." Although A. G. Canada, who led the opposition against Carothers, was "a gifted speaker," Carothers won the debate, and according to Goss, "for most of us the question was settled once and for all."[75] And yet, even in Goss's recollection, the strength of Carothers's "wise and logical deductions" was not quite enough to clinch the victory. In pentecostal-supernatural fashion, Goss had to insist on a type of "inner witness of the spirit" for confirmation of the tongues truth.[76] And in a final adjudication, Carothers's party decided to make a "test case" out of an upcoming meeting in San Antonio. Refraining from preaching

---

72. Bell, "What Is the Evidence," 7.
73. Friesen, *Norming the Abnormal*, 46.
74. "Doctrine of the Pentecostal Movement," 1.
75. Johnston, *Howard A. Goss*, 57–59; emphasis in original.
76. Johnston, *Howard A. Goss*, 57–59.

the tongues evidence doctrine, this group was pleased when those seeking spirit-baptism spoke in tongues.[77]

Assemblies of God historian Carl Brumback claimed that after the Waco convention (which, incidentally, also confirmed a prohibition on eating pork[78]), no pentecostals challenged the Bible evidence doctrine until Bosworth a decade later.[79] Recent historians more accurately identify the connection between tongues and spirit-baptism as "fluid" in the decade after Azusa Street.[80] The sources indicate that before 1918 the issue was not settled: even the Waco convention was ambiguous, with Goss stating that tongues were "not the only evidence."[81] Many pentecostals continued to express dissent or caution against the exclusive tongues doctrine.

The teaching of evidential tongues was particularly contentious among pentecostals with roots in Zion City. According to Voliva, Daniel Bryant, who despite seeking never received tongues, also took issue with the undue emphasis on tongues. Voliva cited Bryant as arguing that "the teaching that tongues must be produced as an evidence of the Baptism in the Holy Spirit, will lead to an unscriptural use of the gift."[82] William H. Piper also questioned the Bible evidence doctrine, leading Voliva to marvel at the pentecostals' inconsistencies. Voliva perhaps strained the evidence when he claimed Piper taught "that the teaching . . . was purely demoniacal," but Voliva clearly saw that Piper did not hold a hard line on tongues.[83] In late summer 1908, Piper came to the conclusion that, "One of the things that has hindered this great movement of God on the face of the earth, and caused many people not to seek the blessing, is the false teaching, that speaking in tongues is the only, essential and necessary evidence of the baptism in the Holy Spirit."[84] Piper's perspective stemmed from his own spirit-baptism experience:

77. Johnston, *Howard A. Goss*, 58–59. That the San Antonio group had no prior knowledge of the tongues doctrine is unlikely, since Parham's network was strong throughout central Texas. Furthermore, one of the participants at the San Antonio meeting was D. C. O. Opperman, who in 1906 had learned of the doctrine directly from Parham himself. See Brumback, *Suddenly . . . from Heaven*, 216–17; Gardiner, *Out of Zion*, 141–43.

78. Anderson, *Vision of the Disinherited*, 156.

79. Brumback, *Suddenly . . . from Heaven*, 216. Brumback may have been following Goss, *Winds of God*, 59.

80. Robeck, "Emerging Magisterium?," 177, 179; Blumhofer, *Assemblies of God*, 240.

81. Words of Howard A. Goss in Lawrence, *Apostolic Faith Restored*, 67. Cited in Anderson, *Vision of the Disinherited*, 162.

82. "Questions Lovingly Addressed," 3.

83. "Questions Lovingly Addressed," 3.

84. Piper, "Manifestations and 'Demonstrations,'" 18.

> Saturday night, while sitting in our chairs communing with God, there came a wave of spiritual power so deep and strong that it seemed to take our breath. This occurred in each of us at exactly the same instant. I am sure that at this time I was baptized in the Holy Spirit, but I would not acknowledge it nor even believe it, because I did not speak in tongues . . . I am now sure that I was grieving the Spirit of God in continuing to ask for that which had already been given to me.[85]

Piper knew of many, like himself, who had a true spirit-baptism without speaking in tongues. These unfortunate people, claimed Piper, "were made to believe that because they had not spoken in tongues they really had nothing and began to question and got into comparative spiritual darkness." Ironically, however, when Piper advised them to believe they had spirit-baptism without tongues, many of them were so freed that tongues speech began to flow naturally.[86] Piper was disturbed by the doctrine's power to create a "sect" out of the pentecostal movement, using the teaching to say "We are the people and you are not." He pointed to the successful ministries of many in church history who had not spoken in tongues. According to Piper, the purpose of spirit-baptism was more important than evidence, and the purpose was "qualifying us for service." He felt that if the tongues doctrine were true, scripture would be clearer on the subject.[87]

William Durham, an outspoken advocate of the tongues evidence doctrine, knew that Piper did not agree with the majority pentecostal position. When the *Household of God* newspaper folded in 1910 and transferred its subscribers to Piper's *Latter Rain Evangel*, Durham felt obligated to let his readers know that his endorsement did not transfer with it. "We cannot recommend a paper that in its first number took a decided stand against tongues being the evidence of the baptism in the Holy Ghost, and other truths for which the Pentecostal movement has stood from the first, and whose editor has not yet received the Holy Ghost, so far as we know."[88] Years before the Assemblies of God labeled the tongues teaching the "distinctive testimony" of the pentecostal movement, Durham recognized it as the unique preserve of pentecostals. Durham indicted Piper and others who denied the teaching, saying, "The work has . . . suffered from the effects of those who claim to be Pentecostal people, and at the same time deny this

---

85. Piper, "Long Weary Months of Spiritual Drought," 5.
86. Piper, "Manifestations and 'Demonstrations,'" 18.
87. Piper, "Manifestations and 'Demonstrations,'" 19.
88. "Criticisms Answered," 11.

great distinguishing truth of the movement."[89] Piper was a major voice of dissent on the tongues teaching and a revered leader in the early movement; the imagination is stirred to think of how the tongues teaching may have evolved if Piper had not died in 1911.

Piper was not alone in challenging the tongues evidence teaching. In his frustration over perceived viciousness of other pentecostals and their unbiblical teachings, William Seymour gradually loosened his stance on evidential tongues, insisting rather on the fruits of the spirit as the true evidence.[90] Agnes Ozman, the first woman to speak in tongues at Parham's Bible school in 1901, also came to the conclusion that tongues was not the only evidence of spirit-baptism. As she told readers of the *Latter Rain Evangel* in 1909, she intended to print an article about it earlier but was hindered. Yet she contented herself with the knowledge that God "might reveal this truth to others who would spread it abroad." Although forsaking the tongues doctrine, she maintained that "My power to speak in tongues has not been lessened by giving up the errors which have become attached to this work, but instead it has increased."[91]

In 1910, the *Pentecost*, edited by J. R. Flower and A. S. Copley, cautioned seekers against preoccupation with tongues, advising them to "keep occupied with Jesus . . . and the new tongue will most likely come when you are least thinking about it."[92] The phrase "most likely" reveals ambivalence toward the tongues evidence teaching. The writer felt that emphasis on tongues would have negative consequences:

> To insist that this is the only evidence of baptism in the Holy Spirit is to compel us to accept all speaking in tongues as divine. Whereas some is purely human and others is certainly satanic. The Scripture . . . records at least three signs of the Spirit's presence . . . Here they are: speaking in tongues, magnifying God, and prophesying.[93]

Copley later developed a strongly Pauline theology of spirit-baptism, arguing that "the whole Church was BAPTIZED in the Spirit once, and all at one time. But individuals receive the ANOINTING as they believe for it." He insisted that "many who speak in tongues put undue stress thereon, boastfully calling it 'the Bible evidence,' and exalting interpretations above

---

89. Durham, "Speaking in Tongues," 9.
90. Robeck, "William J. Seymour," 84.
91. Ozman, "Where the Latter Rain First Fell," 2.
92. *Pentecost* 2.9, 10 (October 1910) 11.
93. *Pentecost* 2.11–12 (December 1910) 9.

the plain Word." Apparently, Copley saw a danger in neat systematization of the pentecostal experience, especially if built upon faulty exegesis.[94]

Another who raised doubts about the teaching was Minnie Abrams, the famed leader of the pentecostal revival in India that predated Azusa Street. Abrams believed "it is God's rule to give speaking in tongues at the time or sometime after one's baptism," but this rule, she averred, "has exceptions." In the end, the seekers must rely on "the witness in our hearts by the power of the Holy Ghost that says, 'I have it.'"[95] In 1916 the *Weekly Evangel* gave guarded advice about the link between tongues and spirit-baptism:

> The question is sometimes asked . . . "Then have not any who have not spoken in tongues been baptized with the Holy Ghost?" I do not feel that we can say that they have not. It is safe, however, to say that they have not had the baptism on scriptural or apostolic lines. I am inclined to think that in these days a person being baptized with the Holy Ghost will generally, if not always, be caused to speak in "tongues."[96]

The writer in fact seemed to endorse a theological vagueness on this issue: "It appears to me, however, that clear theological views of the subject [of the evidences of spirit-baptism], though desirable, are not strictly necessary, for as many have obtained salvation by a simple heart cry to God and without clear apprehension of the way of salvation, so God works in this blessing."[97] The writer listed the plethora of Acts 2 phenomena as "Bible evidences" of spirit-baptism.[98] While most pentecostals endorsed a necessary link between spirit-baptism and tongues, many would not risk the potential damage to consciences or the transgressing of divine liberty by categorically insisting on it.

Several other early testimonies indicate that, in practice, tongues were not as neatly linked to spirit-baptism as pentecostals often supposed. For some, the process was inverted. John G. Lake spoke in tongues on more than one occasion before the experience he labeled his spirit-baptism.[99] Ruth Angstead of Zion City testified in 1907 that she had to wait weeks after

---

94. Copley, *Holy Spirit*, 5.

95. Abrams, "Object of the Baptism in the Holy Spirit," 9. See also McGee and Burgess, "India," 118–26; McGee, "'Latter Rain' Falling in the East," 648–65.

96. Bernard, "Gift of Tongues and the Pentecostal Movement," 5. Cited in Robeck, "Emerging Magisterium?," 179. Bernard is listed as the author at the end of the article as it continued into the June 10 issue.

97. Bernard, "Gift of Tongues and the Pentecostal Movement," 5.

98. Bernard, "Gift of Tongues and the Pentecostal Movement," 5.

99. Lake and Morgan, *John G. Lake's Life & Diary*, 17.

her spirit-baptism before speaking in tongues. She was not ashamed of this. As she wrote, "[T]he conviction that I was baptised [sic] so took hold upon me I constantly affirmed, to those asking if I was baptized, without having spoken in tongues." She claimed that largely she was content with this situation until about six weeks later she "felt the need of so speaking [in tongues] as a witness to others."[100]

Another telling case of "delayed evidence" is that of J. R. Flower.[101] In 1933, Flower, who was at the time assistant general superintendent of the Assemblies of God, published an account of his spirit-baptism experience. After witnessing pentecostal services first hand in Indianapolis in 1907, Flower was converted and began to seek spirit-baptism. After over a year of seeking—several months of which Flower described as in "a real spirit of 'tarry' before the Lord"—he had not received. On his way to minister in Kansas City, he stopped at a faith home in St. Louis:

> I continued to seek the Lord, expecting that when filled with the Spirit, I would speak with other tongues. I now believe this very expectancy drew my eyes from the Baptizer and hindered me from receiving. If I had dared to trust the Lord, I would have received much sooner.[102]

Flower came to the realization that just like salvation and healing, the blessing of spirit-baptism was received by faith—meaning that he ought not to wait for any evidence before claiming it. So claim it he did, determining that "there was to be no more pleading that day . . . I sat on the floor in the corner and praised the Lord for the Baptism in the Holy Ghost, having been received."[103] Although his companions continued to urge him to seek tongues as a sign, they grudgingly accepted his testimony that he had been baptized in the Spirit. Continuing on his ministry in Kansas City, Lincoln, Nebraska, and back in Indianapolis, Flower had still not spoken in tongues. Finally in July of 1910, Flower reported that tongues flowed naturally as he prayed with a woman at a camp meeting.

Flower was testifying to an experience that challenged Assemblies of God dogma, which is why until 1933 he had kept the details of his experience to himself.[104] Robeck rightly lauds Flower's honesty at a time when

100. Angstead, "Grand Experience," 1–2.
101. Robeck, "Emerging Magisterium?," 186–193. The term "delayed evidence" comes from a commentary on Flower's testimony appearing in an Assemblies of God publication in 1957. See Robeck, "Emerging Magisterium?," 193.
102. Flower, "How I Received the Baptism in the Holy Spirit [Part 2]," 6.
103. Flower, "How I Received the Baptism in the Holy Spirit [Part 2]," 6.
104. He referred to his 1933 article as "break[ing] my silence." Flower, "How I

the initial evidence teaching was becoming more entrenched. Still, Flower offered significant qualifications, demonstrating that he shared the concerns that motivated the crystallization of the initial evidence teaching. These qualifications come to light through a comparison of Flower's 1933 testimony to his account from 1910. Flower stated in 1933 that he was reticent about his experience because he was afraid of being "misunderstood" as encouraging seekers to claim spirit-baptism by faith while never having any manifestation. He laid the fault of not experiencing tongues at the feet of those who believe with "only a mental faith." He furthered cautioned that "sometimes there is a need of real heart searching before appropriating faith springs up" and that "it is useless to take a stand of faith until one has first prayed through."[105] But in 1910, writing before he experienced the tongues speech he identified as an indication of "final victories," he presented no such caveats. Because the tongues evidence teaching had not yet become dogma, he felt no need to distinguish "mental faith" from "true faith in the Spirit."[106] Rather, in 1910, Flower simply stressed faith, not any preceding "heart searching" or "pray[ing] through." Without qualifying faith in any way, Flower advised seekers in 1910 to believe they had the experience even if evidence such as tongues was lacking, an approach based on his own experience:

> [A]t last I realized I would seek several years more if I did not step out by faith and claim the promise. I stepped. Nothing happened. Several days later the Lord, to encourage me, gave me a big blessing, but not tongues, and I still had to testify that I had received.[107]

Flower's experience kept him from dogmatically asserting that tongues always immediately accompanies spirit-baptism. He consistently argued that faith was the central factor. But to be more agreeable to the official Assemblies of God position, Flower defined faith more stringently, perhaps suggesting that experiences such as his were—and ought to be—rare. His evolving testimony reveals the fluidity of the tongues evidence doctrine in early pentecostalism and the effects of dogmatization on those whose experiences did not fit the mold.

Many black pentecostals were less rigorous on the tongues evidence doctrine than their white counterparts. The United Holy Church of

---

Received the Baptism in the Holy Spirit [Part 1]," 2.
    105. Flower, "How I Received the Baptism in the Holy Spirit [Part 2]," 7.
    106. Flower, "How I Received the Baptism in the Holy Spirit [Part 2]," 7.
    107. Flower, "God Honors Faith," 1.

America, although identifying with the movement stemming from Azusa Street, preferred to emphasize the many spiritual gifts that are available to the sanctified believer.[108] The Church of God in Christ, although formed out of a dispute over the role of tongues in spirit-baptism, did not retain a strict initial evidence teaching. The split that occurred between C. H. Mason, who embraced the pentecostal message, and C. P. Jones, who rejected it, was about tongues on the surface, but as Estrelda Alexander notes, the conflict was more about what tongues represented: Jones sought a more restrained worship life, while Mason embraced the emotional worship practices of his black heritage. Tongues, in this situation, was shorthand for the divergent approaches to black religiosity in the early twentieth century.[109] While upholding tongues as the apostolic pattern for spirit-baptism, Mason's pentecostal Church of God in Christ would "not presume to teach that no one has the Spirit that does not speak with tongues."[110] In general, black pentecostals refused to be dogmatic about tongues, since their spirituality was oral-associative rather than static and propositional. As Ithiel Clemmons notes, rather than serving as an empirical "evidence" of a personal spiritual experience, for black pentecostals, "speaking in tongues was seen only as the sign of divine power and presence that brings all people together in reconciliation."[111]

Beyond the American scene, the tongues evidence teaching had few staunch advocates. A. A. Boddy, the leader of British pentecostalism, could not insist that tongues always accompanied spirit-baptism, although he reported that it always had in his ministry. Boddy vacillated on the interpretation of his own experiences, finally deciding that his spirit-baptism had occurred in 1892 but was much later "corroborated" by tongues.[112] After a trip to the United States in 1909, Boddy affirmed that he was "in a great measure agreed" with A. B. Simpson's position that tongues should not be considered a singular evidence.[113] Boddy attempted a conciliatory position:

> Evidently some of our German brethren think of the Gift of Tongues as possible apart from the *Baptism* of the Holy Ghost,

---

108. Alexander, *Black Fire*, 163; Turner, *United Holy Church of America*, 10, 126–27; Gregory, *History of the United Holy Church of America*, 52.

109. Alexander, *Black Fire*, 176.

110. Cited in Anderson, *Vision of the Disinherited*, 164. See also Patterson and Church of God in Christ, *History and Formative Years of the Church of God in Christ*, 48.

111. Clemmons, *Bishop C. H. Mason*, 52, 56.

112. Hudson, "Earliest Days of British Pentecostalism," 53. For Boddy's complicated stance on tongues, see Richmann, "Evangelical Unity," 69–79.

113. Boddy, "Visit to Rev. A. B. Simpson," 199.

and this may be so. But if a Seeker has humbly looked to God to give him *this* Sign as a token of his Baptism, and if he is trusting the finished work of the Lord on the Cross (the Blood), then we are pressed into the belief that God would not allow him to be deceived.[114]

Overall, Boddy's was not an enthusiastic endorsement of the tongues evidence doctrine. Boddy was probably influenced in part by influential German pentecostal leader Jonathan Paul. The first issue of Paul's *Pfingstgrüße* in 1909 stated clearly, "We are not of the opinion that only those who speak in tongues have received the baptism of the Holy Spirit."[115] In December of 1912, Paul chaired a session of the International Pentecostal Consultative Council in Amsterdam that produced a statement on spirit-baptism that intentionally avoided the tongues evidence doctrine:

> The Baptism of the Holy Ghost and Fire we hold to be the coming upon and within of the Holy Spirit to indwell the believer in His fulness, and is always borne witness to by the fruit of the Spirit and the outward manifestation, so that we may receive the same gift as the disciples on the Day of Pentecost . . . We do not teach that all who have been baptized in the Holy Ghost, even if they should speak in tongues, have already received the fulness of the blessing of Christ implied in this Baptism.[116]

The Declaration was signed by Boddy, the Dutch leader Gerrit Polman, and the Norwegian pastor T. B. Barratt.[117] One of Barratt's correspondents, Willis C. Hoover, was instrumental in establishing pentecostalism in Chile. He too refused to limit the evidence of spirit-baptism to tongues, as did the churches that trace their roots to his work.[118]

To the chorus of those who openly questioned or qualified the tongues evidence doctrine must be added those who downplayed it. Pentecostal leaders like Carrie Judd Montgomery, Mariah Woodworth-Etter, and Mattie Perry—all of whom had significant contact with Bosworth—never came out strongly for the tongues evidence doctrine. Carrie Judd Montgomery—whose own experience of tongues was delayed about a week after her

---

114. Boddy, "Conference in Germany," 6; emphasis in original.

115. Schmidgall, *European Pentecostalism*, 283.

116. "Declaration, International Pentecostal Consultative Council," 277. Cf. Simpson, "Jonathan Paul," 178–79.

117. Barratt apparently changed his mind many times on the tongues evidence teaching. See Schmidgall, *European Pentecostalism*, 283. See also Bundy, "Spiritual Advice to a Seeker," 164; Anderson, *Introduction to Pentecostalism*, 188–89.

118. Sepulveda, "Another Way of Being Pentecostal," 37–62.

spirit-baptism[119]—refused to be dogmatic about tongues throughout her career and maintained ties to the Christian and Missionary Alliance to her death.[120] Woodworth-Etter time and again avoided doctrinal antagonism, so that her easy adoption of pentecostalism for the sake of a more fruitful ministry makes sense.[121] Her wariness of the tongues evidence doctrine did not stop pentecostals from claiming her as one of their own.[122] Other respected leaders, like F. E. Yoakum and E. W. Kenyon, were embraced by pentecostals but never felt compelled to endorse the tongues evidence doctrine.

Bosworth's Critique and Pentecostal Responses

In an open letter distributed in early 1918, Bosworth outlined his objections to the tongues evidence teaching.[123] Bosworth may have been pressed to publicize his views, since A. G. Garr had likely already circulated a letter attacking Bosworth as a "veritable heretic."[124] Bosworth claimed he was not alone in his position—a claim verified by endorsements from pentecostal ministers published in subsequent editions.[125] While his critiques had previously been voiced by other pentecostals, Bosworth was the first from within the movement to offer a wholesale and systematic challenge to the doctrine. At the outset, he insisted that he was not retracting his pentecostal beliefs or denying his own tongues experience, and he exulted in the good

119. Montgomery, "Promise of the Father," 145–49.
120. Miskov, *Life on Wings*, Kindle locations 7103–94.
121. Warner, *Woman Evangelist*, 174.
122. McMullen, "Maria B Woodworth-Etter," 193. The few pentecostals who spoke against Woodworth-Etter included Charles Parham and Frank J. Ewart, both outspoken advocates of the initial evidence doctrine. Warner, *Woman Evangelist*, 171–72.
123. The earliest edition of Bosworth's open letter that I have found is Bosworth, *Do All Speak with Tongues?* Although undated, this edition asks (p. 22) for pentecostal endorsements that could be included in a second edition to be published May 25, 1918. The letter was widely circulating by the time of the General Council, and it received a published response with specific page references in October 1918. See Kinne, "Open Letter to Elder F. F. Bosworth," 3. Furthermore, in the earliest version of the tract, Bosworth stated that he had been "in the work on Pentecostal lines" for eleven years. He always dated the beginning of his pentecostal ministry to 1907. See, for example, Bosworth, "Wonders of Faith," 8.
124. The timeline is not certain, but Perkins claimed that the letter attacking Bosworth came out before Bosworth's open letter on tongues. Perkins, *Joybringer Bosworth*, 99.
125. Perkins, *Joybringer Bosworth*, 57, 77–79. Brumback notes that M. M. Pinson, Arch P. Collins, and W. T. Gaston (each of whom had worked with Bosworth in Texas) were for a time supporters of Bosworth's position. But after the 1918 General Council, all three fell in line with the Assemblies of God. Brumback, *Suddenly . . . from Heaven*, 220. For Pinson's retraction, see Pinson, "Statement from Bro. Pinson," 9.

that had come out of the pentecostal revival.[126] Yet he identified the "error in teaching" of much of the pentecostal movement as twofold: the belief that baptism in the Spirit is always evidenced by the initial physical sign of tongues, and the distinction between tongues as a sign and tongues as a gift of the Spirit.[127] While he did not evince a broader concern over the growing authority of the Assemblies of God, in this case, he did resent that an erroneous doctrine was made "a test of fellowship and a basis upon which to build a new church."[128] His thorough critique was founded upon pastoral concerns and experience, history, and scripture.[129]

Bosworth believed that the tongues evidence doctrine faltered on the tests of experience and pastoral concerns. Many who receive spirit-baptism do not speak in tongues, and many who "seemingly speak in tongues" have not had the pentecostal experience.[130] Bosworth's overall concern that faith be central to all spiritual experience led him to distrust the tongues evidence doctrine as an inversion that made faith dependent upon a sign.[131] This teaching, "not only leaves no place for faith," railed Bosworth, "but on the other hand destroys faith already Divinely given."[132] While pentecostals searched intently for a sign that would give them divine assurance, Bosworth insisted on the basis of Hebrews 11:1 that "Nothing short of real faith can satisfy the heart and put the soul at rest."[133] As a pastor and evangelist, Bosworth was concerned that the doctrine was divisive and exclusionary, "separating equally devout Christians." Furthermore, the lengthy tarrying for tongues stalls revival, as those who have already received and are empowered to win souls (though perhaps not speaking in tongues) continue to spend their time seeking at the altar, and those who are genuinely interested

---

126. Bosworth's letter is reproduced in Perkins, *Joybringer Bosworth*, 53–77. For Bosworth's recitation of the good that has come of the pentecostal movement (which was not included in the earliest version of the letter), see pp. 53–55. For Bosworth's continued endorsement of his own pentecostal experience with tongues, see p. 73.

127. Perkins, *Joybringer Bosworth*, 56–57.

128. Perkins, *Joybringer Bosworth*, 71. In the midst of the tongues controversy, E. N. Bell demonstrated the nervousness the Council had over its Statement of Fundamental Truths and the growing authority of the denomination. See Bell, "Coming Great Council," 1.

129. My categories for analyzing Bosworth's tract can be contrasted with Jacobsen, *Thinking in the Spirit*, 307.

130. Perkins, *Joybringer Bosworth*, 57.

131. Perkins, *Joybringer Bosworth*, 70.

132. Perkins, *Joybringer Bosworth*, 66.

133. Perkins, *Joybringer Bosworth*, 67.

in spirit-baptism are put off by a God who does not seem eager to fulfill his promise.[134]

Bosworth also looked to history to cast doubt on the tongues evidence teaching. Believing that spirit-baptism was for supernatural empowerment, Bosworth indicted the ministries of so many who spoke in tongues yet fell far short of the great soul winners of history. Bosworth pointed to evangelists like Charles Finney (who claimed spirit-baptism, but not tongues) to demonstrate that the real work of empowerment was accomplished without tongues as evidence.[135] Although he could view the restoration of spiritual gifts as a dispensational sign, he preferred to emphasize the continuity of God's activity throughout history. Furthermore, the doctrine's novelty also made Bosworth uncomfortable. He identified Charles Parham as the originator of the teaching and found Parham's ministry wanting.[136] Bosworth was mistaken in attributing the teaching as he encountered it in the late-1910s to Parham, since Parham did not distinguish between sign and gift and only admitted unlearned recognizable foreign language as tongues speech. But since Bosworth intended to undercut the teaching by pointing to its newness, his argument would have only been strengthened by a more insightful historical gaze.

Bosworth's scriptural critique of the tongues evidence doctrine was his most elaborate. He began with Paul's rhetorical question in 1 Corinthians 12:30: "Do all speak with tongues?", which implied that not all did. Bosworth recognized that in order not to contradict scripture, tongues advocates had to introduce a distinction between tongues as an occasional sign and tongues as a permanent gift. This distinction held that all spoke in tongues at spirit-baptism as a sign, but not all were subsequently endowed with a permanent spiritual gift of tongues.[137] According to Bosworth, defenders of the tongues evidence teaching wrongly interpreted the term "manifestation" in 1 Corinthians 12:7–8 as a reference for the sign of tongues. Bosworth insisted on the basis of context that Paul was using the word as a corporate term for all the spiritual gifts, including wisdom, knowledge, and healing as well

---

134. Perkins, *Joybringer Bosworth*, 69, 71.

135. Perkins, *Joybringer Bosworth*, 75. Bosworth may have been influenced to think this way by William Piper. "Notes: Holding the Truth in Love," 12.

136. Perkins, *Joybringer Bosworth*, 58.

137. This distinction, which was first articulated by W. F. Carothers in 1906, was stated in the General Council of 1917 and expanded in 1918 as a result of Bosworth's contentions. The General Council confessed: "The speaking in tongues in this instance [as a sign at spirit-baptism] is the same in essence as the gift of tongues, but different in purpose and use." *Minutes of the General Council of the Assemblies of God . . . 1917*, 21; *Minutes of the Sixth Annual Meeting of the General Council of the Assemblies of God . . . 1918*, 10; Robeck, "Emerging Magisterium?," 182, 186.

as tongues.[138] Bosworth scolded pentecostals for using their unscriptural distinction between kinds of tongues as an excuse for unscriptural disorder. Bosworth's opponents claimed that tongues as a sign is synonymous with "speaking as the spirit gives utterance." To maintain the sign/gift distinction, tongues advocates claimed that Paul's instructions in 1 Corinthians to silence a tongues speaker who has no interpreter cannot refer to "speaking as the spirit gives utterance," for then Paul would have advocated silencing the Holy Spirit. Bosworth countered that while all true tongues have their origin in the Holy Spirit, the speaker is still in control. God demands order, and this does not mean that one has "quenched the Spirit."[139]

Bosworth also argued that the tongues evidence teaching had no clear scriptural directive. Much as Trinitarians in the Assemblies of God had challenged the Oneness pentecostals in their midst three years earlier, Bosworth charged tongues evidence advocates with having no "thus saith the Lord" for their peculiar doctrine. "It is nowhere taught in the Scriptures," averred Bosworth, "but it is assumed from the fact that in three instances recorded in Acts they spoke in tongues as a result of the Baptism."[140] According to Bosworth, his fellow pentecostals also misunderstood the purpose of tongues. Scripture says that tongues are a sign for the unbeliever, but by requiring tongues as proof of spirit-baptism, pentecostals made the manifestation a sign to believers.[141] Finally, Bosworth challenged a favorite pentecostal proof text. Many believed that John 15:26-27 ("When the Comforter is come . . . He shall testify of me.") referred to tongues speech. Bosworth countered with a proof text of his own: "God also bearing them witness, both with signs and wonders, and with divers miracles, and gifts of the Holy Ghost . . ." (Hebrews 2:4). He argued that this is "how the Holy Ghost testifies": with myriad signs, wonders, miracles and gifts—not the sign of tongues exclusively.[142]

Bosworth's attack on the tongues evidence doctrine was not a retreat from his supernaturalism. He preferred, however, to shift the semantic field. Instead of "evidences," he focused on the "results" of spirit-baptism, which included everything from the nine spiritual gifts of 1 Corinthians 12 to convicting the world of sin and making intercession.[143] Tongues was a valid

138. Perkins, *Joybringer Bosworth*, 58–59.
139. Perkins, *Joybringer Bosworth*, 60–61.
140. Perkins, *Joybringer Bosworth*, 62–63.
141. Perkins, *Joybringer Bosworth*, 63, 66.
142. Perkins, *Joybringer Bosworth*, 65.
143. Perkins, *Joybringer Bosworth*, 70. Anderson's statement that Bosworth "maintained that any of the nine gifts of the Spirit listed in 1 Corinthians was a valid sign of baptism in the Spirit" is misleading. Bosworth was not concerned about the "sign" but

gift, and it often accompanied genuine spirit-baptism. But Bosworth believed that the doctrine impeded God's supernatural work, and he felt that returning the movement to a more scriptural foundation "open[ed] the way for more of the manifestations of the Spirit."[144] "I find," he wrote, "that the people get deeper into God and have more power when they are not taught in such a way that they anchor in tongues."[145] Noting that the apostles never "preached tongues," he found that pressing tongues seemed to have the opposite of the intended effect, and Bosworth claimed that one should "leave the proper place for faith . . . it will bring the real speaking in tongues much quicker, for where any sign is placed before faith, it hinders the Spirit, and lessens the power."[146] And as he had maintained years earlier, the "greatest phase" of spirit-baptism was "soul travail," or intercessory prayer. The work of salvation and revival fueled by such prayer is supremely supernatural: "In this phase of the Baptism," said Bosworth, "there are possibilities whose limits have never been found."[147]

Bosworth's stance created a stir. Over the next few years, the Assemblies of God published numerous articles in defense of their newly-solidified teaching.[148] In October of 1918, Seeley D. Kinne, who pioneered pentecostalism in St. Louis and had worked with Bosworth in Chicago, responded directly to Bosworth's letter.[149] In pentecostal fashion, Kinne looked first to his own experience to verify his beliefs. Kinne had sought for the experience with tongues for months, but rather than causing distress as Bosworth warned, Kinne declared that being "troubled" for a time was worth it. Tongues became the "anchor for my seeking heart," as Kinne testified, and marked the beginning of unprecedented fruitfulness in his ministry. Kinne also claimed that during his seeking period, he received many "additional impartations of the Spirit" that empowered him for ministry. "How could I do other than stand for this truth, seeing the effects in my own life and results that have followed its teaching?" Kinne went so far as to say that Bosworth's ministry was only successful because he had, as Bosworth said, "tenaciously contended" for the tongues evidence teaching. And while

---

rather the usefulness of spirit-baptism. Anderson, *Vision of the Disinherited*, 161–162.

144. Perkins, *Joybringer Bosworth*, 56.
145. Perkins, *Joybringer Bosworth*, 74.
146. Perkins, *Joybringer Bosworth*, 70.
147. Perkins, *Joybringer Bosworth*, 75.
148. A few examples include Kerr, "Do All Speak in Tongues?" 7; Gaston, "Baptism of the Holy Ghost According to Acts 2," 3; Frodsham, "Our Distinctive Testimony," 8–9. For a fuller list, see Robeck, "Emerging Magisterium?," 186.
149. For this and quotations for the next four paragraphs, see Kinne, "Open Letter to Elder F. F. Bosworth," 3.

Bosworth viewed coercive methods like quickly repeating a word or phrase as unscriptural, Kinne, drawing on his own experience under G. B. Cashwell, essentially said that if it works, one should not cast aspersions.

Kinne quarreled with Bosworth's specific arguments. Parham was not the innovator of the tongues evidence doctrine, as Bosworth maintained; Edward Irving and John Chrysostom had taught it. Although Bosworth found no "thus saith the Lord" for the doctrine, Kinne found it clearly in Jesus' words—"these signs shall follow them that believe . . . they shall speak in new tongues" (Mark 16:16–17)—and in the day of Pentecost as a fulfillment of Joel 2. Kinne also argued that the Greek of Acts 19:6 proves that speaking in tongues "was part of the baptism." Bosworth maintained that gifts were for service, not for evidence, but Kinne argued that Jesus often used his gifts to bear witness to his identity and mission. Kinne failed to recognize that Bosworth was insistent that gifts not be used as evidence *to the believer* but only to the unbeliever. In this sense, Bosworth saw no conflict between service and evidence.

Kinne also took personal shots. While Bosworth saw the tongues evidence doctrine as divisive, Kinne accused Bosworth of splitting his own church. Kinne implied that Bosworth dropped the tongues evidence doctrine "to be popular with the popular evangelistic association." "True," said Kinne, "one may obtain to a much wider ministry by coming into fellowship with the common church work of today, but . . . [one does so] at the expense of reality and depth." The charge has a ring of truth, since Bosworth had begun interdenominational work in 1917. But there is no reason to question Bosworth's integrity: Bosworth never hid the fact that he courted a wide audience for the pentecostal message. And if Bosworth had only sought status among non-pentecostals, his attempt to convince his fellow pentecostals of his beliefs seems like a waste of time and effort.

The most insightful critique Kinne leveled at Bosworth came on the issue of faith. If teaching people to wait for tongues stands in the way of faith, argued Kinne, would not teaching the sick to wait for actual physical healing also stand in the way of faith? Claiming healing while still suffering, just like claiming spirit-baptism without tongues, "looks like the dead faith James talks about," argued Kinne. But Bosworth probably would have rejected the premise of Kinne's argument, illustrating a tension in holiness and pentecostal supernaturalism that has never been resolved. Some advocated counterfactual confession, that is, they claimed healing and acted as if healed, even if healing were not yet physically real. Others—notably John Alexander Dowie—ridiculed counterfactual confession as unempirical and evasive.[150] Bosworth insisted that faith was strongest when outward evidence was lacking. *This* was real living faith. While Bosworth's thought was not fully consistent, he leaned toward the counterfactual confession position, which seemed so absurd to Kinne.

Finally, Kinne hit Bosworth on his argument from experience. Bosworth had claimed that some who seemingly speak in tongues did not have the baptism, and some who did not speak in tongues have received "the most powerful Baptisms." Kinne asked, with good reason, how Bosworth could be certain that one has been baptized without a true sign of tongues. This question revealed the heart of the tongues evidence doctrine—providing experiential, verifiable assurance of a significant spiritual experience. So Kinne accosted Bosworth, saying "[you] have just put us back in the old realm of uncertainty, where any who receive a blessing may say they are baptized in the Spirit."

Bosworth's tract was still unnerving doctrinal purists a decade after it was first published.[151] Somewhat disingenuously given his own participation in European pentecostal ambivalence on the tongues evidence doctrine, T. B. Barratt claimed, "There has always been a constant and firm belief in the scriptural statement, that the Baptism has to be followed by speaking in other tongues, just as in the case of the disciples *at the beginning*."[152] To Barratt, Bosworth's argument that the tongues evidence teaching reverses faith was nonsense, since "faith leads up to the divine evidence."[153] Barratt did not seem to share Bosworth's pastoral angst. "We do not press the necessity of seeking the outer sign or proof of the Baptism," insisted Barratt, "because what is needed *is the Baptism itself*, and when *that* comes, the outward proof or sign of the Baptism will follow as a matter of course."[154] Unlike Kinne, Barratt agreed with Bosworth's condemnation of unscriptural methods of coaching seekers, such as rapid repetition of a word. But Barratt considered it a red herring: "I have been over 21 years in this revival and have not yet

---

150. A classic clash of these competing theologies was between A. B. Simpson and John Alexander Dowie. See Robinson, *Divine Healing: The Holiness-Pentecostal Transition Years*, 69.

151. Barratt, *Baptism with the Holy Ghost and Fire*. Although this tract is undated, it appeared as a series of articles in *Pentecostal Evangel* in May of 1928.

152. Barratt, *Baptism with the Holy Ghost and Fire*, 8; emphasis in original. Barratt also seemed to have forgot that he said in 1908, "I believe that many have had, and that people may obtain in our day mighty Baptisms without this sign." Cited in Anderson, *Vision of the Disinherited*, 162.

153. Barratt, *Baptism with the Holy Ghost and Fire*, 17.

154. Barratt, *Baptism with the Holy Ghost and Fire*, 19.

seen it."[155] And unlike Kinne, Barratt did not charge Bosworth with divisiveness. Rather, he matter-of-factly argued that when truth is not accepted, "it will split those who do not accept it, from those who do. This has been the case always."[156]

Both Kinne and Barratt treated Bosworth's resistance to the tongues evidence teaching as a betrayal of pentecostal supernaturalism. Barratt claimed Bosworth was denying the truth "of this world-wide revival . . . that [Bosworth] so heartily commends," and implied that Bosworth's well-respected teachings on healing contradicted his stance on tongues.[157] Kinne went farther, accusing Bosworth's tract of being "calculated to . . . fill men with fear of the supernatural." Kinne asked, "How is it that a sensible man like my brother writes pro and con in the same tract and sometimes in the same sentence?" For Kinne, anyone denying the teaching automatically falls into contradictions and "muddle."

In reaction to Bosworth's challenge, the Assemblies of God further built up its doctrinal walls. New language was introduced. The term "distinctive testimony" had been used in the 1917 General Council but was not designated as referring explicitly to the doctrine of initial evidence.[158] In August of 1918, D. W. Kerr used the term specifically in response to Bosworth's challenge.[159] This usage was enshrined in the 1918 General Council to refer to the initial physical sign doctrine, equating pentecostal identity with the teaching.[160] Other pentecostals, however, sided with Bosworth, and a handful of their anonymous endorsements were included in later editions of Bosworth's open letter. Bosworth clearly had support from among "the more prominent among the Pentecostal ministry" who expressed "unqualified endorsement" of Bosworth's stance, like Bosworth, hoping that pentecostals would "cast aside this gross error." We do not know how many one spoke for when he asked Bosworth, "Why did you not write it sooner?"[161]

In some ways, the antagonists in the tongues controversy were simply talking past one another. Bosworth seemed stubbornly incapable of understanding the sign/gift distinction.[162] And the resolution of the 1918

---

155. Barratt, *Baptism with the Holy Ghost and Fire*, 20.
156. Barratt, *Baptism with the Holy Ghost and Fire*, 32.
157. Barratt, *Baptism with the Holy Ghost and Fire*, 8, 21.
158. *Minutes of the General Council of the Assemblies of God . . . 1917*, 18.
159. Kerr, "Paul's Interpretation of the Baptism of the Holy Ghost," 6.
160. *Minutes of the Sixth Annual Meeting of the General Council of the Assemblies of God . . . 1918*, 8, 10.
161. Perkins, *Joybringer Bosworth*, 78, 79.
162. Bosworth, "F. F. Bosworth to J. W. Welch."

General Council only said that "the baptism of the Holy Spirit is *regularly accompanied* by the initial physical sign of speaking in tongues."¹⁶³ Did this leave room for "irregular" experiences not accompanied by tongues? Furthermore, William Menzies argues that D. W. Kerr's position on tongues as "initial physical evidence" was intended to leave open the possibility of other prior non-physical evidences, under which category Bosworth's concern about "soul travail" would fall.¹⁶⁴ Still, the perceived differences were an impasse. When Bosworth left the General Council in September, he permanently left any formal association with pentecostal denominations. And with him left any other overt opposition to the teaching.¹⁶⁵

Why the Tongues Evidence Doctrine Triumphed

Scholars commonly refer to the initial evidence teaching as the "classical pentecostal" doctrine. This label is misleading, suggesting as it does that the teaching belongs to genuine, original, or normative pentecostalism.¹⁶⁶ But if it can be labeled "classical," it is only as the official position of white American denominational pentecostalism—in other words, having so many qualifiers as to be almost useless. And yet, because this group has historically set the tone for scholarship on pentecostalism, they have successfully "misrepresented the message of the initial leaders of the pentecostal revival," as Ithiel Clemmons argues.¹⁶⁷ If the first decade of pentecostalism is indeed the "heart" of the movement,¹⁶⁸ then the movement has no single position on the relation of tongues to spirit-baptism. Still, historians must reckon with the fact that the tongues evidence doctrine triumphed. Several factors help explain this.

---

163. *Minutes of the Sixth Annual Meeting of the General Council of the Assemblies of God . . . 1918*, 8; emphasis added.

164. Menzies, "Tongues as 'The Initial Physical Sign,'" 184–86.

165. In October of 1918, Burton Bosworth told Welch that he did not believe "that all must speak in tongues as the evidence of the Baptism of the Holy Spirit" and asked Welch to use his judgment with regard to renewing Burton's credentials. Bosworth, "B. B. Bosworth to J. W. Welch," emphasis in original. Warren Collins left the Assemblies of God in 1921 and was identified by E. N. Bell as "dropped in Bosworth class." "Warren Collins Non-Council Files."

166. Blumhofer, *Restoring the Faith*, 136. This identification leads some historians to ignore the development of the tongues evidence doctrine in the first twenty years of pentecostalism. For instance, Alexander, *Black Fire*, 17, 28, 160–62. See also Synan, "Role of Tongues," 67, 71.

167. Clemmons, *Bishop C. H. Mason*, 53–54.

168. Land, *Pentecostal Spirituality*, 1, 37; Hollenweger, "Pentecostals and the Charismatic Movement," 549–54.

Tongues became the focal point for pentecostal spirituality because of the manifestation's multivalent and flexible supernaturalism. Pentecostals were so committed to their supernaturalist worldview that when they were forced to admit that the original theology of tongues as foreign language for missions was untenable, they shifted its meaning and kept the practice rather than abandon it. Pentecostals focused instead on prayer language and "language of angels." In doing this, they kept their supernaturalism intact. Tongues was a meeting point of the two main categories of supernaturalism—the mystical and the miraculous; it is both internal and external. Rare is the testimony of speaking in tongues from the first few decades of pentecostalism that does not describe a concomitant mystical experience—a vision, a feeling of warmth or electricity, or unprecedented joy. But tongues also had an empirical side that proved easier to produce and verify than other miraculous occurrences, like healing, without any apparent diminishing of its supernatural nature. Tongues were immediate, as Barratt put it,

> Even if other gifts are bestowed, it would be impossible to reveal them, the selfsame moment the FIRE FALLS! They must, in the very nature of things, be revealed later on. Tongues because of their character, are the spontaneous and immediate outburst of the inner working of the Spirit. The soul bursts forth in thanksgiving and praise, *and as a general* RULE *in other languages*! That is *the* miracle of the Christian age, and the wondrous result of the Baptism![169]

Pentecostals also defended tongues as the most "severe" test, indicating that the mind (the most stubborn member) submitted to God. And while some might then ask why prophecy cannot be the sign, pentecostals admitted that tongues did not beg verification as prophecy did.[170] The supernaturalism of tongues, combined with the relative ease with which it was produced and verified, ensured its central status in pentecostal spirituality.

Internal developments also affected the meaning of tongues. Pentecostals received from the holiness movement a restorationist view of history. Chiefly, they viewed the doctrine of sanctification as a crucial step in the progressive rehabilitation of apostolic truths leading inexorably to the return of Christ. Baptism in the Holy Spirit with tongues was therefore seen as the final restored doctrine preceding Christ's return. In the early fluid phase, less exactitude was necessary because the main meaning for tongues was

---

169. Barratt, *Baptism with the Holy Ghost and Fire*, 31; emphasis in original. Cf. Friesen, *Norming the Abnormal*, Kindle Locations 3491–3.

170. Flower, "Evidence of the Baptism," 4. Cf. McGee, "Popular Expositions of Initial Evidence," 123.

eschatological: its very presence in the life of the church was sign enough. But when the finished work teaching repudiated the Wesleyan doctrine of sanctification, it also inadvertently cut the progressive-restorationist script off at the knees.[171] As one anxious Wesleyan pentecostal remarked, "Were Wesley, Whitefield . . . wrong?" "Was the entire Methodist Church mistaken?"[172] Durham felt such an argument was misplaced:

> One thing surprised me very much, and that was that those who opposed us utterly refused to meet us with the Scripture, and attempt to point out to us where we were wrong. In contending against us, it was not an attempt to prove from the Bible that we were wrong, but that our teaching reflected on the teaching of some who had lived in the past, and also on the experiences of some who live at present. The question with us was, and is, "Nevertheless, what saith the Scriptures?"[173]

If Wesleyan sanctification were not a true apostolic doctrine restored to the end times church, perhaps the entire view of history that relied on progressive steps from justification to sanctification to divine healing to premillennialism was unreliable. Durham did not abandon the restorationist impulse, but he defined it differently than his holiness brethren.[174] In the holiness progressive-restorationist interpretation, tongues was a sign of spirit-baptism, but in a corporate as well as an individual sense. Tongues testified that apostolic doctrine had been restored to the church and was demonstrated vividly by those who possessed it. But as millennial fervor waned in the 1910s and as the finished work teaching undercut the progressive-restorationist view of history, tongues had to take on different meaning. That Durham was one of the first to assert that the tongues evidence doctrine was what distinguished pentecostals is no coincidence. For Durham, the intensely personal character of the doctrine, rather than its place in a line of providentially-restored doctrines portending the parousia, was its defining characteristic. The doctrine "locates every man that hears it," by

---

171. I owe my thinking along these lines to Faupel, *Everlasting Gospel*, 229–30. Faupel notes the damage to the restorationist creed implied in Durham's message but does not develop it into a discussion of how it might have affected the tongues evidence doctrine.

172. Cited in Faupel, *Everlasting Gospel*, 253.

173. Durham, "Great Battle of Nineteen Eleven," 7.

174. Perhaps as a way of balancing the decreasing eschatological import of sanctification and tongues, Durham emphasized his finished work teaching as restoration of true doctrine. According to Durham, God was "restoring to His people, the church, the portions of truth." Durham, *Articles Written by Pastor W. H. Durham*, 47. For holiness views, see Ware, *Restorationism in the Holiness Movement*, 101.

which he meant that "[God] used it to draw the line between those who had the baptism and those who had not."[175]

W. Jethro Walthall, a Baptist holiness leader who joined the Assemblies of God in 1917, explained that the finished work teaching had helped convince him that pentecostals were "the Lord's general movement." In his defense of the tongues evidence doctrine, Walthall explicitly denied that tongues was a corporate phenomenon. Instead, tongues was an eminently personal experience, either as heavenly languages "exercised between the individual speaking and his God," or unknown human languages "imparted to individuals and not to the Church, as such." This was verified, according to Walthall, in scripture's attention to detail, recording in the majority of cases that those individuals who were spirit-baptized also spoke in tongues.[176] In Walthall's reasoning, tongues had no communal, eschatological, or progressive-restorationist significance; rather, the meaning of tongues was narrowed to a witness to divine blessing for individuals. Thus knowing with certainty that one had been spirit-baptized became increasingly important, and the doctrine of initial evidence was extended to meet this need. This observation is only suggestive and does not explain why certain holiness pentecostals contended for the initial evidence doctrine,[177] but it does help

175. Durham, "Speaking in Tongues Is the Evidence of Spirit Baptism," 9, 10, 11.

176. Walthall, "Do All Speak in Tongues Who Receive the Baptism?" 6. The individualism of American revivalism as well as the developing Baptist consciousness of "soul competency" were probably also factors in this more individualistic interpretation of spirit-baptism with tongues, since so many in the finished work camp came from Baptist traditions. Leading Southern Baptist theologian E. Y. Mullins published his famous work championing the religious authority of the individual, *The Axioms of Religion*, in 1908.

177. Nevertheless, the inner tension produced by the initial evidence doctrine among holiness pentecostal leaders corroborates this interpretation. J. H. King, leader of the Pentecostal Holiness Church, unconsciously revealed that an individual-centered doctrine of initial evidence had an unsettling effect on the larger motif of holiness eschatology. If tongues were primarily an evidence of an individual's experience, some other manifestation or sign would have to fill the eschatological role. King found this in prophecy, which in 1934 he claimed was "distinctively Pentecostal and must be viewed as evidential in character." As Tony Moon argues, this was probably not King's way of equivocating on the initial evidence doctrine, as some have suggested, but of describing prophecy as a unique phenomenon of the "Pentecostal dispensation." Moving beyond Moon's argument, I contend that King was perhaps unknowingly wrestling with the tension between the individualism of the initial evidence doctrine and the corporate nature of the holiness restorationist heritage, which integrated both the broader theme of a New Testament dispensation and the more specific theme of progressive restoration immediately preceding Christ's return. Whereas finished work pentecostals could quietly downplay the eschatological significance of tongues, holiness pentecostals tried to maintain this orientation by pointing to another manifestation of the Holy Spirit—in King's case, prophecy. Moon, "J. H. King on Initial Evidence," 275–76. Moon argues

us to understand why finished work adherents in the Assemblies of God saw Bosworth's challenge to the tongues evidence doctrine as such a threat. In a very real way, Bosworth's attack was personal.

Another reason for the triumph of the initial evidence doctrine was the simple timing of the controversy. Recently returning to stability after the upheavals of the finished work controversy and the Oneness debate, the Assemblies of God had little patience for another doctrinal battle. Just before Bosworth broke the peace, the Assemblies of God celebrated a blessed lack of controversy.[178] In the run-up to the 1918 General Convention, Assemblies of God leaders hoped to put doctrinal strife behind them and get on with the work of building an organization.[179] But the tongues evidence question would not subside, so in the next issue of the *Christian Evangel*, D. W. Kerr adamantly defended the right of the General Council of "expressing its position relative to matters of doctrine and practice."[180] Going into the 1918 Council, Assemblies of God leaders believed that, in order to carry forward the new era of productivity, the only position was one of strength and resistance to doctrinal dissention. As a report in the *Christian Evangel* put it, "In these days of apostasy it was found necessary to insist upon a stricter allegiance to these essential truths which have differentiated us from the surrounding religious bodies and ostracised [sic] us from the pale of so-called orthodoxy."[181]

The growing concern for that which "differentiated" the pentecostals points to probably the strongest explanation for the victory of the tongues evidence doctrine. A decade out from the initial revival, pentecostals had arrived at two realizations. First, Jesus might not return as quickly as anticipated; where imminent eschatology was kept alive, it was tied to geopolitical events as fulfillment of prophecy rather than restorationist views of sacred history.[182] Second, the pentecostal revival would not be welcomed by the existing denominations. Pentecostals concluded that they ought to build institutions that will last into new generations. In the light of these realizations, pentecostals began consciously to craft an identity apart from evangelicalism and the holiness movement. To do this, they had to answer the question: what part of pentecostalism justified its existence as separate

explicitly against Jacobsen, *Thinking in the Spirit*, 190–91.

    178. "Controversy Languishes—Evangelism Spreading," 7, 9; "Council at St. Louis," 2.

    179. Bell, "Coming Great Council," 1.

    180. Kerr, "Paul's Interpretation of the Baptism of the Holy Ghost."

    181. "Council at St. Louis," 2.

    182. For instance, see the "Special Second Coming Edition" of the *Weekly Evangel*, April 10, 1917.

from the rest of Christianity? Most found it in the teaching that tongues always accompanies spirit-baptism. The doctrine, after all, had helped birth the movement, was the majority position, and was the marker that non-pentecostals used to identify pentecostals in their polemics. Seeley Kinne's response in 1918 to Bosworth demonstrates the place of the doctrine in this growing awareness of identity:

> Would this movement ever have existed if it had not been for this teaching[?] After all, is there anything in this movement that is not in other movements? The [Christian and Missionary] alliance, for instance, claimed the baptism before this movement came, and still claims it without tongues, and objects to and disowns missionaries for this teaching. But it is all right if they call it the gift of tongues. Do you wish to pull us down to an old level of spirituality? Has there ever been such a rapid worldwide movement of the gospel through them or any other as has come with this teaching? Missionaries have suffered and been ostracized because they got the baptism with tongues. Now do you propose we shall advise them they had made a mistake and had better return to their old relations and give up the tongues? Shall we drop back to these levels and disappear, as it surely will if we join your teaching? Nay verily. It has cost us too much and brought us too great blessing of God.[183]

The tongues evidence doctrine had seemingly been at the root of pentecostal success, so "Why," as W. H. Pope put it, "at this late hour try to put out the teaching that caused the fire to fall around the world?"[184] Furthermore, for believers who were highly conscious of "levels" of spirituality, denying a doctrine to which many had pinned their high spiritual status was to topple down the spiritual ladder. D. W. Kerr, one of the chief defenders of Assemblies of God orthodoxy, would later verge on holding pentecostal supernaturalism hostage to the doctrine: "whenever we, as a people, begin to let down on this particular point, the fire dies out, the ardor and fervor begin to wane, the glory departs."[185] Assemblies of God leaders did not see

183. Kinne, "Open Letter to Elder F. F. Bosworth," 3.

184. Pope, "Why I Believe," 7.

185. Kerr, "Bible Evidence," 2. Cited in Oliverio, *Theological Hermeneutics in the Classical Pentecostal Tradition*, 102. Durham had made a similar claim in 1912, but with the added force of denominational machinery, Kerr's words carried more weight. Durham, "Speaking in Tongues Is the Evidence of Spirit Baptism," 11. Recent pentecostal historians have tried to tie the initial evidence doctrine positively to church growth. See Synan, "Role of Tongues," 67–82. Synan's argument is unconvincing, however, for at least two reasons. First, Synan tries to adopt categories of "semi-initial evidence" and "near initial evidence" positions. This tact ignores the pastoral concerns that folks like

as clearly as Bosworth did that the pentecostal movement had more to offer than a dogmatic position on spirit-baptism. J. R. Flower's distressed words in 1920 reveal where the question of identity had led:

> If we, as a movement, are wrong in our position [on speaking in tongues as the sign of the baptism in the Holy Spirit], we have no right to an existence as a body of people, as the denominational bodies would possibly take us in if we would drop this one point of contention . . . The very life of the Pentecostal Movement hinges on this point.[186]

Within a few years, the notion that the doctrine was pentecostalism's only contribution to wider Christianity subtly supported the growing sentiment that the teaching was so important that it superseded all other considerations. As D. W. Kerr told readers,

> During the past few years God has enabled us to discover and recover this wonderful truth concerning Baptism in the Spirit as it was given at the beginning. Thus we have all that the others got, and we have got this too. We see all they see, but they don't see what we see. That is why we can't work together with those who oppose or reject this Pentecostal truth. They might invite us to come and labor with them, but you know it would not work. Some have tried and failed. You can not mix Pentecost with denominationalism.[187]

Of course, Bosworth would disagree: he had worked interdenominationally for years and from 1918 embarked on a ministry that mixed with pentecostals and non-pentecostals, without forsaking his pentecostal identity. The tongues controversy was a not a battle of pure versus compromised pentecostalism; it was a fight over the supernatural—how to pursue it, defend it, and disseminate it.[188] Although Bosworth stated that his critique was designed to deepen God's supernatural work and increase manifestations

---

Bosworth have always had with the hard line on tongues evidence. Second, Synan uses the Church of God in Christ as an example of a denomination whose growth correlates with the initial evidence teaching. But the Church of God in Christ did not enforce a hard stance on initial evidence.

186. Flower, "Evidence of the Baptism." Cited in Anderson, *Vision of the Disinherited*, 164.

187. Kerr, "Basis of Our Distinctive Testimony," 4.

188. Tellingly, Bosworth stood at odds with W. F. Carothers on nearly every theological aspect of tongues—the distinction between gift and evidence, the necessity of tongues for all those baptized in the Holy Spirit, and the human role in the spirit-baptism experience. See Carothers, "Baptism with the Holy Ghost," 15.

(even tongues!), some of his denominational colleagues saw him as a traitor to the supernaturalist creed. While the Assemblies of God opted for a doctrinally-based defense of the gospel of the supernatural, Bosworth retained a fluid apology rooted in experience and demonstration.

CONCLUSION

As part of the original delegation that formed the Assemblies of God, F. F. Bosworth was clearly not opposed to the formation of pentecostal organizations. Neither was he outspoken against adopting a statement of faith for the basis of unity in ministry when faced with the threat of the Oneness teaching. On the other hand, as a rising star in the pentecostal movement, Bosworth's success in Chicago, California, and Texas was largely independent of his ties to the new organization. Furthermore, beginning in 1917, Bosworth began intentionally cooperating across denominations in urban evangelism.

As Bosworth's ministry grew in the years after the founding of the Assemblies of God, he ironically became increasingly aware of the challenges of implementing the denomination's dominant position on tongues. His concerns erupted in public rejection of the doctrine and resignation in 1918. Bosworth critiqued the doctrine on experiential, historical, and scriptural grounds. Not the first or the only pentecostal to challenge the doctrine, his opposition nevertheless caused unparalleled controversy. At the heart of the disagreement were differing views of how the supernatural is manifested in the natural world. Bosworth saw pentecostal identity in the broad terms of the gospel of the supernatural, while the Assemblies of God insisted that the tongues evidence doctrine was the narrow gate to the supernatural experience. The doctrine triumphed because it made a distinct supernatural experience accessible and verifiable, offered individual assurance when the finished work attack on Wesleyan restorationism dismantled the corporate and eschatological meaning of spirit-baptism, was the dominant position at a time when the Assemblies of God was wearied by doctrinal controversy, and provided a social demarcation for the young pentecostal movement.

Although the tongues evidence doctrine became the "distinctive testimony" of certain pentecostals, it is an inadequate lens through which to view the pentecostal movement. Not only was the doctrine challenged from within the movement in North America, Europe, and India, but many embraced pentecostalism not because they were enthusiastic about the tongues doctrine, but because the pentecostal churches carried on the supernaturalism of the earlier holiness movement. Bosworth's is not the only story that shows that pentecostal identity is not inextricably linked to the tongues evidence teaching. For example, one might conclude that rather than a reorientation to a new doctrine, Maria Woodworth-Etter simply followed her audience: by 1912, those who sought intense supernatural experiences were more likely to identify with pentecostalism than the holiness movement. This could explain both why Woodworth-Etter did not immediately join the pentecostals when she began to have sustained contact with them in 1908 and why she had such success after identifying with the pentecostals in 1912.

A common characteristic of many who either challenged or remained tacit on the tongues evidence doctrine is the strength of their independent ministries. They did not rely on denominational structures for their ministerial success. This suggests that others—who did not have the resources for independent ministry—possibly remained in the pentecostal denominations because they valued the supernatural gospel proclaimed therein, even if they did not heartily endorse the doctrine. The tongues evidence doctrine may have been necessary for a certain pentecostal denominational identity, but it was not necessary for pentecostal spiritual identity. As Bosworth's ministry would continue to prove, the pentecostal revival in all its chief features could continue without the doctrine.

5

The Healing Evangelist, 1919–1932

> The Bosworths proclaim first, and unceasingly Jesus Christ crucified and risen; but the success of their work is largely due ... to the preaching of the little-known truth, "Jesus Christ the same yesterday, today and forever." This embodies the present experience of bodily healing as a part of the atoning power of the Cross.
>
> —Katherine Elise Chapman, "Times of Refreshing" (1922)[1]

FOLLOWING HIS DEPARTURE FROM the Assemblies of God, F. F. Bosworth could have settled into the quiet life of a pastor. But personal circumstances, cultural forces, and his own ambition led him into an international healing ministry that far eclipsed his success with the Assemblies of God. In fact, the work of Bosworth and a few other pentecostal evangelists "rejuvenated revivalism in North America in a period of history when classical revivalism was in decline."[2] His achievements brought opposition from fundamentalists as well as modernists, compelling him to write his well-known book *Christ the Healer*. In addition to showing Bosworth as a major target of fundamentalist opposition to the full gospel,

1. Chapman, "'Times of Refreshing,'" 361.
2. Robinson, *Divine Healing: The Years of Expansion*, 171.

Bosworth's work during this period illuminates many aspects of 1920s divine healing, such as the tension between the healing and salvation messages, the importance of testimonies and personal networks, the relationship of divine healing to medicine, and the non-fundamentalist critique of modernism. Although affiliated with the Christian and Missionary Alliance for much of this time, his spiritual identity was still pentecostal, seen in the sustained interest in his activities in pentecostal circles, his uneasy relationship with the Alliance, and his own continued focus on the supernatural.

LOSS AND CHANGE, 1919–1920

Bosworth wished to enter evangelism full time when he left his Assemblies of God congregation, but his Dallas parishioners convinced him to stay, forming a congregation that quickly affiliated with the Christian and Missionary Alliance.[3] "The tide of power is continually rising," Bosworth testified of this work in mid-1919.[4] The Alliance gave Bosworth the platform at the Council in 1919 and appointed him Assistant Superintendent for the southern district.[5]

Though Bosworth emerged successful from the professional controversy of 1918, personal tragedy soon struck. On November 6, 1919, his wife died at the age of 37. Estelle had suffered from flu and tuberculosis.[6] Her death may have impelled Bosworth to full-time evangelism, as he soon began meetings in Louisville, Kentucky, and Chicago.[7] But the campaign that began August 12 in Lima, Ohio, was the beginning of a new chapter in his life and ministry.

The Alliance people of Lima had begun a revival under Joseph Hogue of the St. Paul Bible Institute. As Hogue could stay only eleven days, they called upon the Bosworth brothers to continue the work. Bosworth later recalled that the meetings had a "discouraging" start. Only after pastor R.

---

3. Perkins, *Joybringer Bosworth*, 106.

4. "Dallas, Texas," 414. Another sign of success was a baptismal service in April 1919. "Baptismal Service," 9.

5. *Alliance Weekly* 52.10 (May 31, 1919) 146. He spoke on cultivating a prayer life through practice. *Alliance Weekly* 52.11 (June 7, 1919) 167. Bosworth also served as a member of the southern district for young people, which was created at the summer 1920 district conference. "Southern District Organized," 299.

6. Bosworth, "Sister Bosworth with the Lord," 10; Gaston, "Sister Bosworth's Funeral," 10; "Bosworth," (November 19, 1919) 12; "Bosworth," (November 20, 1919) 7; Perkins, *Joybringer Bosworth*, 99, 100; "Editorials," 130.

7. *Alliance Weekly* 53.27 (March 27, 1920) 453.

H. Moon asked Bosworth to change his approach and "preach on Divine Healing," did a "marvelous revival" begin.[8] The tent was overcrowded, and the meetings moved to the 1,800-seat Memorial Hall. These meetings were quite unlike what had transpired under Hogue. As Moon reported, Bosworth was "especially used of the Lord in the matter of healing."[9] Although the Alliance cherished divine healing, one report suggested that this work was extraordinary, pleading for adherents to seek God "for the same mighty out-pouring in every Branch [of the Alliance]" and suggesting Bosworth's ministry as a template.[10]

The success in Lima prompted an invitation from Pittsburgh. The meetings had to be relocated twice to accommodate the crowds. Again divine healing was the key to success. "[Bosworth] preaches the gospel as Peter did at Lydda and as Paul did at Lystra," wrote Pittsburgh Alliance pastor E. D. Whiteside, "and similar results have been vouchsafed."[11] The meetings received a boost from the *National Labor Tribune*, an eight-page weekly that touted itself as the "Official Organ of the American Workmen." During Bosworth's Lima campaign, the *Tribune* (or its editor) underwent a conversion, shifting allegiance from "Russellism to Raderism" and beginning a long relationship with Alliance president and then pastor of the Chicago Moody Tabernacle, Paul Rader.[12] For the next six years, the paper was also the unofficial organ of Bosworth's ministry, giving him the short-lived moniker "Texas Wonder" and relating testimonies, sermons, and eyewitness reports. Recognizing the *Tribune*'s "nation-wide influence," Bosworth credited it with the surge in letters and requests he was receiving.[13]

With two extremely successful campaigns, unprecedented testimonies of healing, and backing from a national newspaper, Bosworth's new career in healing evangelism was secured. From Pittsburgh, Bosworth continued on an unbroken succession of meetings in Detroit, St. Paul, Toronto, Chicago, Toledo, Pittsburgh, and Flint, Michigan—all before the close of 1921.

8. Bosworth, *Bosworth's Life Story*, 11, 12.
9. Moon, "When God Visited Lima, Ohio," 414.
10. Miller, "Revival of Divine Healing," 474.
11. Whiteside, "Apostolic Revival," 616.
12. For years, the *National Labor Tribune* had printed sermons and reports on Charles Taze Russell, the founder of Zion's Watch Tower Tract Society, a precursor to the Jehovah's Witnesses, and of Russell's successor, John F. Rutherford. "How the Tribune Has Fought," 3. The switch may have been prompted by accusations of Bolshevism against the *Tribune*, as Rader's work had a jingoist hue.
13. For "Texas Wonder," see "Gospel Tabernacle Too Small for Crowds," 3. For Bosworth's praise of the *Tribune*, see Bosworth, "Readers of Tribune Request Prayer for Healing," 3.

But Bosworth's success cannot be appreciated in isolation; he represents a trend in American religious culture following the Great War. The careers of faith healers like Anglican James Moore Hickson and pentecostals Aimee Semple McPherson and Raymond Richey blossomed simultaneously and were interconnected with Bosworth's. An often-neglected factor in divine healing history is the post-war influenza pandemic, which peaked in late 1918. At a time when death rates increased tenfold and people died within hours of contracting the virus, an optimistic theology of healing could not be sustained; but the receding of the so-called Spanish flu enabled a renewed emphasis on healing.[14] The post-war economic boom also made a newly confident and high-profile style of healing evangelism financially possible and psychologically attractive.[15] That Hickson's world tour began in 1919 was no coincidence, and it presaged a new movement. In fact, Hickson had finished meetings in Pittsburgh just before Bosworth came to the Steel City.[16] Months before Bosworth's work in Lima, McPherson led a revival seventy miles south in Dayton, Ohio.[17] The Hattiesburg, Mississippi, meetings that set Richey's career path on healing began just after the Lima meetings and are probably indebted to Bosworth's influence.[18]

Aside from the change in prevailing cultural winds, an evolution in Bosworth's approach to evangelism facilitated his new dedication to healing ministry. In a sermon delivered just a few months after the Lima campaign, Bosworth described his "fresh illumination" concerning divine healing. "I knew healing was in the atonement," said Bosworth, "but I was not quite certain that God wanted to make a universal application of it." While some have suggested that Bosworth was struggling to understand whether healing was available to nonbelievers,[19] his further comment makes this less likely. "From some things I had seen," said Bosworth, "I was a little in doubt; enough so that I could not radically and enthusiastically press the point [of universal healing in the atonement]."[20] A clear perspective on the evolution

14. See the interesting but brief discussion of pentecostal responses to the flu epidemic in Alexander, *Pentecostal Healing*, 221–24.

15. Baer, "Perfectly Empowered Bodies," 327.

16. "Evangelist Bosworth, Prayer and Healer," 3.

17. Blumhofer, *Aimee Semple McPherson*, 153.

18. Warren Collins worked with Bosworth in Fort Worth right after the Lima meetings. In Hattiesburg, Richey, who had recently begun assisting Collins, took over the meetings when Collins could not come. *Alliance Weekly* 54.28 (October 9, 1920) 445. For details of the Hattiesburg meetings, see Foxworth, "Raymond T. Richey," 93, 97–102.

19. Hejzlar, *Two Paradigms for Divine Healing*, 21.

20. Bosworth, "They Rehearsed All That God Had Done," 5.

of Bosworth's thought and practice was offered in 1928 by the *Latter Rain Evangel*. After describing how God led Bosworth "into a fuller ministry of Divine Healing" during the Lima campaign, the writer explained that Bosworth "had known for years that God healed the sick" and confidently used the scripture proofs for this teaching. But at some point "looking at human failures to appropriate truth, he became lukewarm and vacillating concerning healing for all."[21] Bosworth did not wrestle with the relation of healing doctrine to unbelievers, but the relation of healing doctrine to apparent failures in healing. This was a concern Bosworth knew firsthand. While grieving for Estelle, he could only limply admonish his sick daughter to "join us in prayer for the supernatural in your recovery."[22] But he now saw that failures did not invalidate truth. This was not so much an "illumination" as a return to first principles, and it translated into—as Bosworth later put it—"preach[ing] this part of the Gospel in a bolder and more public way."[23]

Whatever the nature of this shift, Bosworth was using healing as an evangelistic tool in late 1920 as he never had before. For Bosworth, healing "opens the door into men's hearts as nothing else does."[24] Since committing to preaching healing, claimed Bosworth, "I have often seen more people saved in a week than I formerly saw in a year."[25] The next few years would corroborate Bosworth's bold claim.

MOUNTING SUCCESS, 1921-1924

In January of 1921, Bosworth was appointed field evangelist with the Alliance. The organization spoke of "a year of revivals," thanks in particular to Bosworth.[26] Bosworth agreed that "God is moving . . . in a degree that I have not seen before."[27] The outlines of the meetings remained constant, making a detailed itinerary unnecessary. But the highlights and notorious incidents shed light on Bosworth's ministry and his context.

Bosworth's prestige was lifted by certain incredible testimonies. In Detroit, a young girl whose ear drums had been removed claimed they were "perfectly recreated and restored." A similar testimony came from Mrs. S.

---

21. "Chicago's Visitation of Miracles," 14.

22. Bosworth, "Correspondence—Re: Death of First Wife." Bosworth here presents no case for confidence in divine healing.

23. Quoted in Bosworth, *Christ the Healer*, 73. See also "Binghamton Convert Gone to Writing Poetry," 4.

24. Bosworth, "For This Cause," 8.

25. "1,300 Listen to Bosworths," 16; "Miracles Still Are Performed," 10.

26. Richards, "Annual Report," 261.

27. Bosworth, "They Rehearsed All That God Had Done," 5.

A. Wright of Toronto, who after the regrowth of both kidneys, became a spokesperson for Bosworth.[28] Bosworth defended such events by arguing that since conversion is creation, recreation of organs is "the littlest thing in the world to God."[29] The Detroiters put a Motor City spin on this, saying, "We have a God that can reconstruct and replace any part, the requirement being 'take the machine to the shop and let God have his way.'"[30] Pittsburgh witnessed the healing of John Sproul, who had been gassed in France during the war, causing him to lose his voice, frequently choke, and experience blackouts. Following fourteen unsuccessful operations and eighteen months feeding through a tube, he was released on a disability pension. At a Bosworth meeting, a worker told him to have faith, and he emitted praises that were his first full-voiced words in over three years.[31] Sproul was an instant evangelist, testifying at his former schools, the mayor's office, and even asking strangers "about the Soldier Boy who got his voice back."[32] Sproul frequently assisted in Bosworth's meetings, billed as a particular draw for veterans.[33]

Bosworth's reputation as a speaker also grew. In Toronto, P. S. Campbell, a Greek scholar at McMaster University, endorsed Bosworth's platform performance.[34] Another endorsement came from J. G. Inkster, pastor of Knox Presbyterian Church.[35] The accolades in Toronto boosted Bosworth's stature in the Alliance and with average followers, who called him "the Joybringer" in recognition of the blessings he conveyed.[36] Bosworth's welcome was so great in Chicago in 1921 that he accepted an offering that helped him and his brother relocate to the Windy City.[37]

28. "Revival Campaign in Toronto," 122; "Bosworth Campaign Stirs Toronto," 171–72; Fitch, "Bosworth Campaign," 538.

29. "Bosworth Meetings in Detroit," 3.

30. Perkins, "Detroit Druggists Doomed," 3.

31. "John Sproul to Tell," 5.

32. "Mayor E. V. Babcock," 4.

33. *Alliance Weekly* 56.9 (May 13, 1922) 142; "Alliance Folk Give Dr. Sandford Grand Farewell," 5.

34. Campbell, "How God Worked," 250. See also "Testimonies from Toronto," 586; "Hungry Souls Respond to Invitation," 4.

35. "Testimonies from Toronto," 586. See Inkster's endorsement in "Eminent Minister Endorses Divine Healing," 7.

36. For Alliance recognition, see *Alliance Weekly* 55.12 (June 4, 1921) 177. For "Joybringer," see "Sheraden Church Workers Erect Tabernacle," 4; "'Joybringer' Bosworth and Brother B. B.," 3. Around this time Perkins's biography of Bosworth was published. Perkins's first report was Perkins, "Bosworth's Shaking Detroit," 3.

37. "Bosworth Campaign in Chicago," 490.

Through 1922 and 1923, Bosworth's star continued to rise. In Miami in 1922, Bosworth was asked to fill in for William Jennings Bryan's Sunday school, which had attendance of more than three thousand.[38] Later in Miami, Bosworth boasted the attendance of "leading divines" such as S. D. Gordon and H. C. Morrison.[39] Back in Detroit, Bosworth had his first experience preaching to the "invisible audience" over the radio.[40] Bosworth also caught the attention of the secular press. A 1922 *New York Times* editorial wrote of Bosworth's meetings in Brooklyn, describing him as "resembling Billy Sunday, but without his exuberance of humor or his astonishing acrobatism."[41] Bosworth was also featured in the *Ladies' Home Journal*. Having attended Bosworth's meetings in New York while researching her article, Mabel Potter Daggett showed commendable balance in treating the growing phenomenon of divine healing.[42] Daggett claimed that "[Bosworth's] name has become a household word spoken with reverence and affection."[43] Sproul's case, she said, exemplified "the burning zeal of the people who have been healed, and their determination to pass on the gospel of health and salvation to the rest of the world, that is turning the movement into a crusade."[44] Bosworth publicly approved the piece.[45]

The accolades and attention were impressive, but the stories of lives changed were the heart of Bosworth's success. Hilda Anderson of Brooklyn lost her father to the flu in 1918. While caring for her father she also contracted the flu, spiraling into a "complete breakdown." She was sure that the "devil . . . made me believe I was lost." Threatening suicide, she wanted to be institutionalized. When Bosworth came to Brooklyn, Anderson's sister dragged her to the meetings. A female worker "rebuked the evil spirit" and "victory came at last." She quickly returned to church work and began singing, something her sister had not heard in four years.[46]

---

38. *Alliance Weekly* 55.51 (March 4, 1922) 801; *Alliance Weekly* 56.3 (April 1, 1922) 41. For the attendance figure of Bryan's meetings, see *Alliance Weekly* 55.5 (February 25, 1922) 793.

39. "Americas Leading Divines," 3.

40. Fitch, "Campaign in Detroit," 282.

41. Williams, "Religion On The Corner," 107.

42. "Telling What Happened in the Big Steel Tent," 5; Daggett, "Are There Modern Miracles?," 166–67.

43. Daggett, "Are There Modern Miracles?," 166.

44. Daggett, "Are There Modern Miracles?," 166.

45. "Evangelist Rader Warns 800 College Students," 3. The Bosworth party quoted the article in advertisements. See *Altoona Mirror*, May 2, 1927, 10.

46. "Bosworth Campaign in Jersey," 570; Anderson, "Demented Being," 3.

On April 6, 1924, Bosworth began meetings in Ottawa that marked the high point of his Alliance ministry. Nightly attendance reached 7,000, "the largest crowd ever assembled in Ottawa under one roof at a religious service." Bosworth claimed 12,000 converts, and a parade of thousands gave the Bosworths their sendoff, marching to the train station singing hymns, waving flags, and carrying Bosworth on their shoulders.[47]

Success brought opposition. The Detroit chief inspector of the Board of Health offered a $1,000 charitable donation if Bosworth could heal a hand-selected case. He also dared Bosworth to regrow hair on his own head. To the latter challenge, Bosworth cheekily alluded to the fate of those who were attacked by bears after ridiculing the prophet Elisha for his baldness.[48] Bosworth refused to entertain the more serious challenge but submitted names of some who were healed. The inspector failed to follow up, which Bosworth's supporters scored as a victory.[49] In Toronto and Miami, Bosworth butted heads with Rowland V. Bingham, editor of a leading Canadian fundamentalist magazine.[50] Also in Toronto, a "self-constituted committee of investigation" challenged Alice Baker, who had been healed of lip cancer in the Lima meetings.[51] Baker used the attention as a platform for a public forum, which apparently won many converts.[52]

Working under the auspices of Greene Avenue Baptist Church in Brooklyn in 1923, Bosworth faced criticism from local fundamentalist Baptists, led by I. M. Haldeman.[53] Later in Ottawa, three Catholic priests and a Presbyterian minister challenged the work. The priests were alarmed that as many as 800 Catholics attended one meeting.[54] Telling Catholics it was a "grievous sin" to attend the meetings, the priests said that Bosworth's healings were the result of Coueism.[55] The Presbyterian minister averred that

47. "Remarkable Demonstration," (May 27, 1924) 18; "Member of the House of Commons," 6; "Remarkable Demonstrations," (June 5, 1924) 6, 7. For the sendoff, see "Ottawa Accords a Send-Off," 6. Reprinted from *Ottawa Journal*, May 27, 1924.

48. "Faith Healer Is Challenged," 7; Vitchestain, "Bosworth's Challenge Stands Unrefuted," 7.

49. Vitchestain, "Largest Hall in Detroit," 3; "Want Health Inspector Inoculated," 7; Vitchestain, "Bosworth's Challenge Stands Unrefuted," 7.

50. "Where the Drys and Wets," 3; "Editor's Meetings," 116.

51. Bosworth often repeated Baker's story. See Bosworth, "They Rehearsed All That God Had Done," 6. See Baker's testimony in Miller, "Faithful Girls Grief Stricken," 3; "Testimony of Alice Baker," 3.

52. Fitch, "Bosworth Campaign in Toledo," 538.

53. "Evangelistic Campaign, Bosworth Brothers," 3.

54. Opp, *Lord for the Body*, 154. See "Bosworth Meeting Again Attracts Huge Crowd," 6.

55. Emilie Coue (1857–1926) was a French pharmacist and psychologist who

he had not seen any improvement in those who received prayer. Bosworth responded to these criticisms in turn by insisting that dividing Christians (as the priests seemed to do) was the real sin, that the healings of Coueism pale in comparison to his own, and that "in most miracles, there is nothing to see," since healings are often internal.[56]

RESPONDING TO CRITICS AND ENCOURAGING SUPPORTERS: CHRIST THE HEALER

Weeks after Ottawa, Bosworth began work on a book addressing "the questions so prevalent" and clearing up the "misconstruction placed upon the Scriptures" by Bosworth's opponents. *Christ the Healer*, published in late 1924, became Bosworth's greatest legacy.[57]

Considering the astonishing success of *Christ the Healer* (half a million copies in print; continually in print since 1924), remarkably little is known about the circumstances that compelled Bosworth to write it. This reflects a gap in historical understanding of the fundamentalist critique of divine healing in the 1920s. Because Aimee Semple McPherson has received more scholarly treatment, historians have generally viewed her as the main lightning rod for fundamentalist opposition,[58] while those who recognize Bosworth's role focus on the book itself rather than the years leading up to its publication.[59] Historian Gerald King helpfully places *Christ the Healer* in the context of pentecostal controversy with fundamentalism but makes only a weakly-supported claim that Bosworth's book was a response to R. A. Torrey's *Divine Healing* of the same year.[60] The controversy leading up to the publication of *Christ the Healer* indicates that Bosworth was targeted

---

treated patients through a combination of medicine and training in self-affirmation. His thought centered on overcoming the negative will by strengthening the subconscious mind. His work became known to the English-speaking world in a 1920 translation of his work and particularly in America by his visit to Boston in 1922.

56. "Critics Answered by Evangelist F. F. Bosworth," 77–78. See also "Man Whom God Used," 6. A committee was formed to investigate healings after Bosworth left Ottawa. "Bosworth Revival Campaign Starts," 6.

57. "Farewell to Bosworths," 3. Bosworth's book was released around November. The first advertisement for the book was in *National Labor Tribune*, November 20, 1924, 3. See also "Bosworth Party Starts," 4.

58. Sutton, *Aimee Semple McPherson*, 221–24; King, *Disfellowshiped*, 97.

59. McGee, *Miracles, Missions, and American Pentecostalism*, 182, 188, 192, 299, n.68; Jacobsen, *Thinking in the Spirit*, 294–305; Hejzlar, *Two Paradigms for Divine Healing*. Although Hejzlar refers to the earlier *Discerning the Lord's Body*, he offers no historical context. See pp. 74, 170, 218.

60. King, *Disfellowshiped*, 99; King, "Streams of Convergence," 70.

by fundamentalist opponents to an extent comparable to, if not greater than McPherson. They focused on Bosworth not only because of his notoriety, but also because they saw him as the intellectual representative of the movement. Bosworth's critics read his tracts closely and published direct refutations of his theology, revealing in the process a range of motivations from dispensational cessationism to pastoral concerns to the nature of the atonement. Bosworth was familiar with these critiques and incorporated rebuttals into his preaching and more systematically in *Christ the Healer*. On the other hand, Bosworth approvingly cited Torey's *Divine Healing* in pulpit and print. The earlier written attacks, rather than Torrey's booklet, prompted Bosworth's book and form the proper backdrop for evaluating its significance, while also shedding light on the full range of fundamentalist objections to divine healing in the early 1920s.

The Opposition

In 1921 Rowland V. Bingham published *The Bible and the Body*, which began as a series of articles in 1920 and broadly attacked the teachings and practices of the Christian and Missionary Alliance. Bingham was a former Salvation Army officer who had studied at A. B. Simpson's Missionary Training Institute. He settled in Toronto and became editor of the *Evangelical Christian* magazine.[61] Almost as soon as it was off the press, Bingham encountered Bosworth in Toronto, compelling reactions in the *Christian Evangel* and a revision of his book.[62]

The new edition, published in 1924, took aim at a new batch of healers. Each had their own calling card: McPherson taught that Christ atoned for sickness when he was whipped, since Isaiah says "with his stripes we are healed"; the Bosworth Brothers taught healing through the Eucharist; and Charles Price put people "under the power" through the laying on of hands.[63] But Bosworth was Bingham's target, as Bingham refuted point-by-point each of the thirty-one questions Bosworth published in Toronto newspapers. Bingham ridiculed Bosworth's "redemptive names" theology[64]

61. McKenzie, *Fundamentalism*, 27–75.

62. Bingham attended two of Bosworth's meetings and "later had a long personal interview with him." Bingham, *Bible and the Body*, 105. See also "Healing in the Atonement," (June 1921) 164; "Bosworth Campaign in Toronto," (July 1921) 199–200, 218; Bingham, "Touching the Ark," 714.

63. Bingham, *Bible and the Body*, 22. Bosworth had a near-sacramental understanding of the Lord's Supper. According to Bosworth, Christ's blood cleansed from sins, while Christ's body brought deliverance from disease—if it were properly "discerned."

64. Based on an insight from the *Scofield Reference Bible*, Bosworth argued that God's eternal nature is revealed in God's names. Among the names of God in the Old

and his creative use of Old Testament types like the Day of Atonement. "It is a wonder," cracked Bingham, "that Mr. Bosworth hasn't found in this figure that atonement was made for our mortgages."[65]

Apart from such jabs, Bingham's critique was broad and thoughtful. He was concerned for those who were not healed and found themselves in the wasteland between faith for healing and sanctified suffering.[66] Bingham had rare historical perspective. "The church had almost excluded the Lord from the sick chamber, and talked about the age of miracles being past," noted Bingham, "but in correcting the one extreme of the church, we have made the mistake of going to the other extreme."[67] Unlike staunch dispensationalists, Bingham did not cordon the promise of James 5 as a "Jewish truth."[68] He praised early leaders in the healing movement, like Charles Cullis and A. J. Gordon. But Bingham claimed other healers "pushed to extremes" and made "dogmatic assertion" of what Gordon "wrote suggestively and enquiringly."[69] Bingham faulted A. B. Simpson for teaching that "natural remedies and human help were unnecessary and were to be deprecated by those who took the Lord as their physician."[70] Bingham considered Dowie the most extreme of the early faith healers but noted that Dowie was "logical and consistent." The problem was the "wrong assumptions" all these healers had started with.[71]

Although admitting that some sickness is rooted in personal sin, Bingham denied that healing was "in the atonement," because "then we admit . . . that sickness severs the soul from God."[72] The divine healers, claimed Bingham, had confused cause and effect.[73] Bingham made a distinction between "atonement," which brings "immediate acceptance with God," and "redemption," which waits.[74] Furthermore, Matthew 8 could not refer to the atonement, because at this time, Christ was still three years away from the

---

Testament is "Jehovah-Rapha," which means "the Lord thy healer." Bosworth therefore reasoned that God was always the healer of his people, since it was part of God's nature as revealed in the divine name.

65. Bingham, *Bible and the Body*, 107.
66. "Healing in the Atonement," (June 1921) 164.
67. Bingham, *Bible and the Body*, 51–52.
68. Bingham, *Bible and the Body*, 87.
69. Bingham, *Bible and the Body*, 13, 15–17. Quotes on pp. 16, 17.
70. Bingham, *Bible and the Body*, 19.
71. Bingham, *Bible and the Body*, 22.
72. Bingham, *Bible and the Body*, 37.
73. "The consequences of sin need no atonement." Bingham, *Bible and the Body*, 108.
74. Bingham, *Bible and the Body*, 107.

cross. This distinction—popular among Bosworth's opponents—Bingham called the "difference . . . between Capernaum and Calvary."[75]

Arno C. Gaebelein, the revered editor of *Our Hope* who had assisted with the Scofield Reference Bible, became aware of Bosworth's work in the summer of 1921, when a friend (perhaps Bingham) gave him a copy of the *National Labor Tribune*. Gaebelein was particularly annoyed with the sensationalism coming from the Bosworth camp, and he soon made the attack on divine healing a common feature of *Our Hope*.[76] Although criticizing McPherson (particularly because she was a woman), Gaebelein saw Bosworth as the true theological opponent, since his "dogmatic assertions outstrip even Mrs. McPherson's unscriptural statements."[77] Gaebelien tried to confirm Bosworth's healings; he received one reply and was not impressed.[78] At the Moody Bible Institute in 1922, Gaebelein accused Bosworth of trading in "fake miracles" and called Bosworth's work "a lying delusion." Gaebelein's critique was rooted in dispensationalism: "The age ends not in a restoration of miracles, but it ends in apostasy."[79]

Other *Our Hope* writers targeted Bosworth. F. C. Jennings, having obtained a copy of Bosworth's "most widely circulated" tract *For This Cause*, refuted Bosworth in 1921.[80] Jennings abhorred Bosworth's teaching on the Lord's Supper, saying it was "not far from the bloodless sacrifice of the mass in these ultra-protestant errors."[81] He hit at the heart of Bosworth's message of God's continual supernatural activity: "It is a quite mistaken deduction that because 'He is the same yesterday, today and forever' that His ways with men are ever equally unchanged."[82] Jennings's understanding of Christ's substitutionary atonement led him to see an inconsistency in Bosworth's belief in healing in the atonement. "Can you, by any possibility say," Jennings asked Bosworth, "that 'just as' our sins were on His blessed head, our

75. Bingham, *Bible and the Body*, 55. See also Haldeman, "Did Our Lord By His Death," 486–488; Fitch, *Healing Delusion*, 20–24.

76. "Healing Craze," 139–40; "Self-Deception and Fraud," 140–42; "Believer's Body," 142–44; "Miracles," 207–9; Jennings, "Is Bodily Healing the Work of God," (October 1921) 233–47; "What Power Is It?," 268–71; Jennings, "Is Bodily Healing the Work of God," (November 1921) 286–302; "Is This of God?" 404–7; "Extreme Sensationalism," 466–67.

77. Gaebelein, *Healing Question*, 71.

78. "Self-Deception and Fraud," 141.

79. Gaebelein, "Christianity vs. Modern Cults," 862.

80. Jennings, "Is Bodily Healing the Work of God," (November 1921) 1; Bosworth, *For This Cause*. For "most widely circulated," see *Alliance Weekly* 57.34 (October 20, 1923) 552.

81. Jennings, "Is Bodily Healing the Work of God," (November 1921) 288, 287.

82. Jennings, "Is Bodily Healing the Work of God," (November 1921) 302.

sicknesses were there too; and the judgment of God fell on Him because those sicknesses, pains, griefs . . . were on Him too?"[83]

W. H. Griffith Thomas, who had written the introduction to Bingham's book, swiped at Bosworth while reviewing Alliance writer Kenneth Mackenzie's book on divine healing in 1924.[84] "Mr. Bosworth's position is not only incapable of proof by exegesis," wrote Thomas, "but is perilous in the extreme in practical life."[85] Thomas accused Bosworth of "never properly fac[ing] the question of death," since death was a result of sin as much as sickness.[86] Neither did he satisfactorily answer the issue of broken limbs.[87] The final critique may have been below the belt, as he quoted the death notice of Bosworth's wife. That Estelle died though "much prayer has been offered for [her] healing," was a fact that "tells its own story," wrote Thomas.[88]

In early 1923 I. M. Haldeman, a Baptist preacher in New York, blasted Bosworth in a pamphlet titled *Did Our Lord Jesus Christ by His Death on the Cross Atone for Bodily Sickness and Disease? No! Never!!*[89] Haldeman decried Bosworth's theology as "monstrously false," "the most excuseless, deceiving blunder," an "unspeakable doctrine, this brutal transmutation of the cross of Christ."[90] As a cessationist, Haldeman viewed Christ's miracles as his "credentials," which were unrelated to redemption.[91] Haldeman also relied heavily on the distinction between Jews and Gentiles: James 5 referred exclusively to the Jews; and since "the law was given only to Israel," the atonement did not address the diseases listed in Deuteronomy 28 that Bosworth saw as the "curse of the law" included in redemption.[92] Another plank of Haldeman's attack was the experience of the Apostle Paul. Paul's illness helped him to understand that God's "strength is made perfect in weakness." This, Haldeman declared, was "the authoritative, Heaven sent contradiction" of Bosworth's doctrine.[93] Haldeman summarized his par-

83. Jennings, "Is Bodily Healing the Work of God," (November 1921) 290.

84. MacKenzie's book, *Our Physical Heritage in Christ*, was in part a direct response to Bingham's book. Mackenzie, "Book Review," 506.

85. Thomas, "Divine Healing," 418–19.

86. Thomas, "Divine Healing," 419.

87. Thomas, "Divine Healing," 421.

88. Thomas, "Divine Healing," 422. See also Bingham, *Bible and the Body*, 99, 109, 114.

89. Fitch, *Healing Delusion*, 18–20. Haldeman's pamphlet was first published in *Our Hope*. Haldeman, "Did Our Lord By His Death." See King, *Disfellowshiped*, 105.

90. Haldeman, "Did Our Lord By His Death," 494, 501.

91. Haldeman, "Did Our Lord By His Death," 487.

92. Haldeman, "Did Our Lord By His Death," 494, 491–493.

93. Haldeman, "Did Our Lord By His Death," 497–501. Quote on p. 499.

ticularly Reformed objection to Bosworth's ministry: "Even when it talks of faith, this system is appealing to sight."[94] A pastoral sorrow also gripped Haldeman, who recognized that faith healers would never lack an audience for their instantaneous, free alternative to drugs and operations. The medical establishment, he said, "cannot hope to compete with this system."[95]

A year later, C. E. Putnam, a prolific controversialist with the Moody Bible Institute extension department, published *Modern Religio-Healing*. Reading Bosworth's tracts, attending meetings in Chicago, and interviewing Bosworth, Putnam concluded that Bosworth's teachings were "subtle, misleading, false and unscriptural," as well as "contradictory, illogical, and ridiculous."[96] The critical error of the divine healing creed was Bosworth's message that it is "always God's will to heal."[97] The movement was especially pernicious because its proponents "do not deny the true gospel fundamentals, but being deceived they do add to and try to make a double-gospel."[98] This "double-gospel" was Bosworth's teaching that "healing and forgiveness were provided at the same time, and are offered exactly on the same basis."[99] Since for Bosworth "living faith makes disease impossible," Putnam pounced on what he believed was a contradiction: "it would be utterly impossible for any saved person (for all such must have a 'living faith') to have a disease."[100] For Putnam, Bosworth's teaching implied that believers should never be sick, and failures in healing would cause sufferers to doubt their salvation.[101]

The notion of a multifaceted gospel—whether called a "full gospel," a "fourfold gospel" or a "double gospel"—was silly to Putnam. Healing was a witness to the gospel, which meant it could not be an essential part.[102] Putnam's belief in atonement for sin *only*—which relegated healing to

94. Haldeman, "Did Our Lord By His Death," 502. Gaebelein had a similar complaint, Gaebelein, "Christianity vs. Modern Cults," 862.

95. Haldeman, "Did Our Lord By His Death," 485.

96. Putnam, *Modern Religio-Healing*, 91, 121. For Putnam's visits to Bosworth's meetings (more than eight) and his conversation with Bosworth, see pp. 42, 155–56. Putnam specifically responded to Bosworth's tracts *For This Cause, Discerning the Lord's Body,* and *Do All Speak with Tongues?* Putnam's book came out some time before July of 1924, see *Moody Bible Institute Monthly*, 24.11 (July 1924) 569.

97. Putnam, *Modern Religio-Healing*, 6.

98. Putnam, *Modern Religio-Healing*, 35. See also p. 133.

99. Putnam, *Modern Religio-Healing*, 94.

100. Putnam, *Modern Religio-Healing*, 123, cf. 98.

101. Putnam, *Modern Religio-Healing*, 98, 101–2, 127. For Bosworth's distinction between faith for salvation and faith for healing, see Bosworth, *For This Cause*, 17. See also McCrossan, *Bodily Healing and the Atonement*, 73–75.

102. Putnam, *Modern Religio-Healing*, 154.

"evidence"—was not supported by a strict dispensationalism, but by amassing scriptures.[103] As with Bingham's distinction between "atonement" and "redemption," Putnam argued that salvation from sin was "present tense," but all other "salvation from the results of sin," were "yet future."[104] Putnam also decried Bosworth's methods. The teaching that "God's power . . . will flow from our hearts, through our bodies, and heal," was to Putman "like Spiritism and Demonology."[105] His tactics also led to insincere conversions,[106] and from Putnam's Reformed perspective, Bosworth's many vague "conditions" confused law and grace.[107]

Response from the Bosworth Camp

Bosworth was aware of his opponents. After reading Gaebelein's attack in *Moody Monthly*, Bosworth stormed the Chicago editorial offices, pleading for vindication. Although unswayed, the editor James Gray was impressed by Bosworth, who consented to investigations undertaken "in the right spirit." Gray pledged one hundred dollars toward such work, but nothing came of this challenge.[108] Bosworth also responded to Bingham's criticisms in Miami in 1922.[109] Although Bosworth did not name names, he went on to refute Bingham in *Christ the Healer*.[110] Bosworth probably foresaw an attack from Putnam after their conversation in 1923.[111]

Bosworth's supporters came to his defense. Kenneth MacKenzie refuted Haldeman in the *National Labor Tribune*. While Haldeman rejected Bosworth's syllogism that atonement for sin included immediate redemption from sin's consequences, MacKenzie claimed that Haldeman "totally

103. Putnam, *Modern Religio-Healing*, 106–8.

104. Putnam, *Modern Religio-Healing*, 52.

105. Putnam, *Modern Religio-Healing*, 123.

106. Putnam, *Modern Religio-Healing*, 136, 150.

107. Putnam, *Modern Religio-Healing*, 94. Beginning in Atlanta in 1923, Bosworth required those who wanted prayer for healing to fill out a nine-point questionnaire. These "conditions" may have been made official as a response to Putnam, who had spoken with Bosworth at length in Chicago a few weeks earlier. See Fitch, "Bosworth Campaign in Atlanta," 450; Bingham, *Bible and the Body*, 105.

108. "Visit From Evangelist F. F. Bosworth," 1053. "Evangelism and Bodily Healing," 593. For the moderate stance on divine healing of Gray and Moody Bible Institute, see Baer, "Perfectly Empowered Bodies," 314. See also "Encouraging Endorsements," 401.

109. "Where the Drys and Wets," 3.

110. The "Canadian writer," wrote Bosworth, has "no argument at all." Bosworth, *Christ the Healer*, 19. Cf. Bingham, *Bible and the Body*, 55.

111. At least Perkins was aware of Putnam's book. Perkins, *Fred Francis Bosworth*, 217.

divorced" what God had joined. MacKenzie admitted sympathy for Haldeman's argument on Isaiah 53 and rather than press Bosworth's message of universal healing, he pleaded for Haldeman to "leave this to the personal dealing of the Lord with His child."[112]

Bosworth's response to Haldeman was more direct. He called out the "prominent New York minister" in his sermon "Why All Are Not Healed" and in his "thirty-one questions," which appeared in the weeks after the Brooklyn meetings.[113] Repeating these arguments in *Christ the Healer*, Bosworth called Haldeman's treatment of Paul's sickness an "absurd exposition" and refuted Haldeman's and Bingham's critique centering on Isaiah 53.[114] Bosworth's confident rebuttal of the extreme fundamentalist position challenges the notion that pentecostals begged for a seat at the fundamentalist table.[115]

The Question of R. A. Torrey

Bosworth's publication of *Christ the Healer* was spurred by a growing demand from his followers for clear published exposition on divine healing and the success of the May 1924 Ottawa campaign.[116] The book was also a direct response to Bosworth's many outspoken fundamentalist opponents. But it is not certain that Bosworth was motivated by the appearance of R. A. Torrey's *Divine Healing: Does God Perform Miracles Today?*, as Gerald King

---

112. Mackenzie, "Rev. Kenneth MacKenzie Replies," 3.

113. These thirty-one questions began as twenty-six in the Bridgeport campaign. See Long, "Evangelistic Campaign in Bridgeport," 3. Bosworth's questions as they were preached at Bridgeport (January-February) do not contain any reference to the New York minister (Haldeman) who disputed Bosworth's interpretation of Paul's "thorn." Such responses were added in the expanded version that appeared in the Toronto campaign, which directly followed the Brooklyn campaign. Bosworth quoted Haldeman as referring to the "unspeakable puss, unspeakable looking matter running down over [Paul's] face." (*National Labor Tribune*, July 19, 1923, 5) This exact wording is not in the published versions of Haldeman's critique, but probably came "from a stenographic report of a sermon" Haldeman preached before he published his tract. See Bosworth, *Christ the Healer*, 116. Many of Bosworth's other quotes in *Christ the Healer* against this New York minister are found verbatim in Haldeman's pamphlet, leaving little doubt that Haldeman was the "prominent New York minister" Bosworth had been debating since April of 1923.

114. Bosworth, *Christ the Healer*, 19, 116.

115. Marsden, *Fundamentalism*, 94; Anderson, *Vision of the Disinherited*, 149.

116. Bosworth, *Christ the Healer*, preface, n.p. In July of 1924, Bosworth began publishing a "circular letter" in *National Labor Tribune* and *Alliance Weekly* summarizing key points of his teaching in response to "many inquirers who attend the meetings."

suggests.[117] Despite chastising the divine healing movement, Torrey never named Bosworth, although Torrey did glibly dismiss Bosworth's teaching on the Lord's Supper.[118] Bosworth surely felt the sting of this oblique censure, but rather than taking on the revered fundamentalist, he approvingly cited Torrey's book in June of 1924.[119] Bosworth quoted Torrey again in *Christ the Healer*, claiming they agreed on the basic premise of healing in the atonement.[120] Bosworth did not see Torrey as an opponent, and he did not intend for his book to be a response to Torrey.[121] An unwarranted focus on Torrey risks obscuring the development of Bosworth's thought. As early as May of 1922, he was preaching on "Why Some Fail to Get Healed."[122] Later that year, Bosworth introduced his "covenantal names of God" approach, an elaboration on an insight in the Scofield Reference Bible.[123] The "thirty-one questions" of 1923 were intended as a "challenge" to "various criticisms" and were expanded to refute Haldeman.[124]

Impact of *Christ the Healer*

Once *Christ the Healer* was released, it contributed in its own way to Bosworth's supernatural ministry. Numerous testimonies echoed the man from Indianapolis who wrote, "By the time I finished the book I was sound and well."[125] Simplicity was the key to the book's popularity. May Cole, Bosworth's writing assistant, wanted readers to know how "logical" his exposition was.[126] As one testimony put it, Bosworth's book "made it so plain

---

117. King, *Disfellowshiped*, 99.

118. Torrey, *Divine Healing*, 5–6.

119. "One of America's Leading Exponents of Prayer," 4. Cf. Torrey, *Divine Healing*, 29. Bosworth also recommended Torrey's *The Person and Work of the Holy Spirit* in his campaigns. See *Alliance Weekly* 57.47 (January 19, 1924) 766.

120. Bosworth, *Christ the Healer*, 29. Cf. Torrey, *Divine Healing*, 45. See also Bosworth, "Lame Man at Lystra," 2.

121. Kenneth MacKenzie, ever Bosworth's ally, reviewed Torrey's book in *Alliance Weekly*. Mackenzie, "Book Reviews," 276.

122. "Syracuse Revival: Episcopal Church," 3.

123. "Autos and Busses Crowd Boulevard," 3; Campbell, "Bosworth Campaign in the Alliance Tabernacle," 247; Long, "Evangelistic Campaign in Bridgeport," 3.

124. "Doctrine of Healing Is Promulgated," 3.

125. *Exploits of Faith* 2.8 (August 1929) 12. See, for instance, "Suffered for Five Years," 15; "Bosworth Evangelistic Campaign, Indianapolis, Indiana," 42; "Bosworth Begins in Scranton," 4; *National Labor Tribune*, May 21, 1925, 4.

126. Cole, "Claims Thousands Neglected Rare Opportunity," 4. For more on Cole, see Cole, "End Is Not Yet," 3.

that God wanted to heal me even more than I wanted healing."[127] Although wary of some of Bosworth's methods, Alliance leader Oswald Smith praised *Christ the Healer*. "Its arguments are absolutely unanswerable," said Smith. "It is doubtful if anything simpler or more practical has ever been published on the subject." Smith borrowed heavily from Bosworth for his own defense of divine healing in 1927.[128] The *Alliance Weekly* review was positive but recognized that "many ... do not go to the lengths Mr. Bosworth traces." For both blessing and condemnation, said the reviewer, "Mr. Bosworth has been the cynosure of all eyes."[129]

One condemnation is particularly worth noting, for it came from one who had been very close to Bosworth. May Wyburn Fitch worked at the famous Water Street Mission in New York City with her husband for twenty years, but she became interested in Bosworth's work during the Brooklyn campaign in the summer of 1922. May soon devoted herself full time to Bosworth's campaigns, assisting with prayer ministry, singing, and reporting for *Alliance Weekly*.[130] In 1923 May married Bosworth's campaign manager C. C. Fitch in Bosworth's home.[131] Fitch could not see the irony when, that same year, she praised Bosworth for "all absence of bitterness toward his critics (and they are legion)."[132] Fitch began to have increasing doubts about the way Bosworth interpreted scripture and the effects of his teachings. One of her acquaintances testified to healing of diabetes in the Brooklyn campaign. This woman had returned to a regular diet, encouraged by Bosworth's

---

127. *Exploits of Faith*, 2.2 (February 1929) 15.

128. Smith, *Great Physician*. Quote on p. 21. Oswald took over Bosworth's redemptive names argument (pp. 30–32) and Bosworth's list of "conditions" for healing (pp. 86–94) without attribution.

129. "Book Reviews," 346. *Christ the Healer* was first advertised in *Alliance Weekly* 60.4 (January 24, 1925) 64.

130. Fitch, "Bosworth Campaign in Atlanta," 450; Fitch, "Williamsport Campaign," 760.

131. Perkins, "Bosworths' Farewell Meeting," 3. Fitch was ordained a few weeks later in Chicago. See "Private John Sproul Grips Chicago," 3. C. C. Fitch was the brother of Elmer B. Fitch, pastor of the New York Gospel Tabernacle, the "mother church" of the Christian and Missionary Alliance. Fitch, "Bosworth's Open a Strenuous Month's Campaign," 2. In a later account of the Water Street Mission, May made no reference to her work with Bosworth or her marriage to C. C. Fitch as related to her resignation from the mission. Wyburn, *"But, until Seventy Times Seven,"* 189–191. For May's work with Bosworth, see *Alliance Weekly* 57.9 (April 28, 1923) 151; "Bosworth Campaign in Toronto," (April 28, 1923) 151–52; Fitch, *Healing Delusion*, 12–15; "Mrs. Wyburn Quits McAuley Mission," 23. By mid-1925, C. C. Fitch had been replaced by Floyd Reeve as secretary of the Bosworth party. See "Bosworth Campaign in Scranton, Penna.," 535. But C. C. Fitch rejoined Bosworth by 1929.

132. Fitch, "How Jerry Mc'Auley Mission Worker," 3.

advice to disregard symptoms. But when a cut on her toe refused to heal and gangrene set in, her leg was amputated. Within four months of her "healing," May's acquaintance had died. She unequivocally blamed Bosworth.[133]

In addition to the personal nature of her attack, Fitch presented some concrete arguments. Fitch sided with Haldeman on whether Christ "fulfilled" Isaiah 53 on the cross or amid the throng in Capernaum.[134] She believed Bosworth's contention that "community unbelief" could prevent healing contradicted his argument that God's will is always to heal.[135] Bosworth's attack on the prayer "if it be thy will," was to Fitch both unscriptural and contrary to experience.[136] She believed the list of "conditions" (which Fitch herself had advertised in *Alliance Weekly*) was taxing to seekers. If one used Jesus' ministry as a template, no formula guaranteed healing.[137] While healers argued that Jesus used miracles to draw crowds, Fitch countered that Jesus often urged silence on those healed.[138] Rather than faulting the parents if children were not healed, Fitch argued that Jesus blamed the disciples when they could not cure.[139] Fitch was cynical about Bosworth's evangelistic use of healing, saying that sinners "will do anything, and believe anything, to get healed."[140] Fitch's book was not the only rough handling of Bosworth after the publication of *Christ the Healer*, but hers was the most direct attack, and it continued to resonate with critics of divine healing for years.[141] She summarized the earlier arguments and quoted Bosworth's book to demonstrate that the criticisms stood. With the added force of her intimacy with Bosworth's work, her attack was scathing.

Despite the vitriol against Bosworth, fundamentalists did not present a united front against divine healing. Some were supporters, like J. R. Straton, and more guardedly, William B. Riley. And pentecostals (denominational

133. Fitch, *Healing Delusion*, 8–12.
134. Fitch, *Healing Delusion*, 18–24.
135. Fitch, *Healing Delusion*, 42.
136. Fitch, *Healing Delusion*, 48–51.
137. Fitch, *Healing Delusion*, 28–29, 36–37.
138. Fitch, *Healing Delusion*, 46–47.
139. Fitch, *Healing Delusion*, 47–48.
140. Fitch, *Healing Delusion*, 62. See also p. 53. Fitch applied this to both repentance and baptism.
141. Although undated, *Healing Delusion* was published between June 1927 and February 1928. See Fitch, "Healing Delusion," 688; Gaebelein, "Book Reviews," 512. For later use of Fitch, see Entzminger, *Modern "Divine Healing" Racket*, 43–45. Arno Gaebelein wrote the preface to Fitch's work and in 1925 published *The Healing Question*, again making Bosworth one of his primary targets. Gaebelein, *Healing Question*, 8–9, 42, 86–87, 99–100, 107. Gaebelein shows no familiarity with *Christ the Healer*, quoting rather from earlier tracts. Gaebelein, *Healing Question*, 71–72.

and independent) contributed in their own way to fundamentalism.¹⁴² But for militant anti-pentecostal fundamentalists, Bosworth was the enemy. *Christ the Healer* was a product of this war.

NEW PHASE: INDEPENDENT EVANGELISM, 1924-1932

Christ the Healer increased Bosworth's visibility and influence in full gospel circles. But over the next few years, he leaned toward a new phase of less official cooperation with the Alliance and eventually more meetings close to home in Chicago.

Bosworth went into the second half of 1924 strong. In late August he held a brief series of meetings in his old home town of nearby Zion City—where he was predictably challenged by Voliva.¹⁴³ In November, under the auspices of the Christian Laymen's Committee, he began work in Indianapolis, where he met A. W. Tozer, who would go on to become one of the most admired devotional writers of the century.¹⁴⁴ Over the next two years Bosworth worked in St. Petersburg, Florida, Indianapolis, Ottawa, St. Paul, Minnesota, the coal regions of Pennsylvania, and Philadelphia. Although attendance was still in the thousands, Bosworth's ministry showed signs of change by the end of 1925, and he more frequently returned to Chicago

---

142. Riley, *Divine Healing*; King, *Disfellowshiped*, 110, 114, 131–134; Sutton, "'Between the Refrigerator and the Wildfire,'" 159–88. The fundamentalist coalition that formed in 1942 as the National Association of Evangelicals welcomed pentecostals—a belated recognition of affinity. This organization could be said to demonstrate an evolution and new openness in fundamentalism, but it also made official what had been true for decades: some fundamentalists were open to pentecostal contributions, while others were vehemently opposed. Those fundamentalists who could not countenance cooperation with pentecostals remained committed to their rival organization, the American Council of Christian Churches. This organization should be seen as upholding the legacy of Gaebelein, while the NAE championed the cooperative spirit of Straton. In fact, one of the chief architects of the NAE, William Ayer, was pastor of Straton's Calvary Baptist Church in New York. Although King presents all this evidence, he still sees the NAE mainly as a sign of change in fundamentalist attitudes toward pentecostalism. King, *Disfellowshiped*, 198–200.

143. The Zion City work was hosted by Grace Missionary Church. See "Bosworth Party Starts Old Time Gospel Revival," 4. For Voliva's opposition, see "Zion City Is Again Scene of Holy War," 2. The testimony of Alexander F. Wilson, newspaper editor who was healed during these campaigns, is printed in *Exploits of Faith* 3.12 (December 1931) 7.

144. *Alliance Weekly* 59.24 (December 13, 1924) 410; "Bosworth Meeting in Indianapolis," 450; *Alliance Weekly* 60.9 (February 28, 1925) 142. Lyle Dorsett makes much of Bosworth's influence on Tozer during this period, but Bosworth does not mention Tozer. See Dorsett, *Passion for God*, 73–79.

between campaigns.[145] Possibly due to new requirements that Alliance evangelists actively promote the organization and its publications, Bosworth did not renew his ministerial credentials in 1926.[146] The *Alliance Weekly* and *National Labor Tribune* abruptly ceased their coverage. He filled the publicity gap with a new edition of Perkins's biography and reliance upon local press.[147] More change came in late 1927, as his brother struck out on his own in Clarion, Pennsylvania, while F. F. returned to Lima and then Chicago, where he worked for five months in Paul Rader's Gospel Tabernacle.[148] Coinciding with the Chicago work, Bosworth took two other steps in redeveloping his publicity program. First, with Rader's guidance, he began regularly preaching over the radio.[149] Second, he began publishing *Exploits of Faith*, a monthly paper covering the campaigns and including sermons, holiness and divine healing writings, and testimonies.

Perhaps because Bosworth was no longer affiliated with the Alliance, from mid-1928 on he mostly held meetings in new areas rather than making return trips. After meetings in Washington, D. C., and then Luke Rader's new tabernacle in Minneapolis, Bosworth answered an invitation to Anderson, Indiana, where the meetings were explicitly "independent and interdenominational."[150] From April of 1930, Bosworth held meetings close to home: Bloomington, Joliet, Blue Island, and then the Englewood neighborhood of Chicago. The meetings garnered much attention, but

145. "Bosworth Holds Wonderful Meetings," 7.

146. These new requirements were prompted by concern from leaders in the Central District (Bosworth's home district) over "evangelists who hold Alliance credentials, but whose methods do not rightly represent our work and testimony." The new resolutions also forbade district superintendents from issuing credentials to those who—like Bosworth—ministered outside the boundaries of their home district, referring that duty to the Board of Directors. *Twenty-Ninth Annual Report of the Christian and Missionary Alliance*, 189. The focus on Alliance publications may reflect the fact that Bosworth's *Christ the Healer* was self-published, which meant it did not go through the Alliance vetting process. According to Perkins, beginning with Reading, Pennsylvania, in November of 1925, Bosworth's meetings were "sponsored by an interdenominational honorary Committee of ministers and laymen rather than by any one church organization." She alluded to "denominational limitations" as a factor in this move. Perkins, *Fred Francis Bosworth*, 196. Bosworth is listed again on the Alliance roster in 1931, but no other year from 1925 to 1947.

147. "Regains Hearing After Anointing," 15; "Bosworth Farewell Draws 10,000 People," 16.

148. For B. B.'s ongoing work, see *Alliance Weekly* 62.42 (October 15, 1927) 687. For Bosworth's work with Rader, see "New Year's Tabernacle Camp Meeting," 5.

149. "Fans to Hear Famed Evangelist," 11; *Exploits of Faith* 2, no.3 (March 1929) 19.

150. Fitch, "Bosworth Meetings in Anderson, Indiana," 10, 12. For Minneapolis, see Fitch, "1929 Campaign," 6–8, 12.

Bosworth no longer commanded crowds of many thousands.[151] Another sign of change was the "Bosworth Evangelistic Prayer League," a prayer network for Bosworth's revivals.[152] This was also a way for Bosworth to stay in contact with his supporters. It worked; Joliet became the longest single engagement of Bosworth's career.[153]

Bosworth continued to claim well-publicized successes in healing. Dorothea Bradway had become a "helpless paralytic and cripple" after contracting the flu in 1918 followed by spinal meningitis. While her family prepared for her death, she attended Bosworth's meetings in Indianapolis in late 1924 and had *Christ the Healer* read to her. Eventually she was healed through the prayers of a worker who visited her home, and Bradway entered her own evangelistic ministry.[154] Ruth Pieper was healed in the 1928 Chicago meetings. Born without one ear drum and with the other surgically removed, Pieper also suffered from a curved spine that required a body cast. As Bosworth prayed, she heard "a crackling sound" and could soon hear the world around her. Her back pain also stopped immediately. Greatest of all was the sense of purpose her healings bestowed. "Before my healing life seemed useless to me," said Pieper, "but now it seems like I have been born again into a new life and a new world." Her testimony included a surgeon's verification, and her story was covered by the *Chicago Daily News*, which ran a stirring picture of the 17-year-old beauty using the telephone for the first time.[155]

Bosworth continued to meet opposition. In Scranton, Methodist F. E. Lott argued that belief in healing was better fitted to earlier, superstitious eras.[156] In Corpus Christi, an evangelist denounced Bosworth's teaching on healing and spirit-baptism.[157] Another minister attacked Bosworth during the Blue Island campaign, distributing a circular bearing skull and crossbones and classing Bosworth with cults.[158] Bosworth replied to his critics,

---

151. "Crowds Swarming to Evangelistic Services," 1.

152. Fitch, "More 'Good News,'" 13. In a little over a month, this group numbered around 1,500. This organization formed almost simultaneously with Raymond Richey's "Richey Evangelistic Association." Foxworth, "Raymond T. Richey," 156.

153. Fitch, "Report of the Joliet, Ills., Campaign," (March 1931) 9–10; Fitch, "Report of the Joliet, Ills., Campaign," (April 1931) 6–13.

154. Fitch, "Bloomington, (Ills.) Campaign," 7; Bradway, "Dorothea Ann Bradway's Miraculous, Instantaneous Healing," 12–14.

155. "Healed of Total Deafness," 23–26. Quotes on pp. 25 and 26. See also Fitch, "Bloomington, (Ills.) Campaign," 6; "Deaf Six Years," 5.

156. "Most Healers in Show Business," 4.

157. "Balmy Weather in Corpus Christi," 8.

158. "Opening of Blue Island (Ills.) Campaign," 6–9.

sometimes simply presenting the truth as he saw it.[159] Other times he was less gentle. When Lott suggested Bosworth leave town, Bosworth replied wryly that, "it was Lot who ran from Sodom, not Abraham."[160] Bosworth told the minister in Blue Island that he was "ignorant," and brushed off any debate.[161]

METHODS, MEANS, AND MESSAGE: BOSWORTH AS A HEALING REVIVALIST

Through the course of over a decade of almost constant evangelistic campaigns, Bosworth became a polished revivalist. As the *National Labor Tribune* put it, he was "spiritually capitalizing his forces and the King's business is to be pushed with a zeal that will emulate, aye, probably even rival, the modern business methods."[162] A report of the Toledo meetings describes the preparations that contributed to Bosworth's success:

> A chain of twenty-six county papers, by means of advertisements and write-ups, conveyed the news to a multitude of people in the towns and [indecipherable] surrounding Toledo. Some twenty automobiles bore large banners and announced the meetings as they moved about the city. Trolley cars bore [indecipherable] cards. Arrangements had been made with the city newspapers, all of which had [run?] items before the campaign started. Two of them had news articles every day during the services.[163]

Bosworth was willing to use whatever tools were effective in spreading his message. The Anderson (Indiana) *Herald* set aside three pages for Bosworth's advertisements and increased its circulation by 50,000 for the meetings in the spring of 1929. The residents of Anderson even touted "I have been to the Bosworth meetings" bumper stickers.[164] Music was always central, and around September of 1921 Bosworth released the songbook *Revival Flame*, which included many of the holiness and higher life standards

---

159. "Houston Meetings Close," 11; Bosworth, "Did the Age of Miracles Ever End?" 1–5.

160. "3000 Hear Bosworth Reply to Dr. Lott," 4. For "Lot . . . Abraham," see "Defy Unscriptural," 7.

161. "Opening of Blue Island (Ills.) Campaign," 8, 9.

162. "Combination of Spiritual Forces," 3.

163. Fitch, "Bosworth Campaign in Toledo." See also "Bosworth Meetings Now Under Way," 2; "Toledo Gets a Shake," 3.

164. Fitch, "Bosworth Meetings in Anderson, Indiana," 11, 12.

as well as four songs written by B. B. Bosworth.[165] In the Bloomington meetings in 1930, the Bosworth party engaged a bannered calliope (steam organ) to advertise around the city.[166] As radio became more common in Bosworth's work, he would frequently advertise for a few days over the airwaves before beginning a new campaign.[167] Unlike some fundamentalists who resisted the technology, Bosworth's crew believed that "radio is a mighty channel for the Gospel."[168] Despite Bosworth's use of all the modern means of publicity, the meetings—especially when under a tent—had a nostalgic quality:

> It reminds us of the good old campmeetin' days, years and years ago (!), when Dad would hitch up the old farm horses, and Mother would bundle us all into the big 'spring wagon,' with lunch enough to last a week.[169]

Newly-urbanized Americans yearned for reminders of their rural past, and ironically, the new style of urban evangelism delivered by Bosworth and others met this yearning.

Early on, Bosworth settled into an effective routine. His first main message at each stop was "God's Plan for Successful Revival."[170] He preached once a week on healing, but he prayed with the sick at every service. He nurtured excitement and faith by asking those who had been divinely healed to stand and name their victories. Certainly all the infirm could see themselves in the nearly eighty ailments of which participants claimed healing.[171] The campaigns often closed with Bosworth telling his life story, which, supporters beamed, "reads like a romance."[172]

In an age of proliferating evangelists, Bosworth had his own style and concerns. Unlike many urban revivalists of the Roaring Twenties, Bosworth did not preach against amusements or other vices, a contrast not lost on contemporaries.[173] As A. S. Booth-Clibborn exulted, "His message is not

---

165. "Bosworth Meetings Now Under Way," 2.

166. Fitch, "Bloomington, (Ills.) Campaign Began," 5–6.

167. Fitch, "Battle at Joliet, Illinois," 15.

168. Fitch, "1929 Campaign," 8. For the fundamentalist rejection of radio, see Eskridge, "Only Believe," 114–15.

169. "Scranton Revival Opens," 4.

170. "Reports of God's Working," 26; "St. Paul, Minn.," 14; "Bosworth Campaign, New York City," 394.

171. "Bosworth Campaign, New York City," 394.

172. "Bosworth Bros.: Farewell," 3. For "romance," see Mackenzie, "Are There Modern Miracles?" 493.

173. "Bosworth Campaign Services End Today," 22.

of the negative but of the positive order."[174] Logistical details also set Bosworth apart. Rather than passing out dedication cards and using "personal workers" in the audience to urge the repentant to the altar[175]—techniques made popular by Billy Sunday—Bosworth used private inquiry rooms to counsel converts and urged those who could to claim healing or salvation from their seats.[176] In the counseling work, Bosworth was assisted by his new wife, Florence Valentine, an Alliance Missionary Institute graduate he had married in late 1922.[177]

By 1923, Bosworth systematized the process, possibly in response to criticisms that the "conditions" for healing were not always clear. Those seeking healing were required to attend an inquiry meeting, where they were asked to answer these questions:

1. Have you been born again?
2. Are you committing any known sin?
3. Are you living in obedience to God's will?
4. Are you harboring an unforgiving spirit?
5. Have you any restitution to make, or any wrongs to right?
6. Do you spend some time each day in reading your Bible and in prayer?
7. Are you convinced that it is God's will to heal you?
8. Is your faith based exclusively on the promise of God?
9. What is the nature of your sickness?

Bosworth took these questions seriously and insisted upon attendance at three meetings before praying with those seeking healing.[178] This probably boosted attendance and may have helped to screen the most likely cases to be healed or to appear to be healed.[179] An image of success was important, and by 1924, those who came for prayer were expected to leave all "artificial

---

174. "A. S. Booth-Clibborn London Divine," 4.

175. "Many Converts Crowd Forward," 3.

176. "New Revival to Open Today," 36; "Evangelists Optimistic," 20; "Bosworth's Flint Evangelist Campaign," 3; "Many States Represented," 3.

177. For salvation inquiry, see "Bosworth Revival Campaign Starts," 6. On the marriage, see *Alliance Weekly* 56.36 (November 18, 1922) 566; "Evangelist Fred Francis Bosworth Gone and Done It," 3; "Rice Throwing Clue," 3.

178. Fitch, "Bosworth Campaign in Atlanta."

179. McPherson was criticized for this technique. Gaebelein, *Healing Question*, 88.

means of locomotion" at the end of the platform.[180] The pressure to claim healing was intense.

Balancing a Double Gospel

Bosworth's ministry demonstrated the larger shift in the culture and theology of divine healing. No longer were extended periods of waiting and wrestling for faith in the nourishing environment of a "faith home" necessary. Healings now were more public, more immediate, and rather than being merely a means of empowering a believer to be a soul-winner, were themselves means of winning souls. Bosworth's 1920 "illumination" in Lima was his personal appropriation of this shift. As one supporter put it, "the Lord meant [healings] to be a testimony which should bring soul-healing to many."[181]

A balance was difficult to strike, and supporters worried that healing could eclipse salvation. So they claimed that, "More have been saved when the subject has been Healing than . . . when nothing but Salvation has been proclaimed" and produced plenty of accounts of conversions wrought through the miraculous.[182] In Lima, a woman's healing of goiter "put the husband under deep, pungent conviction," and brought him to salvation. Another "infidel" was convicted when his brother, who had suffered tuberculosis for eighteen years, was healed.[183] Nor was this rare, for often, "whole families were deeply convicted and brought to God through the healing of one member."[184] To combat the perception that "real salvation is not being preached sufficiently in these meetings,"[185] supporters insisted that salvation takes priority to healing in both emphasis and the *ordo salutis*.[186] A *National Labor Tribune* report stated that Bosworth urged "the necessity of soul salvation as a fundamental requirement to healing."[187] But critics said this logic was strained, that it was more for the sake of appearances than

180. "One of America's Leading Exponents of Prayer," 4.

181. Chapman, "'Times of Refreshing,'" 361.

182. "Bosworth Campaign Stirs Toronto," 171. See also Van Arsdale, "Sheridan Campaign," 698.

183. Miller, "Revival of Divine Healing," 473.

184. Whiteside, "Apostolic Revival." This healing is also related in Bosworth, "They Rehearsed All That God Had Done," 8.

185. "Evangelist F. F. Bosworth Opens World's Greatest Religious Campaign," 4.

186. *Alliance Weekly* 55.6 (April 23, 1921) 93.

187. "Evangelist F. F. Bosworth Forced into Larger Hall," 7; *National Labor Tribune*, November 25, 1920, 3. See also Perkins, "Detroit Druggists Doomed," 3; "Evangelist F. F. Bosworth Opens World's Greatest Religious Campaign," 4.

from any carefully wrought theology that salvation was often considered prerequisite for healing.[188] Bosworth was equivocal, saying that healing "*usually* followed those who were perfectly saved."[189] In the heat of debate, one supporter admitted that some who were healed were "ignorant . . . as to God's one and only plan of salvation."[190] Secular papers frankly noted that "the healing side of the work far overshadowed the strictly evangelistic character of the campaign."[191] Bosworth's supporters were betrayed by their reporting. Many accounts disclaimed that the numbers of those converted, rededicated, or spirit-baptized "far outnumber those who have been healed" but then filled the report with healing accounts.[192]

The Culture of Divine Healing

Like most healing evangelists, Bosworth decried any power of healing in himself. In his defense against the health inspector in Detroit, Bosworth declaimed, "I do not have the slightest idea that I could heal a flea."[193] "We are not divine healers in any sense," said Bosworth, "any more than those who preach salvation are divine saviors. We simply proclaim God's will."[194] Bosworth only claimed to "show . . . the way by which those who believe can be healed."[195] This theology led to the conclusion that failure to be healed was the believer's fault rather than God's. Healing did not come as quickly for Dorothea Bradway, because, as she said, "there was some failure upon my part, not the Lord's."[196]

The most common healings dealt with restoration of bodily functions, but healings were not limited to physical infirmities. In Toledo, a woman troubled by "horrible visions and terrifying thoughts" as a result of "close communion with the Ouija board" was cured through Bosworth's prayers.[197] In St. Petersburg, Florida, a spiritualist medium was healed through an exorcism:

---

188. Fitch, *Healing Delusion*, 74.
189. "Every Meeting Crowded with Maimed," 3; emphasis added.
190. "Want Health Inspector Inoculated," 7.
191. "Appeal Made at Bosworth Rally," 4.
192. Chapman, "'Times of Refreshing,'" 361, 367.
193. Vitchestain, "Bosworth's Challenge Stands Unrefuted," 7.
194. "Miracles Still Are Performed," 10.
195. "Revivalists Not Healers," 3. See also "Bosworth in Erie," 6.
196. Fitch, "Bloomington, (Ills.) Campaign Began," 7; Bradway, "Dorothea Ann Bradway's Miraculous, Instantaneous Healing," 14.
197. "Ouija Board Worries Maiden," 3.

His demonic associates were reluctant to go, and for some time remained about the premises not only "rapping," but seemingly "pounding" upon the outside of the house, until in answer to the brother's prayer, they were completely routed and put to flight.[198]

As with Dowie, Bosworth's supporters considered deliverance from harmful habits equally valid as healings. In Joliet, thirty testified to being delivered from tobacco.[199]

Bosworth was the draw for many; but the progress of divine healing relied on networks of personal testimony and service. Three women testified in the pages of the *Alliance Weekly* to healing in connection with Bosworth's ministry. But their healings were also intimately connected to one another. In Pittsburgh in 1921, Mary Long was healed of deafness and chronic pain. She then "asked the Lord to send me to some one who needed healing." Her friend Sadie Robinson immediately came to mind. Robinson suffered from a "nervous breakdown of body and mind." Despite the care of doctors and a country hiatus, her husband feared she was near death. The day after she returned from her rustic outing, Long visited her, giving her testimony, praying with Robinson, and even mending her son's clothes and preparing a meal. Soon Long brought Robinson to Bosworth's services. She was healed immediately. Though she credited her healing to Bosworth's prayers, Long's continuing care made the difference. "Since [my healing] I have been attacked a few times," Robinson admitted, referring to a reappearance of symptoms. "Each time," Robinson continued, "the dear Lord has sent Sister Long to me and she has prayed for me and bless God, each time I have been healed." Robinson's neighbor, Mrs. Bigley, requested a visit from both women. Bigley suffered from varicose veins, high blood pressure, and dropsy. The two women prayed with Bigley and counseled her. Within days she could walk, and her pains and blood pressure decreased. As Bigley's son witnessed this, his heart softened, and he was saved and testified to his own healing of nervous disorders.[200]

---

198. "Bosworth Campaign in St. Petersburgh, Florida," 143. Mysterious "rapping" was a phenomenon associated with spiritualism since the movement's genesis with the Fox Sisters in the late 1840s.

199. Fitch, "Report of the Joliet, Ills., Campaign," (April 1931) 8. See also "Sinus Trouble Cured," 9.

200. "God Honors Faith," 75.

"My Physician Sent Me Here to Be Healed"

Bosworth did not reject medical science *a priori*[201]—a stance even his opponents conceded.[202] The impotence of medical science was, however, a factor in most testimonies—if only because most had tried medicine first. "Bodily healing is not to be accomplished with finding fault with medical skill and surgical genius," commented one supporter, "but patients seeking physical healing are mostly those who are far beyond the aid of medical science."[203] Reports abounded of "the awful tortures through which the patients have passed under the directions of physicians."[204] Some had had "five operations" and others saw as many as "twenty-five doctors."[205] But divine healing was about "what faith can do when drugs fail."[206] This "last resort" mentality added drama to the testimonies. Bosworth's supporters also felt few scruples about having results verified by physicians.[207] Confirmation from physicians was not casting pearls before swine but setting a light on a hill. Physicians often recommended Bosworth's meetings; many of the infirm claimed that "my physician sent me here to be healed"[208] Even if only as a foil or expert witness, physicians were integral to the divine healing narrative.[209]

This relation to the medical profession portended the overall pentecostal development of decreasing antagonism to medical means.[210] For Bosworth, it probably also reflected the socio-economic standing of his audience. As his work centered on thriving industrial centers and was sponsored by the Alliance, the faithful tended to be those with the means for medical help. Alice Baker, whose story of healing from lip cancer was told frequently, claimed to have spent $500 in one year on anesthetics and to

---

201. Vitchestain, "Bosworth's Challenge Stands Unrefuted," 7. Bosworth's attitude toward medicine was more confrontational in his later years. See Bosworth, "Hints Regarding Healing," 13.

202. "Bosworth Campaign in Toronto," (July 1921) 200.

203. Perkins, "Bosworth's Shaking Detroit," 3.

204. "Spiritual Healings at Gospel Tabernacle," 3.

205. "Additional Testimonies," 764; "Testimonies to Divine Healing," 716.

206. "What Faith Can Do," 7.

207. "Bosworth Campaign Stirs Toronto," 171. See also "Marked Movements of God," 186; Bosworth, "They Rehearsed All That God Had Done," 8; "Testimony of Her Physician," 3.

208. "Member of the House of Commons," 6. See also Perkins, "Bosworth's Shaking Detroit," 3; "Crowds Turned Away from Carnegie Hall," 5.

209. This challenges the argument that "physicians find themselves on the periphery of [Bosworth's] thought." Hejzlar, *Two Paradigms for Divine Healing*, 225.

210. Williams, *Spirit Cure*.

have consulted about fifty physicians.[211] A Pittsburgh man testified to seeing nearly thirty doctors and spending $750 before his healing of "nervous trouble."[212]

Yet a mistrust of medicine remained. Rader's comments to Daggett in the *Ladies' Home Journal* succinctly show the mixed signals of the Alliance: "None of us has the least objection to the use of medicine. Only in my own family when anyone is ill there is but one doctor we will have. We run for the Great Physician."[213] Bosworth likewise asserted that "there is no 'fully competent authority' in the matter of diagnosis."[214] Trusting in remedies was not sinful so much as "foolish."[215] Also, a class-based critique of medicine, lingering since the Thomsonian heyday, was always a useful tactic.[216]

Bosworth and other divine healers also indirectly challenged the clinical approach of medical science. As James Opp argues, physicians generally thought of illnesses as scientific cases, while divine healers more deeply appreciated the holistic meaning of sickness and health—what Bosworth referred to as "the full gospel for the full man." These opposing approaches are demonstrated in each camp's use of photographic evidence. Physicians often showed X-rays or headless pictures isolating injured or diseased body parts, but divine healers published full-body photos that emphasized the complete restoration of individuals through healing.[217] A "then and now" collage appeared along with Dorothea Bradway's testimony in *Exploits of Faith*. Both pictures showed her full body, but the "then" photo had the paralytic immobile on her father's lap, while the "now" picture showed her standing on her own in heels, resolutely clutching her Bible. Similarly, Edith Watt, a severely cross-eyed woman healed in Bosworth's meetings in Detroit, was photographed in the *National Labor Tribune* with a headline that testified to her "beauty restored."[218] Another series of photos in the *Tribune* documented the healing of "Little Ruth Bellin," who had been healed of a "lazy foot." In two "before" pictures, she was depicted in devices representing her infirmity—first the plaster casts on her feet, then traveling by wheelbarrow,

211. "Testimony of Alice Baker," 3.

212. "Had Nervous Prostration," 3.

213. Daggett, "Are There Modern Miracles?" 165.

214. He was also happy to cite statistics to the effect that nearly fifty percent of autopsies reveal a misdiagnosis. "3000 Hear Bosworth Reply to Dr. Lott," 4.

215. "Witnesses to the Power of God," 780.

216. Bosworth's supporters reminded readers that while physicians and "fake quack doctors" dope the public and charge a fee, relief is "offered by this evangelist without money and without price." "Spiritual Healings at Gospel Tabernacle," 3.

217. Opp, *Lord for the Body*, 187–95.

218. "Beauty Restored to Girl," 5.

illustrating her "life of torture" and "misery." But the "after" photo showed the girl standing on her own wearing a bright smile, with the caption, "ready to romp and rollick."[219]

The visuals testified to the body-and-soul gospel embraced by Bosworth's followers. As a Presbyterian pastor in Bridgeport, Connecticut, remarked, "In the teaching [of Bosworth] there burst in upon many of us a new light . . . of the sacredness of our bodies, of the beauty and power of life 'every whit whole.' . . . [A] great Gospel in two parts."[220]

Bosworth's message also challenged the epistemological value of symptoms. He taught that "we will miss healing if we allow our symptoms to hinder us from expecting what his Word promises." As one woman declared nearly a year after she was anointed by Bosworth, "All of my symptoms have not disappeared, but I regard them as 'lying vanities,' and praise God just the same." In this way, divine healing undercut a cornerstone of scientific-medical authority.[221]

Bosworth's work exhibited a limited recognition of medical science and did not evince the vituperation against medical means of Dowie or even the ambivalence of A. B. Simpson. In upholding the "sacredness of our bodies," faith healing advocates were on the vanguard of later holistic medicine. They also demonstrated their divergence from other forms of non-medical healing, like Christian Science, which rather than holding the body as sacred, denied its existence. At the same time, by rejecting the import of symptoms, Bosworth and his followers denied the ultimate claims of the materialistic framework.

Non-fundamentalist Critique of Modernism

Full gospel advocates saw themselves as fighting the same war, on the same side, as the fundamentalists. But they also knew they wielded different weapons. Their mutual enemy was modernism in all its guises, encapsulated in the creed that God works through the mechanisms of humanity rather than by revelation and supernatural means.[222] But for Bosworth's supporters, the fundamentalist approach was distant and ineffectual: "What does it profit us to meditate on how Jesus healed the sick nineteen hundred years

219. Bellin, "Little Ruth Bellin," 3.

220. Davenport, "Surely It Was Good to Have Been There," 3.

221. Bosworth, *Christ the Healer*, 91; "Mother and Sons Have a Wonderful Story," 15. "Lying vanities" was probably from Bosworth, *Christ the Healer*, 102.

222. The dichotomy between God and "human means" that led some to reject medicine was fueled in part by the conservative rejection of the overly-immanent God of modernists. Putnam, *Modern Religio-Healing*, 64.

ago if he does not heal us today?"[223] Rather than the intellectual appeal to historical veracity, supporters pointed to the supernatural in their midst to refute modernism.[224] They argued that "to combat the rising tide of apostasy and encroaches of atheism, God is today restoring the gifts of the Holy Spirit and, by mighty signs and wonders, proving that the Bible is true."[225] Proving the Bible was, after all, the ultimate concern for fundamentalists. All recognized that the supernaturalists eclipsed the fundamentalists in their "literal" approach to scripture.[226] Clifton Fowler, outspoken critic of McPherson, wrote that "Once let the protective lines of the dispensational divisions be broken down, and we have departed from God's Word and are at the mercy of the fanatical hordes that are howling for the Bosworthian-McPhersonistic promiscuous divine healing and tongues fiasco."[227] Fundamentalists perceived the vital connection between dispensationalism and their defense against all forms of the supernatural gospel.

Still, the appeal to the supernatural had support from pockets of evangelical Christianity in the 1920s. Bosworth often touted the 1920 Episcopal Commission on Spiritual Healing, which recognized that "healing of the body is an essential element of the gospel."[228] Alliance writers like Kenneth Mackenzie, an Episcopal priest, began to think more deeply about the continuities between Anglican and Alliance approaches to healing. Mackenzie found this continuity in Bosworth's argument for the healing power of Holy Communion, since "a memorial only, does not satisfy [Anglicans] . . . it has a sacramental import which extends to the existing needs of the worshipper, spiritual or otherwise."[229] For MacKenzie, "the truth has been embalmed all through the centuries,

> that the body of the believer as well as his spiritual nature was designed to be a recipient of the correlated results of the crucifixion of our Lord; and that . . . He designed it to be a vitalizing force in the lives of those who . . . should receive it worthily.[230]

223. "Chicago's Visitation of Miracles," 15.

224. "Evangelist F. F. Bosworth Opens World's Greatest Religious Campaign," 4.

225. "Chicago's Visitation of Miracles," 15. See also "Evangelist F. F. Bosworth Opens World's Greatest Religious Campaign," 4; and Perkins, "Detroit Hall Too Small," 3.

226. Bingham, *Bible and the Body*, 45; Miller, "Fundamentalist and Divine Healing," 5–8; Smith, *Great Physician*, 41–42.

227. Fowler, "Anti-Dispensationalism," 329.

228. "Syracuse Revival: Episcopal Church" 3; Wyburn Fitch, *Healing Delusion*, 48. Bosworth approved of Anglican healers Hickson, Charles H. Brent, and others. "Interest Intense at the Great Bosworth's Big Tent Revival," 3.

229. Mackenzie, "Jesus and Our Mortal Flesh," 132–33.

230. Mackenzie, "Jesus and Our Mortal Flesh," 133.

Hopeful to ground the Alliance position in traditional reformation thought to resist modernism, Mackenzie affirmed that "Mr. Bosworth emphasizes what the Church of England has ever stressed" and urged fellow Alliance members "to make of the Holy Communion a fuller medium for the conferment of life for our bodies."[231]

THE FULL GOSPEL AND THE PROBLEM OF CATEGORIZATION

As with many successful evangelists, Bosworth did not fit neatly into one denomination or religious category. He continued to bear the stamp of pentecostal spirituality and was admired in pentecostal circles while working outside the bounds of their denominations. Although affiliated with the Alliance for much of this time, Bosworth's intense supernaturalism made this relationship tense.

Bosworth and Pentecostalism in the 1920s

Many pentecostals agreed with T. B. Barratt, who, with Bosworth in mind, said that those who reject the tongues evidence doctrine "have *placed themselves* outside the whole [Pentecostal] revival and its teaching."[232] But in reality, Bosworth's break from pentecostalism was not so clear. Some pentecostals admired Bosworth from a distance:

> From the north, from the south, from the east, and from the west comes reports of revivals. Pentecostal revivals with signs following . . . F. F. Bosworth, who used to be connected with Pentecost, has been conducting wonderful revival services where many hundreds have been saved and many [experienced] wonderful healings.[233]

Others were less equivocal. A 1921 report in the *Pentecostal Evangel* happily noted that many in Bosworth's meetings "broke out speaking in tongues." Bosworth's work was an occasion to marvel that tongues was "the one generally accepted evidence that one has reached the place where the whole being, *mind and all*, has been brought under the dominion of the Spirit." Denominational pentecostals sanctioned their embrace of Bosworth by suggesting that his results confirmed their dogma.[234]

231. Mackenzie, "Jesus and Our Mortal Flesh," 133.
232. Barratt, *Baptism with the Holy Ghost and Fire*, 8; emphasis in original.
233. "Revival Fires," 1.
234. "Bosworth Meetings," *Pentecostal Evangel*, 7; emphasis in original.

Pentecostal papers gave Bosworth intermittent coverage throughout the decade. Independent pentecostals associated with A. E. Humbard's Church of God read reports of Bosworth's work in the early 1920s.[235] In 1921 and 1922, the *Latter Rain Evangel* published Bosworth's sermons and testimonies from his meetings, as did the *Bridegroom's Messenger* of Atlanta and *Word and Work*, a pentecostal paper billed as "nonsectarian undenominational."[236] The *Pentecostal Evangel* related a testimony of a woman who was healed of gallstones during the Allentown campaign in 1926.[237] The *Latter Rain Evangel* gave Bosworth's work significant attention in the late 1920s. The paper ran the lengthy testimony of Freda Hugh, who was encouraged by her pentecostal housekeeper to read "Discerning the Lord's Body" and *Christ the Healer*. Bosworth's book was the turning point on Hugh's journey from sickness to health and from Methodism to pentecostalism.[238] Bosworth's secretary Rose Meyer reported in the paper on healings in the meetings in Scranton, DuBois and Altoona, Pennsylvania.[239] The periodical also mused on Bosworth's work at Rader's Tabernacle in early 1928.[240]

Just as pentecostals had not given up on Bosworth, Bosworth still evinced a pentecostal ministry. He continued to preach versions of many sermons from his pentecostal days, indicating that his spiritual identity

235. "Evangelist Bosworth's Great Meeting at Lima, Ohio," 1, 3; Bosworth, "Do All Speak with Tongues?" 1, 4; Bosworth, "Brother Bosworth's Minneapolis and St. Paul Meetings," 3. The Lima report is a reprint from *Alliance Weekly*, Miller, "Revival of Divine Healing," 473-74.

236. Bosworth, "For This Cause," 6-9; Bosworth, "Potter and the Clay," 20-23; Mueller, "Blind See," 20-21; "Miracle of Healing of a Gassed Soldier," 22-23; "Wonderful Works of God," (April 1921) 2; "Healed at the Bosworth Meetings," 2; "Revivals in Atlanta, GA.," 2; *Word and Work* 43.14 (October 8, 1921) 7; "Brooklyn, N.Y.," 15; "Bosworth Bros., in New York," 16.

237. "Healed of Gallstones," 8, 17.

238. Hugh, "Divinely Healed of Tuberculosis," 16-22. That Bosworth's book was a catalyst for a pentecostal's healing was to be expected, since *Latter Rain Evangel* and *Pentecostal Evangel* regularly advertised and endorsed *Christ the Healer*. See the following in *Pentecostal Evangel*: no. 637 (March 6, 1926), 15; no. 653 (June 26, 1926) 16; no. 690 (March 26, 1927) 13; and in *Latter Rain Evangel*: 18.6 (March 1926) 24; 18.7 (April 1926) 24; 25.3 (December 1932) 24.

239. Meyer, "When the Good Samaritan Came," 5-8; Rose Meyer, "Child Healed of Sarcoma Cancer," 21-22; Meyer, "Moving Pictures in God's Kaleidoscope," 18-21. See also the brief note of a woman who was healed in DuBois and went on to perform eighteen healings in an insane asylum, *Latter Rain Evangel* 19.11 (August, 1927) 15. That same year, the *Latter Rain Evangel* also published the testimony of a Baptist pastor named Amos Oyer, who had suffered with spinal trouble for eighteen years and had been on the verge of suicide. Oyer, "Healed of Spinal Trouble," 22-23.

240. "Chicago's Visitation of Miracles of Healing," 14.

changed little after leaving the Assemblies of God.²⁴¹ Baptism in the Holy Spirit accompanied by tongues continued to be common in his meetings.²⁴²

In many ways, denominational pentecostals and Bosworth were on the same side. After *Moody Bible Institute Monthly* criticized Aimee Semple McPherson and distanced itself from the Bosworth brothers in 1921, W. F. Carothers came to their defense, saying, "The Bosworth Brothers . . . have the definite experiences for which the [pentecostal] movement stands (and owe their power to it)."²⁴³ When Haldeman attacked Bosworth in February of 1923, Stanley Frodsham took up his defense in the *Pentecostal Evangel*.²⁴⁴ For opponents, divine healing and pentecostalism were so connected that they really represented one threat. There was no question that Bosworth was a pentecostal, since he "endorse[s] the 'gift of tongues' as one of the evidences of having received the Holy Spirit."²⁴⁵ Gaebelein boiled pentecostalism down to "the claim of two manifestations of the supernatural": tongues and healing. And now that "miraculous healings have almost overshadowed the gift of tongues" in pentecostalism, Bosworth clearly fit this mold.²⁴⁶

Bosworth and the Christian and Missionary Alliance

As many pentecostals retreated into their doctrinal enclaves,²⁴⁷ Bosworth freely cooperated with leaders and laity of many denominations.²⁴⁸ He also

---

241. A reprint of "Nothing Can Hinder a Revival" with some additions is Bosworth, "Faint-Hearted Get Go-By," 2, 7. Bosworth preached on "The Potter and the Clay" at seemingly every revival. See, for example, "Syracuse Revival: Indians," 3.

242. For example, an Episcopalian woman with cancer was saved, and "when the spirit that was afflicting her went out, the Holy Spirit came in and she went right over on the floor. She broke out speaking in tongues; didn't even know what it was, and for an hour and a half spoke beautifully in tongues, her eyes filled with tears." Bosworth, "They Rehearsed All That God Had Done with Them," 9.

243. Carothers, "Baptism of the Spirit," 762.

244. Frodsham, "Did Our Lord By His Death," (May 12, 1923) 8–9; Frodsham, "Did Our Lord By His Death," (May 19, 1923) 10. The second installment gives the author as "S.H.F."

245. "Strange Fire," 84–85.

246. Gaebelein, "Christianity vs. Modern Cults," 859.

247. Notwithstanding the extremely guarded relationship of the Assemblies of God with the Foreign Missions Conference beginning in 1920. See Robeck, "Assemblies of God and Ecumenical Cooperation," 107–50.

248. "Baptists, Methodists, Presbyterians and Pentecostal brethren took an active part." Bosworth, "They Rehearsed All That God Had Done with Them," 5. He received musical support from several Salvation Army bands and even one local Lutheran Church. Perkins, "Bosworth's Shaking Detroit," 3.

retained membership in numerous nondenominational associations.[249] This aspect of Bosworth's work reflected his own priorities and the nature of the Alliance, which at this time considered itself a "nondenominational mission society." But Bosworth was working with the Alliance during a "troubled transition."[250] Torn between its evangelistic efforts and the forces of denominationalism, the Alliance severed its relationship with the denominationally-indifferent Paul Rader in early 1924. The presidency of H. M. Shuman (1925–1954) ushered in a denominational phase coinciding with Bosworth's departure.

Earlier signs suggest a troubled partnership. Before Bosworth was invited to Toronto in 1921, an Alliance delegation investigated his work in Detroit, reporting some concern about his understanding of spirit-baptism and the atonement.[251] Despite the debt he owed to Bosworth, Oswald Smith said he was uneasy with the emphasis on healing."[252] Rader too worried that Bosworth was turning the Alliance into a "healing cult" and recommended Bosworth not be invited back to Toronto unless he changed his approach.[253] Alliance adherents were uncomfortable with some of the manifestations at Bosworth's meetings. *Alliance Weekly* went out of its way to describe the "unusual quietness" of the meetings, protesting that "the power of God does not necessarily have to manifest itself in noise or outward emotion." Scholars have often taken such descriptions at face value.[254] Bosworth's words tell a different story:

---

249. In addition to his affiliation with the Alliance, Bosworth was a member of the Ministerial Association, the International Federation of Christian Workers, and the International Association of Evangelists, whose vice president was Billy Sunday. "Gospel Truths, Faith Healing," 1; "Bosworth Brothers Evangelist and Aids," 7.

250. Niklaus, Sawin, and Stoesz, *All for Jesus*, chap. 9.

251. Opp, *Lord for the Body*, 151; Reynolds, *Rebirth*, 60.

252. "Faith Cure Miracle Bubble," 762. For Bosworth's impact on Smith and the ongoing Alliance work in Toronto, see Reynolds, *Rebirth*, 59–60, 66–69.

253. For "healing cult," see Opp, *Lord for the Body*, 153; Reynolds, *Rebirth*, 69. See also "Great Revival in Big Steel Tent," 3. Both Smith and Rader would later come to support Bosworth's brand of divine healing, but also, significantly, both would leave the Alliance. Rader's book on healing was written while Bosworth held a five-month campaign in his Chicago tabernacle. Rader evinces some specific evidence of Bosworth's influence in his use of the redemptive names argument and his discussion of Paul's thorn. Rader, *Man of Mercy*, 36–42, 105. According to one pentecostal controversialist, Rader had confessed that "if he had his life to live over again, he would cast his lot with the Pentecostal people." Perkins, *Baptism of the Holy Spirit*, 27–28.

254. "Bosworth Campaign in Chicago." Hejzlar and Robinson uncritically accept Eunice Perkins's descriptions, see Hejzlar, *Two Paradigms for Divine Healing*, 22; Robinson, *Divine Healing: The Years of Expansion*, 168–69. Even the *National Labor Tribune*, which usually emphasized the decorum of Bosworth's meetings, could not obscure the

People received the baptism of the Holy Spirit right on the platform, the atmosphere was so charged with the power of God. One night, without any suggestion from anyone, three different ones broke out speaking in tongues.[255]

R. V. Bingham happily exploited the tension: "Alliance leaders are decrying the spectacular methods of Mr. Bosworth, while trying to hold onto the addition to their membership largely gleaned . . . through his ministry."[256] This portended changes in the Alliance, which distanced itself not just from pentecostal doctrine (evidential tongues) but also from pentecostal practices like healing, tongues, and other manifestations. Their "full gospel," contracted to "gospel." Bosworth's departure should be seen as an early symptom of this move.[257]

As one of many who moved freely in full gospel circles at this time, Bosworth illustrates the inadequacy of denominational categories.[258] While his doctrine matched the Alliance, his worldview squared with the pentecostals. Bosworth was celebrated by both and kept at an arm's length by both. It is no wonder he felt most comfortable in the role of an independent evangelist.

CONCLUSION

Bosworth's ministry noticeably cooled by the early 1930s. But Bosworth had made his mark, and few could rival his impact on the thought and culture of divine healing in the 1920s. His meetings drew attention and burst attendance records at nearly every location. His "panoramic view of the truth" raised the hopes of the faithful and the ire of the opposition.[259] The abundance of sources and the influence of his writings make Bosworth a wealth of insight into divine healing and its role in the search for certainty that

---

shouts of "glory-glory" in the baptismal service at the end of the Toledo meetings. Fitch, "Great Rush for Baptism" 3.

255. Bosworth, "They Rehearsed All That God Had Done with Them," 9.

256. Bingham, "Healing Movement in Crisis," 39.

257. King, *Genuine Gold*, 234. Without drawing a rigid timeline, King locates this shift in the 1930s. King also suggests that Bosworth "remained with the Alliance for a period of time" after 1927, but this is unsupported by either his ministerial credentials or by coverage in *Alliance Weekly*. King, *Genuine Gold*, 227. For a study of the Alliance shift through the lens of its developing approach to tongues, see Richmann, "Blaspheming in Tongues," 139–55.

258. King describes many of these figures, including Edward Armstrong, Warren Collins, Hardy Mitchell, the Richeys, C. O. Benham, and Carrie Judd Montgomery. See King, *Genuine Gold*, 196–202.

259. "Love Offering to Bosworth Brothers," 4.

characterized the religious controversies of the 1920s. Divine healing was not only a blessing to body and soul, but also a defense against modernism. In this full gospel, personal intimacy combined with the phenomenon of the celebrity evangelist to offer a message that comforted as much as it excited. Although flourishing in independent and interdenominational circles, divine healing was driven by the supernaturalist impulse of pentecostalism. This impulse would soon move Bosworth into a quieter chapter of his ministry and also facilitate his acceptance of a theory of scriptural interpretation that many other full gospel advocates openly rejected.

6

The Lost Years, 1933–1947

> If Israel is not in existence today as "a nation and a company of nations" and a people as numerous as "the stars" and "the sand," then the veracity of Jehovah God, is open to question.
>
> —CHARLES O. BENHAM, "JOSEPH IS YET ALIVE"[1]

As F. F. BOSWORTH turned fifty-six in 1933, he slowed the pace of his ministry. The economic depression also made travel more difficult and decreased his financial base. No longer attached to a denomination or conducting high-profile healing campaigns, Bosworth seems almost to disappear from the historical record. Historians have in fact referred to the period of about 1933 to 1948 as a historical "gap."[2] This relative lack of sources does not mean that Bosworth was inactive, however. Bosworth continued to print *Exploits of Faith*, produced new tracts and booklets, and ministered almost daily on the radio. Perhaps the greatest sign of vitality was his adoption of British-Israelism. Not only did his acceptance of this teaching require active study and discernment, but it also entailed a reconfiguration of Bosworth's professional circle.

This chapter will narrow the historical gap in Bosworth's story, recounting his radio ministry during the Depression and examining his

---

1. Benham, "Joseph Is Yet Alive," 288.
2. Barnes, "F. F. Bosworth," 54–55.

involvement with the controversial British-Israel movement. New sources press new questions, especially since the prior historical gap has been convenient for those who for theological reasons would downplay Bosworth's British-Israelism. In light of the sources indicating his commitment to British-Israelism, any serious study of Bosworth—and American pentecostalism—must deal with the teaching. Historically evaluated, British-Israelism is not inherently contradictory to pentecostalism or an aberration in Bosworth's story. Bosworth and other pentecostals embraced the teaching as a defense against modernism while also rejecting the dominant fundamentalist approach to the scriptures.

MEETINGS, RADIO, AND PRINT, 1933-1940

Bosworth continued to travel occasionally for evangelistic services. In the summer of 1933, he held meetings in the Philadelphia area.[3] In 1938 and 1939, he was a featured speaker at the summer Bible park camp meetings in Oregon, Wisconsin.[4] Also in 1939, Bosworth participated in a "Church and Public Affairs Institute" hosted by River Forest Methodist Church. At this extended public forum for the discussion of religion and political issues, Bosworth was billed as an expert on "Evangelism, the Imperative Task of the Church."[5] In 1939 and 1940, Bosworth led healing and evangelistic services in the Gospel Tabernacle in Freeport, Illinois, attracting participants from dozens of nearby cities.[6]

But by this time, Bosworth did not focus on traditional evangelism. As he said in an address in Chicago in 1937, "the days of revivals are not over and never will be. But the days of the huge tabernacle building program and all that it implied in the way of tremendous physical and financial effort which distracted from the spirituality of the meetings, are definitely past."[7] Uttered in the midst of the Depression, Bosworth's poor predictive skills can be overlooked. Nonetheless, Bosworth turned his focus to radio, which he called the "handmaid of the church of God."[8] Omitting any reference to dwindling crowds or finances, Bosworth's admirers later explained the switch to radio as a calculated decision to reach more hearers with the

---

3. "Evangelistic Services," 4; "Is Conducting Campaign," 15.
4. "Eureka Singers Appear at Oregon," 16; "Oregon Meet Opens Friday," 20.
5. "Speakers at 'Church and Public Affairs Institute,'" 13.
6. "Evangelist Speaks Here Next Sunday," 6; "Freeport Gospel Tabernacle," 6; "At Gospel Tabernacle This Coming Sunday," 6; "Evangelists at Gospel Tabernacle," 7.
7. "River Forest Minister on Radio Often," 46.
8. "Tabernacle Evangelist Now on Radio," 18.

gospel while putting less physical strain on the evangelist.[9] In June of 1935, he began a daily program over Chicago's WJJD, using his home as a satellite studio. In less than a year, Bosworth reported receiving more than 17,000 letters from listeners.[10] His "National Radio Revival" aired on a handful of other Chicago-area stations and eventually on stations in Philadelphia, Salt Lake City, Detroit, North Dakota and even Panama.[11] In the fall of 1938, Bosworth traveled to Haiti to establish his radio program there and then made a trip to Jamaica.[12] His radio broadcasts and *Exploits of Faith* worked in tandem, as listeners would write to Bosworth and then see their testimonies—and those of others—in print. Within the first two years of broadcasting, Bosworth produced a fifty-six-page "National Radio Revival Number" of *Exploits of Faith*.[13] Bosworth also continued writing, no doubt enabled by his constant radio preaching. Between 1932 and 1937, he published several pamphlets, dealing with a wide range of issues including divine healing, sin, the Great Commandment, financial sowing and reaping, and psalm meditations.[14]

About a year before his radio program started in 1935, Bosworth also began interacting with those involved in British-Israelism (or Anglo-Israelism). While this approach to biblical prophecy was fully consistent with Bosworth's overall focus on the continuing supernatural activity of God, it was not viewed favorably by most other Christians at the time, including many full gospel believers. Bosworth continued a fruitful radio and print ministry, but his acceptance of British-Israelism may have alienated him from a large contingent of his potential audience.

THE DISTANT PAST AND THE UNCERTAIN FUTURE: BOSWORTH AND BRITISH-ISRAELISM

Like other premillennial systems, British-Israelism centered on Christ's soon return and the veracity of scripture. British-Israelism differed, however, from other forms of premillennialism in that it took a historicist

9. Blomgren, Jr., "Man of God," 14.

10. Blomgren, Jr., "Man of God," 14.; "Evangelist Rev. F. F. Bosworth," 36; "F. F. Bosworth Heard Over WJJD Daily," 18.

11. *Exploits of Faith* 10.7 (July 1937). See also *Destiny* 7.12 (December 1936) 7; *Herald of Our Race* 2.4 (April 1938) 6; *Destiny* 10.12 (December 1939) 15.

12. "U. S. Evangelists on Visit to Jamaica," 10; "Radio Revivalist Guest Preacher," 10; "Most Pleasurable Experience," 5.

13. This issue is not extant but is advertised in *Exploits of Faith* 10.7 (July 1937) 19, 20.

14. See advertisements in *Exploits of Faith* 10.7 (July 1937) 20.

perspective, meaning it held that most biblical prophecy had been fulfilled in history. It challenged the futurist position of dispensationalism, which posited a prophetic "parenthesis" identified with the church age, postponing the fulfillment of most biblical prophecy to the future. British-Israelism also differed in that it held Anglo-Saxons to be Israelites, or descendants of the biblical Northern Kingdom. From the mid-1930s, Bosworth became involved in the American British-Israel movement, working in its circles, publicizing its work, and contending for the message. Gaining constituents from a diverse base of fundamentalist and full gospel adherents, British-Israelism made its enemies in the same corners.

The British-Israel History and Message

When a handful of British subjects in the last half of the nineteenth century preached that Britain and all who shared her blood were the direct descendants of Israel, they joined a quest that was as old as the Assyrian exile itself. Since antiquity, the clever and the curious have bandied their theories about the fate of the Israelites who were exiled by Assyria in 722 BC. The earliest writers simply affirmed that they were "out there," somewhere.[15] The age of exploration meant they had to be identified among the populations known to exist, such as natives in the New World.[16] Manasseh Ben-Israel's *Hope of Israel* (1652) popularized the notion that although the tribes were still identifiable (i. e., they had not blended into local populations), they had traveled by many routes, and pockets of lost Israel could be found in many locations.[17]

The search for remnants of Israel in existing populations throughout their supposed migrations prepared the way for British-Israelism. The seer Richard Brothers (1757–1823) had many of the bedrock notions that would become currency in British-Israelism, most importantly, the idea that some (though not all) descendants of Israel now lived in Britain. Brothers mainly based his insights on revelation. But a broader movement needed a more scholarly approach. Supported by earlier linguistic studies that identified the lost Israelites with the Scythians—the supposed seed race of Europe—John Wilson's *Our Israelitish Origin* (1840) bowled audiences with innumerable connections between English and Hebrew words and institutions. Such theories also benefited from the developing biological notions of race

---

15. Ben-Dor Benite, *Ten Lost Tribes*, 57, 58, 79, chap. 2.
16. Ben-Dor Benite, *Ten Lost Tribes*, 141; Parfitt, *Lost Tribes of Israel*, 91–114, 142, 159.
17. Parfitt, *Lost Tribes of Israel*, 165–67, 177–81.

and the widely-shared concern to explain scientifically the superiority of European cultures.

What set British-Israelism apart from these early theories was its claim to fulfilled prophecy. British-Israelists argued that Jacob had blessed Ephraim as a "company of nations," a description that fit only Britain and its unprecedented empire. Furthermore, as the early British-Israelist Edward Hine (1825–1891) noted, scripture insisted that the ten tribes would be "consolidated in an Island Nation."[18] Early British-Israelists found in the message a theological argument for the imperial superiority of Britain. Thus, early adherents tended to be the patriotic upper-class (even noble) and belong to the Church of England. As a popular movement in England, British-Israelism's wave crested and broke with the fate of the empire.

British-Israel ideas were present in America as early as the 1870s. Influenced by Wilson and Hine, the New York Congregational minister Joseph Wild sermonized, published books and pamphlets, and organized a local British-Israel society. Charles A. Totten, a military instructor who lectured at Yale, was the most prolific early American adherent. Next to him in influence was J. H. Allen, a holiness minister whose book *Judah's Sceptre and Joseph's Birthright* (1902) became a foundational text for the American movement.[19] Allen's ideas can be taken as representative—although not normative—of American British-Israelism.

According to Allen, understanding the identity of Israel begins with Jacob's blessing to his children and grandchildren (Genesis 48–4 9). Judah is blessed with rule—the "sceptre"—while Joseph (through his sons Ephraim and Manasseh) is blessed with becoming a multitude on earth, thereby perpetuating Jacob's name—the "birthright." Although both blessings seemed threatened by exile—the northern tribes (Joseph's descendants) by the Assyrians in 722 BC and then the southern tribes (Judah's descendants) by Babylon in 587 BC—God had not forgotten his promises. The birthright promise lived on, for after the northern tribes were exiled, they went elsewhere, becoming a multitude to be revealed and brought back to their land in the last days. Allen charted their trip through the "Caucasian Pass" and westward through Europe, placing them finally in Ireland. The scepter promise was maintained through the work of Jeremiah, who preserved the royal line by ushering a Davidic princess to Ireland (Jeremiah 41:10, 43:6).[20]

Allen leaned on a patchwork of scriptures and history. Prophecies of easterly winds, isles, passage through gates, and spreading vines were all

---

18. Cited in Barkun, *Religion and the Racist Right*, 11.
19. Barkun, *Religion and the Racist Right*, 17–21.
20. Allen, *Judah's Sceptre and Joseph's Birthright*, 221, 267–68.

taken to refer to Israel's trek to Britain and establishment of an empire.[21] Although Allen's proof-texting may have been strained, his method was in reality the popular Bible conference and camp meeting "Bible Reading" technique (which "consisted of stringing together a series of scriptural passages on a given topic" with the aid of a concordance[22]), put to the use of British-Israelism. Allen found corroboration in history. In fact, Allen admitted that history is decisive, for while scripture prophesied Jeremiah's work, it did not record it. "Both ancient and modern history," said Allen, "come honestly to the rescue of prophecy."[23] Allen's "history" was, in reality, strained folklore. For instance, the English expression "red-tape" was somehow linked to the prophetic "scarlet thread." Nevertheless, Allen claimed that the secular record confirmed Jeremiah's arrival in Ireland and the identity of the biblical "Stone of Destiny" with the coronation stone of Irish, Scottish, and English monarchs. Historical trace of the tribes' migrations was left in place-names that have some supposed corruption of "Dan," such as *Den*mark, *Dan*ube, and even Lon*don*derry.[24]

British-Israelists were not bothered by the fact that the apparently obvious identity of Israel went unrecognized for centuries. Israel was providentially hidden until God raised up servants to declare its true identity—a quasi-messianic role British-Israelists happily claimed. This entailed a sense of eschatological urgency, for only after Israel had been found could they return to Palestine. With this now happening, Allen believed that Christ's return was "just ahead."[25] The message implicitly demoted the Jews: not only were the scepter and the birthright continued in Israel, but because the Jews rejected Christ, Israel monopolized the gospel message as well.[26]

Upon the foundation of Hine, Trotten, Allen, and others, British-Israelism grew unevenly in the early twentieth century. In the late 1920s Howard B. Rand, a Massachusetts lawyer, began vigorously promoting the

21. Allen, *Judah's Sceptre and Joseph's Birthright*, 223–27, 247–48.

22. Weber, "Two-Edged Sword," 110.

23. Allen, *Judah's Sceptre and Joseph's Birthright*, 224, 225, 247.

24. Allen, *Judah's Sceptre and Joseph's Birthright*. For "red-tape," p. 304; "notable man" and eastern princess, pp. 228–29; Denmark, Danube, etc., pp. 266–67.

25. Allen, *Judah's Sceptre and Joseph's Birthright*, 129, 227, 296–97, 355. Quote on p. 362.

26. Allen, *Judah's Sceptre and Joseph's Birthright*, 220, 246, 283, 362, 367–68. According to Allen, salvation was through Israel, and those who accepted the gospel also need to be adopted into fleshly Israel. What exactly he meant by this is unclear. See p. 337. Scholars who claim that the British-Israel message is not soteriological have missed this, for instance Barkun, *Religion and the Racist Right*, 15. Charles Parham's British-Israelism also had soteriological implications. See Richmann, "Prophecy and Politics."

doctrine, creating a national movement. Inspired by the British-Israel World Federation based in London, Rand organized the Anglo-Saxon Federation of America in 1930. Headquartered in Detroit, soon the Federation had branches spreading across the country and attracted prominent supporters, including Henry Ford's publicity manager William J. Cameron.[27] The Anglo-Saxon Federation also drew Bosworth into its orbit in the mid-1930s.

Bosworth's Involvement

When exactly Bosworth adopted British-Israelism is difficult to pinpoint. The theory was current, although not dominant, in Dowie's Zion City.[28] Dowie himself affirmed that "the Anglo-Saxon race is the lineal descendant of the Ten Tribes of Israel who were scattered abroad."[29] Daniel Bryant, who led a faction in Zion City after Dowie's death, and whom Bosworth quoted in *Christ the Healer*, was also a British-Israelist.[30] Possibly while vacationing in Pasadena in 1929, Bosworth became aware of the work of J. H. Allen, who pastored a church in the city. Bosworth's colleague Luke Rader also began to associate with the Federation in the mid-1930s.[31] Bosworth could have simply been drawn to the movement through local contacts: in the early 1930s, the Federation had a strong presence in Chicago, holding its national convention in the Windy City in September of 1931 and soon after establishing a local branch.[32] More fundamentally, Bosworth's controversies with hardline dispensationalist like I. M. Haldeman and Arno Gaebelein predisposed him to a teaching that directly opposed the dispensationalist hermeneutic.

Regardless of when Bosworth accepted the teaching, by February of 1934, he allowed British-Israelist writer William Pascoe Goard to spread the word in *Exploits of Faith*.[33] In 1935, the Anglo-Saxon Federation advertised Bosworth as a participant in the national convention in Detroit.[34] Later in

---

27. Barkun, *Religion and the Racist Right*, 29–40.

28. "Writer on Anglo-Israel," 367.

29. "Let Us Go Up to Zion," 498. For additional references from Dowie, see Jennings, "Dr. Dowie and the Anglo-Israel Belief."

30. Bryant, "Shiloh and Messiah," 3. Bosworth quoted Bryant's *Christ Among our Sick* (1923). Bosworth, *Christ the Healer*, (1924), 10, 95.

31. Cook, "At Headquarters," 5. Rader said in 1936 that he had studied British-Israelism for eight years. "These Two Letters Speak for Themselves."

32. Stephens, "Our Chicago Convention," 75–76; "New Branch Organizations," 87.

33. Although this issue of *Exploits of Faith* is not extant, Goard's writing is referred to in Thomsen, "Anglo-Israelism," 6.

34. "Convention Program," (May 1935) 2; "Convention Program," (June 1935) 7.

1935, Bosworth, Rader, and Bosworth's associate from years earlier, Charles Benham participated in a Federation conference in Chicago.[35] In preparations for the national convention in 1936, executive secretary S. A. Ackley referred to Bosworth as one of "our old and tried leaders," who is "a convention in himself."[36] Bosworth spoke at another regional convention in 1937 and again with his wife at the national convention in 1938.[37]

The Anglo-Saxon Federation was pleased with the publicity afforded through Bosworth's radio program, calling it one of the "outstanding influences for the extension of our work." Bosworth announced Federation meetings over the airwaves, and the Federation claimed that "a large percentage of our attendants are regular listeners" of Bosworth's program.[38] Bosworth gave over the microphone once a week to Howard B. Rand, the elder statesmen of the American British-Israel movement. Not only did Bosworth give space for the message, "but [he] speaks often upon the Gospel of the Kingdom, in which he is a most sincere believer." In this way, the Federation mused, "much good is being accomplished in thus spreading the Kingdom Truth."[39] Testimonies bore this out. One grateful correspondent told Bosworth in 1937 that the message on "The Proofs of Anglo-Israel Truth" was "convincing as well as inspiring" and said that through Bosworth's work, "this glorious truth grows more and more wonderful despite the sceptics and critics."[40] The Federation returned the favor by periodically advertising Bosworth's tracts.[41]

Bosworth also published articles in the Federation's periodical. In 1936, *Destiny* published "New Covenant Obedience," a standard evangelical message describing the believer's spirit-enabled righteousness.[42] This is one of the few articles in Anglo-Saxon Federation publications that did not focus on the British-Israel message, the Second Coming, or Pyramidology.[43] This article shows that the Federation aligned itself with traditional evangelical concerns and saw Bosworth as an able voice for these concerns.

35. "Plan 2 Regional Conventions," 6; *Messenger of the Covenant* 6, no.72 (December 1935) 3.

36. Ackley, "Detroit Convention," 7. See also "Anglo-Saxon Federation Detroit Convention," 6; "Convention Story," 3.

37. "From Headquarters," 7; *Destiny* 9.10 (October 1938) back cover.

38. Ackley, "Chicago Branch Activities," 3.See also Rand, "Convention Declared Success," 7; Cook, "At Headquarters," 7.

39. "At Headquarters," 10.

40. "Our Hearts Have Been Thrilled and Blessed," 11.

41. *Destiny* 7.1 (January 1936) 5.

42. Bosworth, "New Covenant Obedience," 4.

43. Many British-Israelists (as well as occultists and not a few dispensationalists)

Destiny published another message from Bosworth in 1940. In "The Prophecy of Daniel's 'Seventy Weeks,'" Bosworth refuted the "parenthesis" argument of dispensationalism. According to most dispensationalists, an indeterminate gap existed between the first sixty-nine weeks of the Daniel 9 prophecy (signifying the time from the return of the Jews from exile to the ministry of Christ, with each week a seven-year period in prophetic reasoning) and the final week, which would commence with the return of Christ to gather the saints. Bosworth derided the dispensationalist scheme as "a new interpretation . . . unknown to the Church for the first eighteen centuries."[44] Rather than postponing the fulfillment of Daniel's prophecy, Bosworth argued that "our Lord's personal [i. e., earthly] ministry lay entirely within the seventieth week." For Bosworth, the dispensationalist error amounted to confusing Christ for Antichrist.[45] Bosworth could not abide the removal of these clearly messianic prophecies "from the distant past to the uncertain future" as dispensationalism cavalierly did. "There is not a verse of Scripture in the Bible," Bosworth said, "which suggests a parenthesis of many centuries between the sixty-ninth and seventieth weeks of Daniel." The idea of a prophetic gap was foreign to scripture and risked "destroying the prophecy as a whole." The integrity of biblical prophecy, said Bosworth, was "entirely frustrated by this new idea, that God's measuring line is an elastic one which can be stretched out to a length of thousands of years."[46] As with divine healing, Bosworth argued from the premise that God dealt consistently in human affairs.

Another source for understanding Bosworth's British-Israel sympathies is an undated radio address entitled "The Bible Distinction between the House of Israel and the House of Judah."[47] Bosworth claimed in this sermon that the differentiation between Israel and Judah was divinely

---

believed that the Great Pyramid at Giza contained measurements that corresponded to biblical prophecy. For British-Israelists, the classic text was David Davidson's *The Great Pyramid: Its Divine Message* (1924).

44. Bosworth, "Prophecy of Daniel's 'Seventy Weeks,'" 19. Along with other British-Israelists, Bosworth claimed that the innovative parenthesis theory originated with the Jesuits in the sixteenth century and was brought into Protestant thought by Samuel R. Maitland, a nineteenth-century Anglican cleric. Bosworth, "Prophecy of Daniel's 'Seventy Weeks,'" 21. See Froom, *Prophetic Faith of Our Fathers*, 2:484–502; 3:541–44.

45. Bosworth, "Prophecy of Daniel's 'Seventy Weeks,'" 19.

46. Bosworth, "Prophecy of Daniel's 'Seventy Weeks,'" 20–21.

47. The earliest dated version I have found of this is a reprint, Bosworth, "The Bible Distinction Between the House of Israel and the House of Judah," *New Beginnings* 10.5 (May 1980) 6–10. As this version is not very accessible, I will cite Bosworth, *Bible Distinction*.

ordained, clearly expounded in scripture, and continued to the present day.[48] He rejected the "amalgamation theory," which posited that Israelite exiles were incorporated into the Jewish people after the exile. Only at "the end of the 'latter days,'" claimed Bosworth, would these houses be reunited.[49] Therefore any attempt to assign to Jews (House of Judah) what scripture assigned to Israel was a distortion of scripture. "Until this distinction is clearly understood," said Bosworth, "a great portion of the Bible will remain a closed book."[50] Bosworth claimed that without this distinction, God appeared unfaithful and scripture appeared contradictory, leading to "much of the infidelity of today."[51] Quoting J. H. Allen, Bosworth referred to a willful disregard of this truth as "the great ecclesiastical crime of the ages."[52]

For Bosworth, history was the final arbiter of prophetic interpretation: "That this promise to Israel ['His seed shall become a multitude of nations'] was not to Judah is proven by the fact that Judah has never been a multitude of nations, and never will be."[53] Likewise, prophecy determines that "Israel shall be a great military power" and a "maritime people," neither of which applies to the Jews.[54] Bosworth knew which modern people fit these biblical descriptions: "The Anglo-Saxon Nations are Isaac's sons or Saxons . . . The Promise of 'A Multitude of Nations' was made to Ephraim, not to Judah."[55] For Bosworth, Britain's occupation of the Holy Land following the Great War followed prophecy:

> Obadiah the 17th verse speaks of the soldiers under General Allenby, who delivered Jerusalem from the Turks on the exact day and in the exact manner in which God says Jerusalem would be delivered, as belonging to the House of Jacob . . . The next verse shows us what part of "The House of Jacob" they were—"The House of Joseph." And the next verse shows us what part of the House of Joseph they were—"Ephraim;" and in the same verse He speaks of them as "the children of Israel" . . . To insist that these Scriptures addressed to Israel are to be applied to the Jews is to call the soldiers of General Allenby Jews.[56]

48. Bosworth, *Bible Distinction*, 4.
49. Bosworth, *Bible Distinction*, 8, 9. Also p. 11.
50. Bosworth, *Bible Distinction*, 6.
51. Bosworth, *Bible Distinction*, 1.
52. Bosworth, *Bible Distinction*, 6. This quote is from Allen, *National Number*, 29–30.
53. Bosworth, *Bible Distinction*, 10.
54. Bosworth, *Bible Distinction*, 14, 15.
55. Bosworth, *Bible Distinction*, 16.
56. Bosworth, *Bible Distinction*, 15.

For Bosworth, a rigid hermeneutic combined with global political developments to reinforce his particular historicist approach to scripture.

Historian Paul King claims that Bosworth publicly recanted British-Israelism in 1944, although he offers no documentation for this assertion.[57] On the other hand, British-Israel writers claim that Bosworth held the teaching till his death.[58] Regardless, Bosworth has continued to be revered by pentecostal British-Israelists. Although Bosworth was not directly associated with the Los Angeles British-Israelists who published *Herald of our Race* and ran the Kingdom Bible College, this group advertised Bosworth's radio services and reprinted excerpts from *Christ the Healer*.[59] John A. Lovell, the influential British-Israelist who worked in Texas and California, reprinted a number of Bosworth's articles in his *Kingdom Digest* and his correspondence course.[60] Charles Benham, sometime coworker of Bosworth, often paraphrased and elaborated on Bosworth's British-Israel writings.[61] C. O. Stadsklev, a British-Israel minister in Minnesota, had high praise for Bosworth and republished several of his sermons.[62] Eldon Purvis, who was central to the charismatic movement in the 1960s, published Bosworth's "Bible Distinction" article in his periodical *New Beginnings*.

Bosworth's British-Israelism was typical and somewhat derivative. But he attached great meaning to the teaching as a way to maintain the integrity of biblical prophecy and the consistent supernatural activity of God as contrasted with the "elastic" method of dispensationalism.

Pentecostalism and British-Israelism

The dominant interpretation of British-Israelism as "a religious and emotional expression of British imperialism and American manifest destiny," has obscured the deeper theological concerns that attracted adherents to its

---

57. King, *Genuine Gold*, 235, 239, n. 24, 242, 248, n. 11.

58. Southwick, "Controversy in Zion," 198.

59. Bosworth, "Is God the Author of Disease?," 9.

60. Bosworth, "Recipe for Healing," 33–37; Bosworth, "Is Healing for All?," 18–21; Bosworth, "Windows of Heaven," 14–17. Bosworth, *Judah vs. Israel*. The Anglo-Saxon Federation cited also Bosworth's "Daniel's 'Seventy Weeks,'" in *Destiny* 15.2 (February 1944) 42.

61. "Distinction Between Israel and Judah," 27–29; "Israel vs. Judah," 7–10.

62. Bosworth, "Greatest Sin," 20–30; Bosworth, "Do All Speak with Tongues?," (September 1972) 23–31. Quote on p. 23. Carl Oliver Stadsklev was the brother of Julius Stadsklev, who accompanied Bosworth, Branham, and others in their work in South Africa in 1951. Julius was the author of *William Branham: A Prophet Visits South Africa*.

message.[63] Because early pentecostals do not fit the profile of the "well-to-do and patriotic" that this interpretation implies,[64] British-Israelism is often sidelined by historians of pentecostalism.[65] But the theory was adopted by a significant number of pentecostal leaders in America and Great Britain.

In the logic of the earliest phase of British-Israelism, the reliability of the Bible was the antecedent and British dominance was the consequent:

> Certain it is that this Nation fulfils at the present day the destined role of Israel. This can only be due to the fact that Israel is in Britain: no other nation can have stepped into the promises entailed by God on Israel, for God cannot lie.[66]

Although its political importance never disappeared,[67] the British-Israel theory in the first half of the twentieth century was pressed into the service of the emerging debates over scripture. Particularly, those who embraced the theory in the 1920s and 1930s saw its value as an argument for the authority of scripture. In essence, the antecedent and the consequent were reversed: because England and America were the superior global powers, therefore scripture was vindicated. These later adherents, therefore, were more likely to come from holiness, pentecostal and fundamentalist ranks—those who were concerned about the modernist critique of scripture. As a later pentecostal adherent would claim, "the identity of modern Israel is essential to the vindication of the character of God and to the demonstration of the veracity of the Scriptures."[68]

Pentecostalism emerged as British-Israelism spread in the English-speaking world. Many holiness and pentecostal believers, already freed from denominational constraint, were receptive to theological innovation. Frank Sandford, the ex-Baptist evangelist who influenced early pentecostals Charles Parham and A. J. Tomlinson, incorporated the teaching into his

---

63. Melton, *Melton's Encyclopedia of American Religions*, 565. See also Gonen, *To the Ends of the Earth*, 126–27, 140–43.

64. Wilson, *Sects and Society*, 55.

65. Hollenweger, *Pentecostalism*, 21–23, 185; Robinson, *Pentecostal Origins*, 114, 117, 119, 159–60, 265; Wacker, *Heaven Below*, 115; Goff, *Fields White Unto Harvest*, 57–58, 101–2, 131; Cartwright, *Great Evangelists*.

66. Oxonian, *Israel's Wanderings*, 4. Cited in Ben-Dor Benite, *Ten Lost Tribes*, 196.

67. Thus challenging the common notion that early pentecostals were basically apolitical. Richmann, "Prophecy and Politics."

68. Thomas, *Coming of Christ*, 20. In addition to challenging the imperialistic interpretation, this emphasis also nuances scholarship that sees American British-Israelism primarily as the seed for anti-Semitic political ideologies. Pierard, "Contribution of British-Israelism to Antisemitism," 45–68; Barkun, *Religion and the Racist Right*, 32–40.

Maine community and Bible school.[69] Charles Parham preached and published British-Israelism as integral to his full gospel message.[70] Parham was influenced by J. H. Allen, whose writings occasionally appeared in Parham's *Apostolic Faith* and who in 1927 became associate editor of the paper.[71] In the fluidity of early pentecostalism, leaders like W. H. Cossum could admit "definite sympathy" for Anglo-Israelism, without "speak[ing] dogmatically about it."[72]

John G. Lake, Bosworth's associate from the Zion days, also accepted British-Israel doctrine. The interconnected circles of British-Israelism and pentecostalism are evident in Lake's meeting with Henry Dallimore at a British-Israel conference in 1920 (probably in Vancouver). Lake persuaded Dallimore to enter pentecostal ministry, and Dallimore became a pioneer of pentecostalism in New Zealand, preaching British-Israelism until his death.[73] Around 1925, Lake began work with Philip E. J. Monson, preaching British-Israelism to a San Diego congregation.[74] Lake's younger coworker, Gordon Lindsay, also promoted British-Israelism. According to Lindsay, "the cycles [of Bible Chronology] . . . point unmistakably to the fact that the identity of Britain and the United States of America is to be found in Israel."[75] Lindsay later worked alongside Bosworth in William Branham's ministry. Later pentecostals also proclaimed British-Israelism. George Hawtin, the controversial leader of the Latter Rain movement originating in Saskatchewan in the late 1940s, preached a British-Israelism that evinced some of the anti-Semitism of the later movement. Eldon Purvis, an influential leader in the early charismatic movement, combined his British-Israelism with an independent charismatic ministry.[76]

Several leading British pentecostals were committed to British-Israelism. William Hutchinson, who founded the first pentecostal church

69. Murray, *Sublimity of Faith*, 163.

70. Parham, "Ten Lost Tribes," 10.

71. Parham, "Pleasurable Meeting," 11. See Allen, "What We Saw at Windsor Castle," 10–13; Allen, "What We Saw at Westminster Abbey," 7–10.

72. Cossum, "Mountain Peaks of Prophecy," 3. Anglo-Israelism is assumed but not expounded in Wilson, "Wonderful Signs," 4. A more forthright exposition of British-Israelism was presented in Kellogg, "United States in Prophecy," 3–4, 13–14.

73. Burpeau, *God's Showman*, 219, n. 42.

74. "Did You Know?," 3. For Monson, see Barkun, *Religion and the Racist Right*, 175.

75. Lindsay, "Wonders of Bible Chronology," 3–4, 7. Other articles in the series: Lindsay, "Thirteen Cycles of the United States," 4–5, 12; Lindsay, "Cycles of the 'Sign Woman,'" 9–12; Lindsay, "Cycles of Canada," 3–5, 15. These articles were an early version of Lindsay, *Blueprints of God*.

76. For Hawtin, see Richmann, "Prophecy and Politics." For Purvis, see Melton, *Melton's Encyclopedia of American Religions*, 609.

in Britain, was an ardent British-Israelist. His supporters believed that the pentecostal restoration of apostolic offices "is the sign that we are Israel."[77] Around 1920, the popular evangelist and founder of the Elim Pentecostal Church, George Jeffreys, was won over to British-Israelism. "God is restoring Israel as a servant-nation in the Celto-Anglo-Saxon peoples as the descendants of the ten-tribed Kingdom of Israel," wrote Jeffreys, "just as the Jews are the descendants of the Kingdom of Judah."[78] Jeffreys did not insist on adherence to British-Israelism, but he fought for its right to be considered.[79] His British-Israelism was a dominant factor in Jeffreys' split from the Elim church in 1940.[80] The rejection of British-Israelism reminded Jeffreys of pentecostalism's reception thirty years earlier.[81] American adherents, upon hearing of Elim's censure of the teaching, pleaded with Elim to recognize that "almost every outstanding teacher and deep student of the Bible whose heart has been yearning over souls has accepted and taught this message," including "Dr. F. F. Bosworth."[82] James McWhirter, a colleague of Jeffreys, was also a British-Israelist. His *Britain and Palestine in Prophecy* (1937) was part logbook of his Holy Land tour, part apology for British-Israelism. In the British Mandate for Palestine, McWhirter saw evidence for the return of a portion of British-Israel, which for British-Israelists was an eschatological necessity.[83] This eschatological concern for a "return" was, of course, shared by the Christian Zionism rooted in dispensationalism that was also blossoming at this time—although British-Israelists and dispensationalists fundamentally disagreed about *who* was to return.

The earliest pentecostal British-Israelists, like Parham, focused on the imperialistic implications of the message.[84] But the notion that identifying the tribes vindicated scripture—and that denying the identity of the tribes fueled atheism—was also common.[85] As J. H. Allen put it,

> The failure, hitherto, to identify the Gospel promise as belonging to that branch of the Abrahamic posterity which has the accompanying national characteristics, has been the cause of untold confusion, untold harm, untold skepticism, as well as

77. Cited in Hathaway, "Role of William Oliver Hutchinson," 48.
78. Cited in Edsor, *Set Your House in Order*, 127.
79. Jeffreys, "Israel Question," 301–5.
80. Hudson, "Schism and Its Aftermath," 180.
81. Edsor, *Set Your House in Order*, 126.
82. "Foursquare Leaders Deny Members," 2.
83. McWhirter, *Britain and Palestine in Prophecy*, 26.
84. Parham, "Ten Lost Tribes," 11.
85. Ben-Dor Benite, *Ten Lost Tribes*, 15, 19.

much loudly-told infidelity, both within the pale of Christian denominations and out of them.[86]

"Great violence has been done to the truth of God by those who have tried to spiritualize these prophecies," said Allen, describing the modernist understanding of prophecy, which sought to apply the Israelite promises to the church.[87] Allen would not have it: "Jesus died to confirm the promises made to the fathers, not to transfer them."[88] This was even a concern for the imperialist McWhirter.[89] The modernist-spiritualizing interpretation was not only spiritually unsatisfying, but, said Parham, it begged infidels to point out that "Your God has lied."[90]

As the modernist-fundamentalist controversies intensified, British-Israelist rhetoric focused more on the authority of the Bible. As one adherent put it, "Anglo-Israel truth proves the verbal inspiration of the Scriptures, and makes the Bible a new Book, fascinating and intelligible, revealing a coherent plan from Genesis to Revelation."[91] Texas British-Israelist J. F. Bradford asserted that "in identifying the once lost House of Israel, we are, incidentally, proving the consistent truth of Holy Scripture."[92] In a list of the functions of the message that appeared often in *Herald of Our Race*, the first line read: "Proves the inspiration of the Scriptures."[93] According to Charles Benham, "if we identify Israel as a *national entity* functioning today, the English-speaking nations being the Joseph nations, it becomes unnecessary to question the veracity of the Holy Bible." For Benham, identifying Israel meant that none could "doubt the efficacy of the atoning work of our Lord," as Christ's death provided forgiveness for the national sins of Israel, thereby allowing the Anglo-Saxons to become the world's chief evangelists.[94] Benham believed that the buttressed scriptural authority in the national message also had an eschatological function. Because "the prophecies of God regarding the past have been literally fulfilled," wrote Benham, "we can now look with assurance to the fulfillment of His promises for the future."[95] Like dispensationalists, British-Israelists argued that scripture was so integral to

86. Allen, *Judah's Sceptre and Joseph's Birthright*, 339–40.
87. Allen, *Judah's Sceptre and Joseph's Birthright*, 359.
88. Allen, *Judah's Sceptre and Joseph's Birthright*, 349.
89. McWhirter, *Britain and Palestine in Prophecy*, 70.
90. Parham, *Sermons of Charles F. Parham*, 92.
91. William F. Groom, "Introduction," in Bradford, *Are Anglo-Saxons Israelites?*, 8.
92. Bradford, *Are Anglo-Saxons Israelites?*, 13.
93. See, for example, *Herald of Our Race* 2.(January 1938) 2.
94. Benham, "Joseph Is Yet Alive," 285–86; emphasis in original.
95. Benham, "Joseph Is Yet Alive," 286.

the nature of God that the veracity of scripture implicated God's character. Hawtin was compelled to assert that "*God would not be God* if [the ten tribes] were not *at this very moment* fulfilling every detail of his covenant with them . . ."[96] Aside from historicism, British-Israelism differed from dispensationalism in yearning for a sacred narrative that put proponents in the center of the drama. "We are the people to whom the prophets addressed their message," said Benham.[97]

Pentecostals generally identified with fundamentalists against modernists. But as seen in the previous chapter, these believers also critiqued the fundamentalist defense of scripture, particularly the cessationism of Reformed theologies and dispensationalism. British-Israelism should be seen in the same light—an argument for scripture that rejected both modernism (spiritualism) and fundamentalism (futurism). British-Israelism supported eschatological urgency and an inerrant Bible. Although hermeneutically opposed to dispensationalism, British-Israelism fulfilled a similar role for those wishing to combat modernism.

Opposition to British-Israelism

As a novel approach to scripture, British-Israelism was bound to receive criticism. As an interpretation that appealed to religious conservatives, it was bound to receive its fiercest criticism from other religious conservatives who felt threatened by it.

In the era in which British-Israelism became entangled in the debates over scripture, dispensational fundamentalists were the first to attack British-Israelism in a sustained manner. Not surprisingly, many of the same figures who critiqued Bosworth's divine healing refuted British-Israelism as well. Arno Gaebelein found many scriptures that seemed to contradict the notion of a perpetual distinction between the house of Israel and the house of Judah. From his dispensationalist mindset, Gaebelein took for granted that "all the promises and blessings of Israel are always conditioned in their fulfilment on the Return of the Lord." For Gaebelein, British-Israelism was "worse than post-millennialism" because it confused the dispensations. Both British-Israelists and dispensationalists could affirm that when Jesus sent his disciples "to the lost sheep of the house of Israel" this meant literal descendants, rather than a spiritualized Israel represented by the church.

---

96. Hawtin, *Abrahamic Covenant*, 124. Cited in Richmann, "Prophecy and Politics"; emphasis in original. Benham, "Joseph Is Yet Alive," 288.

97. Benham, "Joseph Is Yet Alive," 288.

But for Gaebelein, this people would only become visible in the coming age, "not the present dispensation as erroneously taught" by British-Israelists.[98]

Gaebelein later accused British-Israelists of "mutilat[ing] God's word," since the only proper method of handling prophecies was to "distinguish between the dispensations." "These are the times of the Gentiles," wrote Gaebelein, "during which Israel cannot be blessed. Israel's blessing cannot begin until the expiration of the seventy weeks of Daniel, the last of which is still future." Despite these efforts, Gaebelein was disappointed to discover that some *Our Hope* readers were British-Israelists.[99] In 1938, Gaebelein published an attack from Anton Darms, an overseer in Dowie's Christian Catholic Church who had previously held the teaching. Like Gaebelein, Darms believed that British-Israelists "lacked the proper understanding of Dispensational truth."[100] Darms blamed modernism for the doctrine's appeal. "In repudiating this wrong allegorical teaching of the Church, British-Israelism declares that Great Britain, not the Church constitutes the Israel entitled to the special favor and blessing of God."[101]

Pentecostals occasionally critiqued British-Israelism. Perhaps because of the strength of British-Israelism in Chicago, those associated with the Stone Church were the first to denounce the teaching. Pastor Philip Wittich off-handedly refuted British-Israelism as "unscriptural and unhistorical" in a sermon in 1926.[102] Around the same time, a brief note in the *Bible Standard* asserted that the teaching had no scriptural support.[103] From mid-1930, the *Latter Rain Evangel* advertised Leonard Sale-Harrison's booklet critique.[104] In 1934, the same paper published a critique of British-Israelism, focusing particularly on the frequent partial biblical citations British-Israelists employed. The writer was "saddened that evangelical, seemingly fundamental teachers" could contend for the false doctrine.[105] The *Latter Rain Evangel* also published a 1936 address Daniel Finestone gave to the Hebrew Christian Conference attacking British-Israelism. Finestone argued that the teaching robbed Jews of their chosen status and their future glory, robbed

---

98. Gaebelein, "British-Israel Invention," 463–68. Quotes on pp. 465, 466. See also Gaebelein, "Anglo-Israel Delusion," 478.

99. Gaebelein, "Anglo-Israelism Once More," 421, 422.

100. Darms, "Fallacy of the British-Israel Delusion," 321. Cf. Darms, *Delusion of British-Israelism*.

101. Darms, "Fallacy of the British-Israel Delusion," 322.

102. Wittich, "Answering the Objections in the Book of Jonah," 6. For another incidental critique, see Klink, "Jew," 8.

103. "Anglo-Israel Movement," 7–8.

104. *Latter Rain Evangel* (August 1930) 24.

105. Thomsen, "Anglo-Israelism," 3.

Christ of his royal prerogative, and robbed the church of its mission and its gospel.[106]

The Assemblies of God was a little later in taking British-Israelism seriously.[107] A brief note in 1936 called the theory "utterly unfounded."[108] A few years later, general superintendent Ernest S. Williams averred that the teaching "provoke[s] racial and national pride and egotism." Without elaborating, Williams said that "the teaching also throws out of balance the correct understanding of prophecy."[109] In 1940, the Assemblies of God's Gospel Publishing House sold Darms's *The Delusion of British-Israelism*, bemoaning that the teaching was "now claiming a number of good people as its dupes."[110] In 1943, the *Pentecostal Evangel*, citing British pentecostal Donald Gee, refused to deal theologically or exegetically with British-Israelism. Instead, the paper encouraged believers to consider such theories "refuse" compared to knowing Christ.[111] The paper also published Australian evangelist Frank Varley's terse critique in 1944.[112]

The Christian and Missionary Alliance also attacked British-Israelism. In 1924, the *Alliance Weekly* summarized for its readers the critique of British fundamentalist D. M. Panton. According to Panton, British-Israelism was "historically impossible," "directly contradicts explicit Scriptures," was an "unconscious betrayal of the Gospel," and a "grave menace to the Jew," as well as "an abandonment of Grace for Law." Besides "[lend]ing itself to the wildest extravagancies," the theory, according to Panton, violated "dispensational truth."[113] Frustrated that the theory had not dissipated, the Alliance ran a full article from Panton in 1933. Panton bemoaned that British-Israelism "numbers some honored evangelical names among its adherents."[114] Oswald Smith, a former associate of Bosworth, wrote against the teaching

---

106. Finestone, "Anglo-Israelism," 13–15.

107. In late 1917, the Assemblies of God organ took notice of Anglo-Israelism, promising to deal with the teaching. No article on the teaching appeared, and no indication was given if a pro or con stance would be taken. *Weekly Evangel* no. 217 (December 1, 1917) 5.

108. "Lost Tribes," 10.

109. *Pentecostal Evangel* no. 1316 (July 29, 1939) 11.

110. "British-Israel Delusion," 7. From the early 1940s, the Assemblies of God also promoted the refutation of British-Israelism written by George L. Rose. *Pentecostal Evangel* no. 1484 (October 17, 1942) 13; *Pentecostal Evangel* no. 1742 (September 27, 1947) 16.

111. "Anglo-Israel Theory," 10.

112. Varley, "Is Britain Israel?," 3.

113. "British Israelism or Anglo Israelism," 315.

114. Panton, "Anglo-Israelism," 500.

in 1936. Smith condemned the teaching for its association with eccentrics like Richard Brothers and its reliance upon pyramidology.[115] Smith's attack struck Luke Rader as odd, since Smith was so indebted to Bosworth's work.[116] Another British-Israelist, Curtis Ewing, apparently thought Bosworth's adherence to the teaching was enough to refute Smith's attack.[117]

In 1934—the same year as the earliest evidence of Bosworth's acceptance of the teaching—respected Alliance missionary John A. MacMillan wrote against British-Israelism. Concerned that the doctrine "of late has been gaining adherents rapidly," MacMillan had no patience for what he identified as a "doctrine of demons" that was "not in any sense Christian." MacMillan saw the menace of British-Israelism to be its truth mixed with error. In describing British-Israelism as "a purely national movement," MacMillan missed the doctrine's scriptural appeal. MacMillan also took issue with some modernists' conflation of fundamentalism and British-Israelism.[118] MacMillan dismantled every pillar of British-Israelism, scriptural, historical and philological.[119] In 1937, the Alliance published Canadian fundamentalist W. F. Roadhouse's refutation of the "now widely-stressed Anglo- or British-Israelism." Disdained by secular scholarship, British-Israelism "stands condemned before the world" and leads to "absurd incredibilities" in biblical interpretation, said Roadhouse.[120]

As united as many full gospel advocates were in their opposition of British-Israelism, they were not agreed on its errors or on how to refute it. One pentecostal could dismiss the teaching with a simple circular argument: "if we knew where they were, they would not be the *lost* tribes!"[121] Another pentecostal critic, however, insisted that "the ten tribes of Israel are not lost, and never have been. The God of Abraham knows where they are, and when his time comes for dealing again with Israel as a nation, they will be forthcoming in fulfilment of his purposes of grace toward them."[122] Some, like Gaebelein, maintained dispensationalist futurism as a sure defense, while others fought the British-Israelists on their own historicist turf. MacMillan

---

115. Smith, "British Israelism," 21. Quote from Smith, *Who Are the False Prophets?*, 35–36. See Darms, *Delusion of British-Israelism*, 223.

116. Rader, "Is British-Israelism a Dangerous Fallacy?" Whatever the personal issues involved, Bosworth was either unphased by Smith's criticism or uniformed, for Bosworth visited Smith's evangelistic services in Jamaica in 1948. "Plane Passengers," 21.

117. Ewing, *Anglo-Israel Belief*, 2, 5.

118. MacMillan, "British-Israelism," (September 1, 1934) 548.

119. MacMillan, "British-Israelism," (September 15, 1934) 580.

120. Roadhouse, "Anglo-Israelism," (September 4, 1937) 563, 564.

121. "Lost Tribes," 10; emphasis in original.

122. Varley, "Is Britain Israel?," 3.

insisted that scripture foretold the overturning of the Semitic people in favor of Gentiles.[123] While some wanted to refute British-Israel claims point-by-point, for others it was enough to critique their haphazard method of proof-texting as "a medley of unconnected passages."[124] Roadhouse and Smith appealed to scholarly historical consensus, thus leaving themselves open to the charge from British-Israelists that they placed human wisdom above God's word.[125]

More than any specific historical or exegetical issue, the materialism of British-Israelism scandalized its critics. "British-Israelism is dangerous," said Oswald Smith, "because it places the emphasis on national instead of individual salvation."[126] Daniel Finestone voiced the concern of many, that, if taken to "its logical conclusion," British-Israelism "is really a gospel of *race* and *place* which has been substituted for a Gospel of grace."[127] In the charged atmosphere of World War II-era nationalism, this was a potentially devastating moral indictment.[128] God's plan, said critics, was "not the going far afield into a purely Gentile race for the perpetuator of David's 'house,' but the lifting it out of the earthly 'seed' into the heavenly."[129] Gaebelein asserted that "the greatest blessing God bestows is the blessing of the new birth, to which the earthly blessings of Israel are only sequel. *This is completely lost sight of by Anglo-Israelism.*"[130] Despite British-Israelist protests to the contrary, opponents felt that British-Israelism "would make identification with Britain or America the only requisite for final salvation."[131] As MacMillan put it, British Israelism's "tendency is placed upon the earthly, whereas the New Testament lays it upon the heavenly . . . [The Christian's] blessed hope is not to be established in this world, but to be caught away out of it."[132] Therefore, the theory "could have no spiritual value for the Christian. The deeper blessings of this age are not for a fleshly Israel, but belong to those redeemed ones."[133] Opponents believed that British-Israelists would inevita-

123. MacMillan, "British-Israelism," (September 22, 1934) 596. See also, Varley, "Is Britain Israel?," 3; Roadhouse, "Anglo-Israelism," (September 4, 1937) 564.

124. Darms, "Fallacy of the British-Israel Delusion," 323.

125. Rader, "Is British-Israelism a Dangerous Fallacy?"

126. Smith, *Who Are the False Prophets?*, 42.

127. Finestone, "Anglo-Israelism," 15; emphasis in original.

128. A 1939 editorial compared British-Israelism with pan-Germanism, for "each proclaims a superior and exclusive nationality as its basis." "Migration Register," 3.

129. Roadhouse, "Anglo-Israelism," (September 11, 1937) 581.

130. Gaebelein, "Anglo-Israel Delusion," 478; emphasis in original.

131. MacLennan, "Anglo-Israelism," 114.

132. MacMillan, "British-Israelism," (September 29, 1934) 612–13.

133. MacMillan, "British-Israelism," (September 1, 1934) 548.

bly lose their simple message of salvation—a critique similar to that leveled against faith healers.[134]

In discussing Charles Parham's legacy, historian Walter Hollenweger says that British-Israelism "has been contradicted by Pentecostalism."[135] Whether this is a historical-descriptive or a theological-normative claim is not clear. In either case, such a position cannot be maintained. Although most pentecostals did not identify with British-Israelism—and a few attacked it—enough pentecostals embraced the teaching to challenge Hollenweger's claim. More important is the nature of the pentecostals' critique of British-Israelism. Never did the opponents call to their support any of the distinctive or favored pentecostal teachings or practices. In other words, those who rejected it did so for reasons other than their pentecostal identity. The pentecostal critique was in no way distinguished from that of other full gospelers or fundamentalists. The rejection of British-Israelism in pentecostal and Alliance circles mirrors the larger trend of fundamentalization in these denominations in the late 1930s and 1940s.

Critics derided British-Israelism as a hopelessly convoluted system of scriptural interpretation, championing themselves as defenders of "the simplicity of Christ."[136] But dispensationalism—the prophetic system favored among British-Israel critics, including pentecostals—had no more claim as a "common-sense" approach to scripture than British-Israelism.[137] And as pentecostal theologians have been recognizing for decades, dispensationalism is in many ways incompatible with the pentecostal worldview.[138] Dispensationalism, however, had the advantage of being a non-refutable hypothesis. One could accept the hermeneutics of dispensationalism or not, but one could not prove or disprove its material claims, because (in terms of the present age) it made none. Critics could attack British-Israelism on historical and philological grounds without fear of reprisal. As valid as historical and philological arguments might be, they were dispensable in light of the larger objection that British-Israelism substituted material for spiritual blessings. That pentecostals and full gospel believers should join with fundamentalists to reprove the teaching for its emphasis on physical blessings is perhaps the greater contradiction.

---

134. MacMillan, "British-Israelism," (September 29, 1934) 612.
135. Hollenweger, *Pentecostalism*, 23.
136. MacMillan, "British-Israelism," (September 1, 1934) 548.
137. Weber, "Two-Edged Sword," 113–17.
138. Sheppard, "Pentecostals and the Hermeneutics of Dispensationalism," 5–33; Althouse, *Spirit of the Last Days*; Thompson, *Kingdom Come*.

Bosworth's British-Israelism, like his stance on tongues, is not sufficient to cast him outside the bounds of pentecostalism, for pentecostalism presented no inherent contradiction of British-Israelism. Scholars are on safer ground recognizing, with Donald Dayton, that pentecostalism's "eschatological motif . . . could coalesce with, or perhaps better, express itself through a variety of distinct eschatological schemes from dispensationalism through British-Israelism that circulated in the fluid, popular Evangelical culture."[139] Both dispensationalism and British-Israelism were honest attempts to deal with Paul's question in Romans 9–11: how will God be faithful to the promises he has made to Israel? Both rejected the spiritualized solution of the modernists. Dispensationalism postponed prophetic fulfillment to another age; British-Israelism claimed that the prophecies had been fulfilled in Anglo-Israel history. Although British-Israelism had its scientific weaknesses, its exegetical merit was comparable to that of dispensationalism. Using the same literalist proof-texting methodology, the two systems simply chose different texts as proofs. Both systems also functioned the same way as a defense against modernism, championing biblical authority and the imminent premillennial return of Christ.

WINDING DOWN? 1940–1947

Bosworth apparently cut ties with the Anglo-Saxon Federation in late 1940. Records do not place him at their conferences, and he no longer advertised or published articles in its journal. Around 1942, Bosworth moved to Philadelphia, perhaps to be closer to his brother, who was working as a regional evangelist for the Alliance. Bosworth continued his radio show for at least another year in Philadelphia, claiming at the end of fourteen years of radio ministry to have received 250,000 letters.[140] He also preached occasionally at local Alliance churches, calling into question the claim that Bosworth was ostracized from the denomination until he allegedly recanted British-Israelism in 1944.[141] Bosworth may have considered himself partially retired by the mid-1940s: he told his wife around this time that he suspected he was "through" with full-time ministry. But he was not done working; he soon received a revelation that "the Lord is my strength," and in April of 1947, Bosworth opened a two-week campaign at an Alliance Tabernacle in Williamsport, Pennsylvania, where parishioners said they were amazed at the "pep" in Bosworth's preaching. The publicity of this campaign also

139. Dayton, *Theological Roots of Pentecostalism*, 145.
140. Bosworth, "Gifts of Healing Plus," B-C; *Harrisburg Telegraph*, January 23, 1943, 2; *Exploits of Faith* 15.3 (March 1942).
141. "Alliance Group to Hear Rev. Bosworth," 10; "Christian Alliance," 12.

suggests that rather than settling into retirement, Bosworth was itching for a fuller return to public ministry.[142]

CONCLUSION

Although Bosworth's ministry slowed, he was not necessarily looking toward retirement in the 1930s and 1940s. He continued to preach, write, and travel. He reevaluated his approach to biblical prophecy—not a small concern for a conservative evangelical. In embracing British-Israelism, Bosworth continued his non-fundamentalist critique of modernism that was so prominent in his divine healing message. Although the teaching was criticized by many conservative Christians in the 1920s and 1930s, British-Israelism was refined by the same concerns for biblical authority and Christ's return that drew so many to dispensationalism. That British-Israelism failed to win a majority of pentecostals reflects its scientific vulnerability and the social forces of fundamentalism, not its exegetical strength or theological integrity.

In their critique of British-Israelism's focus on the material, J. A. MacMillan and Oswald Smith claimed that its adherents would surely weaken in their conviction for spiritual truths and evangelism. But as Luke Rader pointed out, Bosworth's ministry proved otherwise, as he continued to stress evangelism, divine healing, the new birth, and Christian obedience alongside British-Israelism.[143] Furthermore, the next phase of Bosworth's ministry would take him to the greatest heights of his career in promotion of the spiritual truths of the gospel of the supernatural.

---

142. Bosworth, "Be Ye Doers of the Word"; "To Open Campaign," 2. See also advertisements in *Altoona Mirror*, April 19, 1947, 4; and *Williamsport Gazette and Bulletin*, May 3, 1947, 7.

143. MacMillan, "British-Israelism," (September 29, 1934) 612; Smith, "British Israelism," 19, 21; Rader, "Is British-Israelism a Dangerous Fallacy?"

7

The Voice of Healing Years, 1948–1958

> Believe it or not, despite the trend of materialistic thinking that has engulfed the intelligentsia and the schools of learning of our day, there does and always will exist a longing for the manifestation of the power of the supernatural.
>
> —GORDON LINDSAY (1950)[1]

IN LATE 1947, F. F. Bosworth's best years in ministry seemed to be behind him. But as Bosworth entered his seventh decade, pentecostalism entered a period of creativity unseen since its first decade. This transition was driven by social factors, like the passing of most first-generation pentecostals and the postwar economic boom. Independent pentecostalism expressed this creative drive in a divine healing revival that brought Bosworth—through his relationship with William Branham—back into the main current of American pentecostalism.

The postwar healing revival was in many ways a continuation of earlier pentecostal healing ministries, like that of Raymond Richey, Aimee Semple McPherson, Charles Price, and of course, Bosworth himself. What was new in the late 1940s was the cultural support for the healing ministry. The healing evangelists of the late 1940s and 1950s had unprecedented success in conversions, miracles, and income. Hundreds of evangelists hit the trail

---

1. Lindsay, *William Branham*, 20.

from about 1948 to 1958, and they bore the same gospel of the supernatural that Bosworth had cherished since his healing in Fitzgerald, Georgia, in the late 1890s. In the process, they laid the foundation for important developments in twentieth-century Christianity: the charismatic revival, the Word of Faith movement, and signs and wonders evangelism.

A FRESH ANOINTING FROM THE LORD, 1948–1951

Shortly after his meetings in Williamsport, Pennsylvania, in 1947, Bosworth moved to Miami, Florida. There, in January of 1948, Bosworth heard the testimony of two blind boys who had been healed at the local meetings of William Marrion Branham (1909–1965), a Baptist-turned-pentecostal evangelist from Indiana. Although skeptical of Branham's grandiose claims of spiritual giftedness, Bosworth attended a meeting. Bosworth watched as a girl walked the prayer line repeatedly without being healed. Determining that the girl did not have sufficient faith for healing, Branham invited her onstage and told her to grasp his coat and pray until she had enough faith. When Branham discerned that her faith was sufficient, he declared her healed and demanded her braces removed, revealing that her legs were now "perfectly normal."[2] This scene, among others, convinced Bosworth, who reportedly exclaimed: "That's what I've looked for! . . . I've watched the Scriptures for that."[3] The two evangelists began a friendship that would span the final decade of Bosworth's life. Their meeting was propitious for both men; Branham revived the aged Bosworth's career, and Bosworth taught and counseled the enigmatic Branham.

William Branham: The Healer-Prophet

On May 7, 1946, an angel commissioned William Branham "to take the gift of divine healing to the peoples of the world."[4] This was not the first time Branham had entertained a "supernatural visitor." When Branham was seven, an angel had commanded him never to drink or smoke, causing the peculiar boy to live the life of a modern Nazirite. Branham had grown up in poverty and obscurity, miraculously escaping death on more than one occasion, and his ministerial life continued the trend of despair balanced with divine assurance.[5] His first pastorate was at a Baptist church with pentecostal

2. Branham, "Diseases and Afflictions."
3. Branham, "Mary's Belief."
4. Lindsay, "Story of the Great Restoration Revival, Part I," 5.
5. Lindsay, *William Branham*, 27–35. Like Bosworth, Branham frequently told the story of his life during his campaigns. See Lindsay, *William Branham*, 132.

leanings, but he was also exposed more directly to pentecostalism when he attended a Oneness conference in 1936.[6]

By the early 1940s, Branham was working as a small-time healing evangelist. A Oneness minister in St. Louis asked Branham to pray for his sick daughter. The healing of Betty Daugherty was pivotal for Branham's career, as Branham returned to St. Louis for a successful campaign and began receiving invitations to minister in Arkansas. After this success, the 1946 visitation became the center of Branham's personal narrative. In many ways, it fulfilled the same function as Bosworth's "revelation" of the universality of divine healing in 1920: both events provided a biographical and theological justification for a successful healing ministry, and both occurred shortly after the end of a world war and on the eve of a major revival of divine healing.[7]

Some of the participants in Branham's Arkansas meetings brought word of what they had witnessed to their pastor, Jack Moore, in Louisiana. Moore, also a Oneness pentecostal, assisted Branham in meetings in Texas, Arizona, and California. In the spring of 1947, Moore wrote of Branham to his friend Gordon Lindsay. Lindsay was an independently-minded and well-connected pentecostal whose family had ties in Dowie's Zion City. Lindsay remarked that Branham's meetings were "different from any we had ever been in before."[8] Moore and Branham thought Lindsay could help Branham's ministry grow, since Lindsay's "associations have been in the larger Full Gospel circles."[9] Branham's work with Lindsay began in the Pacific Northwest in the fall of 1947. Under Lindsay's guidance, Branham's work was conducted on an "inter-evangelical basis," reaching beyond the confines of Oneness pentecostal groups and influencing countless pentecostal leaders.[10]

---

6. Weaver, *Healer-Prophet*, 32–33; Lindsay, *William Branham*, 46–50.

7. For conflicting stories of Branham's angelic visitations, see Duyzer, *Heterodox Tsunami*, 53, 540. Cf. William Branham, "I Was Not Disobedient Unto the Heavenly Vision."

8. Lindsay, "Story of the Great Restoration Revival, Part I," 5.

9. Lindsay, "Story of the Great Restoration Revival, Part I," 22.

10. Lindsay, *William Branham*, 127–28.

Bosworth, Branham, and the Early Voice of Healing Network

When Branham met Bosworth in Miami, "it was 'love at first sight.'"[11] Later witnesses delighted in the "harmony" between the evangelists.[12] For the rest of his life, Branham spoke of "Daddy Bosworth" in loving and respectful terms. To Branham, Bosworth was "my old saintly dad" and "one of the greatest teachers on Divine healing that I ever heard in my life." Branham likened their friendship to Jonathan and David or Elijah and Elisha.[13] According to Lindsay, Bosworth received in Branham's meetings "a fresh anointing from the Lord, and a renewed vision," and "nearly ten years of added ministry after his supposed time of labor was over."[14]

Bosworth preached at least once in Branham's Miami meeting and soon began traveling with the younger evangelist.[15] Over the next few months, Bosworth accompanied Branham in meetings in Phoenix, Florida, Missouri, Illinois, Washington, and Oregon. In these meetings, Bosworth led the daily teaching sessions, while Branham handled the more intense evening healing services.[16] Healings also continued to occur as a direct result of Bosworth's work.[17] Since Branham, in the early years of the revival, viewed his role as primarily praying for the sick, rather than preaching, Bosworth's preaching and teaching skills were a welcome complement to the ministry. Along with Ern Baxter, Bosworth was part of the "dynamic revival trio," that helped take "Branham to the pinnacle of success" in the early postwar healing movement.[18] Seasoned pentecostals like Stanley Frodsham determined that a general revival was brewing in Branham's ministry.[19] Historians have agreed that in the postwar divine healing movement, Branham was the "initiator," "visionary," and "pacesetter."[20]

---

11. Lindsay, *William Branham*, 110.

12. Freligh, "Pastor Reports Continuation of Revival," 1.

13. Branham, "Queen of Sheba"; Branham, "Africa Trip Report"; Branham, "Our Hope Is in God"; Branham, "Jehovah-Jireh," (June 12, 1957).

14. Lindsay, "Story of the Great Restoration Revival, Part II," 18.

15. "Conversations with F. F. Bosworth," 4.

16. "Elgin, Ill., Unable to Accommodate Crowds," 1. See also Weaver, *Healer-Prophet*, 68.

17. "Woman Completely Healed," 12; "Elgin, Ill., Unable to Accommodate Crowds," 2; "Minister Is Healed as Brother Bosworth Prays," 10.

18. Weaver, *Healer-Prophet*, 52.

19. Frodsham, "Remarkable Healing Campaigns," 5.

20. Harrell, *All Things Are Possible*, 25, 165; Weaver, *Healer-Prophet*, ix.

As Branham's ministry grew, publicity became more important.[21] In April of 1948, Lindsay began publishing *Voice of Healing*, and from the beginning, Bosworth was heavily involved in the work. The magazine styled itself an "Inter-evangelical publication of the Branham healing campaigns," signifying both the modesty and ambition of the early Voice of Healing machine: to promote only Branham, but also reaching across denominational boundaries. To the dismay of many, Branham announced in May of 1948—just as the first issue of *Voice of Healing* was reaching subscribers—that he would have to cease his ministry due to nervous exhaustion. Branham's health had been a concern since the previous fall, and in early 1948, a rumor even began circulating that the evangelist had died.[22] Suffering from bouts of "nervous attack" at least since April, Branham explained that his leave "might be a year or it might be forever."[23] Branham's announcement caused a brief crisis for *Voice of Healing*. Luckily, several other ministries—mostly inspired by Branham—had emerged. The magazine quickly enlarged its scope to "the latter-day sign-gift ministries" of a growing number of healing evangelists, such as William Freeman, Richard Vineyard, and Velmer Gardner. Branham's health problems did not interrupt the success of the paper that had been created for him: according to Lindsay, within a year of the paper's inception, it had 100,000 readers, and double that figure within two years.[24]

While Branham continued his indefinite leave, Bosworth engaged in a reinvigorated ministry, becoming an "associate editor" for *Voice of Healing*.[25] By July, he had produced a revised and enlarged seventh edition of *Christ the Healer*, which was advertised in *Voice of Healing* as a "classic."[26] In October, Bosworth conducted his own meetings in Seattle.[27]

Branham's leave of absence would not last forever or a year. In July, Branham briefly joined Bosworth on a lakeside vacation and received spiritual nourishment from the elder evangelist. His five-day visit with Bosworth was, according to their colleague John Sharritt, a turning point on Branham's road to wellness. Emboldened by Bosworth's counsel, Branham "placed his

21. Weaver, *Healer-Prophet*, 47.
22. Lindsay, *William Branham*, 126, 129–30.
23. Lindsay, "Story of the Great Restoration Revival, Part II," 18.
24. Lindsay, *William Branham*, 147.
25. "Latest News of Rev. Branham," 5. Although "associate editor" was something of an honorific title that was later extended to dozens of evangelists, Bosworth was one of just a handful of those labeled as such in the first few years.
26. *Voice of Healing* 1.10 (January 1949) 6; "Bosworth Book Off Press," 6. *Christ the Healer* was chosen as "book of the month" in *Voice of Healing* 4.6 (September 1951) 18.
27. *Voice of Healing* 1.7 (October 1948) 6.

feet firmly on the Word of God and the promises of God" and began to eat regularly, thanks in part to Mrs. Bosworth's cooking.[28] Around this time, Branham also asserted that his faith was encouraged by reading Bosworth's tract on "Christian Confession."[29]

In August, Branham told Lindsay that "a miracle was wrought," although he was not yet to his full strength or weight.[30] True to style, Branham's return to full ministry was aided by an angelic visitation, this time giving him a mandate to preach overseas. Branham reentered the itinerant ministry in late October with meetings in Fresno, California, after which he joined Bosworth in Seattle.[31] With Branham's health restored, he and Bosworth continued working together. In early February of 1949, Bosworth joined Branham's campaign in Miami.[32] The next month, the two ministered in Zion, Illinois. Bosworth spent a few days before Branham joined the meetings teaching Zionites and undoubtedly renewing old acquaintances.[33] While in Zion, the two evangelists visited the grave of John A. Dowie, to whose pioneering ministry both owed a great debt.[34] Bosworth often prayed with the sick after Branham grew exhausted.[35]

Although Bosworth's ministry was closely tied to Branham, Bosworth continued to nourish contacts throughout full gospel circles. In January of 1949, Bosworth lent his approval to Oral Roberts, who began his own successful healing ministry shortly after Branham. Roberts was conducting meetings in Miami, where he welcomed Bosworth to the platform. Bosworth gave Roberts a glowing endorsement, and Roberts returned the favor, rehearsing Bosworth's fabled ministry successes. Most important for Roberts was the fact that Bosworth "said that he was thrilled beyond words to see the marvelous healing and discernment gift in my humble life."[36] Around this time, Bosworth's work with Branham came to the attention of

28. "Latest News of Rev. Branham," 5.

29. Lindsay, *William Branham*, 206.

30. "Word from Bro. Branham," 1. For Branham's activities during his leave and his return to health, see "Editorial," 6; "God Performs Operation," 12; Branham, "Life Story of Rev. Wm. Branham," 1, 13.

31. "Flash!" 1; "Brother Branham on the Field Again," 1; "Fresno, California, and Seattle, Washington," 2; Freligh, "Pastor Reports Continuation of Revival," 1, 5.

32. Sam Perry, brother of Mattie Perry, who had healed Bosworth of tuberculosis about fifty years earlier, reported on the meetings. "Branham-Bosworth Reunite," 1.

33. "Special Notice to Illinois Subscribers," 16; Nelson, "Dowie's Followers Relive Glorious Days," 1, 16.

34. "Branham-Bosworth Campaign Successful," 2.

35. Nelson, "Dowie's Followers Relive Glorious Days," 1.

36. Bosworth, "F. F. Bosworth Rejoices," 4.

Bosworth's old coworker Charles Benham, who gloried in the "supernatural revival of miracle power" evident in the Branham-Bosworth meetings."[37] Benham visited the Zion meetings and even relived old times with Bosworth by leading the congregation in song on his cornet.[38] In May of 1949, Bosworth teamed up with Benham and T. L. Osborn for work in Flint and Detroit, Michigan.

Osborn, inspired by Branham, started his deliverance ministry in 1947. The following year, Bosworth told the young evangelist that "the only way to whip the devil is to move into town and stay until he gives up and leaves." Osborn followed Bosworth's advice to great results in a Jamaica campaign in late 1948 and early 1949. Hearing of Osborn's success in Jamaica, Bosworth invited Osborn to fill Branham's spot in the remaining days of their Flint meetings, bringing Osborn into the *Voice of Healing* orbit.[39] According to Branham, Bosworth counseled Osborn when Osborn was struggling with his vocation. At Branham's cabin in Jeffersonville, Indiana, Bosworth counseled Osborn in "all the techniques of how to use the Scriptures," ensuring that Bosworth's didactic and homiletic approach to divine healing would have a strong advocate in the second half of the century.[40] As Branham put it, "Brother Osborn is a young Brother Bosworth."[41] Like Bosworth, Osborn claimed no healing gift, but considered himself a proclaimer of divine healing truths.

Bosworth also took part in the first convention of the *Voice of Healing* revivalists, held in Dallas in late 1949. Here Bosworth, the "respected, seasoned warrior," recalled his own ministry struggles and victory in Dallas over thirty years earlier.[42]

---

37. Benham, "God Answers the Present World Crisis," 4. S. A. Ackley, another British-Israelist who knew Bosworth personally, endorsed the "Bosworth-Branham campaigns." See *Voice of Healing* 1.6 (September 1948) 6.

38. "Dr. Charles O. Benham," 9.

39. Osborn and Osborn, *Faith Library*, 1:93, 120–21; "North Michigan Rocked by Mighty Revival," 1, 15; Harrell, *All Things Are Possible*, 64; Lindsay, *William Branham*, 25–26.

40. Branham, "Early Spiritual Experiences." See also Branham, "Palmerworm, Locust, Cankerworm and Caterpillar." Osborn, "God in Flesh Again"; Branham, "Basis of Fellowship"; Branham, "Expectations and What Love Is."

41. Branham, "Wedding Supper."

42. Moore, "Historic Conference of Evangelists," 1–3. See also Branham, "Deity of Jesus Christ."

Houston, 1950: A Harangue and a Halo

In January of 1950, Branham, Bosworth, Lindsay and Jack Moore teamed up for a memorable series of meetings in Houston. They eventually drew five thousand nightly and the ire of a local Baptist minister, W. E. Best. Best challenged the authenticity of Branham's ministry and divine healing in general, requesting a public debate. Bosworth urged Branham to answer the challenge for the sake of the believing public. Branham declined, saying that "God never sent me to debate. He sent me to pray for the sick, and that's what my duty is. I do not argue religion with anyone. It isn't supposed to be argued—it's supposed to be lived." Branham suggested that debates only cause confusion. But behind the principled posturing was Branham's insecurity: "I can't go down there and debate, for if I do, it throws me all off."[43] Branham consented, however, for Bosworth to take up the challenge.

Bosworth and Best debated before an audience of eight thousand on January 24. This was not the most dignified occasion: the opponents often talked at the same time, at least two members of the audience came to blows, and tempers flared to the point that Raymond Richey dramatically removed his seat from the platform to distance himself from Best.[44] Best, who apparently had the backing of the Houston Baptist Pastors Conference, denied that Christ bore physical infirmities on the cross and that anyone today had the gift or power of healing as in apostolic times. For all his defense of divine healing in the past, this was probably the first time Bosworth had debated before an audience.[45] Although Bosworth quoted his usual scriptures, made his familiar appeal to the "redemptive names" of God, and argued that Christ "bore our sicknesses" on the cross, his more dramatic (and effective) tactic was to call upon audience members who had been healed to stand when Best asserted that the day of miracles was past. In this way, reported one writer for the *Houston Press*, the "suave" Bosworth "used the audience itself to prove that miracles of healing are accomplished every day."[46] According to *Voice of Healing*, Best found that "few were in sympathy with his cold denial of the promises of God."[47]

Although Bosworth ably defended the supernatural gospel, supporters claimed the challenge to Branham's ministry "was answered by God

---

43. Branham, *William Branham Sermons*, 25. See also Branham, "At Thy Word."
44. "News Clip: Houston Press, 1950," 1, 3–5.
45. Branham, "Testimony."
46. "News Clip: Houston Press, 1950," 3. See also "Houston Newspaper Accounts," 4.
47. "God Vindicates Branham," 1.

himself."⁴⁸ Best had hired two photographers to capture his performance. After developing the film of numerous shots of Best and one of Branham, the photographers were amazed at the results. In Branham's picture, a blurry, glowing specter hovered a few inches above Branham's head. For supporters, the sight could only be described as a halo. And not only was Branham's photo supernaturally adorned, but all of the shots of Best turned out blank. The metaphor was not subtle: those who opposed the supernatural gospel were as nothing, while ministers of the miraculous were assured of God's powerful presence, what Branham here called a "sacred sign."⁴⁹ This was not the first—or last—time a photograph captured a supernatural attendant of Branham's ministry, but the publicity and charged setting made this "the most famous relic in the history of the revival."⁵⁰ Because supporters felt that their supernatural gospel was on trial, they touted this vindication. Bosworth, in arranging and performing in the debate, played a central role in the production of this relic.

AT HOME AND ABROAD, 1951-1955

Like most dramatic events in Branham's life, his "call" to South Africa was an intricate and miraculous series of events. And again, Bosworth played a key role. According to Branham, on the same night during which the famous halo photograph was taken, Bosworth showed Branham a picture of a woman from Durban named Florence Nightingale Shirlaw (perhaps a distant relative of the famous English nurse). Shirlaw was suffering from stomach cancer and reportedly weighed sixty pounds. Branham, with Bosworth's urging, determined that if God healed Shirlaw, he would take that as a sign that he was to minister in South Africa. As providence would have it, while Branham was in England on his way to Scandinavia shortly after the Houston meetings, he met Shirlaw and prayed for her. Eight months later, she wrote to Branham, testifying to healing and enclosing a picture showing her at a healthy 155 pounds.⁵¹

48. "God Vindicates Branham," 1.

49. Branham, "God Revealing Himself to His People." See also Branham, "Early Spiritual Experiences."

50. For other supernatural photos, see Bosworth, "Gifts of Healing Plus," C; Lindsay, *William Branham*, 43, 71. Quote from Harrell, *All Things Are Possible*, 35.

51. For Branham's story of his call to South Africa, see Branham, "How God Called Me to Africa, Part I," 5, 8; Stadsklev, *William Branham*, 48–50. See also Branham, "Who Hath Believed Our Report?" Some of these details were refuted by Gwilam I. Francis, a minister who was present at the time Branham prayed for Shirlaw, in "Vindication of William Branham," 8. According to Peter Duyzer, *Legend of the Fall*, Branham's first mention of Shirlaw was Branham, "Works That I Do Bear Witness of Me." The first

Making good on the vow, Bosworth, Ern Baxter, and Branham traveled to South Africa in the fall of 1951. Bosworth and Baxter arrived a few days before Branham in early October, jumping right into the work of teaching and healing.[52] The meetings were sponsored in part by the Apostolic Faith Mission—the pentecostal organization that John G. Lake had helped build fifty years earlier.[53] Although the party spent most of their time among "Europeans," they made room to work with natives and Indians; Bosworth even noted that a Zulu prince endorsed the meetings.[54] At their first stop in Johannesburg, sixty pentecostal churches cooperated in organizing and supporting the meetings.[55] The party then went to Klerksdorp, Kimberley, Durban and a total of about a dozen cities, holding over one hundred meetings. During this trip, Baxter usually gave the salvation message while Bosworth, referred to as "a dean of the divine healing ministry," assumed his role of teacher.[56] During their ten weeks in South Africa, they ministered to a reported 500,000 people. At one meeting in Durban, the crowd was estimated at forty-five to sixty thousand—the largest crowd Bosworth had ever addressed by far.[57] Bosworth led several services on his own in South Africa and also prayed for many who received healing. Most often, the healings dealt with deafness.[58] In one meeting among "natives," Bosworth resisted praying for many of the sick, instead encouraging them to grasp healing in the atonement without mediation. In this case, this tactic was employed to differentiate divine healing from the "old heathen methods" that were common among the native population.[59]

This work continued to raise Bosworth's profile. A group in Chicago offered Branham and Bosworth a salaried co-pastorate. After discussing the possibility, the evangelists determined that their call to overseas work was

---

publicized photo of Shirlaw is in *Voice of Healing* 4.7 (October 1951) 8.

52. du Plessis, "International Fellowship Column," 16; Stadsklev, *William Branham*, 151–52.

53. Stadsklev, *William Branham*, 75.

54. Stadsklev, *William Branham*, 142, 153; Bosworth, "God's Visitation to South Africa," 1.

55. Schoeman, "Great Revivals in Africa," 8. Cf. Stadsklev, *William Branham*, 121.

56. Stadsklev, "Greatest Religious Meetings in History," 14; Stadsklev, *William Branham*, 119, 138, 148, 149, 150, 154.

57. Stadsklev, "Greatest Religious Meetings in History," 14; "4,000 Letters," 7. See also Bosworth, "God's Visitation to South Africa," 1.

58. Stadsklev, *William Branham*, 94, 130, 136, 140, 142, 144, 172, 176, 192. At least one healing dealt with restoration of vision, see pp. 111–12.

59. "More on the South African Revival," 9.

too strong to allow a settled pastorate.⁶⁰ In early 1953, Bosworth took part in the opening of the Miami chapter of the Full Gospel Business Men's Fellowship International (FGBMFI). Formed in 1951, the organization was the outgrowth of Oral Roberts's desire to organize support from prominent laymen in the communities of his campaigns.⁶¹ Demos Shakarian, the genius behind the association that significantly raised the profile of pentecostalism, referred to Bosworth as "one of the greatest writers of our time."⁶²

Even in his mid-seventies, Bosworth could conduct overseas missions on his own. In the summer of 1953, Bosworth returned to South Africa for ten months. "I just had such a taste, such a craving and yearning for those poor souls who had never heard [the gospel]," Bosworth later recalled, "that I just had to go back."⁶³ Bosworth prayed for dozens of cases of cancer each night. "The greatest victories over sin and sickness took place among the non-Europeans; especially the Zulus," reported an eyewitness for *Voice of Healing*.⁶⁴ In addition to his meetings, Bosworth visited the homes in poorer regions to bring to them the gospel of the supernatural.⁶⁵ With barely a rest after his South Africa trip, Bosworth traveled to Japan, spending several months ministering in Naraken with L. W. Coote, a pioneering pentecostal missionary.⁶⁶

After Bosworth's work in Japan, he took on managing duties for Branham's crusades.⁶⁷ In January and February of 1955, Bosworth worked with Branham in Lubbock, Texas, and also conducted his own meetings in cooperation with the FGBMFI.⁶⁸ In August, Branham's party—under the direction of the FGBMFI—requested Bosworth for work in Switzerland and

60. Branham, "Faith Once Delivered to the Saints."

61. Harrell, *All Things Are Possible*, 49.

62. Shakarian, "Two Chapters Organized in Florida," 10. For the founding and early history of the FGBFI, see Tallman, "Demos Shakarian," 206–56.

63. Bosworth, "Be Ye Doers of the Word."

64. Laggar, "Report on Evangelist F. F. Bosworth," 11. See also Branham, "Jesus Christ the Same Yesterday, Today, and Forever"; Branham, "Speak to This Rock."

65. Bosworth, "Be Ye Doers of the Word."

66. Branham, "It Is I, Be Not Afraid"; Branham, "Prophet Elisha"; *Voice of Healing* (August 1954) 22. At some point, Bosworth also ministered in Cuba, but I have been unable to find any details on this work. Osborn, "He Prayed Earnestly for Himself," 25.

67. Branham, "Expectation." See also Branham, "At Thy Word, Lord, I'll Let Down the Net"; Branham, "How the Angel Came to Me, and His Commission."

68. "Attention People of All Faiths," 26; "Lubbock, Texas, Sponsors Branham-Bosworth Meet," 22.

Germany.⁶⁹ Bosworth continued in his supporting role and saw miracles in his own ministry.⁷⁰

To the flood of testimonies of healing and the inflated statistics of the healing evangelists must be added the voices of those who were not healed or who grew worse after attending Branham and Bosworth's campaigns.⁷¹ Regardless of empirical results, however, for the postwar healing revival, Bosworth was a living link with the pentecostal past, a doctrinal authority, and a vibrant and dedicated evangelist in his own right.

BOSWORTH AND BRANHAM: REFLECTIONS ON A SUCCESSFUL PARTNERSHIP

As Bosworth's success in his final decade of life was inseparable from his ministry relationship with William Branham, an investigation into the contours of that relationship is in order. This relationship rested on mutual admiration and a shared pursuit of the supernatural within the context of admittedly different styles and emphases.

Branham saw Bosworth as a living saint, a fount of wisdom in divine healing and a moral example. Branham's respect for Bosworth was unbounded. "[I]f ever [there] was a man that ever represented Pentecost and was a true apostle, it was F. F. Bosworth," Branham commented from the pulpit. For a movement that Branham saw as hampered by dogmatism, Bosworth "was a man who brought dignity and power to the Pentecostal church."⁷² Branham admired how Bosworth suffered "for preaching the baptism of the Holy Ghost" during his beating in Texas in 1911.⁷³ Branham frequently told the story of John Sproul, the soldier who had been healed under Bosworth and entered into his own traveling ministry.⁷⁴ To Branham, Bosworth was a living symbol of the truth of divine healing, and any attack on Bosworth was an attack on the supernatural gospel. When a preacher tried to indict divine healing as ineffectual by claiming that the

---

69. Bosworth, "Branham Meetings in Germany and Switzerland," 4. During these meetings, another supernatural photograph was taken of Branham.

70. Bosworth, "Branham Meetings in Germany and Switzerland," 7–8. See also "William Branham in Lausanne," 7.

71. Hollenweger, *Pentecostals*, 355–56.

72. Branham, "Manifested Sons of God (Series, Part 2 of 4)"; Branham, "Greater than Solomon Is Here."

73. Branham, "Israel at the Red Sea."

74. Branham, "By Faith, Moses"; Branham, "Jehovah-Jireh," (March 9, 1957).

Bosworth brothers had both died young, Branham called to set the record straight.[75]

Bosworth was drawn to Branham because of Branham's demonstration of the gospel of the supernatural. The central conviction of Branham's ministry was "Jesus Christ the same yesterday, today, and forever" (Hebrews 13:8).[76] This teaching on the immutability of Christ had been a cardinal tenet of pentecostal healing ministries. According to Lindsay, Branham brought "a fresh revelation of the reality of the power of God and the intrinsic truth of the miraculous in the scriptures."[77] Branham's life revealed one supernatural occurrence after another. Always given to visions, Branham recorded numerous instances when he had seen a person's demise or healing beforehand.[78] As Bosworth related, Branham knew when it was unnecessary to pray for some, since he foresaw that they would be healed without prayer.[79] Branham's gift as a "seer" was also displayed in mundane events like travel details.[80] In short, as healer and prophet—one who frequently communed with angels, foresaw events, discerned sins, and was a vessel for healing—Branham embodied the supernatural gospel on a scale unseen since Dowie.

Bosworth was an untiring supporter of Branham. As W. F. Mullan put it, Bosworth's "loyalty to the Branham Party won every heart."[81] This support probably owed to the way Branham reinvigorated Bosworth's ministry. Bosworth said that after their meetings together in Miami, he was "just a kid living in an old house."[82] Bosworth fell naturally into the role of Branham's apologist, insisting that "the message of the angel is verified in Branham's Meetings nightly, before the eyes of thousands" and confirmed the countless times when Branham correctly identified a person's ailment without any previous knowledge of his or her condition.[83] Bosworth told Charles Benham that "in all his long career he had never witnessed such a high percentage of healing miracles."[84] He claimed of Branham's ministry, "there has never

---

75. Branham, "Divine Healing."
76. Weaver, *Healer-Prophet*, 61.
77. Lindsay, *William Branham*, 12.
78. Lindsay, *William Branham*, 181–206.
79. Bosworth, "Looking at the Unseen," 4.
80. Lindsay, *William Branham*, 139.
81. Branham, *William Branham Sermons*, 127.
82. Branham, "To Whom Is the Arm of the Lord Revealed?"
83. "Fresno, California, and Seattle, Washington," 1, 2. See also Lindsay, *William Branham*, 168–80; Stadsklev, *William Branham*, 37–47.
84. Benham, "God Answers the Present World Crisis," 4.

been anything like it since the time when Christ was here on earth."[85] Often when Bosworth taught in Branham's campaigns, he not only expounded the "truths of Divine Healing" but also "explained the gift which God has given to William Branham."[86] According to Bosworth, Branham's gift as a "seer" allowed him to describe and quote the surgeons who had operated on the sick who attended his meetings. Seven years after he began working with Branham, Bosworth claimed that Branham's gift of discernment was "100% correct. Not a single time was he mistaken."[87]

Bosworth and Branham shared many qualities that made them good ministry partners. Observers often referred to Branham's humility and gentleness—qualities that Bosworth's supporters also prized.[88] Yet both evangelists were excellent showmen. Bosworth had often increased the drama of healings of deaf-mutes by whispering numbers into the ear of the newly healed for the person to repeat for the audience.[89] When Branham healed the blind, he asked them to follow him as the evangelist walked silently up and down the platform.[90]

Although Branham became doctrinally adventurous in his later years, the two evangelists approached theology the same way: an insider's critique of pentecostalism combined with a desire to spread pentecostal blessings to all. Branham lambasted pentecostalism for its doctrinal instability, its hampering denominational machinery, and its dogmatism on the tongues evidence doctrine.[91] Branham even deferred to Bosworth on tongues.[92] Branham preferred to think of gifts rather than evidence: "So if speaking in tongues then is an evidence of the Holy Ghost, all these other things [spiritual gifts listed in 1 Corinthians 12] has to be evidence of the Holy Ghost too." If forced to speak of "evidence" of the Holy Spirit, Branham pointed to love.[93] Branham's meetings—like Bosworth's—were interdenominational,

---

85. Stadsklev, *William Branham*, 81. See also p. 88.

86. Stadsklev, "Greatest Religious Meetings in History," 14.

87. Bosworth, "Branham Meetings in Germany and Switzerland," 4.

88. Lindsay, *William Branham*, 12; Harrell, *All Things Are Possible*, 38, 39; Weaver, *Healer-Prophet*, 55.

89. In fact, Bosworth continued this technique while working with Branham in South Africa. Stadsklev, *William Branham*, 92–93.

90. Sitton and Lindsay, "Branham in Houston," 16.

91. Branham, "Where I Think Pentecost Failed."

92. Branham, "I Will Restore."

93. Branham, "Debate on Tongues." See also Lindsay, *William Branham*, 42; Weaver, *Healer-Prophet*, 115, 134–35.

with a "conscious avoidance of doctrinal conflict."[94] Branham's early messages stressed "the unity of the body of Christ."[95]

Like Bosworth, Branham viewed signs and wonders as supportive for the work of salvation. Branham frequently quoted Bosworth in referring to healing as "bait" for conversion.[96] Nonetheless, Branham's supporters unambiguously identified the "MINISTRY OF THE MIRACULOUS" as "a most vital and potent force in the spiritual awakening of the countries of the world."[97] They also had a similar position on medicine, encouraging those healed to have their miracles verified by physicians.[98] Bosworth would have agreed with Branham, who said that "doctors are able to assist nature, but they are only men . . . God is almighty."[99] Branham possibly laid more stress on the role of demons in sickness than Bosworth had earlier in his career.[100] Perhaps connected to this, under Branham's more dynamic (rather than propositional) approach to healing, Bosworth viewed medicine with increasing suspicion in his final years.[101]

Bosworth was not uncritical of the younger evangelist. Branham's habit of refusing to sell gospel books on Sunday annoyed Bosworth.[102] Bosworth also tried to expand Branham's technique to enable Branham to pray for more people.[103] In South Africa, Branham received a revelation warning him not to go to the next stop on their itinerary. Bosworth told Branham he was mistaken and that Satan could have given him a false vision. Branham responded that Bosworth "was looking at it from the natural, ministerial stand point." According to Branham, God "permitted" him to go along with Bosworth's counsel, but the party paid for their disobedience, as many got

---

94. Weaver, *Healer-Prophet*, 52; Harrell, *All Things Are Possible*, 39, 95.

95. Lindsay, "Story of the Great Restoration Revival, Part I," 22. See also Lindsay, *William Branham*, 15.

96. Weaver, *Healer-Prophet*, 47–48, 60, 108; Stadsklev, *William Branham*, 134, 149. See also Branham, "God's Provided Way"; Branham, "We Would See Jesus," (April 22, 1959). Similarly, Raymond Richey spoke of healing as the "dinner bell" bringing sinners to salvation. Harrell, *All Things Are Possible*, 93.

97. Stadsklev, *William Branham*, 135; emphasis in original. See also Weaver, *Healer-Prophet*, 58, n. 94; Harrell, *All Things Are Possible*, 6.

98. Stadsklev, *William Branham*, 84, 146.

99. Lindsay, *William Branham*, 78. See also Stadsklev, *William Branham*, 60.

100. Weaver, *Healer-Prophet*, 62.

101. Weaver, *Healer-Prophet*, 66–67.

102. Branham, "Maniac of Gadara."

103. Branham, "I Have a Greater Witness than John." See also Branham, "Africa Trip Report."

sick and some of their meetings were cancelled because of storms.[104] A few other differences were apparently not strong enough to threaten the bond between the ministers. Branham rejected the doctrine of British-Israelism.[105] Branham was also uninterested in Bosworth's focus on the Lord's Supper as a conduit of healing power.[106]

In two main areas, Branham's work impressed Bosworth as different from his own. First, Bosworth never claimed the gift of healing, which he freely ascribed to Branham. As Branham told the story, Bosworth had prayed that someday the gift of healing would be restored to the church, rather than "just somebody preaching Divine Healing."[107] This longing was met in Branham's ministry. Second—and relatedly—crowds were large from the outset of Branham's meetings in each new location, and along with the large crowds, miracles and healings usually occurred on the first night of meetings. Bosworth, on the other hand, claimed he often spent many days in a location before a sizeable crowd developed, and he had usually encouraged those seeking healing to attend numerous meetings before coming through the prayer line.

These contrasts, said Bosworth, stemmed from "the difference between the Gift of Healing and the prayer of faith."[108] These two paths to healing were complementary. The "prayer of faith" continued to be the route of healing for many, but the increase in the "gift of healing" signaled the nearness of the end times. The two also worked in tandem: as Branham detected diseases and hidden sins, such signs "raise the faith of the afflicted to the level where the 'gift of healing operates for their deliverance.'"[109] Branham described his differences with Bosworth:

> Now, Brother Bosworth, many other ministers, they preach the Word. And through the Word, you believe. And then when I

---

104. The narrative here is compiled from Branham, "How God Called Me to Africa, Part I," 8. See also Branham, "Early Spiritual Experiences"; Branham, "Africa Trip Report"; Branham, "Faith (Africa Trip Report)."; Branham, "How Faith Acts (Africa Trip Report)."

105. Yet, many of Branham's ideas seemed compatible with British-Israelism, such as his pyramidology and "two-seed-in-the-spirit" soteriology. Branham, "Sign of His Coming." See Barkun, *Religion and the Racist Right*, 12–14, 160–62; Weaver, *Healer-Prophet*, 125.

106. Harrell, *All Things Are Possible*, 92.

107. Branham, "Diseases and Afflictions."

108. "Rev. and Mrs. F. F. Bosworth Work with Branham Party," 5.

109. Bosworth, "Gifts of Healing Plus," B. See also Schoeman, "Great Revivals in Africa with Branham Party," 8; Bosworth, "Branham Meetings in Germany and Switzerland," 4.

was put in the world, I was given a gift. That gift brings the— brings God in view of everyone. So you can see, you understand, that something supernatural is moving with the people.[110]

Although Bosworth believed that healing was available to all on the basis of faith, often his enthusiasm for Branham's ministry placed more emphasis on contact with the prophet than simple faith. When one father in South Africa asked Bosworth how "his child might receive the healing which he realized Christ had purchased," Bosworth advised him to pray that Branham would receive a vision of the child.[111] Still, Bosworth was not willing to concede what critics of divine healing often charged: that healing evangelists claimed power to heal in themselves.[112] Branham's supporters still held that healing was chiefly a matter of "God's universal laws."[113]

BOSWORTH'S IMPACT ON THE POSTWAR HEALING REVIVAL AND THE WORD OF FAITH MOVEMENT

Bosworth was among select revivalists of the 1920s and 1930s who were "the legitimate ancestors of the charismatic revivalists of the post-World War II period."[114] To the younger generation of believers in the gospel of the supernatural, Bosworth was an "Apostle of Faith"[115] and a "20th century pioneer of the ministry of the miraculous."[116] But Bosworth was more than a distant and revered ancestor, he was a living conduit of "inspiration and instruction in pentecostal doctrine" for the healing revival.[117]

Branham took over a number of theological ideas that were central to Bosworth's healing message, such as faith as a "sixth sense" and the distinction between God's will and God's ability.[118] Branham also made much of Bosworth's slogan "faith comes by hearing."[119] Bosworth and Branham had a similarly ambivalent attitude toward the relationship of saving faith to

110. Branham, "Blind Bartimaeus."
111. Stadsklev, *William Branham*, 86.
112. "News Clip: Houston Press, 1950," 10.
113. Stadsklev, *William Branham*, iv.
114. Harrell, *All Things Are Possible*, 12–13. Harrell identifies Charles Price as "the man who probably influenced the healing revivalists of the postwar period most directly." Harrell, *All Things Are Possible*, 17. Both Richey and Bosworth have a greater claim to direct influence, since these two worked with the new generation of healers.
115. Stadsklev, *William Branham*, 130.
116. Stadsklev, *William Branham*, 136.
117. Harrell, *All Things Are Possible*, 34.
118. Stadsklev, *William Branham*, 54–55, 61.
119. Stadsklev, *William Branham*, 126. See also Osborn, *Frontier Evangelism*, 34–35.

healing faith, and Branham's theology of healing, like Bosworth's, generally placed the blame on the seeker for lack of faith if healing was not forthcoming.[120] Although less refined theologically, Branham echoed Bosworth's claim that healing was on the "same basis" as salvation.[121]

Aside from Branham, T. L. Osborn was the evangelist most influenced by Bosworth. Osborn described the 1949 campaign in Detroit with Bosworth as "a practical training school" in divine healing as Bosworth spent long hours coaching Osborn. Bosworth encouraged Osborn to write and provided him with his first publisher—J. J. Scruby, who had published Bosworth's biography in 1921 and managed Bosworth's *Exploits of Faith*.[122] Osborn adopted Bosworth's legal language, likening atonement blessings to a bank account.[123] Osborn acknowledged that many of his insights in "One Hundred Divine Healing Facts" came directly from Bosworth's *Christ the Healer*.[124] Osborn's best-known work, *Healing the Sick* (1950), included numerous references to and direct quotations from Bosworth.[125] This book also lifted many of Bosworth's key ideas without attribution, such as the "redemptive names" argument, the Lord's Supper as a focus for healing, and symptoms of disease as "lying vanities."[126]

A notable development in the revival connected to Bosworth is "healing *en masse*." According to this approach, many could be healed simultaneously—without laying on of hands, prayer cards, or prayer lines—if they apprehended God's power and willingness to heal. Proponents argued that "if a thousand people wanted to accept Christ and be saved, I would not pray for each one individually; I would teach them all to call on the Lord and to believe at one time . . . I knew the same method should be followed in ministering to the sick."[127] This solved many practical problems: healing large numbers during short visits, "demonstrating the Gospel on a mass evangelistic scale," and keeping seekers' focus on God instead of the evangelist.[128]

---

120. Weaver, *Healer-Prophet*, 66.

121. Stadsklev, *William Branham*, 60.

122. Osborn and Osborn, *Faith Library*, 1:104, 151–154.

123. Osborn, *Healing En Masse*, 88; emphasis in original. See also p. 45 and Osborn, *Healing the Sick*, 39, 61.

124. Osborn, *Frontier Evangelism*, 57–58, 62–78.

125. Osborn, *Healing the Sick*, 7, 23, 57, 64, 79, 82, 83, 120–22, 145–46, 284.

126. Osborn, *Healing the Sick*, 176, 180–86, 191–94. For "lying vanities," see Osborn, *Healing the Sick*, 283; Osborn, *Healing En Masse*, 75.

127. Osborn, *Healing En Masse*, 13.

128. Osborn, *Healing En Masse*, 15–16.

Historians regard the mass healing technique as an innovation and identify Osborn as the originator, while recognizing that Bosworth and Branham also used the method.[129] Osborn recalled that while in Flint, Michigan, with Bosworth in 1949, "like a light from heaven the truths of mass healing suddenly shined into my soul."[130] He tested the revelation by praying simultaneously for fifty-four deaf people, all of whom were soon healed. Emboldened by success, Osborn repeated the practice in Puerto Rico shortly after Flint. Mass healing became a cornerstone of Osborn's ministry: he boasted in rarely praying individually for the sick.[131]

Several facts complicate Osborn's rather polished account from 1954. First, Osborn's "light from heaven" concerning mass healing significantly occurred while working with Bosworth. Osborn listened attentively to Bosworth's theological musings on how the Israelites were all healed by looking to the serpent, rather than through the individual ministrations of Moses. As Osborn later recalled, "God chose Mr. Bosworth to seed us with these and many other biblical reasons for faith to help multitudes to be healed at the same time."[132] In an honest moment, Osborn only claimed to have "pioneered the concept of *Mass-Miracle Evangelism on mission fields*," that is, taking the "seed" of Bosworth's theology and applying it in crusades in "heathen" nations.[133] Second, Osborn's diary confirms that in May of 1949 he prayed a "mass prayer" for fifty-three deaf people, but at the time he did not seem to regard this as an innovation and continued to use prayer lines in his services.[134] Third, Bosworth's own discussions of mass healing centered on Branham, not Osborn. Bosworth's earliest mention of the technique was in connection with Branham's early 1950 meetings in Louisville, Kentucky. As Bosworth had hoped, Branham used the technique again in Houston a few days later, and from then it probably became a staple of the Branham meetings.[135]

---

129. Harrell, *All Things Are Possible*, 66; Barnes, "F. F. Bosworth," 183–84, 194; Stadsklev, *William Branham*, 145, 152.

130. Osborn, *Healing En Masse*, 11.

131. Osborn, *Healing En Masse*, 14–22, 65.

132. Osborn and Osborn, *Faith Library*, 1:127–29; quote on p. 129.

133. Osborn and Osborn, *Faith Library*, 1:137; emphasis in original.

134. Osborn and Osborn, *Faith Library*, 1:135, 141–43. In *Healing the Sick*, Osborn's diary is greatly edited, leading to some chronological discrepancies. See Osborn, *Healing the Sick*, 250–52, 254.

135. Bosworth, "Gifts of Healing Plus," C; "Profound Confirmation by Catholic Convert," 4; Stadsklev, *William Branham*, 92–93, 142; William Branham, "Healing (What Cancer Is)."

Furthermore, when speaking of mass healing, Bosworth and Osborn may not have been talking about precisely the same thing. While Osborn described mass healing as a simple numerical extension of the basic premise of healing by faith, Bosworth tended to invest greater significance in the "cumulative power of mass faith," suggesting that the power of an individual's faith is supernaturally and exponentially increased when it is combined with that of others.[136] This theory necessitated a distinction in "levels" of faith, where a certain level makes healing possible. According to Bosworth in 1950, faith could also "pull" on the gift of healing within a healer like Branham—essentially a spiritual method of tapping the healer on the shoulder. If the healer then noticed and identified the one whose faith "pulled" on his gift, that person's faith was likely to rise to "healing level" due to the supernatural confirmation.[137]

Historian Roscoe Barnes suggests that Bosworth's adoption of new techniques and terminology like healing *en masse* "indicate[s] a new phase in Bosworth's understanding of divine healing."[138] Bosworth himself seemed to suggest that the method was novel.[139] But such comments reflect rather the pentecostal penchant for emphasizing ordinary developments as supernatural revelations in order to sanction one's ministry. Healing *en masse* was a development in magnitude, not kind. Bosworth had always expected those seeking healing to be healed without direct intervention, based on faith in the atonement for healing. His long-held teaching that healing could come through participation in the Lord's Supper also suggested that those seeking healing needed no human intervention or prayers. Bosworth frequently rejoiced that seekers were healed simply by reading his writings and believing God's promises therein. Often Bosworth told the infirm they could be healed during the sermon. In 1948, before any supposed breakthrough in the healing *en masse* approach, Bosworth spoke glowingly of the call for "corporate faith" for healing voiced by the Episcopal Church in Australia.[140] The same year, he gave advice compatible with the later "level of faith" language and the premise that healing requires no human intervention, saying that "We receive only in a measure, as we accept and believe."[141] Although evangelists like Osborn and Branham, working in

---

136. Osborn, *Healing En Masse*, 33; Bosworth, "Mass Faith." See also Bosworth, "Be Ye Doers of the Word."

137. Bosworth, "Looking at the Unseen," 4–5.

138. Barnes, "F. F. Bosworth," 184.

139. Bosworth, "Mass Faith."

140. Bosworth, *Christ, the Healer*, (1948) 177.

141. Bosworth, "Hints Regarding Healing," 4; emphasis in original.

their prime, developed mass healing as a definite technique and put their own stamp on it, the technique should be seen as a large-scale application of Bosworth's healing theology and practice.

Bosworth also influenced the revival with his focus on financial blessings. A. A. Allen was probably the first to make prosperity a central theme in 1953. Roberts followed with his principle of sevenfold return.[142] Kate Bowler claims that "Bosworth never preached about prosperity,"[143] but Bosworth was already preaching in the 1920s,

> Many people do not know that God has laws in regard to financial blessing just the same as he has in regard to spiritual blessings. If they sow money, give it to the Lord, in the right spirit, it will bring a fruitful harvest. Some people say "I cannot afford to give." They stay poor. Everything you give out will increase. You always reap more than you sow.[144]

Also, in a 1930s tract, Bosworth detailed many themes of financial blessing that would appear with force decades later.[145] The full bloom of the prosperity gospel probably awaited corresponding economic showers, but Bosworth may have pioneered the prosperity message.

The Word of Faith movement, a theological development integrating pentecostal healing theology with metaphysical thought, arose in the 1960s after the excitement of the postwar healing revival abated. The movement identified faith with spoken confession and stressed the creative power of faith for healing and material prosperity. Kenneth Hagin, often described as the father of the Word of Faith movement, was clearly influenced by Bosworth. An independent-Baptist-turned-pentecostal minister, Hagin came into the *Voice of Healing* orbit around 1953, and his writings were very popular.[146] Hagin attended Bosworth's meetings, the last time in 1954, and visited with Bosworth as late as 1956. According to Hagin, Bosworth had a peculiar anointing from God to heal the deaf. Acknowledging his debt to Bosworth—and especially admiring Bosworth for proving his teaching of divine healing by living in health—Hagin taught from *Christ the Healer* in his RHEMA Bible Training Center in Tulsa.[147]

---

142. Harrell, *All Things Are Possible*, 49, 74, 105, 200; Bowler, *Blessed*, 47.

143. Bowler, *Blessed*, 22.

144. "Syracuse Revival Promises Big Success," 3.

145. Bosworth, *Key to the Windows of Heaven*, 11–12. This tract was originally published as Bosworth, "God's Financial Plan," 7–13. For another early sermon on financial blessing, see Bosworth, "Grace of Liberality," 1–2.

146. Hejzlar, *Two Paradigms for Divine Healing*, 25–28.

147. Hagin, *Name of Jesus*, preface; Hagin, *Understanding the Anointing*, 41–42;

Another instance of Bosworth's influence on the Word of Faith movement is seen in Hagin's son, Kenneth Hagin, Jr. In a detailed analysis of the elder Hagin's plagiarism of E. W. Kenyon, D. R. McConnell cites numerous passages that reprinted Kenyon with a few words changed. Hagin, Jr., seems to have continued the practice, preferring to plagiarize Bosworth:[148]

Bosworth	Hagin, Jr.
"The opening of the prison" is God's own figurative illustration of our release from bondage or imprisonment to sin, and sickness and everything else that reached us through the fall. (*The Opening of the Prison*)	"The opening of the prison" is God's figurative way of describing that you have been released from the bondage of Satan: from sin, sickness, disease, torment—all that is involved with the prison house of Satan himself. (*The Prison Door is Open*)
[T]he first thing God requires of man is that he forsake his way and thoughts and accept God's way and thoughts . . . Faith requires no evidence but the Word. (*The Opening of the Prison*)	The first thing God requires is that man forsake his own ways and accept God's ways . . . Faith requires evidence. Evidence of feeling or touch? No, evidence of the Word. (*The Prison Door is Open*)
Hope is *expecting* a blessing some time in the *future*; but *faith* is *taking now* what God offers. (*The Past Tenses of God's Word*)	Hope expects it "sometime." Faith takes it now. *Faith takes what God has already offered us and makes it a reality in our lives.* (*The Past Tense of God's Word*)
It is important for seekers after the mercies of God to see that appropriating faith is *taking* and *using* what God offers to us. (*The Past Tenses of God's Word*)	It is important as we seek after the mercies and benefits of God to appropriate them by faith. This means actually taking them. (*The Past Tense of God's Word*)

Apparently, for Hagin, no improvement could be made upon Bosworth's teaching.

HISTORICAL ASSESSMENT OF THE POSTWAR HEALING REVIVAL

The decade following World War II was a time of religious revival in America. According to contemporary pentecostal observers, Branham and the divine healing revival fit into a larger awakening that included the salvation focus of Billy Graham and the growth of the pentecostal denominations.[149]

Hagin, *Prevailing Prayer to Peace*, 70.

148. Hagin, *Prison Door Is Open*; Hagin, *Past Tense Of God's Word*; Bosworth, *Opening of the Prison*; Bosworth, *Christ, the Healer*, (1948), chap. 8; Bosworth, *Past Tenses of God's Word*. Hagin does quote Bosworth with a citation once in *Past Tense*, but most of the booklet is a sort of unattributed paraphrase of Bosworth's tract.

149. "Letter from J. Mattsson Boze," 13.

The healing revival was also eminently pentecostal, conveying the same gospel of the supernatural that had been the pentecostal core for half a century and exhibiting the familiar tensions between independent and denominational expressions. And yet, the healing revival was also a pivotal moment in pentecostalism, American religion, and world Christianity.

Discontinuities and Continuities

Scholars describe the healing revival as an unexpected and unparalleled era.[150] And due to the unprecedented success of Branham, Roberts, and others, the participants often emphasized the "new thing" God was doing. Even Lindsay—who appreciated the debt the revival owed to its precursors—touted a "new era" in pentecostal revivalism. This interpretation was symbolically buttressed by the deaths of the leading lights of the 1920s: Price, McPherson, and Smith Wigglesworth.[151] A much-touted prophecy that Price gave in 1945 also fed this perspective.[152] The need for a new revival was also signaled by American pentecostalism's apparent spiritual drought; according to Lindsay, "ninety per cent . . . had never previously witnessed a single miracle." To full gospel adherents who had grown up on the stories of the supernatural but never witnessed it, Branham's ministry signaled that they were coming into their spiritual inheritance. To those beyond the full gospel fold, this supernaturalism was a rebuttal of scientific materialism and an antidote to overly-cerebral faith. Either way, after witnessing Branham's work, the church "began to demand the ministry of the supernatural to be in action in its midst."[153] As Donald Gee noted, this same sense of spiritual lack was at the foundation of the Latter Rain revival.[154]

As monumental as the postwar healing revival was, its distinctiveness should not overshadow its connection and parallels with earlier pentecostalism, particularly independent healing ministries. According to Gee, the evangelists of the mid-1950s did not "manifest any essentially new features within the Pentecostal Revival" and were simply carrying on the legacy of

150. Common terms for the description of the revival are "erupted," or "explosion." Harrell, *All Things Are Possible*, 25.

151. Lindsay, "Story of the Great Restoration Revival, Part I," 4; Lindsay, "Story of the Great Restoration Revival, Part IV," 18.

152. *Golden Grain* 20.6 (September 1945) 30; cf. Grant, "Is This the Beginning," 1, 4–5. Branham referred to a prophecy by Dowie. Branham, "I Was Not Disobedient to the Heavenly Vision."

153. Lindsay, "Story of the Great Restoration Revival, Part II," 17.

154. "The 'Latter Rain,'" 17. See also Brumback, *Suddenly . . . from Heaven*, 331. For the origin and early development of the Latter Rain revival, see Faupel, "Everlasting Gospel," 397, 400–422.

Woodworth-Etter, Lake, Wigglesworth, McPherson, Price, and others.[155] The revival nurtured an appreciation for earlier pentecostal movements that operated outside the bounds of "classical" pentecostalism. Bosworth and Raymond Richey were the most prominent living connections of this pentecostalism in which tongues was a constituent, but not crucial part. Gordon Lindsay, reared in a Dowieite home, converted under Charles Parham, and apprenticed under John Lake, did much to foster an interest in this earlier independent gospel of the supernatural, publishing reprints of Lake's sermons, Woodworth-Etter's writings, and a biography of Dowie. As such, he made it a conspicuous factor of pentecostal self-identity for the second half of the century.

Tensions between Independent and Denominational Pentecostalism

Pentecostal denominations showed cautious approval of both the Latter Rain revival and the divine healing movement. In the late 1940s, the Assemblies of God again took notice of Bosworth.[156] In 1952, M. E. Collins, president of the Assemblies of God Southwestern Bible Institute, reminisced in *Voice of Healing* on how he had been brought into the ministry of divine healing during Bosworth's meetings at Rader's Tabernacle in Chicago in 1928.[157] In 1952, Branham claimed that the Assemblies of God had offered to sponsor his work in India.[158] Three years later, Bosworth spoke at a Pentecostal Holiness camp meeting in Atlanta.[159]

But this cooperation with the denominations dwindled as the revival wore on. Some denominational observers faulted Bosworth for his credulity and the healing evangelists in general for creating followers who "never go further than the excitement of the campaign."[160] Professional jealousies,

155. "'Deliverance Campaigns,'" 17.

156. Bosworth, "Hints Regarding Healing," 4, 13. For advertisement of *Christ the Healer*, see *Pentecostal Evangel* no. 1779 (June 12, 1948) 16. A reprint of a chapter of *Christ the Healer* appeared in early 1947. Bosworth, "Faith That Takes," 6–7.

157. Collins, "Divine Healing in the Bible College, Part V," 8. See also Collins, "How I Learned the Truth About Divine Healing," 3.

158. Branham, "Heathen Believe as Power Is Shown," 7.

159. "Beulah Heights Camp Meeting—1955," 4. This paper also published an excerpt from Bosworth's "Christian Confession," in the same issue (p. 2). Another excerpt from *Christ the Healer* was published in *Bridegroom's Messenger* 46.1 (September-October 1955) 1–2.

160. Gee, *Wind and Flame*, 244–45. Harrell argues that denominational support stopped around 1952. Harrell, *All Things Are Possible*, 107–16. A notice for Branham's meetings still appears in *Pentecostal Evangel* May 31, 1953, p. 16. A brief report

competition for offerings, and disagreement over things like diagnosing diseases were the sorest spots. To outspoken revivalists, the denominations' criticism simply showed that the denominations had begun to "fight those who preached signs, wonders and miracles."[161] This uneasiness also appeared in Bosworth's relationship with the Christian and Missionary Alliance. Four years after reestablishing his credentials with the Alliance in 1947, Bosworth and his wife quietly left their official designation as workers in the Southeastern District.[162] The tensions between an independent and broadcast supernatural gospel and the concerns for order and control of the denominations must have seemed familiar to Bosworth.

The Distinctiveness of the Revival

Despite the familiarity and continuity of the healing revival with its predecessors, at least three factors made this movement distinct. First, the sheer numbers of the attendance at the healers' meetings—especially overseas—were unprecedented. Although estimates of crowds were probably exaggerated, attendance in some meetings numbered in the hundreds of thousands.[163] Through its contact with large audiences, the healing revival played a major role in introducing the American public to pentecostal beliefs and practices.[164] Second, the interdenominational character of the meetings within the pentecostal context directly inspired the ecumenical experiment that became the charismatic movement.[165]

Finally, with the exception perhaps of xenolalia in the first years of pentecostalism, the healing revival brought into sharper focus than any earlier effort the place of the supernatural in evangelism and missions—what

---

appeared in March 25, 1954, p. 12.

161. Quote from A. A. Allen in Harrell, *All Things Are Possible*, 114.

162. *Annual Report for 1947*, 189; *Minutes of the General Council, 1949*, 219; *Minutes of the General Council, 1950*, 219; "Pastoral Personnel," 13. The last time Bosworth was listed on the Alliance roster published with the annual report was *Annual Report for 1950*, 242.

163. Lindsay, "Story of the Great Restoration Revival, Part I," 4.

164. "New Revivalist," 73–7 4, 76, 78; Van Dusen, "Third Force in Christendom," 113–24.

165. The best-known pentecostal ecumenist and international promoter of the charismatic movement was David du Plessis, who greatly admired the independent healing ministries of the 1950s. See Ziefle, *David Du Plessis*, 37, 41. See also Harrell, *All Things Are Possible*, 5. The clearest organizational tie between the healing revival and the charismatic movement was the Full Gospel Business Men's Fellowship International. See Tallman, "Demos Shakarian," 257–307.

historian Gary McGee called the "radical strategy" of missions.[166] Beginning with Gordon Lindsay's work in Mexico in March of 1949 and T. L. Osborn's campaign in Jamaica the same year, the healing evangelists "saw that from now on we must encourage World-Wide Revival through healing and miracles."[167] Together they set the tone for a global outreach stemming from the healing revival. Lindsay was the most articulate in noting that the unprecedented audiences were "drawn together through the demonstration of the ministry of the supernatural."[168] For Lindsay, the healing revivals were the first necessary step toward world evangelization.[169] Experience confirmed this for Bosworth, who said that "seeing these miracles was breaking" the hard-hearted Hindus of South Africa.[170] Osborn believed that, "Without world-wide evangelization by miracles, Pentecost has no purpose."[171] This approach implicated both twentieth-century missions and pentecostal self-understanding.

The supernaturalist mission strategy was, of course, an extension of Bosworth's own belief that healing was "bait" for the gospel of soul-salvation. But the scope with which this miracle-driven evangelism was promulgated in the postwar healing revival initiated a new phase in the theory and practice of missions. As a witness of T. L. Osborn's ministry put it, "Who would want to go back to the old traditional missionary methods which for years had proved to be ineffective in winning the masses[?]"[172] This strategy strengthened pentecostal work and planted new ministries across the globe. As Harrell observes, "the balance of world religion has been changed" by ministries stemming from the healing revival.[173]

FAILING HEALTH AND DEATH

While in South Africa in 1953, Bosworth experienced prostate trouble that brought him close to death. Doctors advised surgery; Bosworth preferred divine healing and wired a prayer request to Branham. According to Branham, "the Lord Jesus Christ healed him without any operation."[174] In the summer

166. McGee, "'Power from on High,'" 317–36.
167. Lindsay, "Story of the Great Restoration Revival, Part II," 18.
168. Lindsay, "Story of the Great Restoration Revival, Part I," 4.
169. "World-Wide Revival Crusade," 2–3. Lindsay also wrote a book on the subject, entitled *World Evangelization Now by Healing and Miracles*.
170. Bosworth, "God's Visitation to South Africa," 1.
171. Osborn, *Frontier Evangelism*, 24.
172. Osborn, *Healing En Masse*, 104.
173. Harrell, *All Things Are Possible*, 228.
174. Branham, "Be of Good Cheer."

of 1956, Bosworth had another health scare. Bosworth's wife told Branham that Bosworth, suffering from a blood clot, had "death rattles" in his throat and was unconscious in an oxygen tent. At this time, the Bosworths made it clear that they wanted Branham to preach Bosworth's funeral.[175] A year later, Bosworth was again ill. Again Florence called on Branham for prayer. In December, Branham visited Bosworth one last time.[176]

On Thursday, January 23, 1958, F. F. Bosworth died at his home in Miami. According to Branham, Bosworth—who turned eighty-one less than a week earlier—died well, full of faith and hope. In fact, Bosworth did not believe his looming death was due to sickness but that he was simply "wore out; and I just want to go home."[177] Branham was unable to preach Bosworth's funeral, so Osborn filled in, commemorating the man who "dedicated himself to preach the Word of faith." Osborn said that he was always surprised at how many in his audiences had been converted under Bosworth's ministry. Such was Bosworth's legacy that "if we would begin to consider the chain reaction . . . of his ministry, we would never find the end of it."[178] As he was faithful in ministry, so he was faithful in death. Bosworth's last word were a testimony to his spiritual fortitude: "Everything is clear! Perfect trust! Nothing but the blood!"[179]

CONCLUSION

After Bosworth's death, his personal Bible was discovered. Tucked inside were thirty prayers Bosworth prayed daily while ministering overseas. As he had his entire life, he prayed that his "preaching be 'in demonstration of the Spirit and of power.'"[180] Such prayers witness to the fixed core of Bosworth's fifty-year ministry: a gospel that is more than words, but a vivid encounter with the supernatural. During the postwar healing revival, Bosworth's style and language adapted to new challenges, opportunities, and personalities. William Branham's strange and exciting prophetic ministry allowed Bosworth to witness and promote what he had earlier only prayed for. And the

---

175. Branham, "Law Having a Shadow"; Branham, "Divine Love."

176. Branham, "Life Is the Healer." See also Branham, "Mighty Conqueror"; Branham, "Questions and Answers on Hebrews (Series, Part 2 of 3)"; Branham, "Sirs, We Would See Jesus."

177. William Branham, "Who Is This?"

178. For Branham unable to preach the funeral, see Branham, "Queen of Sheba"; Branham, "Jehovah-Jireh," (June 12, 1957). For Osborn's funeral sermon, see Osborn, "Commemoration," 17–18.

179. Osborn, "F. F. Bosworth Promoted to Eternal Reward," 25.

180. Osborn, "He Prayed Earnestly for Himself," 25.

masses of people in their meetings forced a more facilitating approach in the "mass healing" technique. But the center of Bosworth's ministry—and that of popular pentecostalism—never shifted: the experience and pursuit of the supernatural.

While one can conceive of the postwar healing revival without Bosworth's direct involvement, the revival would be unimaginable without Bosworth's earlier ministry and writings. In Bosworth, the new generation of healing evangelists saw a pioneer but also a co-laborer. If Bosworth never rose to the postwar stardom that Branham, Osborn, or Oral Roberts achieved, it was due to the limitations of his age. As cultural and religious conditions in America evolved, the healing evangelists—"preach[ing] with F. F. Bosworth's *Christ the Healer* tucked under their arm"[181]—reached more people with the gospel of the supernatural than ever before. In the process, they changed Christianity in America and around the world.

---

181. Bowler, *Blessed*, 43.

8

Theologian of the Supernatural Gospel

> Real unadulterated faith is one hundred per cent supernatural.
> —F. F. Bosworth, "The Wonders of Faith" (1913)[1]

Aside from his critique of the tongues evidence doctrine, F. F. Bosworth is most known for his theology of divine healing. Explicitly or implicitly, scholars have frequently taken divine healing to be the center of Bosworth's thought. But to do so is to mistake prominence for centrality. Divine healing is not the generative center but the logical conclusion of Bosworth's thought. While space does not permit an exhaustive treatment or a logical, biblical, or theological critique of Bosworth's thought, the corpus of Bosworth's writings reveals a broader theme. Bosworth's central theological conviction was that God continues to engage in human history in identifiable, predictable, and often supernatural ways. Bosworth's concern for the dependability of divine intervention led him to a theological corollary that stressed the power of faith to appropriate divine acts. This paradigm brings into a cohesive whole Bosworth's most conspicuous theological positions on spirit-baptism, divine healing, and British-Israelism.

---

1. Bosworth, "Wonders of Faith," 11.

THE MIRACLE-WORKER'S AGE

Like other full gospel adherents, Bosworth believed that "The Book of Acts ... is the only unfinished book of the New Testament" and that the church was to continue the supernatural story.[2] As with the early church, modern Christians could expect the Holy Spirit to empower this work in miraculous and tangible ways. "If you want to know how the Spirit acts now, just read how He *did* act when he had full possession of the Church."[3] Bosworth spoke of dispensations, but whereas fundamentalists used the term to eliminate supernatural activity from the modern world, Bosworth saw in the concept the premier argument for ongoing supernatural activity:

> There is but one dispensation of the Holy Spirit, and that one lies between the First and Second Advents of our Lord. It is true that we are living in the Laodicean, or lukewarm, period of the Spirit's Dispensation. At the beginning of the Age, the Church was in her Spirit-filled period, and we are now in the Laodicean, or lukewarm period; but for one (Thank God there are many others!), I am going to base my teachings and practices on the teachings and practices of the Church in her Spirit-filled period rather than in her lukewarm period. I would rather labor to build the Church up to the Bible standard than to try to make the Bible fit the Church of the Twentieth Century.[4]

Bosworth argued that the Holy Spirit was responsible for all miracles in every age but "entered office" at Pentecost, making miracles and spiritual gifts more common. Furthermore, since this same period was thought to be "the Dispensation of Grace" by dispensational thinkers, Bosworth argued that it would be absurd for Christ's mercies for the sick to be suspended during this time.[5]

Spirit-baptism was also key to full life in the Spirit's age. So adamant was Bosworth that this experience be dependable and predictable that he attacked any teaching that delayed its reception or caused doubts that it had been received. In critiquing the majority pentecostal position on tongues, Bosworth was not only rejecting the reigning biblical hermeneutic that supported the tongues evidence doctrine, nor was he only publicizing a pastoral response to the disparity he witnessed between doctrine and practice.

---

2. Bosworth, "Did the Age of Miracles Ever End?," 2.

3. Bosworth, *Christ, the Healer*, (1948), 176. Italics in original.

4. Bosworth, "Did the Age of Miracles Ever End?," 2. Cf. Bosworth, *Christ, the Healer*, (1948), 185–86.

5. Bosworth, "Did the Age of Miracles Ever End?," 2.

Bosworth was also placing spirit-baptism on a different theological footing than many of his pentecostal peers.

Bosworth insisted that believers could expect a spirit-baptism experience essentially similar to that of the apostles. In this he did not differ from other pentecostals. But Bosworth asserted different grounds for believers to claim the pentecostal experience. While most other pentecostals saw this through the lens of tongues, for Bosworth, spirit-baptism meant that, "not only the manifestations of tongues and healing, but all the other signs that accompanied the first outpouring of the Spirit, have been more or less in evidence."[6] While many other pentecostals insisted on an essential link between tongues and spirit-baptism, eventually to the point that believers were discouraged from claiming spirit-baptism until they had spoken in tongues, Bosworth argued that faith alone is the ground for the experience and serves as its own verification:

> Nothing short of real faith can satisfy the heart and put the soul at rest. The word "evidence" in the Scriptures is never used in connections with a spiritual gift, or manifestation, making faith dependent upon any sign or physical manifestation, but the Apostle distinctly states that "*faith* is the evidence."[7]

Bosworth's stress on faith meant that spirit-baptism did not have to wait for evidence. In this way, a supernatural encounter was not only more likely, it was assured. "Proper instruction followed by consecration and prayer will, in every instance, bring down the Baptism in the Holy Spirit, but it will not always bring down the manifestation of tongues."[8]

FAITH: PUTTING GOD TO WORK

The faith that could claim spirit-baptism was the key for bringing all the Spirit's supernatural power to fruition. Simple doctrine did not suffice; seekers must "take a general truth and make it our own by personal faith."[9] True faith meant for Bosworth, "importunity" in prayer, or praying with "purpose of heart," which was the same as getting "in tune with God." When this was done, supernatural results were guaranteed, whether the prayer was for salvation, healing, spirit-baptism, or revival. All worked according to divine law.[10] This rational confidence echoed Charles Finney's claim that

---

6. Perkins, *Joybringer Bosworth*, 54.
7. Perkins, *Joybringer Bosworth*, 67. Italics in original.
8. Perkins, *Joybringer Bosworth*, 69.
9. Bosworth, *Meditations on the Ninety-First Psalm*, 11.
10. Bosworth, "Nothing Can Hinder a Revival," 6. For the phrase "in proper tune

revivals are the predictable result of the "right use of constituted means." But while Bosworth *likened* God's laws for revivals to the laws of nature, Finney believed revivals were the *result* of natural laws. Both revivalists spoke of "laws" as divine guarantees, but they had markedly different conceptions of the natural and the supernatural, the mundane and the miraculous.[11] Bosworth believed that because Jesus had taught that those who believe shall receive (Mark 11:24), "It is faith that releases the power of God . . . Since God's power is at our disposal we are as responsible for its exercise, through our faith, as though we possessed the power ourselves."[12] According to Bosworth, faith was not just powerful, but omnipotent, because through faith the divine nature was imparted to humans. "Our power to act in the name of Jesus," said Bosworth, "depends upon the measure of the divine nature within us. To ask in the *name* of Jesus is to ask in the nature or Spirit of Jesus."[13] Bosworth's former coworker John Lake would be well-known for the doctrine of "God-men," but Bosworth also spoke on occasion of the "manifestation of the sons of God" that was effected by faith. Such musings were as inspired by the mystical tradition as by New Thought.[14]

Of course, faith was often challenged by sense experience, for which reason Bosworth said, "It honors God to believe Him while every sense contradicts Him!"[15] Bosworth used Jonah as the great example of this counterfactual confession: "Jonah did not wait until he got out of the fish before thanking God, but he thanked Him before he got out." This resulted in a straightforward admonition: "take your eyes off the symptoms and put them on the Lamb and praise God for your deliverance."[16] Bosworth did not deny the reality of sense experience (a stance he criticized as Christian Science) but insisted on a higher truth: "Symptoms are real, but God's word is true, and by means of God's word symptoms can be made to disappear. But

---

with the infinite," see "Anointments for Night Reach 100," 1. Such phrases strongly suggest Bosworth's familiarity with New Thought as popularized by Ralph Waldo Trine's *In Tune with the Infinite* (1897). Bosworth's one-time coworker Cyrus Fockler published a similarly-titled book: Fockler, *Tuning In with the Infinite*.

11. For Bosworth, salvation was the "greatest miracle," while for Finney, "when mankind become religious, they are not enabled to put forth exertions which they were unable to put forth." Bosworth, *Christian Confession*, 29; Finney, *Lectures on Revivals of Religion*, 12.

12. "Clergymen Impressed by Revivals in City," 4. Cf. Bosworth, *Christ, the Healer* (1948), 136.

13. Bosworth, "Wonders of Faith," 6–7.

14. "Great Outpouring at Last Meeting," 22. For the mystical influence, see, Bosworth, "Practice of the Presence of God," 6, 8.

15. Bosworth, *Christ, the Healer* (1948), 118. See also 142.

16. Bosworth, "Wonders of Faith," 9.

if you try to feel right first and then have faith, that's doing it backward."[17] Thanking and praising God for a blessing before it materializes "always puts God to work."[18]

Bosworth's early insistence on praising God for deliverance despite sense experience later translated into a focus on the power of words. Bosworth criticized those who "insist on looking at their bites, pains and aches, on talking about and nursing them."[19] The fear that acknowledging symptoms was detrimental to faith and therefore granted legitimacy to sickness led Bosworth to exhort, "Talking health will hasten recovery, while allowing the mind to rest on disease and talking about disease will cause doubts to arise in ourselves and in others; as doubt is the opposite of faith, healing is hindered."[20] Bosworth did not advise believers to say they were healed before healing was "fully manifested," but he urged the sick to say "I'm standing on the Word of God." Words were not magical but could either feed or deplete faith. But that made right words no less important, for "Wrong confession shuts the Father out and lets Satan in."[21]

Denying sense experience was an act of obedience. Such "yieldedness" to God was a constituent part of faith for Bosworth, who, in the vein of New School Presbyterianism (Finney was one of his favorite theologians), believed that "Salvation [is] the work of God and man."[22] "Everyone who meets His conditions can be healed," said Bosworth.[23] Faith often required corresponding acts—"visible expression[s] of faith"—which were behaviors that specifically denied sense experience and could imply forgoing medicine.[24] "Make your dead faith walk and it will live," urged Bosworth.[25] "Attempting the seeming impossible opens the channel through which the supernatural current flows," claimed Bosworth, "and healing is the result."[26] This determination to "act faith" led to multiple victories in Bosworth's own health.[27]

17. "Evang. Bosworth Preaches Strong Sunday Message," 3.
18. Bosworth, *Christ, the Healer*, (1948), 145.
19. Bosworth, "Hints Regarding Healing," 4.
20. Bosworth, "Hints Regarding Healing," 13.
21. Bosworth, *Christ, the Healer*, (1948), 150.
22. "Thousands Come to Hear Bosworth's Final Message," 3. For obedience and yieldedness, see Bosworth, "Wonders of Faith," 7, 8.
23. Bosworth, "Discerning the Lord's Body," 2.
24. Bosworth, *Christ, the Healer*, (1948), 193. See also Bosworth, *Meditations on the Ninety-First Psalm*, 18.
25. Bosworth, "Wonders of Faith," 10.
26. Bosworth, "Hints Regarding Healing," 13.
27. Bosworth, "Discerning the Lord's Body," 4.

Why Some Are not Healed: A Theology for Failure

Bosworth usually explained lack of healing by lack of faith or failure to meet conditions; God was cleared of any failures. Yet his approach was also pastoral and sympathetic. Those who did not have sufficient faith were not to be faulted, but were simply ignorant of the Gospel, which was to be remedied by preaching and teaching.[28] "If a person did not know what God's word taught he had no basis for his faith."[29] Bosworth also claimed that "Community unbelief is a great hindrance to people being healed."[30] If a particular area had a preponderance of doubt or opposition to the gospel of healing, God would not perform miracles there, as with Christ in Mark 6:5. According to Bosworth, widespread unbelief was usually the result of the "traditions of men," such as "the days of miracles are past," or that "God is the author of disease."[31]

Bosworth also turned to demonology to explain healing failures. "Sometimes people are not healed because their affliction is not a sickness but an evil spirit."[32] To be sure, Bosworth believed—like Dowie—that all sickness was the work of the devil, but he also believed that God sometimes allowed sickness for the sake of a person's soul.[33] Sometimes demonic influence was more acute, however, and dealing with evil spirits presumably called for different techniques; faith alone was not enough.[34] Believers should not underestimate the demonic threat. "The devil has always hidden his identity," warned Bosworth, "and most Christians fail to realize that the real spiritual battle is against the devil and the hosts of darkness. The devil has put on a program of sin, sickness and demon possession period."[35] Encountering demonic forces was not a rare occurrence for true believers. "There are just as many demons in the world today as there were in Christ's day," he told an audience in Erie, Pennsylvania, "and they have had almost two thousand years of experience in dealing with human beings."[36]

---

28. "Woman Tells of Cure," 22.

29. "Evangelist Bosworth Hands Out One," 4.

30. "Why Are Not All Who Are Prayed For Healed?," 3.

31. Bosworth, *Christ, the Healer*, (1948), 183–84.

32. "Why Are Not All Who Are Prayed For Healed?," 3. This section should nuance Hejzlar's claim that "demonology is not a prominent feature of Bosworth's doctrine of divine healing." Hejzlar, *Two Paradigms for Divine Healing*, 200.

33. Bosworth, "For This Cause," 6; Bosworth, *Christ, the Healer*, (1948), 133, 191–92; "Blessings More Abundantly," 458.

34. "Final Meetings of the Bosworth Brothers at Detroit, Mich.," 3.

35. "Bosworth Party Opens in Canada," 4.

36. "Erie Revival Campaign Increases in Power," 3.

Bosworth's musings on demonic powers led him to a suggestive, yet undeveloped theology of territorial spirits:

> We may have to get victories over the prince of Ottawa, for just as there was a prince of Persia there is undoubtedly a prince of Ottawa. There is a great difference in the spiritual atmosphere in various localities. Why? Because there is a spiritual conflict in progress and the victory is won in some places while it is not in others, on the part of God's people.[37]

Bosworth saw Satan at work in general opposition to God's message of healing. "[The devil's hosts] control the policies of men and such instrumentalities as newspapers and other means of making the work of God known."[38] No matter how much human opposition to the supernatural gospel Bosworth encountered, he determined to see the devil behind it rather than individuals.[39]

Atonement: The Purchase of Blessings for Spirit, Soul, and Body

Faith could only appropriate those things that God had promised, because—as Bosworth never tired of saying—"faith comes by hearing." In fact, Bosworth seemed almost to limit God's sovereignty when he said, "God's way of doing everything is by making promises and then by fulfilling them wherever they produce faith."[40] The promises were those associated with Christ's redemptive work. Bosworth preached that "We cannot have any spiritual blessings except those we get through Calvary."[41] As earlier divine healing advocates had explained, salvation and healing were both "in the atonement," since Christ's work restored all that was lost through the fall. The "past tense" nature of Christ's work meant that the believer could be certain that from God's perspective, healing is a done deal.[42] Healing was unqualifiedly a promise stemming from the atonement and therefore always God's will. For this reason, Bosworth frequently railed against the prayer for healing that was couched in "if it be thy will" as destructive of faith.[43]

---

37. Bosworth, "Triumphant Faith," 459.
38. "Paul Rader Issues Warning," 3.
39. "Evangelistic Campaign, Bosworth Brothers Opens in Brooklyn," 3.
40. Bosworth, *Christ, the Healer*, (1948), 113.
41. "Bosworth Campaign; Interest Growing," 3.
42. Bosworth, *Christ, the Healer*, (1948), 135.
43. Bosworth, *Christ, the Healer*, (1948), 15.

Bosworth's scriptural argument for healing rested on many prooftexts, but three passage-pairs were particularly central. First, from Isaiah 53:4—interpreted through Matthew 8:16–17—Bosworth argued that human sickness was vicariously laid on Christ. Second, Bosworth believed on the basis of Galatians 3:13—interpreted through Deuteronomy 28:22—that Christ redeemed believers from the sicknesses that are part of the "curse of the law."[44] Third, considering the Old Covenant always to be a shadow of the New, Bosworth frequently appealed to the healing of the Israelites in Numbers 21 as a type for Christian healing. Although all Israelites were afflicted, all were healed by looking to the brazen serpent (cf. John 3:14) rather than their symptoms.[45]

The New Covenant provisions of the atonement meant that healing was even more certain, leading Bosworth toward a mechanical or transactional view of healing. Bosworth told believers to "claim" healing, since it was included in the atonement.[46] He therefore stressed the legal nature of God's work in Christ, likening Christ's death to a will and stressing that on the basis of this will, faith "sees the health and strength bequeathed to us as already belonging to us because of the death of the Testator."[47] Such legal understanding of healing was common among divine healing advocates from many backgrounds, from pentecostal to Episcopal to New Thought and Christian Science.[48] In Bosworth's words, "Learn to realize your birthright, that you belong to the Kingdom of God and are under its supernatural laws."[49]

The blessings provided by Calvary surpassed salvation, spirit-baptism, or healing. "The Atonement," said Bosworth," is the only ground for any benefit to fallen man."[50] Bosworth told audiences that "Calvary insures

---

44. These passages occur frequently in Bosworth's writings, but the arguments associated with both passage-pairs is concisely laid out in Bosworth, "For This Cause," 7. As discussed in chapter one, earlier expositions on divine healing, like that of R. A. Torrey, focused on James 5:16–17. Bosworth claimed—with some justification—that he never used James 5 or Mark 16 as the basis of his teachings. (The issue with Mark 16 was its textual unreliability.) In general, Bosworth saw James 5 as a commandment and a blueprint rather than a theological argument for healing. "3000 Hear Bosworth Reply to Dr. Lott," 4. Still, the standard critique of divine healing in the 1920s centered on James 5: Gaebelein called it the "star text for all 'divine healers.'" Gaebelein, *The Healing Question*, 49.

45. Bosworth, *Christ, the Healer*, (1948), 52.
46. Bosworth, "For This Cause," 7.
47. Bosworth, *Christ, the Healer*, (1948), 137.
48. Daggett, "Are There Modern Miracles?," 165.
49. Bosworth, "Hints Regarding Healing," 13.
50. Bosworth, *Christ, the Healer*, (1948), 29.

for us our clothes and our food just as surely as it does our salvation."[51] According to Bosworth, "In His substitutionary work for us He anticipated every possible need of Adam's race, and opened the way for mercy to reach every phase of human need." Bosworth's doctrine of the redemptive names of God indicated that through the atonement God was "provider" as well as "righteousness" and "physician" for those with faith.[52]

Bosworth's view of Christ's atonement combined penal substitution with a *Christus Victor* approach: "When the Devil drove the nails into the hands of Jesus Christ he was defeating himself and he was conquered. You and I now have the right to come and ask for all that God has ever done in the way of showing His love and mercy and to be avenged of our adversary."[53] Faith in the precise benefits of the atonement explains Bosworth's focus on the Lord's Supper as a conduit of healing. Christ's blood effected soul salvation while Christ's body effected bodily healing. The believer appropriated these benefits not *ex opera operato*, but by "discerning" what the elements bestowed (cf. 1 Corinthians 11:29–30).

The Same in Any Age: Divine Love and Divine Immutability

Historian Douglas Jacobsen argues that "Bosworth's theology revolved around the conviction that God is love." Jacobsen is correct to identify divine love as indispensable in Bosworth's thought, but to see it as the central conviction overstates the case. Most importantly, divine love does not help the historian or theologian fully appreciate Bosworth's distinct approach to spirit-baptism or his adoption of British-Israelism.[54] Rather than divine

---

51. Armstrong, "Bosworth Evangelistic Campaign," 674.

52. Bosworth, *Christ, the Healer*, (1948), 85–86.

53. "Bosworth Campaign in Toronto," (April 28, 1923) 152.

54. Jacobsen, *Thinking in the Spirit*, 294. Jacobsen does not sustain the argument for the centrality of divine love in Bosworth's thought, and he is more accurate when he argues a bit further on that "Bosworth's great desire—the core of his ministry and message—was to tell Christians, and indeed all people, how to appropriate God's blessings, and how to do so without any delay" (p. 300). On the issue of spirit-baptism, Jacobsen rightly argues that for Bosworth, the purpose of spirit-baptism was "to make the recipient more like God—more loving and more able to demonstrate that love for others in powerful and effective ministry" (p. 308). But this would not have been disputed by other pentecostals and so sheds little light on Bosworth's attack on the tongues evidence doctrine. Bosworth did feel that the tongues evidence teaching sometimes distracted seekers from this more important function of the experience, but this is not the same as saying that Bosworth believed the tongues evidence teaching was contradictory to the missional import of spirit-baptism. The teaching did, however, contradict Bosworth's understanding of how faith ensures the experience of the continual supernatural

love, Bosworth's central conviction was the ongoing supernatural activity of God. Divine love was a key element in the argument for this supernatural gospel but functioned more as support than foundation.

Bosworth wanted to correct an imbalance he saw in the Christianity of his day that emphasized God's power rather than God's love. To this end, he stressed that the Bible clearly states that "God is love" and argued that "benevolence is the great attribute of God."[55] Bosworth wanted believers to picture God's love as if an ocean were set above humanity, pressured by gravity "to find an outlet through which it might pour its ocean-tides over all the earth."[56] God's love was depicted most clearly in the gospels, which record Jesus healing many solely out of compassion. Likewise, recognition of God's faithfulness and experience of its effects should bring the believer into "a state of rapture." "Love is an emotion," said Bosworth, "and Divine love is the most exquisite emotion possible to the human heart."[57]

But for Bosworth, the divine-human relationship of love was not an end in itself. Rather, God's love signaled most of all God's continuing willingness to save and heal and thus was inextricably bound up with Bosworth's insistence that Christ did not change.[58] As Bosworth often assured his audiences, "Christ's compassion for them is just as great as it was for those in Apostolic days." God offered healing in every age, said Bosworth, but now, through the atonement, "His provisions for this work to be done today are perfect."[59] Bosworth preferred to work with logical rather than emotional categories, and even God's love was subsumed under the larger theme of "principles": "All that God does is done in faithfulness to principles of love and mercy acting under varying circumstances so far as we are concerned; but unchanging as to His own attitude."[60] "God is the most reasonable being in the universe,"[61] proclaimed Bosworth, and the central plank of God's reasonableness was his "immutability."[62] Since Christ's

---

activity of God. On the issue of Bosworth's British-Israelism, Jacobsen is silent.

55. Bosworth, *Christ, the Healer*, (1948), 72.

56. Bosworth, *Christ, the Healer*, (1948), 73.

57. "Blessings More Abundantly," 458.

58. The first sentence of the chapter that Jacobsen bases much of his argument on is: "In the study of the Lord's compassion, we have, to my mind, a complete revelation of the Lord's willingness to heal." Bosworth, *Christ, the Healer*, (1948), 70. See also pp. 71, 82.

59. "Bridgeport People Attend Brooklyn Meeting," 3; Bosworth, "Wonders of Faith," 6.

60. "Blessings More Abundantly," 458.

61. Bosworth, "Triumphant Faith," 459.

62. Bosworth frequently preached on "The Unchangeableness of Christ," contrasting

promises were essentially his nature, "the results of fulfilment of divine promises are the same in any age."⁶³ Furthermore, knowing what God in his compassion willed to do in the present tense created faith, the ever-important link between what God has provided and its reception. "It is not what God *can* do," said Bosworth, "but what we know He *yearns* to do, that inspires faith."⁶⁴ For this reason, Bosworth stated, "I would rather doubt God's power than his willingness to meet our needs."⁶⁵ Bosworth could see no reason to withhold supernatural blessings for God's people. "Since God wants to pour out His blessings, and His riches upon us in profusion, why not give Him a chance? Why not say 'I am going to come into the possession in this life, of all the eternal riches I can enjoy.'"⁶⁶ In Bosworth's concern for the dependability of healing and other atonement blessings, God's love met God's reliable promise.

Bosworth and E. W. Kenyon

In discussions of the prosperity gospel movement, scholars tend to emphasize Bosworth's importance as a conduit of E. W. Kenyon's theology and have assumed that any meeting between the two ministers resulted in Kenyon's influence on Bosworth.⁶⁷ This perspective has, in part, been used to support the broader argument that the Word of Faith theology does not arise organically out of the pentecostal mindset but is a foreign implantation of cultic metaphysical thought.⁶⁸ Unfortunately, these arguments have been made with limited appreciation for the scope of Bosworth's thought. Previously unrecognized sources from Bosworth's works add more precise chronological details and nuance claims of Bosworth's dependence on Kenyon.

Assertions of any supposed meeting between Bosworth and Kenyon are tenuous. Based on recollections of Kenyon's daughter in an interview, Dale Simmons claims that Bosworth met Kenyon sometime before 1910 in

---

Christ's immutability with the mutability of all other things. "Many Converts Crowd Forward," 3; "Bosworth Brothers Winning Many Hearts," 3; "Bosworths in Miami," 3; "Bosworth Bros. Broadcasted," 3.

63. Bosworth, *Christ, the Healer*, (1948), 176.

64. Bosworth, *Christ, the Healer*, (1948), 71; emphasis in original.

65. "Bosworths in Miami," 3.

66. "Soldier Boy's Testimony Makes Hit," 8.

67. McConnell, *Different Gospel*, 68. See also Simmons, *E. W. Kenyon*, 294–96; Kinnebrew, "Charismatic Doctrine of Positive Confession," 132. The exception is McIntyre, *E. W. Kenyon*, 131.

68. McConnell, *Different Gospel*, xviii, 16, 22–24.

Chicago.⁶⁹ The first definite date showing Bosworth's knowledge of Kenyon comes from the reprint of Kenyon's "The New Kind of Love" published in *Exploits of Faith*, October 1928.⁷⁰

Aside from Bosworth's admission in the 1948 edition of *Christ the Healer* that he drew on Kenyon's concept of "confession," nothing compels historians to argue that when Bosworth and Kenyon interacted, influence flowed only in one direction. Around the same time in 1912, both evangelists began testing more specific legal language to describe the believer's authority—Bosworth with the phrase "power of attorney" and Kenyon speaking of the "right of attorney."⁷¹ Although Kenyon put his slogan in print about seven months before Bosworth, Kenyon did not use the more familiar "power of attorney" phrase in print until 1914.⁷² The ambiguity is sufficient to suggest that, if Bosworth and Kenyon had interacted, influence could have been mutual. If they had not yet interacted, they could have come to these insights independently or from contact with a common third source.

Regardless of chronology or any proposed chart of dependence, Bosworth, in endorsing Kenyon, did not offer a theology that was fundamentally different from his own as reconstructed from the earliest sources. Like Bosworth, Kenyon spoke in tongues but critiqued pentecostals as overly dependent on manifestations rather than having faith in the plain word of God.⁷³ In particular, the notorious legal language usually associated with Kenyon was an early staple of Bosworth's message of certainty in God's continuing supernatural activity:

---

69. Simmons, *E. W. Kenyon*, 295. See also McIntyre, *E. W. Kenyon*, 68, 132, 325–26, n. 17.

70. Kenyon, "New Kind of Love," 15–16. Bosworth also may have interacted with Kenyon in the summer of 1929 when he vacationed in Pasadena with the Richeys. Foxworth, "Raymond T. Richey," 159. For Bosworth's time in California, see "Evangelist and Mrs. Bosworth Enjoy Vacation," 8.

71. Bosworth, "Pentecostal Outpouring in Dallas, Texas," 11. See also Bosworth, "Wonders of Faith," 6. Kenyon, "Prayer," 74; Kenyon, "Heart," 93; Kenyon, "Deferred Answers," 147–48. Kenyon's sudden and repeated use of the phrase in early 1912 suggests that this was new language for him at the time, meaning that he may not have been using the phrase before 1910, when he supposedly met Bosworth. Kenyon recalls the moment when the notion of believers' rights as "power of attorney" came to him while holding meetings in Tennessee, but he does not give a date for this event. Kenyon, *Wonderful Name of Jesus*, 4. If Kenyon's account is credible, this event may have occurred in spring 1906. See *Reality* 3.4 (May 1906) 78.

72. Kenyon, "Legal Authority," 2.

73. Simmons, *E. W. Kenyon*, 43. See also McConnell, *Different Gospel*, 28; Lie, *E. W. Kenyon*, 15.

Do you ever stop to think that the Bible is a legal document, the Old Testament and New Testament legal terms? God treated the devil rightly. He defeated the adversary on legal grounds and Satan has no legal authority over the new creation. The Church has legal authority over demons of all ranks and kinds.[74]

Compare a typical passage from Kenyon: "You have been delivered out of the authority of Satan. Satan has no authority or legal right to reign over you. You are the absolute master of satanic forces in the name of Jesus."[75] Bosworth's later espousal of Kenyon's "confession" language represents a refinement of thought rather than the adoption of a new theology. As Kate Bowler hints, Bosworth's earlier theology of "appropriating faith" through praise and "thinking [God's] thoughts" was fully congruent with the later "confession" theology.[76] Kenyon's thought led Bosworth to more precise language but did not alter his basic theology, which suggest that the "metaphysical" doctrines of the Word of Faith movement can be seen as logical extensions of pentecostal divine healing theology.

CATEGORIZING BOSWORTH: SCHOLARLY PARADIGMS OF DIVINE HEALING

In tracing the history and theology of modern divine healing, scholars have suggested several interpretive categories. These categories have varying merit for interpreting Bosworth's thought and his role in the divine healing story.

Faithfulness and Freedom

In a seminal theological essay, Henry Knight situates healing theologies on a spectrum between the "two poles of God's faithfulness and God's freedom."[77] Knight identifies the "faith confession" movement—exemplified by Hagin and implicating Bosworth—as a prime example of "emphasiz[ing] God's faithfulness at the expense of God's freedom."[78] Toward the other end are those—like Kathryn Kuhlman—who emphasize God's freedom, while the Catholic Francis MacNutt and the "third wave" charismatic John Wimber

---

74. Bosworth, "Triumphant Faith," 460.
75. McIntyre, *E. W. Kenyon*, 265.
76. Bowler, *Blessed*, 21. Bosworth, "Practice of the Presence of God," 6.
77. Knight, "God's Faithfulness and God's Freedom," 65, 66.
78. Knight, "God's Faithfulness and God's Freedom," 69. Knight recognizes other styles are also found at this end of the pole.

occupy the middle ground. Knight's work is mainly descriptive and theologically constructive and betrays little interest in historical origins.[79] The usefulness of Knight's paradigm lies in its ability to account for all healing theologies without cumbersome qualifications and its promise for discovering patterns that only become apparent when healing theologies are located on the faithfulness/freedom spectrum.

Wesleyan and Finished Work

Kimberly Alexander might be said to be working broadly within the paradigm established by Knight, but with specific attention to early pentecostalism and the soteriological origins of healing theologies. According to Alexander, those pentecostals identified with the "finished work" teaching on sanctification (which presumably includes Bosworth) place themselves in a stream of divine healing thought that differs significantly from those in the Wesleyan stream. Wesleyans, working from a broad trinitarian perspective, stressed divine freedom, understood faith as "faithfulness," and viewed healing as a proleptic sign of complete restoration. Finished work pentecostals, more narrowly christological, adhered to a "positional" model that emphasized God's faithfulness, understood faith as "reckoning," and saw redemption—including healing—as an accomplished fact.[80] Alexander demonstrates that early pentecostal healing was far from monolithic.[81] In descriptive terms, the finished work school seems to fit Bosworth. But Alexander's categories are less helpful as a historical-theological explanation of the "positional" model of divine healing that stresses Durham's soteriological "paradigm shift" in 1910.[82]

For several reasons, the theological connections between Durham's "finished work" theology and the "positional" approach to healing are not as simple as they might appear. First, as Alexander admits, William Durham never applied the principles of his theology of sanctification to divine healing—an omission that requires explanation if one wishes to contend that Durham "chang[ed] the face of pentecostalism," including its healing

---

79. Knight, "God's Faithfulness and God's Freedom," 69.

80. Alexander, *Pentecostal Healing*, 230-42.

81. Correcting those who focus on the positional model. Wacker, "Pentecostal Tradition," 522.

82. Alexander, *Pentecostal Healing*, 196. Alexander's argument concerning Durham's role is hard to pinpoint. At times she implies that Durham's theology was crucial to the split in divine healing models (p. 230, see also pp. 6, 150.) However, she is also clear that Durham neither invented the teaching nor was the first pentecostal to adhere to it, an honor she gives to Carrie Judd Montgomery, see pp. 45-4 6, 151, 160, 227.

theology.⁸³ Second, not all who fit Alexander's description of the finished work healing model showed concern for—or even awareness of—the finished work theology of sanctification. Therefore, putting such thinkers in the "finished work" camp can be misleading. For Bosworth, the issue of sanctification was peripheral, and when he did discuss it, he preferred the non-Durhamite terminology of "consecration."⁸⁴ In other words, Bosworth was not a follower of Durham in any significant theological sense. Finally, the concept of "finished work" in radical evangelical rhetoric was highly idiosyncratic, and scholarly discussions have often not been sufficiently nuanced.⁸⁵ By lumping thinkers together under a slogan-banner of "finished work," scholars do a disservice to these leaders' individuality of thought and cloud further investigation into the positional approach to healing. For example, the two chief candidates for a pre-Durham "finished work" theology—E. W. Kenyon and Carrie Judd Montgomery—were also proponents of the positional approach to healing; yet they did not speak of sanctification in the same way as Durham.⁸⁶ This suggests that rather than extrapolating from a theological "finished work" core on sanctification, these leaders arrived at their positions on divine healing in response to other common concerns.

---

83. Alexander, *Pentecostal Healing*, 46, 70, 211. Alexander offers no argument or speculation on this matter.

84. For Durham, "consecration" refers to dedication to service rather than sanctification in the soteriological sense. Durham, "Some Other Phases of Sanctification," 7–9.

85. Perhaps Alexander's appeal to "models" in her methodological approach absolves her somewhat of this charge. Alexander, *Pentecostal Healing*, 197. But the loss of the individual shades of meaning given to "finished work" are at least equal to the gains achieved through her "integrative approach."

86. For Kenyon's finished work teaching pre-dating Durham, see Simmons, *E. W. Kenyon*, xi–x, 28–29, 292–96. Kenyon used the concept of "finished work" in a very broad sense, as a foundational proposition for justification, sanctification, and "legal authority" over demonic powers. Kenyon, *Father and His Family*, 195. Furthermore, Kenyon more specifically expressed his doctrine of sanctification as the "vital part" of "new birth" in which we "receive the nature of God." Kenyon, *Father and His Family*, 159. Kenyon out-finished Durham's finished work teaching by going so far as to say personal appropriation of death to sin does not need be repeated. Kenyon, "One Secret Victory," 71. Compare Durham, "Sanctification," 2.

For Montgomery's finished work teaching pre-dating Durham, see Alexander, *Pentecostal Healing*, 45, 151, 160, 227, 230. Yet the similarities here are also superficial, since Montgomery's teaching generally focused on healing rather than sanctification. And while Durham understood sanctification as qualitatively different from spirit-baptism, for Montgomery "Spirit baptism [was] a fuller measure of something that has already been given in small portions (sanctification being one of these.)" Miskov, *Life on Wings*, Kindle location 7247.

Ironically, Alexander provides the material for the strongest refutation of her argument by claiming that Carrie Judd Montgomery's "finished work" healing theology was forged under the influence of Phoebe Palmer.[87] This suggests that the pentecostal tradition did not need Durham (or anyone else) to introduce a Reformed "finished work" soteriology in order to give rise to a strong positional theology of healing in the movement.[88] Rather, the desire to stress the dependability of God's blessings and grounds for faith led rationally-oriented leaders like Palmer to her "shorter way" for sanctification just as it led Bosworth to the categorical "healing in the atonement" doctrine. Alexander rightly points to a correlation between the positional model and the practice of itinerant healing evangelism, while the Wesleyan model fostered the healing ministry within the framework of long-term congregational support.[89] But Alexander possibly inverts the cause and effect; ministers like Bosworth may have been led to embrace the positional model as a result of their style of ministry. Unable to spend long hours with those seeking healing and less confronted on a personal pastoral level with the many cases of long-term failures of healing due to the itinerant nature of his ministry, Bosworth stressed the immediate availability and certainty of healing and sought theological and scriptural support for this view. In connection to this, it is probably significant that Bosworth came to his "revelation" about the universality of healing in the atonement when he was on the cusp of a career-altering success in traveling revivalism in 1920. Although Bosworth had always argued for universal healing, he chose to emphasize this in conjunction with his new identity as a successful itinerant evangelist. This also would explain why an evangelist like Oral Roberts, although raised in the Wesleyan pentecostal tradition, increasingly embraced a positional model as his traveling ministry expanded. The soteriological consequences of this approach clearly diverged from Wesleyan "crisis-process," but this need not implicate Durham's finished work theology.[90]

Healing Evangelists and Pastoral Healing Ministers

Pavel Hejzlar's categories take into account pentecostal and charismatic approaches to divine healing. Hejzlar identifies two broad "paradigms" for

87. Alexander, *Pentecostal Healing*, 12.

88. One could, of course, consider Palmer a sort of proto-finished work adherent, which Alexander seems almost to suggest. Alexander, *Pentecostal Healing*, 213. But to do so undercuts the broader argument that the finished work theology was born of Reformed/Baptist thought. Alexander, *Pentecostal Healing*, 196.

89. Alexander, *Pentecostal Healing*, 207, 213–14.

90. For "crisis-process," see Alexander, *Pentecostal Healing*, 205.

the healing ministry: "healing evangelism," exemplified by Bosworth and Kenneth Hagin; and "pastorally oriented healing ministry," exemplified by Episcopalian Agnes Sandford and Francis MacNutt. According to Hejzlar, the healing evangelists are characterized by the doctrine of healing in the atonement, the sufficiency of individual faith, the immediacy of healing, and a demeaning of medicine (if only implicitly). In reaction, the pastoral healing ministers emphasized the role of the Holy Spirit (rather than the cross) in healing, laid less stress on individual faith, allowed for more complexity with regard to the cause and cure of sickness, and viewed medical science more positively.[91]

As a basic schema of generalization, Hejzlar's categories are useful. Although, as he admits, on some issues, such as the necessity of faith, a neat line cannot be drawn between representatives of the two paradigms. Hejzlar recognizes that representatives in both camps have affinity with the Word of Faith movement and links to the movement's New Thought origins. Yet Hejzlar tries to distance Bosworth from the Word of Faith movement, arguing that Bosworth "processed what he read [in Kenyon] and chose not to follow Kenyon's distinctives that have become part of the unique genetic make-up of the Word of Faith Movement."[92] For example, Hejzlar claims that Bosworth did not use Kenyon's terms of "sense knowledge" and "revelation knowledge." But if Bosworth did not take over these terms literally, the same concepts are at play.[93] Furthermore, Kenyon's theology of "confession"—which Bosworth endorsed—should be considered a conspicuous (if not "unique") part of the "genetic make-up" of the Word of Faith movement.

Although recognizing Alexander's categories, Hejzlar prefers to treat Bosworth as "Wesleyan" because his doctrine of healing in the atonement was the result of late nineteenth-century Wesleyan "perfectionism, applied to deliverance from sickness."[94] The fact that Bosworth was not a proponent of Wesleyan sanctification therefore forces Hejzlar to conclude that Bosworth was "inconsistent" since he "drop[ped] the Wesleyan perfectionism that gave birth to the healing in the atonement doctrine."[95] But

91. Hejzlar, *Two Paradigms for Divine Healing*, 11.
92. Hejzlar, *Two Paradigms for Divine Healing*, 109.
93. Bosworth, *Looking at the Unseen*, 38. Bosworth, *Christ, the Healer*, (1948), 143. Hejzlar is correct, however, in noting that Bosworth did not adopt Kenyon's more speculative "spiritual death of Jesus" teaching or his disparagement of mind or soul. Hejzlar, *Two Paradigms for Divine Healing*, 189.
94. Hejzlar, *Two Paradigms for Divine Healing*, 64.
95. Hejzlar, *Two Paradigms for Divine Healing*, 81, see also pp. 110, 256–57. Bosworth still saw a connection between salvation from sin and salvation from disease, but rather than drawing the parallel between sanctification and healing Bosworth likened

Hejzlar has confused historical dependence with theological consistency. One can reach a theological commitment without necessarily endorsing all the propositions that historically led to it. If pursuit of the supernatural be the fundamental motive for theologies of sanctification, spirit-baptism, healing, and the like, full gospel thinkers are allowed the peculiar emphases that arise from their own personal story, historical context, and theological leanings without being guilty of inconsistency.

Gifted Healers, Facilitators, Heroes, and Victors

In a socio-historical approach, Jonathan Baer identifies four categories of divine healing leaders. "Gifted" healers, who flourished in the first burst of divine healing just before and after the Civil War, stressed the importance of their own spiritual endowment and faith in effecting healing for their patients.[96] Although dramatic, this style left many seekers unsettled, since they had to rely on the healer and "impressions, leadings, and personal promises."[97] In the 1870s, the "facilitating" healing style arose to meet these uncertainties and corresponded to an increase in the popularity of divine healing and its transfer into the middle class. Healers like Charles Cullis nourished healing faith "through teaching, encouragement, and prayer." For the facilitating healers, "individual faith, not any gift or degree of assurance within the healer, elicited the power of God for healing."[98] And it was available for all. The visibility of divine healing in the 1880s attracted criticism, which led some to soften their stance and others to become more radical. One radical approach Baer labels "heroic," which combined elements of the gifted and facilitating styles. This "incipient pentecostalism" came to the fore in the late 1890s with Charles Parham, John Alexander Dowie, Frank Sandford, and Maria Woodworth-Etter.[99] While the personality cults of the heroic healers were unsustainable, their methods continued in the "victorious" healing of early pentecostalism. According to Baer, victorious healers like John G. Lake and Smith Wigglesworth differed only in that they traded the eschatological focus on divinely-appointed messengers for the end-times imperative to spread the pentecostal experience.[100] But by the 1920s the facilitating approach again ascended, reflecting American affluence and

---

forgiveness and healing. Bosworth, *Christ, the Healer*, (1948), 28, 29.
  96. Baer, "Perfectly Empowered Bodies," 42.
  97. Baer, "Perfectly Empowered Bodies," 50.
  98. Baer, "Perfectly Empowered Bodies," 55.
  99. Baer, "Perfectly Empowered Bodies," 202, 203.
  100. Baer, "Perfectly Empowered Bodies," 263.

a reaction to the "confrontational tone of victorious healing."[101] Baer locates Bosworth in this renewed facilitating approach, which helped seekers appropriate healing through their own faith.

Baer's analysis has great explanatory power because it emphasizes the importance of cultural factors for the development of divine healing. Healing, while itself a substantive phenomenon, can be seen as a metaphor for believers' relation to their surrounding culture. The facilitating approach with broader cultural appeal ruled during periods of abundance like the 1880s and 1920s, while a more confrontational and isolated approach dominated during less affluent times. Put differently, where healing advocates felt embattled by the world around them, healing took on a tone of triumph, but where they saw themselves in greater harmony with their culture, they stressed the theme of abundance.[102] This helps explain Bosworth's emphases and the context of his success in the 1920s. Nevertheless, Bosworth's career also seems to blur Baer's categories. In particular, Bosworth's embrace of "heroic" healers like Maria Woodworth-Etter and William Branham shows the compatibility of different approaches and suggests that personality may have played just as large a role.[103] Furthermore, Baer's analysis does not explain the differences between the facilitating approach of 1870s, with its Victorian domesticity and patient counseling, and that of Bosworth in the 1920s, with its mass meetings and fast-moving prayer lines.

Summary

Each of these scholarly paradigms sheds light on Bosworth's thought, but none fully accounts for the complexities of his theology and career. Not feeling himself to have the certainty afforded by a healing gift and operating within the fast-paced and impersonal framework of itinerant evangelism, Bosworth sought to guarantee, experience, and share the supernatural work of God through a positional theological model that emphasized God's faithfulness over God's freedom. But because the pursuit of the supernatural was the center of Bosworth's thought, he also could easily work alongside and heartily endorse those whose practice and theological foundation for divine healing were remarkably different from his.

---

101. Baer, "Perfectly Empowered Bodies," 289–90.

102. Baer, "Perfectly Empowered Bodies," 327–30.

103. In part, Baer may not recognize this because he claims that divine healing was not prominent in Bosworth's ministry in the 1910s. Baer, "Perfectly Empowered Bodies," 291. Bosworth's work with Woodworth-Etter and Branham also challenges Ronald Kydd's categories. Kydd, "Healing in the Christian Church," 699. This article is a condensation of Kydd, *Healing through the Centuries*.

BRITISH-ISRAELISM: REFLECTIONS ON HISTORICISM AND THE SUPERNATURAL

As seen in chapter one, the gospel of the supernatural often expressed itself in particular eschatological systems. These could vary widely, as suggested by the transition from postmillennialism to premillennialism within the holiness movement. But this does not mean that the supernaturalist impulse is equally comfortable in all eschatologies. In fact, historically, a correlation exists between a historicist approach (or at least a rejection of a strict futurist approach) and intense supernaturalism. As a British-Israelist, Bosworth championed a historicist view of biblical prophecy that complemented his foundational pursuit of the supernatural.

A classic example of the eschatological-supernaturalist correlation comes from England in the 1830s. The futurist John N. Darby rejected the idea of the continuance of the spiritual gifts and other miracles. Darby in many ways wanted to remove God from history, so much so that he viewed the entire Christian era as a parenthesis. Darby's heirs, known as fundamentalists, continued the charge, as seen in the exchanges between Bosworth and his opponents in the 1920s. On the other hand, Darby's British rival, Edward Irving, argued for a historicist approach to prophecy and embraced a supernatural gospel replete with spiritual gifts such as healing and tongues.[104]

British-Israelists like Bosworth, although promulgating a very different kind of historicism than Irving, consistently placed the supernatural at the center of their message. As George Southwick, a pentecostal British-Israelist who revered Bosworth greatly, told one researcher, "I am talking about a supernatural God; a supernatural Book; a supernatural Creator; redemption, providence."[105] Gordon Lindsay, who worked closely with Bosworth during the *Voice of Healing* years, advocated his peculiar form of British-Israelism—which he called "Bible Chronology"—as a "link which bridges the gap between the Bible and modern times":

> We are given a vision of the scope, uniformity, and progressive manifestation of Divine Providence in the affairs of man. History becomes but a continuation of the Bible narrative; ever, there is divine continuity.[106]

---

104. Flegg, *"Gathered under Apostles,"* 423–36; Grass, *Lord's Watchman*, 149–73, 302; Robinson, *Divine Healing: The Formative Years*, 15–16; Dixon, "Have the 'Jewels of the Church' Been Found Again," 78–92.

105. "George W. Southwick to Michael Barkun."

106. Lindsay, *Wonders of Bible Chronology*, 35.

Lindsay considered his "Bible Chronology" a way to harmonize the futurist and historicist schools of interpretation. If he continued to hold these views during the time he worked with Bosworth, this may explain why Bosworth and Lindsay did not make an issue of British-Israelism when they began working with others, like Branham, who did not hold this teaching.[107]

While most pentecostals adopted a modified futurist dispensational eschatology, several of the most intensely supernatural groups rejected dispensationalism. For example, the British pentecostal William Hutchinson and his Apostolic Faith Church, the Latter Rain movement in North America in the late 1940s, and the later charismatic Kingdom Now theology all combined a refutation of futurism with an uncompromising expectation of supernatural experience.[108] Like Bosworth, these movements recognized (sometimes more intuitively than critically) that futurism contradicts the full gospel. In response, they offered a more integrated eschatological view that celebrated God's supernatural activity throughout human history, refusing to cordon God and the important end-time events to a time outside of time. Although generally rebuffed by the pentecostal establishment, such ideologies are perhaps more consistently supernaturalist than that of the pentecostal denominations.

CONCLUSION

In his pursuit of the supernatural, Bosworth taught that Christ's atonement purchased God's blessings while faith appropriated them on a personal level. He also looked for God's ongoing activity in human history, corroborated by biblical prophecies. According to Bosworth, believers had no excuse not to be living in full victory over sin, disease, and want, since God's love ensured his desire to bestow redemption blessings while God's immutability made his promises more dependable evidence than anything perceived by the five senses. Bosworth's theology did not always align neatly with that of the pentecostal denominations, but the same motivations were at its root. Pentecostals, distinguished in American religion for their pursuit

107. Lindsay, *Wonders of Bible Chronology*, 2–4, 33.
108. Hathaway, "Role of William Oliver Hutchinson," 40–57. The Latter Rain movement also rejected some of the tenets of Darbyism and blurred the prophetic lines demarcating the eschaton from the victorious Christian life. See Faupel, "Everlasting Gospel," 450–54. The Latter Rain movement helped birth Kingdom Now theology, the socially-oriented charismatic ideology that denies the dispensationalists' rapture and "[views] Revelation as a message of Christians' victory—on earth as well as at the end of time—in the cosmic battle of good and evil." Like the Latter Rain movement, Kingdom Now puts a premium on the gift of prophecy and openness to new spiritual truth. Barron, "Rechristianizing America," 53–79; quote on 53.

of the supernatural, gravitated to theologies like Bosworth's that provided some type of guarantee that God's direct intervention could be immediately experienced.

Conclusion

F. F. BOSWORTH IS a provocative lens through which to view the phenomenon of American pentecostalism from its beginnings in the late-nineteenth century holiness movement to its rise as a major cultural force in the decade after World War II. Although his story is unique, the chronological span and rare success of his ministry justifies the claim that he epitomizes and brings to the fore some dominant and often overlooked themes in the pentecostal story.

No significant pentecostal leader other than Bosworth serves as a true living link between the stirring supernatural gospel of the 1890s and the high-profile miracle ministries of the 1950s.[1] Healed under the ministry of the holiness evangelist Mattie Perry toward the end of the nineteenth century and occupying a position of leadership in the utopian project of divine healing demagogue John Alexander Dowie, Bosworth has as good a claim as any to have been nourished in the crosscurrents of the full gospel that gave rise to pentecostalism. His spirit-baptism under the ministry of Charles Parham substantively connects him to the "theological founder" of the new pentecostal movement.[2] As an early itinerant pentecostal evangelist and later settled pastor in Dallas who helped foster the greatest extended pentecostal revival in the decade after Azusa Street, Bosworth made an important contribution to early pentecostal religious culture, reminding believers that the pursuit of the supernatural, rather than doctrinal

---

1. Carrie Judd Montgomery has often been identified as a unique connection between the late-nineteenth century holiness movement and the postwar healing revival. Alexander, *Pentecostal Healing*, 25; Chappell, "Divine Healing Movement in America," 229; Miskov, *Life on Wings*, Kindle location 14513. While Montgomery was more thoroughly involved than Bosworth in the leadership of the pre-pentecostal movement, she died in July of 1946, just as William Branham was beginning his epochal itinerant ministry. The significance of Bosworth's chronological span is suggested, but downplayed by Hejzlar, *Two Paradigms for Divine Healing*, 8.

2. Baer, "Perfectly Empowered Bodies," 232.

exactitude, was its *raison d'être*. As a founding delegate of the Assemblies of God, Bosworth represented the work of coalescence and the drive toward organization in the new movement. The fact that Bosworth's development as an influential early pentecostal leader can be told virtually without mention of Azusa Street helps challenge the notion that the famed Los Angeles revival is the central point of origin for worldwide pentecostalism. Bosworth's success in itinerant divine healing ministry in the 1920s attests to his ongoing influence and pentecostalism's broader impact on American culture. His career quieted in the 1930s and 1940s, but he remained an authoritative and inspirational voice for many in the full gospel subculture while also presaging the later pentecostal attraction to broadcast media with his long-running radio program. His reappearance on the national and international scene after World War II provided the emerging healing revivalists with a live connection to the origins of the movement. This continuity could not be better portrayed than in the remarkable photograph of the aging Bosworth, standing next to Branham in his prime, as the two visited Dowie's grave. In content, this continuity consisted of the pursuit of the supernatural, which was articulated and experienced in a variety of ways. Being of a rational bent, not believing himself to be endowed with the gift of healing, having little appreciation for traditional Wesleyan concerns of assurance or crisis, and pursuing a type of ministry that necessitated quick results, Bosworth centered his theology on propositions that seemingly guaranteed God's supernatural intervention.

As a product of American revivalism, pentecostalism could not resist the tendency toward organization and forming denominations. Yet it also exhibited another characteristic of American revivalism, the independent minister who, although embodying the ethos of the organized movement, is not beholden to it. Perhaps more than most forms of American revivalism, pentecostalism—due to its focus on supernatural guidance—embraced independence of thought and leadership. Pentecostalism was born in an expectation of the restoration of forgotten teachings and practices and the unfolding of new revelation. Such pursuits by definition required thinking outside of the inherited theological box. Only pentecostalism could have produced a well-regarded denominational leader who argued that, "We need the extremist to start things moving, but we need the balanced teacher to keep them moving in the right direction."[3] Bosworth embodies this independence, with only transitory affiliations with pentecostal and full gospel denominations. Yet his success on the national and later global stage

---

3. Gee, "Extremes Are Sometimes Necessary," 9; cited in Harrell, *All Things Are Possible*, 109.

suggests that leaving the denominations does not signal a falling out with the main impulses of popular pentecostalism. Like Maria Woodworth-Etter, Raymond Richey, Aimee Semple McPherson, and Oral Roberts, Bosworth operated outside of the pentecostal establishment while sitting squarely in its popular stream.

In two main areas, Bosworth demonstrated the pentecostal penchant for independence of thought—his rejection of the majority tongues evidence doctrine and his adoption of British-Israelism. Although these were minority positions for pentecostalism, both positions testify to the underlying pursuit of the supernatural that was at the heart of the pentecostal movement as a whole. According to Bosworth, the tongues evidence doctrine detracts from the centrality of faith as the efficient cause and validation of supernatural activity. Bosworth observed that waiting on tongues to verify the experience of spirit-baptism had the effect of delaying or in some cases arresting altogether the supernatural experience. In the same way, Bosworth could not square the dominant dispensational eschatology with his desire to discern God's activity throughout history. British-Israelism provided an eschatological alternative that preserved the "any moment" expectation of premillennialism without sacrificing the church age as a supernaturally-devoid "parenthesis."

Bosworth is rightly known for his ministry of divine healing. Although healing was not the center of his thought, it was the spotlight for his public profile. In this respect, Bosworth embodies a distinctive that rivals tongues in its centrality to pentecostal practice and identity.[4] That Bosworth did not endorse the tongues evidence doctrine hardly mattered to opponents and supporters alike, for whom his ministry of healing was the preeminent claim for the supernatural gospel. The key role of divine healing in the postwar pentecostal revival demonstrates that throughout his career, Bosworth was championing that which was the crucial element to pentecostalism's broad cultural impact and appeal. Seekers did not fill auditoriums and arenas holding ten, twenty, or fifty thousand to receive tongues, but to receive healing. Filling these auditoriums were those harboring the radical evangelical desire for supernatural experiences that would "prove" their faith against encroaching scientific materialism sitting alongside those desperate for supernatural intervention for their broken bodies who might otherwise look askance at the pentecostals. The story of twentieth-century pentecostalism is the story of how this supernatural gospel was nurtured in local assemblies and broadcast for the masses alike.

---

4. Wacker, "Pentecostal Tradition," 515.

Bibliography

PRIMARY SOURCES

"1,300 Listen to Bosworths, Evangelists." *Syracuse Herald*, May 8, 1922, 16.
"3000 Hear Bosworth Reply to Dr. Lott." *National Labor Tribune*, September 3, 1925, 4.
"4,000 Letters from Those Helped by William Branham's Meetings in South Africa." *Pentecost* no. 22 (December 1952) 7.
Abrams, Minnie F. "The Object of the Baptism in the Holy Spirit." *Latter Rain Evangel* 3.8 (May 1911) 8–11.
Ackley, S.A. "Chicago Branch Activities." *Destiny* 7.4 (April 1936) 3.
———. "Detroit Convention." *Destiny* 7.4 (April 1936) 7.
"Additional Testimonies to God's Response to Faith." *Alliance Weekly* 54.48 (February 26, 1921) 764.
Allen, J. H. *Judah's Sceptre and Joseph's Birthright: An Analysis of the Prophecies of Scripture in Regard to the Regard to The Royal Family of Judah and the Many Nations of Israel*. 18th ed. 1902. Reprint, Merrimac, MA: Destiny, n.d.
———. *The National Number and Heraldry of the United States of America*. Boston, Beaumont, 1919.
———. "What We Saw at Westminister Abbey." *Apostolic Faith* 2.11 (December 1926) 7–10.
———. "What We Saw at Windsor Castle." *Apostolic Faith* 2.11 (November 1926) 10–13.
"Alliance Folk Give Dr. Sandford Grand Farewell." *Syracuse Herald*, May 20, 1922, 5.
"Alliance Group to Hear Rev. Bosworth." *Pottstown Mercury*, February 14, 1942, 10.
"All Night with God in Zion." *Leaves of Healing* 16.12 (January 7, 1905) 372.
"Americas Leading Divines Attend Bosworth Revival." *National Labor Tribune*, March 6, 1924, 3.
"The Anglo-Israel Error." *Pentecostal Evangel* no. 1392 (January 11, 1941) 12.
"The Anglo-Israel Movement." *Bible Standard* 7.2 (1926) 7–8.
"The Anglo-Israel Theory." *Pentecostal Evangel*, January 16, 1943, 10.
"Anglo-Saxon Federation Detroit Convention." *Destiny* 7.5 (May 1936) 6.
Angstead, Ruth. "A Grand Experience." *Pentecost* 1.2 (September 1908) 1–2.
Anderson, Hilda. "A Demented Being, Would Kill Self." *National Labor Tribune*, November 2, 1922, 3.
Annual Report for 1947. The Christian and Missionary Alliance, 1948.

Annual Report for 1950 and Minutes of the General Council. The Christian and Missionary Alliance, 1951.
"Anointments for Night Reach 100." *Altoona Mirror,* May 18, 1927, 1.
"Apostolic Faith World-Wide Camp Meeting." *Triumphs of Faith* 33.2 (February 1913) 45–46.
"Apostolic Faith World-Wide Camp Meeting." *Bridegroom's Messenger* 6.129 (March 15, 1913) 2.
"Appeal Made at Bosworth Rally for Money to Build Tabernacle." *Ottawa Citizen,* May 19, 1924, 4.
"A Refutation." *Latter Rain Evangel* 7.8 (May 1915) 14–15.
Argue, Zelma. "Chosen of God: The Story of Mrs. Robert A. Brown, Chapter One." *Christ's Ambassadors Herald* 13.6 (June 1940) 3, 12.
Armstrong, B. F. "Bosworth Evangelistic Campaign." *Alliance Weekly* 57.41 (December 8, 1923) 674.
Armstrong, Edward. "The Newark Convention." *Weekly Evangel* no. 88 (May 1, 1915) 4.
"A.S. Booth-Clibborn London Divine, Assisting Bosworth at Toledo, Ohio." *National Labor Tribune,* September 22, 1921, 4.
"As Dr. Speicher Sees It." *Zion City News,* June 28, 1907, 2.
Assembly, Pentecostal Church of the Nazarene General, Phineas Franklin Bresee, Robert Pierce, and Holiness Church of Christ. *Manual of the Pentecostal Church of the Nazarene, [1908].* Los Angeles: Nazarene Publishing, 1908.
"A Strange Fire." *Our Hope* 28.2 (August 1921) 83–85.
"At Gospel Tabernacle This Coming Sunday." *Freeport Journal Standard,* October 30, 1940, 6.
"At Headquarters." *Destiny* 7.4 (April 1936) 10.
"Attention People of All Faiths." *Lubbock Avalanche-Journal,* January 30, 1955, 26.
"Autos and Busses Crowd Boulevard for Bosworth Meetings in Beer Garden—Police Guard Meetings." *National Labor Tribune,* October 12, 1922, 3.
"Balmy Weather in Corpus Christi, Texas As the Meetings Close." *Exploits of Faith* 3.4 (April 1930) 8–9.
"Bandmaster Bosworth Surprised." *Zion Banner,* November 14, 1905, 58.
"Baptismal Service." *Dallas Morning News,* April 20, 1919, 9.
Barratt, Thomas B. *Baptism with the Holy Ghost and Fire: What Is the Scriptural Evidence?.* Springfield, MO: Gospel Publishing House, n.d.
Barth, Hattie. "The Dallas Revival." *Bridegroom's Messenger* 5.119 (October 15, 1912) 1.
"Beauty Restored to Girl Robbed by Affliction." *National Labor Tribune,* February 17, 1921, 5.
Beecher, Lyman. *A Plea for the West.* Cincinnati: Truman & Smith, 1835.
"The Believer's Body." *Our Hope* 28.3 (September 1921) 142–44.
Bell, E. N. "Bible Order Versus Fanaticism." *Word and Witness* 10.3 (March 20, 1914) 2–3.
———. "Editor's Field Report." *Weekly Evangel* no. 101 (July 31, 1915) 1.
———. "The Coming Great Council." *Christian Evangel* no. 250–251 (August 10, 1918) 1, 4.
———. "What Is the Evidence of the Baptism in the Spirit." *Word and Witness* 9.6 (June 20, 1913) 7.
Bellin, Fred A. "Little Ruth Bellin and Her Lazy Foot; Suffered in Miserable Plaster Paris Cast; More Operations Seemed Her Fate." *National Labor Tribune,* July 20, 1922, 3.

Benham, Charles O. "Joseph Is Yet Alive." In *Who Hath Believed Our Report?: A Biblical-Historical Defense of the Anglo-Israel Message Through the Lives, Testimonies, and Ministries of Many Outstanding Men of God!*, edited by Charles A. Jennings, 284–90. Owasso, OK: Truth in History, 2010.

———. "God Answers the Present World Crisis with Miracles of Healing." *Voice of Healing* 2.1 (April 1949) 4.

Bernard, W. "The Gift of Tongues and the Pentecostal Movement." *Weekly Evangel* no. 142 (June 3, 1916) 4–6.

"Beulah Heights Camp Meeting—1955." *Bridegroom's Messenger* 45.6 (August 1955) 4.

Bingham, Rowland V. *The Bible and the Body: Healing in the Scriptures*. 4th ed. 1921; repr.,Toronto: Evangelical Publishers, 1952.

———. *The Bible and the Body, Or, Healing in the Scriptures*. Toronto: Evangelical Publishers, 1921.

———. "The Healing Movement in Crisis." *Evangelical Christian* 18.2 (February 1922) 39–40.

———. "Touching the Ark." *Moody Bible Institute Monthly* 22.4 (December 1921) 714.

"Binghamton Convert Gone to Writing Poetry." *National Labor Tribune*, October 16, 1924, 4.

Birdsall, Elias G. "Revival News in Home Land: Dallas, Texas." *Word and Witness* 9.11 (November 20, 1913) 1.

———. "Application Blank for Ordination Certificate." 1916. Flower Pentecostal Heritage Center.

"Blessings More Abundantly." *Alliance Weekly* 56.29 (Sptember 1922) 458.

Boardman, William Edwin. *Record of the International Conference on Divine Healing and True Holiness Held at the Agricultural Hall, London . . . 1885*. London: Snow, 1885.

Boddy, A.A. "A Visit to Rev. A.B. Simpson." *Confidence* 2.9 (September 1909) 199.

———. "The Conference in Germany." *Confidence* 2.1 (January 1909) 5–6.

———. "The Pentecostal Movement." *Confidence* 3.8 (August 1910) 194–197.

"Book Reviews." *Alliance Weekly* 60.21 (May 23, 1925) 346.

"Bosworth." *Dallas Morning News*, November 19, 1919, 12.

"Bosworth." *Dallas Morning News*, November 20, 1919, 7.

"Bosworth Begins in Scranton." *National Labor Tribune*, June 18, 1925, 4.

"Bosworth Book Off Press." *Voice of Healing* 1.4 (July 1948) 6.

"Bosworth Bros. Broadcasted—Detroit Free Press Pull Enterprising Stunt—Thousands Hear the Message." *National Labor Tribune*, June 15, 1922, 3.

"Bosworth Bros.: Farewell—Cure for the Blues." *National Labor Tribune*, June 8, 1922, 3.

"Bosworth Bros., in New York." *Word and Work* 44.12 (December 1922) 16.

"Bosworth Brothers Evangelist and Aids Ready for Big Time; Great Crowds Waiting." *National Labor Tribune*, December 30, 1920, 7.

"Bosworth Brothers Here to Assist in Revival in Soldiers Tabernacle." *Houston Chronicle*, January 8, 1918, 8.

"Bosworth Brothers Winning Many Hearts in Sunny Southland." *National Labor Tribune*, February 16, 1922, 3.

Bosworth, Burton B. "Application Blank for Ordination Certificate." March 23, 1917. 30/2/8. Flower Pentecostal Heritage Center.

250 BIBLIOGRAPHY

———. "B.B. Bosworth to J.W. Welch." March 23, 1917. 30/2/8. Flower Pentecostal Heritage Center.
———. "B.B. Bosworth to J.W. Welch." October 13, 1918. 30/2/8. Flower Pentecostal Heritage Center.
"Bosworth Campaign in Chicago." *Alliance Weekly* 55.31 (October 15, 1921) 490.
"The Bosworth Campaign; Interest Growing in the Bosworth Revival and Healing Campaign; Prominent People Attend." *National Labor Tribune*, December 29, 1921, 3.
"Bosworth Campaign in Jersey." *Alliance Weekly* 56.36 (November 18, 1922) 570.
"Bosworth Campaign in Scranton, Penna." *Alliance Weekly* 60.31 (August 1, 1925) 535.
"Bosworth Campaign in St. Petersburgh, Florida." *Alliance Weekly* 60.9 (February 28, 1925) 143.
"Bosworth Campaign in Toronto." *Alliance Weekly* 57.9 (April 28, 1923) 151–52.
"The Bosworth Campaign in Toronto." *Evangelical Christian* 17.7 (July 1921) 199–200, 218.
"Bosworth Campaign, New York City." *Alliance Weekly* 56.25 (September 2, 1922) 394, 399.
"Bosworth Campaign Services End Today." *Syracuse Herald*, May 28, 1922, 22.
"Bosworth Campaign Stirs Toronto." *Alliance Weekly* 55.11 (May 28, 1921) 171–72.
"Bosworth Evangelistic Campaign, Indianapolis, Indiana." *Alliance Weekly* 60.3 (January 17, 1925) 42.
"Bosworth Farewell Draws 10,000 People." *Altoona Mirror*, July 26, 1927, 1, 16.
Bosworth, F. F. "A Continuous Revival in Dallas, Texas." *Weekly Evangel* no. 145 (June 24, 1916) 8.
———. "A Wonderful Revival." *Bridegroom's Messenger* 5.118 (September 15, 1912) 1.
———. "Beating in Texas Follows Ministry to Blacks: F. F. Bosworth's 1911 Letter to His Mother." *Assemblies of God Heritage* 6 (June 1, 1986) 5, 14.
———. "Be Ye Doers of the Word." Sermon, Chicago, Illinois, July 22, 1954. http://www.brothermel.org/audio-video/74.
———. *Bosworth's Life Story: The Life Story of Evangelist F. F. Bosworth, as Told by Himself in the Alliance Tabernacle, Toronto*. Toronto: Alliance Book Room, n.d.
———. "Branham Meetings in Germany and Switzerland." *Full Gospel Men's Voice* 3.6 (September 1955) 3–11.
———. "Brother Bosworth's Minneapolis and St. Paul Meetings." *Word and Witness* (Pangburn, Arkansas (3.2 (January 15, 1922) 3.
———. "Brother F.F. Bosworth About the Dallas Revival." *Bridegroom's Messenger* 5.119 (October 15, 1912) 1.
———. *Christ the Healer*. Grand Rapids, MI: Fleming H. Revell, 2000.
———. *Christ, the Healer: Messages on Divine Healing*. 7th edition. Miami Beach, FL, 1948.
———. *Christ the Healer: Sermons on Divine Healing*. Chicago, 1924.
———. "Clay in the Hands of the Potter." *Triumphs of Faith* 35.11 (November 1915) 254–259.
———. "Confirming the Word By Signs Following." *Latter Rain Evangel* 1.3 (December 1908) 7–8.
———. "Correspondence—Re: Death of First Wife." November 20, 1919. 3/8/5. Flower Pentecostal Heritage Center.
———. "Dallas and Bridgeport, Texas." *Weekly Evangel* no. 81 (March 13, 1915) 1.

———. "Did the Age of Miracles Ever End?" *Exploits of Faith* 3.3 (March 1930) 1–5.
———. "Discerning the Lord's Body." *Latter Rain Evangel* 6.9 (June 1914) 2–7.
———. "Do All Speak with Tongues?" *Word and Witness* (Pangburn, Arkansas) 3.2 (January 15, 1922) 1, 4.
———. "Do All Speak with Tongues?" *Truth and Liberty*, September 1972, 23–31.
———. *Do All Speak with Tongues? An Open Letter to the Ministers and Saints of the Pentecostal Movement*. Dallas: Williams Printery, n.d.
———. "The Enthronement of Self the Great Sin." *Latter Rain Evangel* 7.11 (August 1915) 3.
———. "Faint-Hearted Get Go-By; Ask, Stand Pat and Watch; Beg Big Things and Run; Golden Chance Awaiting." *National Labor Tribune*, February 17, 1921, 2, 7.
———. "F.F. Bosworth Rejoices Over Roberts' Meeting in Miami, Florida." *Healing Waters* 2.3 (February 1949) 4.
———. "F.F. Bosworth to J.W. Welch." July 24, 1918. 30/4/1. Flower Pentecostal Heritage Center.
———. *For This Cause: Or Why Many Are Weak and Sickly and Why Many Die Prematurely*. New York: Christian Alliance Publishing, n.d.
———. "For This Cause Was the Son of God Manifest That He Might Destroy the Works of the Devil." *Latter Rain Evangel* 13.8 (July 1921) 6–9.
———. "From Farm to Pulpit." *Bread of Life* 29.6 (June 1980) 5–6, 8, 11.
———. "Gifts of Healing Plus." *Voice of Healing* 2.10 (March 1950) B–C.
———. "God's Financial Plan Insures the Prosperity of His People." *Exploits of Faith* 2.5 (May 1929) 7–13.
———. "God's Visitation to South Africa." *Herald of His Coming* 11.2 (n.d.) 1.
———. "The Greatest Sin; Or, the Sin of Omission." *Truth and Liberty*, October 1956, 20–30.
———. "Healing in the Atonement." *Triumphs of Faith* 35.10 (October 1915) 226–31.
———. "Hints Regarding Healing." *Pentecostal Evangel* no. 1776 (May 22, 1948) 4, 13.
———. "How To Appropriate the Redemptive and Covenant Blessing of Bodily Healing." *Alliance Weekly* 59.23 (December 6, 1924) 397, 401.
———. "Is God the Author of Disease?" *Herald of Our Race* 2.4 (April 1938) 9. Flower Pentecostal Heritage Center.
———. "Is Healing for All?" *Kingdom Digest*, September 1949, 18–21.
———. *Judah vs. Israel*. Kingdom Study Course, Advanced Series: Lesson No. 4, n.d. Flower Pentecostal Heritage Center.
———. "Letter from Dallas, Texas." *Triumphs of Faith* 34.3 (March 1914) 72.
———. "Living Faith in the Power of God." *Triumphs of Faith* 35.2 (February 1915) 29–33.
———. "Looking at the Unseen." *Voice of Healing* 2.10 (January 1950) 4–5.
———. *Looking at the Unseen: Or, The Mental Habit of Faith*. Miami Beach: Bosworth, n.d.
———. "Mass Faith." Sermon, Chicago, Illinois, July 21, 1954. http://www.brothermel.org/audio-video/74.
———. *Meditations on the Ninety-First Psalm*. Miami Beach: Bosworth, n.d.
———. "Miracles in Texas." *Triumphs of Faith* 32.9 (September 1912) 202–5.
———. "New Covenant Obedience." *Destiny* 7.12 (December 1936) 4–5, 12.
———. "Nothing Can Hinder a Revival." *Weekly Evangel* no. 135 (April 15, 1916) 6–8.

———. "Pentecostal Outpouring in Dallas, Texas." *Latter Rain Evangel* 4.11 (August 1912) 10–11.
———. "Power in the Holy Ghost." *Triumphs of Faith* 34.11 (November 1914) 244–47.
———. "Readers of Tribune Request Prayer for Healing." *National Labor Tribune*, November 11, 1920, 3.
———. "Recipe for Healing." *Kingdom Digest*, August 1950, 33–37.
———. "Revival News in Home Land." *Word and Witness* 9.9 (September 20, 1913) 3.
———. "Revival News in Home Land: Bro. Bosworth, Texas." *Word and Witness* 9.12 (December 20, 1913) 3.
———. "Sin and Repentance." *Word and Witness* 10.5 (May 20, 1914) 2.
———. "Sister Bosworth with the Lord." *Pentecostal Evangel* no. 316–317 (November 29, 1919) 10.
———. *The Bible Distinction Between the House of Israel and the House of Judah.* Owasso, OK: Truth in History, 2002.
———. "The Call to Love." *Weekly Evangel* no. 218 (December 8, 1917) 2.
———. *The Christian Confession; Or, How to Obtain All Redemptive Blessings.* Miami: Bosworth, n.d.
———. "The Enthronement of Self the Great Sin." *Latter Rain Evangel* 7.11 (August 1915) 2–6.
———. "The God of All the Earth Working at Dallas." *Word and Witness* 8.10 (December 20, 1912) 1.
———. "The Grace of Liberality." *Exploits of Faith* 3.2 (February 1930) 1–2.
———. "The Greatest Revival in Dallas." *Weekly Evangel* no. 143 (June 10, 1916) 7.
———. "The Greatest Sin; Or, the Sin of Omission." *Truth and Liberty*, October 1956.
———. "The Faith That Takes." *Pentecostal Evangel* no. 1707 (January 25, 1947) 6–7.
———. "The Holy Spirit." *Pentecostal Herald* 3.12 (April 1918) 1.
———. *The Key to the Windows of Heaven, or God's Financial Plan.* Miami: Bosworth, n.d.
———. "The Lame Man at Lystra." *Exploits of Faith* 3.6 (June 1930) 1–4.
———. "The Ministry of Intercession." *Latter Rain Evangel* 5.8 (May 1913) 2–5.
———. *The Opening of the Prison: A Message to the Sick.* Miami Beach: Bosworth, n.d.
———. *The Past Tenses of God's Word*, n.d.
———. "The Potter and the Clay." *Latter Rain Evangel* 13.10 (September 1921) 20–23.
———. "The Practice of the Presence of God." *Latter Rain Evangel* 7.5 (February 1915) 5–8.
———. "The Practice of the Presence of God." *Triumphs of Faith* 35.3 (March 1915) 51–55.
———. "The Promise of the Father." *Latter Rain Evangel* 8.5 (February 1916) 2–7.
———. "The Prophecy of Daniel's 'Seventy Weeks.'" *Destiny* 11.10 (October 1940) 16–22.
———. "The Revival at Dallas, Tex." *Bridegroom's Messenger* 6.123 (December 1912) 2.
———. "The Sinfulness of Procrastination." *Latter Rain Evangel* 6.11 (August 1914) 7–11.
———. "The Will of God Boiled Down into Five Words. 'Be Filled with the Spirit.'" *Weekly Evangel* no. 229 (March 2, 1918) 1.
———. "The Windows of Heaven." *Kingdom Digest*, January 1948, 14–17.
———. "The Wonders of Faith." *Latter Rain Evangel* 5.9 (June 1913) 5–11.
———. "The Wonders of God in Dallas." *Word and Witness* 8.6 (August 20, 1912) 3.

———. "They Rehearsed All That God Had Done with Them." *Latter Rain Evangel* 13.6 (March 1921) 5–10.

———. "Tide Still Rising in Dallas, Texas." *Christian Evangel* 2.19 (May 9, 1914) 6.

———. "Triumphant Faith." *Alliance Weekly* 60.27 (July 4, 1925) 459–60.

"Bosworth Holds Wonderful Meetings in St. Paul—In East Next." *National Labor Tribune*, November 19, 1925, 7.

"Bosworth in Erie; No Fanaticism in His Manner; A Smile Always." *National Labor Tribune*, April 13, 1922, 6.

"Bosworth Meeting Again Attracts Huge Crowd and Many Remarkable Healing Testimonies Delivered." *Ottawa Citizen*, May 17, 1924, 6.

"The Bosworth Meetings." *Pentecostal Evangel* no. 386–387 (April 2, 1921) 7.

"The Bosworth Meetings in Detroit." *National Labor Tribune*, January 27, 1921, 3.

"Bosworth Meetings Now Under Way; No Sham Battle; Healing Taught." *National Labor Tribune*, September 8, 1921, 2.

"Bosworth Meeting in Indianapolis." *Alliance Weekly* 59.26 (December 27, 1924) 450.

"The Bosworth Party in Atlanta, Georgia." *Alliance Weekly* 60.10 (March 7, 1925) 167.

"Bosworth Party Opens in Canada." *National Labor Tribune*, April 5, 1923, 4.

"Bosworth Party Starts Old Time Gospel Revival." *National Labor Tribune*, August 21, 1924, 4.

"The Bosworth Revival Campaign in Houston, Texas." *Weekly Evangel* no. 213 (November 3, 1917) 14.

"Bosworth Revival Campaign Starts in Sheraden Tabernacle." *National Labor Tribune*, June 1924, 6.

"Bosworth's Flint Evangelist Campaign in Full Blast; Tabernacle Too Small; People Turned Away." *National Labor Tribune*, December 15, 1921, 3.

"Bosworths in Miami." *National Labor Tribune*, March 2, 1922, 3.

Bradford, Jesse F. *Are Anglo-Saxons Israelites? The Greatest Religious Question of the Day Discussed from a Bible Standpoint and Identifies the Ten Lost Tribes of Israel as the English Speaking Race, and God's Appointed Servants*. Dallas: Bradford, 1932.

Bradway, Dorothea Ann. "Dorothea Ann Bradway's Miraculous, Instantaneous Healing." *Exploits of Faith* 3.6 (June 1930) 12–14.

"Branham-Bosworth Campaign Successful in Zion, Illinois." *Voice of Healing* 2.1 (April 1949) 2.

"Branham-Bosworth Reunite for Miami, Florida, Campaign." *Voice of Healing* 1.12 (March 1949) 1–2.

"Branham Visits Roberts Campaign." *Voice of Healing* 2.1 (April 1949) 2, 16.

Branham, William. "Africa Trip Report." Sermon, Owensboro, Kentucky, November 9, 1953. http://churchages.com/en/sermon/branham/53-1 109-Africa-trip-report.

———. "A Greater than Solomon Is Here." Sermon, Bloomington, Illinois, April 12, 1961. http://churchages.com/en/sermon/branham/61-0 412-Greater-than-Solomon-is-here.

———. "At Thy Word." Sermon, Minneapolis, Minnesota, July 14, 1950. http://churchages.com/en/sermon/branham/50-0 714-at-Thy-Word.

———. "At Thy Word, Lord, I'll Let Down the Net." Sermon, Johnson City, New York, December 7, 1954. http://churchages.com/en/sermon/branham/54-1 207-at-Thy-Word-Lord-Ill-let-down-the-net.

———. "A Wedding Supper." Sermon, Chicago, Illinois, October 6, 1956. http://churchages.com/en/sermon/branham/56-1 006-wedding-supper.

———. "Believest Thou This?" Sermon, Tulsa, Oklahoma, April 2, 1960. http://churchages.com/en/sermon/branham/60-0402-believest-thou-this.

———. "Believest Thou This?" Sermon, Houston, Texas, January 15, 1950. http://churchages.com/en/sermon/branham/50-0115-believest-thou-this.

———. "Be of Good Cheer." Sermon, Chicago, Illinois, July 21, 1954. http://churchages.com/en/sermon/branham/54-0721-be-of-good-cheer.

———. "Blind Bartimaeus." Sermon, Karlsuhe, East Germany, August 18, 1955. http://churchages.com/en/sermon/branham/55-0818-blind-Bartimaeus.

———. "By Faith, Moses." Sermon, Jeffersonville, Indiana, July 20, 1958. http://churchages.com/en/sermon/branham/58-0720M-by-faith-Moses.

———. "Debate on Tongues." Sermon, Yakima, Washington, August 7, 1960. http://churchages.com/en/sermon/branham/60-0807-debate-on-tongues.

———. "Diseases and Afflictions." Sermon, Louisville, Kentucky, January 1950. http://churchages.com/en/sermon/branham/50-0100-diseases-and-afflictions.

———. "Divine Healing." Sermon, Jeffersonville, Indiana, December 19, 1954. http://churchages.com/en/sermon/branham/54-1219M-Divine-healing.

———. "Divine Love." Sermon, Jeffersonville, Indiana, August 26, 1956. http://churchages.com/en/sermon/branham/56-0826-Divine-Love.

———. "Do You Now Believe?" Sermon, West Palm Beach, Florida, December 6, 1953. http://churchages.com/en/sermon/branham/53-1206-do-you-now-believe.

———. "Early Spiritual Experiences." Sermon, Hammond, Indiana, July 13, 1952. http://churchages.com/en/sermon/branham/52-0713A-early-spiritual-experiences.

———. "Expectation." Sermon, Binghamton, New York, December 6, 1954. http://churchages.com/en/sermon/branham/54-1206-expectation.

———. "Expectations and What Love Is." Sermon, Phoenix, Arizona, February 28, 1954. http://churchages.com/en/sermon/branham/54-0228A-expectations-and-what-Love-is.

———. "Faith (Africa Trip Report)." Sermon, Zion, Illinois, July 25, 1952. http://churchages.com/en/sermon/branham/52-0725-faith-Africa-trip-report.

———. "God Revealing Himself to His People." Sermon, Cleveland, Ohio, August 13, 1950. http://churchages.com/en/sermon/branham/50-0813E-God-revealing-Himself-to-His-people.

———. "God's Provided Way." Sermon, Los Angeles, California, April 15, 1959. http://churchages.com/en/sermon/branham/59-0415A-Gods-Provided-Way.

———. "Healing (What Cancer Is)." Sermon, Chicago, Illinois, September 4, 1953. http://churchages.com/en/sermon/branham/53-0904-healing-what-cancer-is.

———. "How Faith Acts (Africa Trip Report)." Sermon, Battle Creek, Michigan, August 16, 1952. http://churchages.com/en/sermon/branham/52-0816-how-faith-acts-Africa-trip-report.

———. "How God Called Me to Africa, Part I." *Voice of Healing* 5.4 (July 1952) 5, 8.

———. "How the Angel Came to Me, and His Commission." Sermon, January 17, 1955. http://churchages.com/en/sermon/branham/55-0117-how-the-Angel-came-to-me-and-His-commission.

———. "I Have a Greater Witness than John (How the Angel Came to Me)." Sermon, Owensboro, Kentucky, November 7, 1953. http://churchages.com/en/sermon/branham/53-1107-I-have-a-Greater-Witness-than-John-How-the-Angel-came-to-me.

———. "Israel at the Red Sea." Sermon, Jeffersonville, Indiana, March 26, 1953. http://churchages.com/en/sermon/branham/53-0326-Israel-at-the-Red-Sea-1.

———. "It Is I, Be Not Afraid." Sermon, Chicago, Illinois, July 20, 1954. http://churchages.com/en/sermon/branham/54-0720E-it-is-I-be-not-afraid.

———. "I Was Not Disobedient to the Heavenly Vision." Sermon, Zion, Illinois, July 18, 1949. http://churchages.com/en/sermon/branham/49-0718-i-was-not-disobedient-to-the-heavenly-vision.

———. "I Was Not Disobedient Unto the Heavenly Vision." http://tosworg.globat.com/Special/I%20Was%20Not%20Disobedient.htm.

———. "I Will Restore." Sermon, Owensboro, Kentucky, November 10, 1953. http://churchages.com/en/sermon/branham/53-1110-I-will-restore.

———. "Jehovah-Jireh." Sermon, Phoenix, Arizona, March 9, 1957. http://churchages.com/en/sermon/branham/57-0309E-Jehovah-Jireh.

———. "Jehovah-Jireh." Sermon, Indianapolis, Indiana, June 12, 1957. http://churchages.com/en/sermon/branham/57-0612-Jehovah-Jireh.

———. "Jesus Christ the Same Yesterday, Today, and Forever." Sermon, Jonesboro, Arkansas, May 6, 1953. http://churchages.com/en/sermon/branham/53-0506-Jesus-Christ-the-same-yesterday-and-today-and-forever.

———. "Life Is the Healer." Sermon, Indianapolis, Indiana, June 11, 1957. http://churchages.com/en/sermon/branham/57-0611-Life-is-the-healer.

———. "Life Story of Rev. Wm. Branham." *Voice of Healing* 1.7 (October 1948) 1, 13.

———. "Manifested Sons of God (Series, Part 2 of 4)." Sermon, Jeffersonville, Indiana, May 18, 1960. http://churchages.com/en/sermon/branham/60-0518-manifested-sons-of-God.

———. "Mary's Belief." Sermon, Phoenix, Arizona, March 11, 1960. http://churchages.com/en/sermon/branham/60-0311-Marys-belief.

———. "Our Hope Is in God." Sermon, New York, September 29, 1951. http://churchages.com/en/sermon/branham/51-0929-our-hope-is-in-God.

———. "Palmerworm, Locust, Cankerworm and Caterpillar." Sermon, Connersville, Indiana, June 12, 1953. http://churchages.com/en/sermon/branham/53-0612-palmerworm-locust-cankerworm-and-caterpillar.

———. "Sirs, We Would See Jesus." Sermon, Newark, New Jersey, December 11, 1957. http://churchages.com/en/sermon/branham/57-1211-sirs-we-would-see-Jesus.

———. "Speak to This Rock." Sermon, Jonesboro, Arkansas, May 12, 1953. http://churchages.com/en/sermon/branham/53-0512-speak-to-this-Rock.

———. "Testimony." Sermon, West Palm Beach, Florida, November 29, 1953. http://churchages.com/en/sermon/branham/53-1129E-testimony.

———. "The Basis of Fellowship." Sermon, Long Beach, California, February 14, 1961. http://churchages.com/en/sermon/branham/61-0214-basis-of-fellowship.

———. "The Deity of Jesus Christ." Sermon, Jeffersonville, Indiana, December 25, 1949. http://churchages.com/en/sermon/branham/49-1225-Deity-of-Jesus-Christ.

———. "The Faith Once Delivered to the Saints." Sermon, West Palm Beach, Florida, November 29, 1953. http://churchages.com/en/sermon/branham/53-1129A-faith-that-was-once-delivered-to-the-saints.

———. "The Heathen Believe as Power Is Shown." *Voice of Healing* 5.5 (August 1952) 6–7, 18.

———. "The Law Having a Shadow." Sermon, Chicago, Illinois, June 21, 1956. http://churchages.com/en/sermon/branham/56-0621-Law-having-a-shadow.

———. "The Maniac of Gadara." Sermon, Chicago, Illinois, July 20, 1954. http://churchages.com/en/sermon/branham/54-0 720A-maniac-of-Gadara.

———. "The Marriage of the Lamb." Sermon, Phoenix, Arizona, January 21, 1962. http://churchages.com/en/sermon/branham/62-0 121E-marriage-of-the-Lamb.

———. "The Mighty Conqueror." Sermon, Edmonton, Alberta, Canada, August 8, 1957. http://churchages.com/en/sermon/branham/57-0 808-Mighty-Conqueror.

———. "The Prophet Elisha." Sermon, Chicago, Illinois, July 23, 1954. http://churchages.com/en/sermon/branham/54-0 723-prophet-Elisha.

———. "Questions and Answers on Hebrews (Series, Part 2 of 3)." Sermon, Jeffersonville, Indiana, October 2, 1957. http://churchages.com/en/sermon/branham/57-1 002-questions-and-answers-on-Hebrews-2.

———. "The Queen of Sheba." Sermon, Waterloo, Iowa, January 25, 1958. http://churchages.com/en/sermon/branham/58-0 125-Queen-of-Sheba.

———. "The Sign of His Coming." Sermon, Cleveland, Tennessee, April 7, 1962. http://churchages.com/en/sermon/branham/62-0 407-sign-of-His-coming.

———. *The William Branham Sermons: How God Called Me to Africa and Other Sermons*. Dallas: Voice of Healing Publishing, 1960.

———. "The Works That I Do Bear Witness of Me." Sermon, Phoenix, Arizona, April 13, 1951. http://churchages.com/en/sermon/branham/51-0 413-works-that-I-do-bear-witness-of-me.

———. "To Whom Is the Arm of the Lord Revealed?" Sermon, Cleveland, Ohio, August 24, 1950. http://churchages.com/en/sermon/branham/50-0 824-to-whom-is-the-arm-of-the-Lord-revealed.

———. "We Would See Jesus." Sermon, San Jose, California, April 22, 1959. http://churchages.com/en/sermon/branham/59-0 422-we-would-see-Jesus.

———. "We Would See Jesus." Sermon, Bloomington, Illinois, April 9, 1961. http://churchages.com/en/sermon/branham/61-0 409-we-would-see-Jesus.

———. "Where I Think Pentecost Failed." Sermon, San Fernando, California, November 11, 1955. http://churchages.com/en/sermon/branham/55-1 111-where-I-think-Pentecost-failed.

———. "Who Hath Believed Our Report?" Sermon, Toledo, Ohio, July 19, 1951. http://churchages.com/en/sermon/branham/51-0 719-who-hath-believed-our-report.

———. "Who Is This?" Sermon, Jeffersonville, Indiana, May 10, 1959. http://churchages.com/en/sermon/branham/59-0 510E-who-is-this.

"Bridgeport People Attend Brooklyn Meeting to Hear Evang. Bosworth." *National Labor Tribune*, February 22, 1923, 3.

"The British-Israel Delusion." *Pentecostal Evangel* no. 1357 (May 11, 1940) 7.

"British Israelism or Anglo Israelism." *Alliance Weekly* 59.19 (November 8, 1924) 315.

"Bro. Bosworth at Houston, Tex." *Weekly Evangel* no. 206 (September 8, 1917) 11.

"Brooklyn, N.Y." *Word and Work* 44.10 (October 1922) 15.

"Brother Branham on the Field Again." *Voice of Healing* 1.8 (November 1948) 1.

Bryant, Daniel. "Baptism of Holy Spirit." *Zion City Independent*, December 13, 1907.

———. "Shiloh and Messiah." *Zion City News*, December 24, 1909, 3.

Bundy, David. "Spiritual Advice to a Seeker: Letters to T B Barratt from Azusa Street, 1906." *Pneuma* 14.2 (September 1, 1992) 159–70.

"Bureau of Information." *Word and Witness* 9.10 (October 20, 1913) 1.

Bushnell, Horace. *Nature and the Supernatural: As Together Constituting the One System of God*. London: Dickinson, 1880.

Calvin, John. *Institutes of the Christian Religion*. Peabody, MA: Hendrickson, 2008.
Campbell, P.S. "How God Worked in Toronto." *Alliance Weekly* 55.16 (July 2, 1921) 250.
———. "The Bosworth Campaign in the Alliance Tabernacle, Toronto." *Alliance Weekly* 57.15 (June 9, 1923) 247.
"Camp Meeting Notes." *Bridegroom's Messenger* 2.40 (June 15, 1909) 3.
"Campmeetings." *Latter Rain Evangel* 2.9 (June 1910) 9.
"Campmeetings." *Latter Rain Evangel* 3.9 (June 1911) 12.
"Campmeetings and Conventions." *Latter Rain Evangel* 5.6 (March 1913) 16.
Carothers, W. F. "The Baptism of the Spirit and Speaking with Tongues." *Moody Bible Institute Monthly* 22.5 (January 1922) 761–62.
———. "The Baptism with the Holy Ghost." *Apostolic Faith* (Baxter Springs) 1.9 (May 1906) 14–15.
———. *The Baptism with the Holy Ghost and Speaking in Tongues*. Houston; Zion City, IL, 1906.
Cather, Willa. *The Life of Mary Baker G. Eddy and the History of Christian Science*. Lincoln: University of Nebraska Press, 1993.
Chapman, Katherine Elise. "'Times of Refreshing': The Bosworth Revival Campaign in Detroit." *Alliance Weekly* 56.23 (August 19, 1922) 361, 367.
"Cheering Words from Zion's Guests." *Leaves of Healing* 4.15 (February 5, 1898) 295.
"Chicago Convention." *Word and Witness* 9.6 (June 20, 1913) 5.
"Chicago's Visitation of Miracles of Healing." *Latter Rain Evangel* 20.5 (February 1928) 14–17.
"Christian Alliance." *Pottstown Mercury*, March 6, 1943, 12.
"The Christian Assembly." *Zion City News*, December 25, 1908, 4.
"Church Notes." *Dallas Morning News*, March 15, 1914, 4.
"Citizens' Mid-Week Rally." *Leaves of Healing* 16.22 (March 18, 1905) 701.
"Clergymen Impressed by Revivals in City." *National Labor Tribune*, September 25, 1924, 4.
"Close of Third Feast." *Zion Banner*, July 24, 1903, 155.
"Closing Service of the Feast." *Leaves of Healing* 13.18 (August 22, 1903) 576.
"The Cloud of His Glory Upon Us." *Latter Rain Evangel* 5.9 (June 1913) 2–5.
Cody, Sadie. "A Miracle of Healing." *Latter Rain Evangel* 3.8 (May 1911) 19–22.
———. "Report from Los Angeles Convention." *Triumphs of Faith* 34.11 (November 1914) 262–63.
Cole, May A. "Claims Thousands Neglected Rare Opportunity." *National Labor Tribune*, May 28, 1925, 4.
———. "The End Is Not Yet—More Healings Reported." *National Labor Tribune*, June 19, 1924, 3.
Collins, M.E. "Divine Healing in the Bible College, Part V." *Voice of Healing* 4.11 (February 1952) 8.
———. "How I Learned the Truth About Divine Healing." *Pentecostal Evangel* no. 2129 (February 27, 1955) 3.
"A Combination of Spiritual Forces to Sweep New England." *National Labor Tribune*, January 18, 1923, 3.
Combined Minutes of the General Council of the Assemblies of God . . . 1914. St. Louis: Gospel Publishing, 1914.

Constitution and By-Laws of the General Council of the Assemblies of God . . . Minutes 1929 with List of Ministers and Missionaries. Springfield, MO: General Council of the Assemblies of God, 1929

"Controversy Languishes—Evangelism Spreading." *Christian Evangel* no. 193 (June 9, 1917) 7, 9.

"Convention at Osborne, Kans." *Weekly Evangel*, February 12, 1916, 14.

"The Convention Program." *Messenger of the Covenant* 6.65 (May 1935) 2.

"Convention Program." *Messenger of the Covenant* 6.66 (June 1935) 7.

"Convention Story." *Destiny* 7.7 (July 1936) 3.

"Conversations with F.F. Bosworth." *Voice of Healing* 1.1 (April 1948) 4.

"Conway, S.C." *Bridegroom's Messenger* 2.44 (August 15, 1909) 2.

Cook, C.R. "At Headquarters." *Messenger of the Covenant* 6.66 (June 1935) 5.

———. "At Headquarters." *Messenger of the Covenant* 6.71 (November 1935) 7.

Coote, Leonard W. *Impossibilities Become Challenges: A Record of God's Faithfulness, in Saving, Baptizing with the Holy Spirit, Leading out into Missionary Work and Supplying of Daily Needs*. Ikoma, Japan: Ikoma Bible College, 1965.

Copley, A.S. *The Holy Spirit, The One Baptism, The Anointing—Personal and Practical*. Accessed April 7, 2014. http://www.gracegod.com/pamphlet_and_articles/pamphlets/The%20Holy%20Spirit%20-%20The%20One%20Baptism%20and%20the%20Anointing.pdf.

Cossum, W.H. "Mountain Peaks of Prophecy and Sacred History: Prophecy Fulfilled and Unfulfilled." *Latter Rain Evangel* 2.6 (March 1910) 3–7.

"The Council at St. Louis." *Christian Evangel* no. 210 (October 13, 1917) 2–3.

"Criticisms Answered." *Pentecostal Testimony* 1.5 (July 1, 1910) 11.

"The Critics Answered by Evangelist F.F. Bosworth." *Alliance Weekly* 59.5 (August 2, 1924) 77–78.

"Crowded with Blessing." *Zion City News*, September 18, 1908, 1, 3.

"Crowds Swarming to Evangelistic Services on Lot." *Southtown Economist*, August 11, 1931, 1.

"Crowds Turned Away from Carnegie Hall; Evangelist Bosworth Extends His Date." *National Labor Tribune*, December 2, 1920, 5.

Daggett, Mabel Potter. "Are There Modern Miracles?" *Ladies' Home Journal*, June 1923, 166–6 7.

"Dallas, Texas." *Alliance Weekly* 52.26 (September 20, 1919) 414.

Darms, Anton. *The Delusion of British-Israelism: A Comprehensive Treatise*. New York: Publication Office "Our Hope." 1938.

———. "The Fallacy of the British-Israel Delusion." *Our Hope* 45.5 (November 1938) 321–27.

Davenport, Henry A. "Surely It Was Good to Have Been There." *National Labor Tribune*, March 22, 1923, 3.

"Deaf Six Years, Faith Cures Her." *Chicago Daily News*, March 28, 1928, 5.

"Declaration, International Pentecostal Consultative Council." *Confidence* 5.12 (December 1912) 277.

"Defy Unscriptural—But Is Willing to Have Dr. Lott Pick Out Any Healed." *National Labor Tribune*, December 17, 1925, 7.

Delaney, Maude M. "God's Mighty Power." *Word and Witness* 8.8 (October 20, 1912) 3.

———. "More About the Revival in Dallas, Texas." *Bridegroom's Messenger* 5.120 (November 1, 1912) 2.

"The 'Deliverance Campaigns.'" *Pentecost* no. 37 (June 1956) 17.
"Did You Know?" *Herald of Our Race* 4.8 (August 1940) 3.
"Directory of the Ordained Officers of the Christian Catholic Church in Zion." *Leaves of Healing* 14.20 (March 5, 1904) 618.
"The Dirtiest and Biggest Lie Since the Death of Ananias and Sapphira." *Zion Herald*, December 23, 1908, 3.
"The Distinction Between Israel and Judah." *Kingdom Digest*, June 1952.
"Doctrine of Healing Is Promulgated." *National Labor Tribune*, May 3, 1923, 3.
"Doctrine of the Pentecostal Movement." *Bridegroom's Messenger* 2.37 (May 1, 1909) 1.
"Dowie and His Host." *Dallas Morning News*, October 17, 1903, 3.
Dowie, John Alexander. *Doctors, Drugs and Devils; Or, The Foes of Christ the Healer. A Sermon Delivered in The Auditorium, Chicago, March 29, 1896*. Chicago: Zion, 1897.
"Dowie Rails at Churches." *Waukegan Daily Sun*, July 21, 1902, 2.
"Dr. Charles O. Benham." *Voice of Healing* 2.2 (May 1949) 9.
Du Plessis, David J. "A Faithful Pioneer Passes." *World-wide Revival* 11.1 (April 1958) 10.
———. "The International Fellowship Column." *Voice of Healing* 4.9 (December 1951) 16.
Durham, William H. *Articles Written by Pastor W.H. Durham Taken from Pentecostal Testimony*, n.d.
———. "The Great Battle of Nineteen Eleven." *Pentecostal Testimony* 2.1 (January 1912) 6–8.
———. "The Pentecostal Revival at Azusa Street—How It Began and How It Ended." *Pentecostal Testimony* 1.8 (1911) 3–4.
———. "Sanctification: The Bible Does Not Teach It as a Second Definite Work of Grace." *Pentecostal Testimony* 1.8 (July 1911) 2.
———. "Some Other Phases of Sanctification." *Pentecostal Testimony* 2.2 (May 1912) 7–9.
———. "Speaking in Tongues Is the Evidence of Spirit Baptism." *Pentecostal Testimony* 2.2 (May 1912) 9–12.
"Early Morning Sacrifice of Praise and Prayer." *Leaves of Healing* 14.1 (October 24, 1903) 14.
"Early Morning Sacrifice of Praise and Prayer." *Leaves of Healing* 15.16 (August 6, 1904) 515.
Eddy, Mary Baker. *Retrospection and Introspection*. Boston: Joseph Armstrong, 1892.
———. *Science and Health: With Key to the Scriptures*. Boston: A. V. Stewart, 1906.
"Editorial." *Voice of Healing* 1.6 (September 1948) 6.
"Editorials." *Alliance Weekly* 53.9 (November 22, 1919) 130.
"The Editor's Meetings." *Evangelical Christian* 18.4 (April 1922) 116.
"Elgin, Ill., Unable to Accommodate Crowds Attending Meeting." *Voice of Healing* 1.3 (June 1948) 1–2, 12.
"Eminent Minister Endorses Divine Healing—-Rejoices and Suggests Shaking Up." *National Labor Tribune*, June 23, 1921, 7.
"Encouraging Endorsements." *Our Hope* 32.7 (January 1926) 400–401.
Entzminger, Louis. *The Modern "Divine Healing" Racket: Are Bible Miracles to Be Performed by the People of God Today?*. Houston: L. Entzminger, 1938.

"Epoch in History of Zion." *Zion City News*, September 4, 1908, 1. Zion Historical Society.
"Erie Revival Campaign Increases in Power." *National Labor Tribune*, April 27, 1922, 3.
"Eureka Singers Appear at Oregon." *Madison Wisconsin State Journal*, August 17, 1938, 16.
"Evang. Bosworth Preaches Strong Sunday Message." *National Labor Tribune*, March 1, 1923, 3.
"Evangelism and Bodily Healing." *Moody Bible Institute Monthly* 24.12 (August 1924) 593–95.
"Evangelist and Mrs. Bosworth Enjoy Vacation." *Exploits of Faith* 2.8 (August 1929) 8.
"Evangelist Bosworth Hands Out One to Skeptics and Critics." *National Labor Tribune*, November 17, 1921, 4.
"Evangelist Bosworth, Prayer and Healer, Invites Sick and Afflicted to Come." *National Labor Tribune*, October 21, 1920, 3.
"Evangelist Bosworth's Great Meeting at Lima, Ohio." *Word and Witness* (Pangburn, Arkansas (3.2 (January 15, 1922) 1, 3.
"Evangelist F.F. Bosworth Answers Multitudes of Anxious Folks." *National Labor Tribune*, July 24, 1924.
"Evangelist F.F. Bosworth Answers Multitudes of Anxious Folks." *National Labor Tribune*, July 31, 1924.
"Evangelist F.F. Bosworth Answers Multitudes of Anxious Folks." *National Labor Tribune*, August 7, 1924.
"Evangelist F.F. Bosworth Answers Multitudes of Anxious Folks." *National Labor Tribune*, August 14, 1924.
"Evangelist F.F. Bosworth Forced into Larger Hall; Tribune Writers Seek and Write to Find Out How." *National Labor Tribune*, November 4, 1920, 7.
"Evangelist F.F. Bosworth Opens World's Greatest Religious Campaign; Bring the Sick." *National Labor Tribune*, June 23, 1921, 4.
"Evangelist Fred Francis Bosworth Gone and Done It—He's Married." *National Labor Tribune*, November 22, 1922, 3.
"Evangelistic Campaign, Bosworth Brothers Opens in Brooklyn on February 11th." *National Labor Tribune*, February 15, 1923, 3.
"Evangelistic Services." *Chester Times*, June 24, 1933, 4.
"Evangelist Rader Warns 800 College Students against Suicide." *National Labor Tribune*, June 21, 1923, 3.
"Evangelist Rev. F.F. Bosworth." *Oak Park Leaves*, June 6, 1935, 36.
"Evangelists at Gospel Tabernacle." *Freeport Journal Standard*, October 7, 1940, 7.
"Evangelists Optimistic in Revival Here." *Syracuse Herald*, May 14, 1922, 20.
"Evangelist Speaks Here Next Sunday." *Freeport Journal Standard*, November 16, 1939, 6.
"Every Meeting Crowded with Maimed, Halt, Blind Seeking Divine Aid—Many Souls Saved." *National Labor Tribune*, November 18, 1920, 3.
"Evil Men Wax Worse." *Zion Herald*, April 8, 1908, 1.
Ewing, Curtis Clair. *The Anglo-Israel Belief: Is It a Cult?*. Pasadena, CA, n.d. Flower Pentecostal Heritage Center.
———. *The Distinction between Judah and Israel as Shown by the Weight of Scholarship.* Chicago: Curtis Clair Ewing, n.d.

Excell, J.G. "Notes of Thanksgiving from the Whole World." *Leaves of Healing* 12.26 (April 18, 1903) 827.
Executive Presbytery of the General Council of the Assemblies of God. "Certificate of Ordination, Fred F. Bosworth." 1916. 30/4/1. Flower Pentecostal Heritage Center.
"Extracts from a Very Important Letter from Bro. J.G. Lake." *Confidence* 2.3 (March 1909) 74–75.
"Extreme Sensationalism." *Our Hope* 28.8 (February 1922) 466–67.
"Faith Cure Miracle Bubble Is Bursting." *Our Hope* 28.12 (June 1922) 760–63.
"Faith Healer Is Challenged." *National Labor Tribune*, February 17, 1921, 7.
"Fans to Hear Famed Evangelist Over WJBT." *Freeport Journal Standard*, January 6, 1928, 11.
"Farewell to Bosworths, Gone Back to Chicago, Will Answer Critics." *National Labor Tribune*, June 19, 1924, 3.
"F.F. Bosworth Fully Recovered." *Zion City Independent*, September 22, 1911, 4.
"F.F. Bosworth Heard Over WJJD Daily." *Oak Park Leaves*, February 20, 1936, 18.
"F.F. Bosworth, Raymond T. Richey, and B.B. Bosworth at Evangelistic Temple." *Exploits of Faith* 3.2 (February 1930) 8–10.
"F.F. Bosworth to His Mother." August 11, 1911. 3/8/5. Flower Pentecostal Heritage Center.
"Fifteen Days with God." *Latter Rain Evangel* 7.9 (June 1915) 13.
"The Final Meetings of the Bosworth Brothers at Detroit, Mich., Soul-Inspiring—Many Saved, Cured and Baptized." *National Labor Tribune*, July 6, 1922, 3.
Finestone, Daniel. "Anglo-Israelism—Fact or Fancy?" *Latter Rain Evangel*, May 1936, 13–15.
Finney, Charles G. *Memoirs of Rev. Charles G. Finney*. New York: Barnes-, 1876.
———. *Lectures on Revivals of Religion*. New York: Leavitt, Lord & Company, 1835.
Fitch, C.C. "Bloomington (Ills.) Campaign Began on Easter Sunday." *Exploits of Faith* 3.5 (May 1930) 5–7.
———. "Bosworth Campaign in Toledo." *Alliance Weekly* 55.34 (November 5, 1921) 538.
———. "The Bosworth's Open a Strenuous Month's Campaign in Brooklyn, N.Y." *National Labor Tribune*, August 10, 1922, 2.
———. "Campaign in Detroit." *Alliance Weekly* 56.18 (July 15, 1922) 282.
———. "Great Rush for Baptism; Presbyterians in Line; Candidates Rejoice; Hundreds Join In." *National Labor Tribune*, October 18, 1921, 3.
———. "More 'Good News' from Joliet, Illinois, Meetings." *Exploits of Faith* 3.10 (October 1930) 13–18.
———. "Report of the Joliet, Ills., Campaign." *Exploits of Faith* 4.3 (March 1931) 7–10.
———. "Report of the Joliet, Ills., Campaign." *Exploits of Faith* 4.4 (April 1931) 6–13.
———. "The 1929 Campaign in 'The Twin Cities.'" *Exploits of Faith* 2.2 (February 1929) 6–8, 12.
———. "The Battle at Joliet, Illinois." *Exploits of Faith* 3.8 (August 1930) 15–17.
———. "The Bosworth Meetings in Anderson, Indiana." *Exploits of Faith* 2.3 (March 1929) 10–14, 16.
———. "The Bosworth's Open a Strenuous Month's Campaign in Brooklyn, N.Y." *National Labor Tribune*, August 10, 1922.
Fitch, May Wyburn. "Bosworth Campaign in Atlanta." *Alliance Weekly* 57.28 (September 8, 1923) 450.

———. "The Healing Delusion." *Our Hope* 33.11 (May 1927) 687–90.

———. *The Healing Delusion: Dealing with the Doctrine, the Methods Prevailing and the Claims Made in the Present-Day Healing Campaigns*. New York: Loizeaux Bros., n.d.

———. "How Jerry Mc'Auley Mission Worker Sees Evangelist F.F. Bosworth." *National Labor Tribune*, September 20, 1923, 3.

"Flash!" *Voice of Healing* 1.7 (October 1948) 1.

Flexner, Abraham. *Medical Education in the United States and Canada: A Report to the Carnegie Foundation for the Advancement of Teaching*. Carnegie Foundation for the Advancement of Teaching, 1910.

Flower, J. Roswell. "Evidence of the Baptism." *Pentecostal Evangel* no. 336–337 (April 17, 1920) 4.

———. "God Honors Faith." *Pentecost* 2.3 (February 1, 1910) 1.

———. "How I Received the Baptism in the Holy Spirit [Part 1]." *Pentecostal Evangel* no. 982 (January 21, 1933) 2–3.

———. "How I Received the Baptism in the Holy Spirit [Part 2]." *Pentecostal Evangel* no. 983 (January 28, 1933) 6–7.

Fockler, Cyrus B. "A Message to Seekers: How I Sought and Received the Baptism of the Holy Ghost." *Good News* 17.12 (December 1926) 16–17.

———. "Big Meeting in Milwaukee, Wis." *Weekly Evangel* no. 96 (June 26, 1915) 2.

———. *Overcomers*. Milwaukee, 1933.

———. "The Church at Milwaukee." *Weekly Evangel* no. 146 (July 1, 1916) 11.

———. *Tuning in with the Infinite*. Milwaukee: Gospel Tabernacle, 1925.

"Foursquare Leaders Deny Members a Fuller Gospel." *Kingdom Voice* 2.5 (March 10, 1940) 1–2.

Fowler, Clifton L. "Anti-Dispensationalism." *Grace and Truth* 6.11 (November 1928) 329–30.

"Fred Bosworth in City." *Zion City News*, January 8, 1909, 4.

"Freeport Gospel Tabernacle." *Freeport Journal Standard*, November 21, 1939, 6.

Freligh, Paul E. "Pastor Reports Continuation of Revival After Campaign Closes." *Voice of Healing* 1.9 (December 1948) 1, 5.

"Fresno, California, and Seattle, Washington, Visited by Party." *Voice of Healing* 1.9 (December 1948) 1–2.

Frodsham, Stanley. "Did Our Lord By His Death on the Cross Atone for Bodily Sickness and Disease? Yes! Praise the Lord!!" *Pentecostal Evangel* no. 496 (May 12, 1923) 8–9.

———. "Did Our Lord By His Death on the Cross Atone for Bodily Sickness and Disease? Yes! Praise the Lord!!" *Pentecostal Evangel* no. 497 (May 19, 1923) 10.

———. "Glorious Victories of God in Dallas, Texas." *Word and Witness* 9.1 (January 20, 1913) 1.

———. "The 1918 General Council." *Christian Evangel* no. 256–257 (October 5, 1918) 2–3.

———. "Our Distinctive Testimony." *Pentecostal Evangel* no. 320–321 (December 27, 1919) 8–9.

———. "Remarkable Healing Campaigns." *Pentecost* no. 4 (June 1948) 5.

———. *"With Signs Following": The Story of the Latter-Day Pentecostal Revival*. Springfield, MO: Gospel Publishing House, 1928.

"From Africa." *Bridegroom's Messenger* 2.33 (March 1, 1909) 1.

"From Headquarters." *Destiny* 8.3 (March 1937) 7.
Froom, LeRoy E. *Prophetic Faith of Our Fathers*. 4 vols. Washington, DC: Review and Herald Publishing Association, 1946.
"Fruits of Parhamism." *Zion Herald*, September 20, 1907, 1.
Gaebelein, Arno Clemens. "A Divine Healing Suicide." *Our Hope* 32.2 (August 1925) 81–82.
———. "Anglo-Israelism Once More." *Our Hope* 38.7 (January 1932) 421–424.
———. "Christianity vs. Modern Cults." *Moody Bible Institute Monthly* 22.3 (March 1922) 858–62.
———. "The Anglo-Israel Delusion." *Our Hope* 34.8 (February 1928) 476–80.
———. "The British-Israel Invention." *Our Hope* 27.7 (February 1921) 463–68.
———. *The Healing Question: An Examination of the Claims of Faith-Healing and Divine Healing Systems in the Light of the Scriptures and History*. New York: Our Hope, 1925.
Gaebelein, Frank E. "Book Reviews." *Our Hope* 34.8 (February 1928) 512.
Garr, A.G. "Tongues: The Bible Evidence to the Baptism with the Holy Ghost." *Pentecostal Power*, March 1907, 2–6.
Gaston, W.T. "Sister Bosworth's Funeral." *Pentecostal Evangel* no. 316–317 (November 29, 1919) 10.
———. "The Baptism of the Holy Ghost According to Acts 2: Some Objections Answered." *Christian Evangel* no. 302–303 (August 23, 1919) 3.
"Gave a Fine Concert." *Waukegan Daily Sun*, June 8, 1904, 7.
Gee, Donald. "Extremes Are Sometimes Necessary." *Voice of Healing* 6.1 (April 1953) 9.
———. *Wind and Flame: Incorporating the Former Book The Pentecostal Movement, with Additional Chapters*. Croydon, England: Assemblies of God, 1967.
"General Convention of Pentecostal Saints and Churches of God in Christ." *Word and Witness* 10.1 (January 20, 1914) 4.
"General Convention of Pentecostal Saints and Churches of God in Christ." *Word and Witness* 10.3 (March 20, 1914) 1.
General Council of the Assemblies of God...1917. St. Louis, MO: Gospel, 1917.
"George W. Southwick to Michael Barkun." September 5, 1991. Flower Pentecostal Heritage Center.
"The Gift of the Holy Spirit." *Zion Herald*, July 6, 1907, 3.
"Given the Right Hand of Fellowship." *Leaves of Healing* 15.16 (August 6, 1904) 523.
"God Honors Faith in Bosworth Meetings." *Alliance Weekly* 56.5 (April 15, 1922) 75.
"God Approved Man Condemned." *Zion City News*, November 4, 1910, 3.
"God Performs Operation after Anointed Ribbon Is Sent to Minister's Wife." *Voice of Healing* 1.8 (November 1948) 12.
"God's Witnesses to Divine Healing." *Leaves of Healing* 14.26 (April 16, 1904) 745–747.
"God's Witness to Divine Healing." *Leaves of Healing* 3.39 (July 24, 1897) 609–611, 621.
"God's Witness to Divine Healing." *Leaves of Healing* 9.8 (June 15, 1901) 225–28.
"God Uses Diaconate." *Zion Banner*, November 18, 1902, 1.
"God Vindicates Branham in Houston by Most Amazing Photograph Ever Taken." *Voice of Healing* 2.12 (March 1950) 1.
"Good Tidings from Marion, N.C." *Bridegroom's Messenger* 1.4 (December 15, 1907) 1.
Gordon, Adoniram Judson. *The Ministry of Healing: Miracles of Cure In All Ages*. Whitefish, MT: Kessinger, 2006.

"Gospel Tabernacle Revival Campaign to Continue." *Dallas Morning News*, October 21, 1917, 3.
"Gospel Tabernacle Too Small for Crowds; Phenomenal Healing Astounds Multitudes." *National Labor Tribune*, October 28, 1920, 3.
"Gospel Truths, Faith Healing." *Chicago Heights Star*, January 19, 1922, 1.
Goss, Howard A. "Jehovah Still Working at Hot Springs, Ark." *Word and Witness* 9.11 (November 20, 1913) 1.
―――. *The Winds of God: The Story of the Early Pentecostal Days (1901–1914) in the Life of Howard A. Goss*. New York: Cornet, 1958.
Grant, Del. "Is This the Beginning of the Predicted 'Spiritual Explosion That Will Rock the World'?." *Voice of Healing* 1.7 (October 1948) 1, 4–5.
Graves, Fred A. "Prayer for Persecutors." *Assemblies of God Heritage* 6 (June 14, 1986) 5.
"Great Outpouring at Last Meeting." *Altoona Mirror*, July 25, 1927, 22.
"Great Revival in Big Steel Tent Closes Monday, July 30, 1923." *National Labor Tribune*, July 19, 1923, 3.
"A Great Revival in Dallas, Texas." *Pentecostal Testimony* 1.8 (1911) 14.
"Had Nervous Prostration; 28 Drs. in 21 Months; Went and Heard Bosworth; Prayed for Instantly Healed." *National Labor Tribune*, November 17, 1921, 3.
Hagin, Kenneth E. *Prevailing Prayer to Peace: [26 Prayer Lessons]*. Tulsa: K. Hagin Evangelistic Association, 1973.
―――. *The Key to Scriptural Healing*. Tulsa: Faith Library Publications, 1978.
―――. *The Name of Jesus*. Faith Library Publications. Tulsa: Kenneth Hagin Ministries, 1979.
―――. *Understanding the Anointing*. Tulsa: Faith Library, 1983.
Hagin, Kenneth W. *The Past Tense Of God's Word*. Tulsa: RHEMA Bible Church, 1980.
―――. *The Prison Door Is Open—What Are You Still Doing Inside?* Tulsa: Faith Library, 2013.
Haldeman, I.M. "Did Our Lord By His Death on the Cross Atone for Bodily Sickness and Disease No! Never!!" *Our Hope* 29.8 (February 1923) 484–503.
Harlan, Rolvix. "John Alexander Dowie and the Christian Catholic Apostolic Church in Zion." Ph.D. diss., University of Chicago, 1906.
"Has Pentecost Come to Johannesburg?" *Confidence* 2.2 (February 1909) 27–31.
Hawtin, George. *The Abrahamic Covenant*. Thousand Oaks, CA: Artisan Sales, 1988.
"Healed at the Bosworth Meetings." *Bridegroom's Messenger* 14.232 (September 1921) 2.
"Healed of Fever." *Leaves of Healing* 16.22 (March 18, 1905) 709.
"Healed of Gallstones." *Pentecostal Evangel* no. 673 (November 20, 1926) 8, 17.
"Healed of Total Deafness, Running Ear and Curvature of the Spine." *Exploits of Faith*, Special Healing Number, n.d., 23–26.
"The Healing Craze." *Our Hope* 28.3 (September 1921) 139–40.
"Healing in the Atonement." *Evangelical Christian* 17.6 (June 1921) 164.
"Hell Is a Reality and Full of Sorrows, Says Evangelist Bosworth." *Houston Chronicle*, August 31, 1917, 8.
Hess, Benjamin G. "Frenzied Religion." *Zion Herald*, August 2, 1907, 3.
Hines, R. P. "Tongues Are for a Sign." *Weekly Evangel* no. 85 (April 10, 1915) 2.
"History of Pentecost." *Faithful Standard*, November 1922, 8, 14.
"Horror in Zion City." *Zion City News*, September 27, 1907, 2.
"Hot Springs Assembly: God's Glory Present." *Word and Witness* 10.4 (April 20, 1914) 1.

"Houston Meetings Close; Bosworth Party Opens at Corpus Christi." *Exploits of Faith* 3.3 (March 1930) 9–11.
"Houston Newspaper Accounts of the Service That Produced the Remarkable Photograph." *Voice of Healing* 2.12 (March 1950) 4.
"How the Tribune Has Fought." *National Labor Tribune*, September 30, 1920, 3.
Hugh, Freda. "Divinely Healed of Tuberculosis: How the Lord Used the Printed Page." *Latter Rain Evangel* 19.1 (October 1926) 16–22.
"Hungry Souls Respond to Invitation without Sermon and No Pleading Hundred Say 'Yes,'" *National Labor Tribune*, May 19, 1921, 4.
In Loving Memory, Marie Estelle Brown Founder and Pastor Glad Tidings Tabernacle, New York City, 1907–1971. New York: Glad Tidings Tabernacle, 1971.
"Interest Intense at the Great Bosworth's Big Tent Revival." *National Labor Tribune*, August 31, 1922, 3.
"Invasion of the Barbarians." *Zion Herald*, August 9, 1907, 1, 4, supplement.
"Is Conducting Campaign. *Altoona Mirror*, July 17, 1933, 15.
"Is It Not Awful?." *Zion Herald*, December 9, 1908, 3.
"Is It the Latter Rain?." *Zion City News*, August 1, 1907. Flower Pentecostal Heritage Center.
"Israel vs. Judah." *Kingdom Digest*, May 1947, 7–10. Flower Pentecostal Heritage Center.
"Is This of God?" *Our* 28.7 (January 1922) 404–7.
"Jacobs-Wasson Marriage." *Dallas Morning News*, November 27, 1913, 16.
Jamieson, S.A. "God Still in Dallas." *Word and Witness* 9.2 (February 20, 1913) 2.
———. "How a Presbyterian Preacher Received the Baptism." *Pentecostal Evangel* no. 883 (January 31, 1931) 2–3.
———. "Revival on at Dallas, Texas." *Weekly Evangel* no. 141 (May 27, 1916) 14.
Jeffreys, George. "The Israel Question." In *Who Hath Believed Our Report?: A Biblical-Historical Defense of the Anglo-Israel Message Through the Lives, Testimonies, and Ministries of Many Outstanding Men of God!*, edited by Charles A. Jennings, 301–5. Owasso, OK: Truth in History, 2010.
Jennings, Charles. "Dr. Dowie and the Anglo-Israel Belief." http://www.johnalexanderdowie.com/attachments/File/british_Israelism_charles_jennings.pdf.
Jennings, F.C. "Is Bodily Healing the Work of God That Characterizes Our Day?" *Our Hope* 28.4 (October 1921) 233–47.
———. "Is Bodily Healing the Work of God That Characterizes Our Day?" *Our Hope* 28.5 (November 1921) 286–302.
Johnson, Floyd B. "Bosworth Evangelistic Campaign, Lima, Ohio." *World-Wide Christian Courier* 2.10 (October 1927) 13–14.
"John Sproul to Tell How Voice Came Back Again." *Syracuse Herald*, May 13, 1922, 5.
"'Joybringer' Bosworth and Brother B.B. Opens Campaign in Sheraden in Great Tabernacle." *National Labor Tribune*, October 20, 1921, 3.
Judd, Carrie. "The Work and the Workers." *Triumphs of Faith* 10.1 (January 1890) 19–22.
———. "The Work and the Workers." *Triumphs of Faith* 10.9 (September 1890) 212–15.
Judd Montgomery, Carrie. "Special Meetings in Oakland." *Triumphs of Faith* 35.9 (September 1915) 216.
———. "The Mighty Power of God at Dallas, Texas." *Triumphs of Faith* 32.12 (December 1912) 267–70.

———. "The Promise of the Father: A Personal Testimony." *Triumphs of Faith* 28.7 (July 1908) 145–49.
Kellogg, Jay. C. "The United States in Prophecy." *Bible Standard Overcomer* 15.9 (September 1934) 3–4, 13–14.
Kenyon, Essek William. *The Wonderful Name of Jesus*. Seattle: Kenyon's Gospel Publishing Society, 1964.
———. "Deferred Answers." *Reality* 8.9 (May 1912) 147–48.
———. "Dying to Self." *Reality* 7.8 (April 1912) 120–22.
———. "Legal Authority." *Reality* 9.1 (January 1914) 1–5.
———. "Legal Authority." *Triumphs of Faith* 34.12 (December 1914) 281–85.
———. "One Secret Victory." *Reality* 7.5 (January 1912) 70–73.
———. "Prayer." *Reality* 7.5 (January 1912) 73–76.
———. *The Father and His Family, the Story of Man's Redemption*. Seattle: Kenyon's Gospel Publishing Society, 1964.
———. "The Heart." *Reality* 7.6 (February 1912) 93.
———. "The New Birth." *Reality* 7.12 (November 1912) 181–83.
———. "The New Kind of Love." *Exploits of Faith* 1.10 (October 1928) 15–16.
Kerr, D.W. "Do All Speak in Tongues?" *Christian Evangel* no. 270–271 (January 11, 1919) 7.
———. "Paul's Interpretation of the Baptism of the Holy Ghost." *Christian Evangel* no. 252–253 (August 24, 1918) 6.
———. "The Basis of Our Distinctive Testimony." *Pentecostal Evangel* no. 460–461 (September 2, 1922) 4.
———. "The Bible Evidence of the Baptism of the Holy Ghost." *Pentecostal Evangel* no. 509 (August 11, 1923) 2–3.
"The Kingdom of God Is Come." *Leaves of Healing* 7.14 (July 28, 1900) 427–35.
Kinne, Seeley D. "Open Letter to Elder F.F. Bosworth." *Pentecostal Herald* 4.6 (October 1918) 3.
Klink, Otto J. "The Jew." *Latter Rain Evangel* 26.7 (March 1935) 6–9.
Knapp, Martin Wells. *Lightning Bolts from Pentecostal Skies: Or, Devices of the Devil Unmasked*. Cincinnati: Office of the Revivalist, 1898.
Laggar, William. "A Report on Evangelist F.F. Bosworth in Durban, South Africa." *Voice of Healing* 6.9 (December 1953) 11.
Lake, John G. *John G. Lake: The Complete Collection of His Life Teachings*. Edited by Roberts Liardon. Tulsa: Albury, 1999.
———. "South Africa." *Confidence* 2.8 (August 1909) 185.
Lake, John G., and Talbert Morgan. *John G. Lake's Life & Diary*. Bloomington, IN: AuthorHouse, 2006.
"Large Audience Greets Evangelist Bosworth at Initial Service." *Houston Chronicle*, August 6, 1917, 3.
"Latest News of Rev. Branham Just Receive from Bro. John Sharritt." *Voice of Healing* 1.5 (August 1948) 5, 7.
"Latest Word from Dallas." *Zion City Independent*, September 20, 1912, 1.
"Latest from Dallas, Tex." *Zion City Independent*, October 4, 1912, 2.
"The 'Latter Rain.'" *Pentecost* no. 20 (June 1952) 17.
"The 'Latter Rain' in Zion City." *Apostolic Faith* (Los Angeles (1.9 (September 1907) 1.
Lawrence, Bennett Freeman. *The Apostolic Faith Restored*. St. Louis: Gospel Publishing House, 1916.

Lee, Bernice C. "A Holy Jubilee." *Bread of Life* 5.11 (November 1956) 3–4, 9–10.
———. "Be Not Anxious for the Morrow." *Latter Rain Evangel* 1.5 (February 1909) 8.
———. "I Will Be Within Thee a Well of Water." *Latter Rain Evangel* 1.7 (April 1909) 20–21.
"Letter from F.F. Bosworth: Zion's Former Well Known Band Leader Writes to News." *Zion City News*, August 21, 1908, 1, 2.
"A Letter from J. Mattsson Boze." *Pentecost* no. 17 (September 1951) 13.

"Let Us Go Up to Zion." *Leaves of Healing* 8.16 (February 9, 1901) 498–501.
Lindsay, Gordon. "Cycles of Canada." *Anglo-Saxon World* 2.5 (May 1, 1940) 3–5, 15.
———. "Cycles of the 'Sign Woman'—Israel." *Anglo-Saxon World* 2.3 (April 1, 1940) 9–12.
———. *John G. Lake, Apostle to Africa*. Dallas: Christ for the Nations, 1978.
———. *Sketches from the Life and Ministry of John G. Lake*. Shreveport: Voice of Healing, 1952.
———. *The Blueprints of God: Wonders of Bible Chronology*. Vol. 1. Portland, OR: Cosbys, 1940.
———. *The Life of John Alexander Dowie, Whose Trials, Tragedies, and Triumphs Are the Most Fascinating Object Lesson of Christian History*. Shreveport, LA: Voice of Healing, 1951.
———. "The Story of the Great Restoration Revival, Part I." *World-Wide Revival* 10.12 (March 1958) 4–5, 22.
———. "The Story of the Great Restoration Revival, Part II." *World-Wide Revival* 11.1 (April 1958) 4, 17–18.
———. "The Story of the Great Restoration Revival, Part IV." *World-Wide Revival* 11.3 (June 1958) 4, 18–19.
———. "The Thirteen Cycles of the United States." *Anglo-Saxon World* 2.3 (March 1, 1940) 4–5, 12.
———. "The Wonders of Bible Chronology." *Anglo-Saxon World* 2.2 (February 1, 1940) 3–4, 7.
———. *William Branham: A Man Sent from God*. Jeffersonville, IN: William Branham, 1950.
———. *Wonders of Bible Chronology*. Blueprints of God, vol. 1. Abridged. Portland, OR: Cosbys, 1940.
"Local Notes." *Dallas Morning News*, April 12, 1912, 11.
Lockhart, G.D. *Weekly Evangel* no. 185 (April 14, 1917) 11.
Long, Lewis J. "Evangelistic Campaign in Bridgeport Was of Estimable Value." *National Labor Tribune*, April 26, 1923, 3.
"Lost Tribes." *Pentecostal Evangel* no. 1175 (November 14, 1936) 10.
"Love Offering to Bosworth Brothers." *Ottawa Citizen*, May 26, 1924, 4.
"Lubbock, Texas, Sponsors Branham-Bosworth Meet." *Full Gospel Men's Voice* 2.10 (February 1955) 22.
Luther, Martin. "Commentary on Galatians." In *Martin Luther: Selections from His Writings*, edited by John Dillenberger. Garden City, NY: Doubleday, 1962.
Mackenzie, Kenneth. "Are There Modern Miracles?" *Alliance Weekly* 57.31 (September 29, 1923) 492–493.
———. "Book Review." *Alliance Weekly* 55.32 (October 22, 1921) 506.

———. "Book Reviews: Dr. Torrey's 'Divine Healing.'" *Alliance Weekly* 59.17 (October 25, 1924) 276.
———. "Jesus and Our Mortal Flesh." *Alliance Weekly* 56.9 (May 13, 1922) 132–133.
———. "Rev. Kenneth MacKenzie Replies to the Attack Made Upon Evangelist Fred Francis Bosworth by Rev. I.M. Haldeman, D.D." *National Labor Tribune*, July 5, 1923, 3.
MacLennan, Stewart P. "Anglo-Israelism." *Our Hope* 38.2 (August 1931) 105–114.
MacMillan, J.A. "British-Israelism—A Latter-Time Heresy." *Alliance Weekly* 69.35 (September 1, 1934) 548–49.
———. "British-Israelism—A Latter-Time Heresy." *Alliance Weekly* 69.37 (September 15, 1934) 580–81.
———. "British-Israelism—A Latter-Time Heresy." *Alliance Weekly* 69.38 (September 22, 1934) 596–97, 602.
———. "British-Israelism—A Latter-Time Heresy." *Alliance Weekly* 69.39 (September 29, 1934) 612–13.
MacMullen, Ramsay. *Christianizing the Roman Empire: A.D. 100–4 00*. New Haven, CT: Yale University Press, 1984.
Mahan, Asa. *Scripture Doctrine of Christian Perfection: With Other Kindred Subjects, Illustrated and Confirmed in a Series of Discourses Designed to Throw Light on the Way of Holiness*. D.S. King, 1839.
"A Man Born Blind Now Sees." *Latter Rain Evangel* 6.9 (June 1914) 19–21.
"Mansfield, Ohio." *Leaves of Healing* 7.12 (July 14, 1900) 371.
Manual of the Pilgrim Holiness Church: Containing Form of Government and Ritual for Churches; Also Location of Ministers. Etcetera. Easton, MD: Easton, 1922.
"The Man Whom God Used to Put to Flight Higher Critics and Unbelievers in Ottawa, Canada." *National Labor Tribune*, June 12, 1924, 6.
"Many Converts Crowd Forward." *National Labor Tribune*, November 3, 1921, 3.
"Many States Represented at Bosworth Meeting; Some Travel Long Way to Hear Healing Message." *National Labor Tribune*, April 20, 1922, 3.
"Marked Movements of God in Healing." *Alliance Weekly* 55.12 (June 4, 1921) 186.
"Mayor E.V. Babcock Believes in Miracles." *National Labor Tribune*, October 27, 1921, 4.
McAlister, R.E. *The Pentecostal Movement: What It Is and What It Stands For*. Springfield, MO: Gospel Publishing House, n.d.
McCrossan, T.J. *Bodily Healing and the Atonement*. Seattle, WA: McCrossan, 1930.
McPherson, Aimee Semple. *This Is That: Personal Experiences, Sermons and Writings of Aimee Semple McPherson, Evangelist*. Los Angeles: Bridal Call, 1919.
McWhirter, James. *Britain and Palestine in Prophecy*. London: Methuen & Co., 1937.
"Member of the House of Commons Joins in Bodily Healing Meetings." *National Labor Tribune*, May 22, 1924, 6.
"Messages of the Moment." *Weekly Evangel* no. 162 (October 28, 1916) 8.
Meyer, Rose. "Child Healed of Sarcoma Cancer." *Latter Rain Evangel* 19.10 (July 1927) 21–22.
———. "Moving Pictures in God's Kaleidoscope." *Latter Rain Evangel* 19.12 (September 1927) 18–21.
———. "When the Good Samaritan Came to Altoona." *Latter Rain Evangel* 19.9 (June 1927) 5–8.
"Midwinter Pentecostal Convention." *Weekly Evangel* no. 164 (November 11, 1916) 11.

"A Migration Register." *Alliance Weekly* 74.1 (January 7, 1934) 2–3.
Miller, B.C. "The Fundamentalist and Divine Healing." *Golden Grain* 1.5 (July 1926) 5–8.
Miller, F. Bertram. "Faithful Girls Grief Stricken; Overwhelmed by Unexpected Joy; People Baffled by Case." *National Labor Tribune*, May 19, 1921, 3.
Miller, F.B. "A Revival of Divine Healing." *Alliance Weekly* 54.30 (October 23, 1920) 473–74.
"Minister Is Healed as Brother Bosworth Prays." *Voice of Healing* 1.4 (July 1948) 10.
"Minutes of the Executive Presbytery." General Council of the Assemblies of God, November 25, 1914. Flower Pentecostal Heritage Center.
Minutes of the General Council, 1949 and Annual Report for 1948. The Christian and Missionary Alliance, 1949.
Minutes of the General Council, 1950 and Annual Report for 1949. The Christian and Missionary Alliance, 1950.
Minutes of the General Council of the Assemblies of God . . . 1915. n.p., 1915.
Minutes of the General Council of the Assemblies of God . . . 1916. St. Louis, MO: Gospel, 1916.
Minutes of the General Council of the Assemblies of God . . . 1917. St. Louis, MO: Gospel, 1917.
Minutes of the Sixth Annual Meeting of the General Council of the Assemblies of God...1918. Springfield, MO: Gospel, 1918.
"A Miracle of Healing." *Leaves of Healing* 1.9, 10, 11 (1891) 220–222.
"Miracles of Healing in Dallas." *Latter Rain Evangel*, October 1912, 13–14.
"A Miracle of Healing of a Gassed Soldier." *Latter Rain Evangel* 15.4 (January 1922) 22–23.
"Miracles." *Our Hope* 28.4 (October 1921) 207–9.
"Miracles Still Are Performed, Bosworth Says." *Syracuse Herald*, May 9, 1922, 10.
"Missionaries to Johannesburg, South Africa." *Apostolic Faith* (Los Angeles (11.13 (May 1908) 4.
Mitchell, Hardy. "Milwaukee, Wis." *Weekly Evangel* no. 103 (August 14, 1915) 1.
"Mob Victim Improving." *Zion City Independent*, August 25, 1911, 3.
"The Montwait Meeting: Testimonies Under Oath." *Bridegroom's Messenger* 8.142 (October 15, 1913) 4.
Moomau, Antoinette. "China Missionary Receives Pentecost." *Apostolic Faith* (Los Angeles (1.11 (January 1908) 3.
Moon, R. H. "When God Visited Lima, Ohio." *Alliance Weekly* 54.26 (September 25, 1920) 414.
Moore, Anna Jeanne. "Historic Conference of Evangelists Conducting Great Healing Campaigns Convened in Dallas December 22–2 3." *Voice of Healing* 2.11 (February 1950) 1–3.
Moorehead, Max Wood. "A Personal Testimony." *Cloud of Witnesses to Pentecost in India* no. 2 (September 1907) 36–38.
"More Musicians for Zion City Band." *Zion Banner*, September 12, 1905, 411.
"More on the South African Revival with Bros. Branham, Baxter and Bosworth." *Herald of Faith* 17.6 (June 1952) 9–10.
"Most Healers in Show Business, Says Rev. Lott." *National Labor Tribune*, August 13, 1925, 4.
"Most Pleasurable Experience in 16 Years." *Daily Gleaner*, October 24, 1938, 5.

"Mother and Sons Have a Wonderful Story." *Exploits of Faith* 4.4 (April 1931) 15–16.
"Mother Tortured in Religion's Name: Aged Woman Dies at the Hands of Son and Daughter and Three Other Parhamites. Tried to Cast Out Devils After Death Members of the Sect Attempt to 'Resurrect' Victim—All Are Arrested." *New York Times*, September 21, 1907, 7.
"Mrs. Wyburn Quits McAuley Mission to Wed; Romance with Evangelist Started at Revival." *New York Times*, March 13, 1923, 23.
"Mt. Auburn Revival Campaign Will Continue This Week." *Dallas Morning News*, September 30, 1917, 10.
Mueller, Rose. "The Blind See, the Deaf Hear, Cancers Healed." *Latter Rain Evangel* 15.7 (April 1922) 20–21.
"Musicians Meet at Shiloh Tabernacle." *Zion Banner*, January 17, 1906, 129.
Myland, D. Wesley. *The Latter Rain Covenant and Pentecostal Power*. Springfield, MO: Temple, 1910.
Nelson, Thomas H. "Dowie's Followers Relive Glorious Days of Past as Branham and Bosworth Minister in Zion." *Voice of Healing* 2.2 (May 1949) 1, 16.
"New Branch Organizations." *Bulletin of the Anglo-Saxon Federation of America* 2.23 (November 1931) 87.
"New Leader in Zion City: Says a Voice He Heard in a Vision Inspired Him—Voliva Alarmed." *New York Times*, September 27, 1906, 7.
"A New Revivalist." *Life*, May 7, 1951, 73–7 4, 76, 78.
"New Revival to Open Today in Tabernacle." *Syracuse Herald*, May 7, 1922, 36.
"News Clip: Houston Press, 1950." Living Word Press, n.d., 1, 3–5. 30/4/1. Flower Pentecostal Heritage Center.
"New Tracts." *Latter Rain Evangel* 6.10 (July 1914) 11.
"New Year's Tabernacle Camp Meeting." *World-Wide Christian Courier* 3.1 (January 1928) 5.
"New York Visitation of Elijah the Restorer and Zion Restoration Host." *Leaves of Healing* 14.5 (November 21, 1903) 139–50.
"North Michigan Rocked by Mighty Revival." *Voice of Healing* 2.3 (June 1949) 1, 15.
"Notes." *Latter Rain Evangel* 6.11 (August 1914) 12.
"Notes from Zion's Harvest Field." *Leaves of Healing* 7.13 (July 21, 1900) 410.
"Notes from Zion's Harvest Field." *Leaves of Healing* 8.10 (December 29, 1900) 314.
"Notes from Zion's Harvest Field." *Leaves of Healing* 8.23 (March 30, 1901) 713.
"Notes from Zion's Harvest Field." *Leaves of Healing* 12.24 (April 4, 1903) 760.
"Notes from Zion's Harvest Field." *Leaves of Healing* 14.23 (March 26, 1904) 693.
"Notes: Holding the Truth in Love." *Latter Rain Evangel* 2.5 (February 1910) 12.
"Not I But Christ: Fourth Annual Convention in the Stone Church." *Latter Rain Evangel* 4.9 (June 1912) 2–6.
"Notice." *Bridegroom's Messenger* 2.44 (August 15, 1909) 2.
"Obeying God in Baptism." *Leaves of Healing* 11.17 (August 16, 1902) 576.
"Obeying God in Baptism." *Leaves of Healing* 11.19 (August 30, 1902) 644.
"Obeying God in Baptism." *Leaves of Healing* 12.2 (November 1, 1902) 60.
"Obeying God in Baptism." *Leaves of Healing* 13.15 (August 1, 1903) 487.
"Obeying God in Baptism." *Leaves of Healing* 13.15 (August 1, 1903) 486.
"Obeying God in Baptism." *Leaves of Healing* 13.23 (September 26, 1903) 742.
"Obeying God in Baptism." *Leaves of Healing* 14.1 (October 24, 1903) 29.
"Obeying God in Baptism." *Leaves of Healing* 15.4 (May 14, 1904) 111.

"Obeying God in Baptism." *Leaves of Healing* 15.15 (July 30, 1904) 490, 491.
O'Connor, Edward. "Pentecost and Catholicism." *Ecumenist* 6.5 (August 1968) 161–64.
Official List of Ministers and Missionaries of the General Council Assemblies of God, Revised November 1, 1930. Springfield, MO: General Council Assemblies of God, 1930.
O'Neal, Thomas J. "Announcement." *Weekly Evangel* no. 231 (March 16, 1918) 15.
"One of America's Leading Exponents of Prayer and Faith Astounds Tremendous Crowds." *National Labor Tribune*, June 26, 1924, 4.
"Opening of Blue Island (Ills.) Campaign." *Exploits of Faith* 4.6 (June 1931) 6–9.
Opperman, Daniel C.O. "Our Lord Is Giving the Victory." *Bridegroom's Messenger* 4.84 (April 15, 1911) 3.
———. "God Stretching Out His Hand to Heal." *Word and Witness* 9.10 (October 20, 1913) 1.
"Ordained Elders, Pastors, Ministers, Evangelists and Missionaries of the Churches of God in Christ with Their Stations for 1914." *Word and Witness*, December 20, 1913, 4.
"Ordained Ministers of the Churches of God in Christ with Their Locations." August 1, 1912. Flower Pentecostal Heritage Center.
"Ordained Ministers of the Churches of God in Christ with Their Locations (revised)." February 1, 1913. Flower Pentecostal Heritage Center.
"Oregon Meet Opens Friday." *Madison Wisconsin State Journal*, August 10, 1939, 20.
Osborn, T. L. "Commemoration." *Faith Digest* 3.3 (March 1958) 17–18.
———. "F.F. Bosworth Promoted to Eternal Reward." *Full Gospel Business Men's Voice* 6.3 (April 1958) 25.
———. *Frontier Evangelism: God's Indispensable Method for World Evangelism*. Tulsa: Osborn Foundation, 1955.
———. "God in Flesh Again: Memorial Message for William Branham." Sermon, Phoenix, Arizona, January 26, 1966. http://www.williambranhamhomepage.org/wbmtos.htm.
———. *Healing En Masse*. Tulsa: Osborn, 1958.
———. *Healing the Sick and Casting out Devils, the Message and Ministry of a Bible Discipline Now Living. Christ's Power of Attorney Exercised Today*. Tulsa: Osborn, 1950.
———. "He Prayed Earnestly for Himself." *Full Gospel Business Men's Voice* 6.4 (May 1958) 25–26.
Osborn, T. L, and Daisy Osborn. *Faith Library in 23 Volumes: 20th Century Legacy of Apostolic Evangelism*. Tulsa: OSFO International, 1997.
"Other Cases of Torture: Further Arrests of Parhamites May Be Made at Zion City." *New York Times*, September 22, 1907, C5.
"Ottawa Accords a Send-Off to the Bosworth Bros. Such as Rarely Seen Here." *National Labor Tribune*, June 5, 1924, 6.
"Ouija Board Worries Maiden; Cured of Habit; Haunted No More." *National Labor Tribune*, September 22, 1921, 3.
"Our Hearts Have Been Thrilled and Blessed." *Exploits of Faith* 10.7 (July 1937) 11.
"Our Summer Meetings." *Latter Rain Evangel* 5.11 (September 1913) 12–13.
"Our Trip East." *Apostolic Faith* (Baxter Springs, KS) 3.3 (March 1927) 7.
"Overflowing Audience Hears Rev. Mr. Bosworth on 'The Holy Spirit.'" *Houston Chronicle*, August 13, 1917, 8.

Oxonian (Walter Metcalfe H. Milner). *Israel's Wanderings; Or, The Sciiths, the Saxons, and the Kymry*. London: Heywood, 1885.
Oyer, Amos. "Healed of Spinal Trouble After Years of Suffering." *Latter Rain Evangel* 20.3 (December 1927) 22–23.
Ozman, Agnes. "Where the Latter Rain First Fell." *Latter Rain Evangel* 1.4 (January 1909) 2.
Palmer, Phoebe. *Phoebe Palmer: Selected Writings*. Edited by Thomas Oden. New York: Paulist, 1988.
"Paul Rader Issues Warning Against the Anvil Chorus and Knockers Brigade." *National Labor Tribune*, June 7, 1923, 3.
Panton, D.M. "British Israelism or Anglo Israelism." *Alliance Weekly* 59.19 (November 8, 1924) 315.
———. "Anglo-Israelism." *Alliance Weekly* 68.32 (August 12, 1933) 500–501, 506.
Parham, Charles F. "A Pleasurable Meeting." *Apostolic Faith* 2.4 (April 1926) 11.
———. *The Sermons of Charles F. Parham*. Edited by Donald W. Dayton. The Higher Christian Life. New York: Garland, 1985.
———. "The Ten Lost Tribes." *Apostolic Faith* 4.2 (February 1928) 10–11.
Parham, Sarah E. *The Life of Charles F. Parham, Founder of the Apostolic Faith Movement*. Baxter Springs, KS: Apostolic Faith Church, 1930.
"Pastoral Personnel." *Alliance Weekly* 86.48 (December 5, 1951) 13.
"Paulding and Oceola, Ohio." *Leaves of Healing* 12.15 (January 31, 1903) 477.
Perkins, Eunice May. "Bosworths' Farewell Meeting; Eunice M. Perkins Sends a Flash of Bosworth Bros. Gospel Revival." *National Labor Tribune*, January 5, 1922, 3.
———. "Bosworth's Shaking Detroit with Monster Evangelistic Meetings; Crowds Bring Sick." *National Labor Tribune*, January 13, 1921, 3.
———. "Detroit Druggists Doomed; Medicine Chests Ruined; Family Remedies Gone; Sick Saved and Healed." *National Labor Tribune*, January 27, 1921, 3.
———. "Detroit Hall Too Small; Seeking Larger Quarters; Men from Workshops Turn out in Numbers." *National Labor Tribune*, January 20, 1921, 3.
———. *Fred Francis Bosworth (the Joybringer)*. River Forest, IL: F.F. Bosworth, 1927.
———. *Joybringer Bosworth: His Life Story*. Dayton, OH: John J. Scruby, 1921.
Perkins, Jonathan Ellsworth. *The Baptism of the Holy Spirit*. Los Angeles: B.N. Robertson, 1945.
Perry, Mattie E. "A Call to Prayer." *Latter Rain Evangel* 12.5 (February 1920) 8–9.
———. *Christ and Answered Prayer*. Nashville: Benson, 1939.
"Personal Mention." *Zion Banner*, April 28, 1903, 370.
"Personal Testimony of Pastor Durham." *Pentecostal Testimony*, March 1909, 7.
Pinson, M.M. "A Statement from Bro. Pinson." *Christian Evangel* no. 280–281 (March 22, 1919) 9.
———. "Trip to the Southwest." *Word and Witness* 8.6 (August 20, 1912) 1.
Piper, William H. "Long Weary Months of Spiritual Drought." *Latter Rain Evangel* 1.1 (October 1908) 3–6.
———. "Manifestations and 'Demonstrations' of the Spirit." *Latter Rain Evangel* 1.1 (October 1908) 16–20.
"Plan 2 Regional Conventions." *Messenger of the Covenant* 6.68 (August 1935) 6.
"Plane Passengers." *Daily Gleaner*, January 17, 1948, 21.
"Poor Piper." *Zion Herald*, November 11, 1908, 2.

Pope, W.H. "Great Times of Refreshing at Pawhuska, Oklahoma." *Weekly Evangel* no. 171 (January 6, 1917) 16.

———. "Why I Believe All Who Receive the Full Baptism Will Speak in Other Tongues." *Christian Evangel* no. 244–245 (June 15, 1918) 6–7.

"Preliminary Statement Concerning the Principles Involved in the New Issue." *Word and Witness* 12.6 (June 1915) 1.

"Private John Sproul Grips Chicago Folk with Testimony That Sinks into Doubters." *National Labor Tribune*, January 26, 1922, 3.

"Profound Confirmation by Catholic Convert of Supernatural Light." *Voice of Healing* 2.12 (March 1950) 4.

Putnam, Charles Elsworth. *Modern Religio-Healing, Man Theories Or God's Word?*. Chicago: C.E. Putnam, 1924.

"Questions Lovingly Addressed to the Gift of Tongues People in Zion City." *Zion Herald*, December 2, 1908, 3.

Rader, Luke. "Is British-Israelism a Dangerous Fallacy?" *Sunshine News*, An Excerpt from the Sunshine News, July 16, 1936. Flower Pentecostal Heritage Center.

Rader, Paul. *The Man of Mercy*. Chicago Gospel Tabernacle, Chapel Book Stall, 1928.

"Radio Revivalist Guest Preacher at City Tabernacle." *Daily Gleaner*, October 24, 1938, 10.

"Ranchman Offers $25,000 Wager on Fallacy of Claim." *Belvidere Daily Republican*, May 21, 1928, 7.

Rand, Howard B. "Convention Declared Success." *Messenger of the Covenant* 6.67 (July 1935) 1, 7.

"Regains Hearing After Anointing." *Altoona Mirror*, May 26, 1927, 15.

Reiff, Anna C. "The Day of Chicago's Visitation." *Latter Rain Evangel* 5.10 (August 1913) 2–11.

"A Relentless War Against Iniquity of Every Kind!!!." *Zion Herald*, July 25, 1907, supplement.

"Remarkable Demonstrations When Evangelists Finish Campaign and Say Farewell." *National Labor Tribune*, June 5, 1924, 6, 7.

"Remarkable Demonstration When Evangelists Conclude Campaign and Say Farewell." *Ottawa Citizen*, May 27, 1924, 18.

"Report of Meeting: Newton, N.C., July 18, 1910." *Bridegroom's Messenger* 3.67 (August 1, 1910) 4.

"Reports of God's Working." *Alliance Weekly* 55.2 (March 26, 1921) 26.

"Revivalists Not Healers." *National Labor Tribune*, September 15, 1921, 3.

"Rev. and Mrs. F.F. Bosworth Work with Branham Party." *Voice of Healing* 1.2 (May 1948) 1, 5.

"The Revival Campaign in Toronto: Services Marked by Simplicity." *Alliance Weekly* 55.8 (May 6, 1921) 122.

"Revival Fires." *Bridegroom's Messenger* 14.227 (February 1921) 1.

"Revivals in Atlanta, GA." *Bridegroom's Messenger* 16.246 (August 1923) 2.

"Rice Throwing Clue to Wedding of Evangelist." *National Labor Tribune*, November 9, 1922, 3.

Richards, E.J. "Annual Report of Secretary of Home Department." *Alliance Weekly* 55.17 (July 9, 1921) 261.

Richey, Raymond T. "A Telegram from Houston, Texas." *Weekly Evangel* no. 225 (February 2, 1918) 3.

———. "Work Amongst the Soldiers." *Weekly Evangel* no. 220 (December 22, 1917) 10.
Riley, W.B. *Divine Healing, Or, Does God Hear Prayer for the Sick?*. Minneapolis: L.W. Camp, n.d.
"River Forest Minister on Radio Often." *Oak Park Leaves*, September 16, 1937, 46.
Roadhouse, W.F. "Anglo-Israelism." *Alliance Weekly* 62.36 (September 4, 1937) 563–65.
———. "Anglo-Israelism." *Alliance Weekly* 62.37 (September 11, 1937) 581–83.
Roberts, Oral. *Miracle of Seed-Faith*. Tulsa: Roberts, 1970.
———. "Personal Word from Oral Roberts About F.F. Bosworth." *Healing Waters* 2.3 (February 1949) 4.
"Rominger a Parhamite!!!" *Zion Herald*, October 25, 1907, 2.
"Said to Be Religion: Strange Scenes at 'Revival Meetings' Held in Indiana." *New York Times*, January 24, 1885, 1.
Salvation Army. *Orders and Regulations for Field Officers of the Salvation Army*. London: Headquarters of the Salvation Army, 1891.
Sandford, Frank. "Who God's Ancient People Are." In *Who Hath Believed Our Report?: A Biblical-Historical Defense of the Anglo-Israel Message Through the Lives, Testimonies, and Ministries of Many Outstanding Men of God!*, edited by Charles A. Jennings, 255–63. Owasso, OK: Truth in History, 2010.
Schoeman, A.J. "Great Revivals in Africa with Branham Party." *Voice of Healing* 4.10 (January 1952) 8.
"Scranton Revival Opens on Ideal Day." *National Labor Tribune*, June 25, 1925, 4.
"Second Special Conference of Ordained Officers of the Christian Catholic Church in Zion." *Leaves of Healing* 15.21 (September 10, 1904) 740.
"Self-Deception and Fraud." *Our Hope* 28.3 (September 1921) 140–42.
"A Sensible Talk." *Zion City News*, September 25, 1908.
"Seventh Anniversary of the Christian Catholic Church in Zion." *Leaves of Healing* 12.19 (February 28, 1903) 593.
Sexton, E.A. "Sanctification the Necessary Preparation for the Pentecostal Baptism." *Bridegroom's Messenger* 3.65 (July 1, 1910) 1.
Shakarian, Demos. "Two Chapters Organized in Florida." *Full Gospel Men's Voice* 1.1 (February 1953) 6–11.
"Sheraden Church Workers Erect Tabernacle for Use During Bosworth Revival Campaign." *National Labor Tribune*, October 3, 1921, 4.
"Signs Following in Milwaukee." *Latter Rain Evangel* 7.11 (August 1915) 14–15.
Simpson, Albert B. *The Gospel of Healing*. Harrisburg, PA: Christian Publications, 1915.
Simpson, Albert Benjamin. *Days of Heaven upon Earth*. Nyack, NY: Christian Alliance, 1897.
"Sinus Trouble Cured." *Exploits of Faith* 4.2 (February 1931) 9.
Sisson, Elizabeth. "A Series of Baptisms." *Latter Rain Evangel* 6.8 (May 1914) 10–11.
———. "Four Years' Continuous Revival." *Confidence* 8.4 (April 1915) 69, 71–72.
———. "Healing a Man Born Blind: The Power of the Word in Dallas, Texas." *Latter Rain Evangel* 6.7 (April 1914) 2–4.
———. "The Council and Missionary Conference." *Weekly Evangel* no. 208 (September 29, 1917) 4.
"Sister Etter Now in St. Louis." *Weekly Evangel* no. 96 (June 26, 1915) 1.
Sitton, Rev., and Gordon Lindsay. "Branham in Houston; City Sees 'Something Different.'" *Voice of Healing* 2.11 (February 1950) 3, 16.

"Six Able to Speak and Hear Through Faith and Prayer." *Los Angeles Times*, May 6, 1928, sec. 1, 7.

"Smallpox? No! Something Ten Thousand Times Worse Has Invaded Zion City." *Zion Herald*, October 21, 1908, 1.

Smith, Oswald J. "British Israelism, A Dangerous Fallacy." *Defender*, July 1936, 16–19, 21.

———. *The Great Physician*. Christian Alliance Publishing Company, 1927.

———. *Who Are the False Prophets?*. Toronto: Peoples Press, 1953.

"Soldier Boy's Testimony Makes Hit with Soldiers." *National Labor Tribune*, November 29, 1923, 8.

"Some Figures of the Feast." *Zion Banner*, July 24, 1903, 158.

"Southern District Organized." *Alliance Weekly* 54.19 (August 7, 1920) 299.

Southwick, George W. "Controversy in Zion: For the Benefit of Our Pentecostal Brethren." In *Who Hath Believed Our Report?: A Biblical-Historical Defense of the Anglo-Israel Message Through the Lives, Testimonies, and Ministries of Many Outstanding Men of God!*, edited by Charles A. Jennings, 191–99. Owasso, OK: Truth in History, 2010.

"Special Notice to Illinois Subscribers." *Voice of Healing* 1.12 (March 1948) 16.

"Speakers at 'Church and Public Affairs Institute.'" *Oak Park Leaves*, September 21, 1939, 13.

"Spiritual Healings at Gospel Tabernacle and Carnegie Hall Astound Multitude." *National Labor Tribune*, November 11, 1920, 3.

Spitz, Lewis William, ed. "The Geneva Confession." In *The Protestant Reformation: Major Documents*. St. Louis: Concordia, 1997.

"Splendid Music By Zion Band." *Zion Banner*, February 2, 1904, 145.

Stadsklev, Julius. "Greatest Religious Meetings in History of South Africa Inspired by Wm. Branham." *Voice of Healing* 4.12 (March 1952) 14–15.

———. *William Branham: A Prophet Visits South Africa*. Minneapolis: Julius Stadsklev, 1952.

Stephens, John W. "Our Chicago Convention." *Bulletin of the Anglo-Saxon Federation of America* 2.22 (October 1931) 75–76.

"Stone Church Meetings." *Latter Rain Evangel*, April 1913, 12.

"The Story of Zion's Victory Over the Devil and the Pig in Minnesota." *Leaves of Healing* 5.41 (August 5, 1899) 792–99.

"St. Paul, Minn." *Alliance Weekly* 55.1 (March 19, 1921) 14.

"Suffered for Five Years." *Exploits of Faith* 4.3 (March 1931) 15.

"Syracuse Revival: Episcopal Church Awakes, Pray and Expect Answer, Cut Out 'If Thy Will Be Done,' Pray for Sick and Watch." *National Labor Tribune*, June 1, 1922, 3.

"Syracuse Revival Promises Big Success, John Sproul Testifies, Three Meetings Held." *National Labor Tribune*, May 18, 1922, 3.

"Tabernacle Evangelist Now on Radio." *Chicago Daily Herald*, September 17, 1937, 18.

"Tabernacle Warmed for Night Service; Blustery Weather No Bar." *Houston Chronicle*, January 11, 1918, 9.

"Telling What Happened in the Big Steel Tent." *National Labor Tribune*, June 28, 1923, 3, 5.

"Tent Revival Has Begun." *Dallas Morning News*, July 26, 1912, 4.

"Testimonies from Toronto." *Alliance Weekly* 55.37 (November 26, 1921) 586.

"Testimonies to Divine Healing from the Bosworth Meetings." *Alliance Weekly* 54.45 (February 5, 1920) 716.
"Testimonies Under Oath." *Word and Witness* 9.10 (October 20, 1913) 1.

"Testimony of Alice Baker." *National Labor Tribune*, October 20, 1921, 3.
"Testimony of Her Physician, Dr. C.A.D. Fairfield." *National Labor Tribune*, July 5, 1923, 3.
"These Two Letters Speak for Themselves." *Sunshine News*, An Excerpt from the Sunshine News, July 16, 1936. Flower Pentecostal Heritage Center.
"Third Anniversary of the Consecration of the Zion Temple Site." *Leaves of Healing* 13.14 (July 25, 1903) 426.
Thomas, Rupert C. *The Coming of Christ and Israel-Britain's Identity*. London: Covenant, 1935.
Thomas, W.H. Griffith. "Divine Healing: A Criticism of 'Our Physical Heritage in Christ' by Kenneth MacKenzie." *Our Hope* 31.7 (January 1925) 418–22.
Thomsen, N.P. "Anglo-Israelism, Under the Searchlight of God's Word." *Latter Rain Evangel* 26.8 (May 1934) 3–6.
"Thousands Come to Hear Bosworth's Final Message; Many Unable to Get In; The Arena Too Small." *National Labor Tribune*, May 4, 1922, 3.
"Toledo Gets a Shake; Bosworth's Jolt City; Some Real Revival with All the Frills." *National Labor Tribune*, September 15, 1921, 3.
"To Open Campaign." *Williamsport Sun Gazette*, April 19, 1947, 2.
"To Preachers." *Word and Witness* 9.10 (October 20, 1913) 4.
Torrey, R. A. *Divine Healing; Does God Perform Miracles Today?*. 1924; repr., Grand Rapids, MI: Baker, 1974.
"A Tragedy." *Zion Herald*, September 27, 1907, 1.
"Trance Evangelism." *Leaves of Healing* (First Series) 1.5, 6, 7 (December 1890) 98–100.
Twenty-Ninth Annual Report of the Christian and Missionary Alliance for the Year 1925. New York, 1926.
"U.S. Evangelists on Visit to Jamaica." *Daily Gleaner*, October 17, 1938, 10.
"The Value of Speaking in Tongues." *Bridegroom's Messenger* 1.12 (April 15, 1908) 4.
Van Arsdale, Chas. N. "The Sheridan Campaign." *Alliance Weekly* 55.44 (January 14, 1922) 698.
Van Dusen, Henry P. "The Third Force in Christendom." *Life*, June 9, 1958, 113–2 4.
Varley, Frank. "Is Britain Israel?" *Pentecostal Evangel* no. 1551 (January 29, 1944) 3.
"Victim of Race Prejudice." *Zion City Independent*, August 18, 1911, 4.
"A Visit From Evangelist F.F. Bosworth." *Moody Bible Institute Monthly* 22.10 (June 1922) 1053.
"Vindication of William Branham of Attack by 'Prophecy Magazine.'" *Voice of Healing* 7.8 (November 1954) 8.
Vitchestain, J.H. "Bosworth's Challenge Stands Unrefuted; Major Roehl Fails to Report on Cases." *National Labor Tribune*, February 10, 1921, 7.
Vitchestain, J.H. "Largest Hall in Detroit Packed with Seekers." *National Labor Tribune*, February 3, 1921, 3.
"Voice of Children Praising God" *Leaves of Healing* 8.3 (November 10, 1900): 80.
"Voliva Drives Out Deacons." *Waukegan Daily Gazette*, October 22, 1906, 15/2/5, Flower Pentecostal Heritage Center.

Walthall, W. Jethro. "Do All Speak in Tongues Who Receive the Baptism?" *Christian Evangel* no. 248–248 (July 27, 1918) 6.
"Want Health Inspector Inoculated with Leprosy and Tuberculosis Germs Then Try Bible Truths." *National Labor Tribune*, February 3, 1921, 7.
"Warning to Zion: Parhamites Seeking to Rule." *Zion Herald*, October 25, 1907, 1.
"Warren Collins Non-Council Files." n.d. 30/2/8. Flower Pentecostal Heritage Center.
Welch, J.W. "A Visit Among the Saints in Oklahoma, California and Texas." *Weekly Evangel* no. 173 (January 20, 1917) 8.
"West End Revival Campaign Closes." *Houston Chronicle*, September 3, 1917, 6.
Wesley, John. *The Works of John Wesley*. 3rd ed., complete and unabridged. Grand Rapids, MI: Baker, 1978.
"What Faith Can Do When Drugs Fail." *National Labor Tribune*, October 15, 1925, 7.
"What Power Is It?" *Our Hope* 28.5 (November 1921) 268–71.
"Where the Drys and Wets May Quaff a Draught and Maintain the Law Begging to Come and Drink." *National Labor Tribune*, April 27, 1922, 3.
Whiteside, E.D. "An Apostolic Revival." *Alliance Weekly* 54.39 (December 25, 1920) 616.
"Why Are Not All Who Are Prayed For Healed?" *National Labor Tribune*, October 26, 1922, 3.
"Will Conduct Meeting Here." *Dallas Morning News*, July 23, 1912, 14.
"William Branham in Lausanne." *Pentecost* no. 34 (December 1955) 7.
Williams, Mark W. "Religion On The Corner: This Year's Revivals Are Like Those of Old Times. Army Hard at Work. Gospel in All Tongues." *New York Times*, September 24, 1922, sec. Special Features, 107.
Wilson, Everett. "Wonderful Signs: Soon Coming Christ." *Bible Standard* 3.3 (1922) 4.
"Witnesses to the Power of God." *Alliance Weekly* 54.49 (March 5, 1921) 780.
Wittich, Philip. "Answering the Objections in the Book of Jonah." *Latter Rain Evangel*, March 1926, 5–8.
"Woman Completely Healed While Bro. Bosworth Is Preaching." *Voice of Healing* 1.8 (November 1948) 12.
"Woman Tells of Cure Wrought Through Faith." *Syracuse Herald*, May 23, 1922, 22.
"The Wonderful Works of God." *Bridegroom's Messenger* 14.229 (April 1921) 2.
"The Wonderful Works of God." *Zion City Independent*, September 13, 1912, 1, 3.
Woodworth-Etter, Maria Beulah. *Signs and Wonders God Wrought in the Ministry for Forty Years*. Indianapolis, IN: [Mrs. M.B.W. Etter], 1916.
———. *Acts of the Holy Ghost: Or The Life, Work, and Experience of Mrs. M. B. Woodworth-Etter, Evangelist*. Dallas: John F. Worley, 1912.
———. "Neglect Not the Gift That Is In Thee." *Latter Rain Evangel* 5.10 (August 1913) 13–17.
"Woodworth-Etter Meetings in Dallas (Texas)." *Confidence* 5.11 (November 1912) 258–59.
"Word from Bro. Branham." *Voice of Healing* 1.5 (August 1948) 1.
"World-Wide Revival Crusade." *Voice of Healing* 6.4 (July 1953) 2–3.
———. "Williamsport Campaign." *Alliance Weekly* 57.47 (January 19, 1924) 760.
"A Writer on Anglo-Israel." *Zion Banner*, August 9, 1904, 367.
Wyburn, Susie May Patterson. *"But, until Seventy Times Seven": Jeremiah, Samuel, John*. New York: Loizeaux Brothers, 1936.
Yeomans, Lilian B. *Healing from Heaven*. Springfield, MO: Gospel, 1973.

Yeomans, Lillian B. "Out of the Depths: A Testimony." *Christian and Missionary Alliance* 29.20 (February 15, 1908) 330–331.

———. "This Is the Rest . . . and This Is the Refreshing." *Pentecostal Evangel* no. 845 (April 26, 1930) 1.

"Zion City Band." *Zion Herald*, May 15, 1907, 2

"Zion City Band Concert." *Zion Banner*, April 25, 1905, 246.

"Zion City Band to Give Concerts." *Zion Banner*, June 7, 1904, 289.

"Zion City Bands for Next Visitation." *Zion Banner*, November 20, 1903, 10.

"Zion City Brass Band." *Zion Banner*, February 17, 211.

"Zion City, Ill." *Christian Evangel*, August 10, 1913, 8.

"Zion City Is Again Scene of Holy War." *Freeport Journal Standard*, August 29, 1924, 2.

"Zion City Subscribers." *Household of God* 4.12 (December 1908) 8.

"Zion Musical Organizations." *Zion Banner*, February 3, 1903, 178.

"Zion's Birth Record for 1903." *Zion Banner*, January 12, 1904, 122.

"Zion vs. Parhamism and the Municipal League." *Zion Herald*, October 25, 1907, 2.

SECONDARY SOURCES

Alexander, Thomas G. "Wilford Woodruff and the Changing Nature of Mormon Religious Experience." *Church History* 45.1 (March 1, 1976) 56–69.

Althouse, Peter. *Spirit of the Last Days: Pentecostal Eschatology in Conversation with Jürgen Moltmann*. Journal of Pentecostal Theology Supplement Series, 25. London: T & T Clark, 2003.

Anderson, Allan. *An Introduction to Pentecostalism: Global Charismatic Christianity*. New York: Cambridge University Press, 2004.

Anderson, Robert Mapes. *Vision of the Disinherited: The Making of American Pentecostalism*. Peabody, MA: Hendrickson, 1992.

Atkinson, William. *The "Spiritual Death" of Jesus: A Pentecostal Investigation*. Leiden: Brill, 2009.

Baer, Jonathan R. "Perfectly Empowered Bodies Divine Healing in Modernizing America." PhD diss., Yale University, 2002.

Barkun, Michael. *Religion and the Racist Right: The Origins of the Christian Identity Movement*. Chapel Hill: University of North Carolina Press, 1997.

Barnes, Roscoe. "F.F. Bosworth: A Historical Analysis of the Influential Factors in His Life and Ministry." PhD diss., University of Pretoria, 2009.

———. *F.F. Bosworth: The Man Behind "Christ the Healer."* Newcastle Upon Tyne: Cambridge Scholars, 2009.

———. "Why F.F. Bosworth and His Family Moved to Fitzgerald, Ga." Accessed November 6, 2013. http://www.academia.edu/2281739/Why_F._F._Bosworth_and_His_Family_Moved_to_Fitzgerald_Ga.

Barron, Bruce A. "Rechristianizing America: The Reconstruction and Kingdom Now Movements in American Evangelical Christianity." PhD diss., University of Pittsburgh, 1991.

Bassett, Paul. "The Theological Identity of the North American Holiness Movement." In *The Variety of American Evangelicalism*, edited by Donald W. Dayton and Robert K. Johnston, 72–108. Knoxville: University of Tennessee Press, 2001.

Ben-Dor Benite, Zvi. *The Ten Lost Tribes: A World History*. New York: Oxford University Press, 2009.

Berger, Peter L. "The Sociological Study of Sectarianism." *Social Research* 21.4 (December 1, 1954) 467–85.
Blomgren, Jr., Oscar. "Man of God: Fred F. Bosworth, Part VII: The National Radio Revival." *Herald of Faith*, May 1964, 14–15.
Blumhofer, Edith L. "A Pentecostal Branch Grows in Dowie's Zion: Charles F. Parham's 1906 Invasion." *Assemblies of God Heritage* 6 (September 1, 1986) 3–5.
———. "A Woman Used by the Spirit." *Paraclete* 21.3 (June 1, 1987) 5–9.
———. "The Christian Catholic Apostolic Church and the Apostolic Faith: A Study in the 1906 Pentecostal Revival." In *Charismatic Experiences in History*, edited by Cecil M. Robeck, 126–46. Peabody, MA: Hendrickson, 1985.
Blumhofer, Edith Waldvogel. *Aimee Semple McPherson: Everybody's Sister*. Library of Religious Biography. Grand Rapids, MI: W.B. Eerdmans, 1993.
———. *Restoring the Faith: The Assemblies of God, Pentecostalism, and American Culture*. Urbana: University of Illinois Press, 1993.
———. *The Assemblies of God: A Chapter in the Story of American Pentecostalism*. Vol. 1. Springfield, MO: Gospel, 1989.
Bonk, Jon. *Between Past and Future: Evangelical Mission Entering the Twenty-First Century*. William Carey Library, 2003.
Bowler, Kate. *Blessed: A History of the American Prosperity Gospel*. New York: Oxford University Press, 2013.
Brown, Kenneth O. *Inskip, McDonald, Fowler: "Wholly and Forever Thine": Early Leadership in the National Camp Meeting Association for the Promotion of Holiness*. Hazleton, PA: Holiness Archives, 1999.
Brumback, Carl. *Suddenly . . . from Heaven: A History of the Assemblies of God*. Springfield, MO: Gospel, 1961.
Burpeau, Kemp Pendleton. *God's Showman: A Historical Study of John G. Lake and South African/American Pentecostalism*. Oslo: Refleks, 2004.
Cartwright, Desmond W. *The Great Evangelists: The Lives of George and Stephen Jeffreys*. Basingstoke: Marshall Pickering, 1986.
Chappell, Paul Gale. "The Divine Healing Movement in America." PhD diss., Drew University, 1983.
Cho, Kyu-Hyung. "The Move to Independence from Anglican Leadership: An Examination of the Relationship between Alexander Alfred Boddy and the Early Leaders of the British Pentecostal Denominations (1907–1930)." PhD diss., University of Birmingham (United Kingdom (2009.
Clemmons, Ithiel C. *Bishop C.H. Mason and the Roots of the Church of God in Christ*. Bakersfield, CA: Pneuma Life, 1996.
Cook, Philip L. *Zion City, Illinois: Twentieth-Century Utopia*. Syracuse, NY: Syracuse University Press, 1996.
Cox, Harvey Gallagher. *Fire from Heaven the Rise of Pentecostal Spirituality and the Reshaping of Religion in the Twenty-First Century*. Cambridge, MA: Da Capo, 2001.
Creech, Joe. "Visions of Glory: The Place of the Azusa Street Revival in Pentecostal History." *Church History* 65.3 (September 1, 1996) 405–24.
Cunningham, Raymond J. "From Holiness to Healing: The Faith Cure in America 1872–1892." *Church History* 43.4 (December 1, 1974) 499–513.
Curtis, Heather D. "A Sane Gospel: Radical Evangelicals, Psychology, and Pentecostal Revival in the Early Twentieth Century." *Religion and American Culture* 21.2 (June 1, 2011) 195–226.

———. *Faith in the Great Physician: Suffering and Divine Healing in American Culture, 1860-1900*. Baltimore: Johns Hopkins University Press, 2007.

———. "'God Is Not Affected by the Depression': Pentecostal Missions during the 1930s." *Church History* 80.3 (September 1, 2011) 579-589.

Dayton, Donald W. "Asa Mahan and the Development of American Holiness Theology." *Wesleyan Theological Journal* 9 (March 1, 1974) 60-69.

———. "From Christian Perfection to the 'Baptism of the Holy Ghost.'" In *Aspects of Pentecostal-Charismatic Origins*, 39-54. Plainfield, NJ: Logos International, 1975.

———. *Theological Roots of Pentecostalism*. Studies in Evangelicalism no. 5. Metuchen, NJ: Scarecrow, 1987.

Dieter, Melvin E. *The Holiness Revival of the Nineteenth Century*. 2nd ed. Lanham, MD: Scarecrow, 1996.

———. "The Wesleyan/Holiness and Pentecostal Movements: Commonalities, Confrontation, and Dialogue." *Pneuma* 12.1 (March 1, 1990) 4-13.

Dixon, Larry E. "Have the 'Jewels of the Church' Been Found Again: The Irving-Darby Debate on Miraculous Gifts." *Evangelical Journal* 5.2 (Fall 1987) 78-92.

Dorsett, Lyle W. *A Passion for God: The Spiritual Journey of A.W. Tozer*. Chicago: Moody, 2008.

Duyzer, Peter. *Heterodox Tsunami: The Theology of William Branham, Scriptural or Heretical?*. Delta, BC: Peter Duyzer, 2004.

Edsor, Albert W. *Set Your House in Order: God's Call to George Jeffreys as the Founder of the Elim Pentecostal Movement*. Chichester, West Sussex: New Wine, 1989.

Eskridge, Larry K. "Only Believe: Paul Rader and the Chicago Gospel Tabernacle, 1922-1933." MA thesis, University of Maryland, 1985.

Espinosa, Gastón. *William J. Seymour and the Origins of Global Pentecostalism: A Biography and Documentary History*. Durham: Duke University Press, 2014.

Faupel, David W. *The Everlasting Gospel: The Significance of Eschatology in the Development of Pentecostal Thought*. Journal of Pentecostal Theology Supplement Series 10. Sheffield, England: Sheffield Academic, 1996.

Faupel, D. William. "The Everlasting Gospel: The Significance of Eschatology in the Development of Pentecostal Thought." Ph.D. diss., Department of Theology, University of Birmingham, 1989.

———. "The Function of 'Models' in the Interpretation of Pentecostal Thought." *Pneuma* 2.1 (March 1, 1980) 51-71.

Flegg, Columba Graham. *"Gathered under Apostles": A Study of the Catholic Apostolic Church*. Oxford: Clarendon, 1992.

Foxworth, John David. "Raymond T. Richey: An Interpretive Biography." PhD diss., Regent University, 2011.

Friesen, Aaron T. *Norming the Abnormal: The Development and Function of the Doctrine of Initial Evidence in Classical Pentecostalism*. Eugene, OR: Pickwick, 2013.

Fudge, Thomas. *Daniel Warner and the Paradox of Religious Democracy in Nineteenth-Century America*. Lewiston, NY: Mellen, 1998.

Gardiner, Gordon. "A Herald of Glad Tidings: Part One." *Bread of Life* 3.5 (May 1954) 3-4, 8-10.

———. "Herald of Glad Tidings: Part Two." *Bread of Life* 3.6 (June 1954) 5-6, 9-10.

———. "Herald of Glad Tidings: Part Three." *Bread of Life* 3.7 (July 1954) 9-10.

———. "Herald of Glad Tidings: Part Four." *Bread of Life* 3.8 (August 1954) 5-6.

———. "The Apostle of Divine Healing." Bread of Life, 6.3 (March 1957) 3-9, 11-15.

---. *Out of Zion into All the World*. Shippensburg, PA: Companion, 1990.
Gill, Gillian. *Mary Baker Eddy*. Cambridge, MA: Perseus, 1998.
Goff, James R. *Fields White Unto Harvest: Charles F. Parham and the Missionary Origins of Pentecostalism*. Fayetteville: University of Arkansas Press, 1988.
Gonen, Rivka. *To the Ends of the Earth: The Quest for the Ten Lost Tribes of Israel*. Northvale, NJ: Jason Aronson, 2002.
Grass, Tim. *Lord's Watchman: A Life of Edward Irving (1792-1834)*. Eugene, OR: Pickwick, 2012.
Gregory, Chester W. *The History of the United Holy Church of America, Inc., 1886-2000*. Baltimore, MD: Gateway, 2000.
Guelzo, Allen C. "Oberlin Perfectionism and Its Edwardsian Origins, 1835-1870." In *Jonathan Edwards's Writings: Text, Context, Interpretation*, edited by Stephen J. Stein, 159-74. Bloomington: Indiana University Press, 1996.
Haines, Michael R. "Selected Population Characteristics – Median Age, Sex Ratio, Annual Growth Rate, and Number, by Race, Urban Residence, and Nativity: 1790-2000, Table Aa22-3 5." In *Historical Statistics of the United States, Earliest Times to the Present: Millennial Edition*, edited by Susan B. Carter, Scott Sigmund Gartner, et al. New York: Cambridge University Press, 2006. http://dx.doi.org/10.1017/ISBN-9780511132971.Aa1-1 0910.1017/ISBN-9780511132971.Aa1-1 09.
Hardesty, Nancy. *Faith Cure: Divine Healing in the Holiness and Pentecostal Movements*. Peabody, MA: Hendrickson, 2003.
Harrell, David Edwin. *All Things Are Possible: The Healing and Charismatic Revivals in Modern America*. Bloomington: Indiana University Press, 1975.
Hathaway, Malcolm R. "The Role of William Oliver Hutchinson and the Apostolic Faith Church in the Formation of British Pentecostal Churches." *Journal of the European Pentecostal Theological Association* 16 (January 1, 1996) 40-57.
Heath, Elaine A. *Naked Faith: The Mystical Theology of Phoebe Palmer*. Princeton Theological Monograph Series, 108. Eugene, OR: Pickwick, 2009.
Hejzlar, Pavel. *Two Paradigms for Divine Healing: Fred F. Bosworth, Kenneth E. Hagin, Agnes Sanford, and Francis Macnutt in Dialogue*. Global Pentecostal and Charismatic Studies, 4. Leiden: Brill, 2010.
Hindmarsh, D. Bruce. *The Evangelical Conversion Narrative: Spiritual Autobiography in Early Modern England*. New York: Oxford University Press, 2007.
Hollenweger, Walter J. *Pentecostalism: Origins and Developments Worldwide*. Peabody, MA: Hendrickson, 1997.
---. "Pentecostals and the Charismatic Movement." In *The Study of Spirituality*, edited by Cheslyn Jones, Geoffrey Wainwright, and Edward Yarnold, 549-54. New York: Oxford University Press, 1986.
---. *The Pentecostals*. Peabody, MA: Hendrickson, 1988.
---. *The Pentecostals: The Charismatic Movement in the Churches*. Minneapolis: Augsburg, 1972.
Hudson, David Neil. "A Schism and Its Aftermath: An Historical Analysis of Denominational Discerption in the Elim Pentecostal Church, 1939-1940." PhD diss., King's College London (University of London (1999.
---. "Dealing with the Fire: Early Pentecostal Responses to the Practices of Speaking in Tongues and Spoken Prophecy." *Journal of the European Pentecostal Theological Association* 28.2 (January 1, 2008) 145-57.

———. "The Earliest Days of British Pentecostalism." *Journal of the European Pentecostal Theological Association* 21 (January 1, 2001) 49–67.

Jacobsen, Douglas. *Thinking in the Spirit: Theologies of the Early Pentecostal Movement.* Bloomington: Indiana University Press, 2003.

Johnston, Robin. *Howard A. Goss: A Pentecostal Life.* Hazelwood, MO: Word Aflame, 2010.

Jones, Charles Edwin. *Perfectionist Persuasion: The Holiness Movement and American Methodism, 1867–1936.* ATLA Monograph Series no. 5. Metuchen, NJ: Scarecrow, 1974.

King, Gerald W. *Disfellowshiped: Pentecostal Responses to Fundamentalism in the United States, 1906–1943.* Eugene, OR: Wipf and Stock, 2011.

———. "Streams of Convergence: The Pentecostal-Fundamentalist Response to Modernism." *PentecoStudies* 7.2 (2008) 64–84.

King, Paul L. *Genuine Gold: The Cautiously Charismatic Story of the Early Christian and Missionary Alliance.* Tulsa: Word and Spirit, 2006.

Kinnebrew, James M. "The Charismatic Doctrine of Positive Confession: A Historical, Exegetical, and Theological Critique." ThD diss., Mid-America Baptist Theological Seminary, 1988.

Kline-Walczak, Kenneth Richard. *Testimonies of Signs and Wonders: Evangelistic Crusade of Maria Buelah Woodworth-Etter in Moline, Rock Island, Illinois and Davenport, Iowa in the Years 1902 - 1903 - 1907: Or Redigging the Wells of Holy Spirit Renewal: Our Forgotten Heritage in the Quad Cities.* Davenport, IA: Kenneth Richard Kline-Walczak, 2006.

Knight, Henry H., III. "God's Faithfulness and God's Freedom: A Comparison of Contemporary Theologies of Healing." *Journal of Pentecostal Theology* no. 2 (1993) 65–89.

Kostlevy, William. *Holy Jumpers: Evangelicals and Radicals in Progressive Era America.* New York: Oxford University Press, 2010.

Kydd, R. A. N. "Healing in the Christian Church." In *The New International Dictionary of Pentecostal and Charismatic Movements,* edited by Stanley M. Burgess and Ed M. Van der Maas, 698–711. Grand Rapids, MI: Zondervan, 2002.

Kydd, Ronald A. N. *Healing through the Centuries: Models for Understanding.* Grand Rapids, MI: Baker Academic, 1995.

Laan, Cornelis van der. "The Proceedings of the Leaders' Meetings (1908–1911) and of the International Pentecostal Council (1912–1914)." *Pneuma* 10.1 (March 1, 1988) 36–49.

Land, Steven J. *Pentecostal Spirituality: A Passion for the Kingdom.* Cleveland, TN: CPT, 2010.

Liardon, Roberts. *God's Generals: The Healing Evangelists.* New Kensington, PA: Whitaker House, 2011.

Lie, Geir. *E.W. Kenyon: Cult Founder or Evangelical Minister?* Oslo: Refleks, 2003.

Loftis, Carrie Frances Wagliardo. *A History of First Assembly of God; Dallas, Texas, 1912–1992, 80 Years.* Dallas: First Assembly of God, 1992.

Lovett, L. "Black Holiness Pentecostalism." In *New International Dictionary of Pentecostal and Charismatic Movements,* edited by Stanley M. Burgess and Eduard M. Van Der Mass, 419–428. Grand Rapids, MI: Zondervan, 2002.

Lowery, Kevin T. "A Fork in the Wesleyan Road: Phoebe Palmer and the Appropriation of Christian Perfection." *Wesleyan Theological Journal* 36.2 (September 1, 2001) 187–222.

Marsden, George M. *Fundamentalism and American Culture: The Shaping of Twentieth Century Evangelicalism, 1870-1925*. New York: Oxford University Press, 1980.

McConnell, D. R. *A Different Gospel: A Historical and Biblical Analysis of the Modern Faith Movement*. Peabody, MA: Hendrickson, 1988.

McDonnell, Kilian. "Holy Spirit and Pentecostalism." *Commonweal*, November 8, 1968.

McGee, Gary B. "'Latter Rain' Falling in the East: Early-Twentieth-Century Pentecostalism in India and the Debate over Speaking in Tongues." *Church History* 68.3 (September 1, 1999) 648–65.

———. *Miracles, Missions, and American Pentecostalism*. American Society of Missiology Series 45. Maryknoll, NY: Orbis, 2010.

———. "Popular Expositions of Initial Evidence in Pentecostalism." In *Initial Evidence: Historical and Biblical Perspectives on the Pentecostal Doctrine of Spirit Baptism*, edited by Gary B. McGee, 119–30. Peabody, MA: Hendrickson, 1991.

———. "'Power from on High': A Historical Perspective on the Radical Strategy in Missions." In *Pentecostalism in Context: Essays in Honor of William W. Menzies*, edited by Wonsuk Ma and Robert P. Menzies, 317–36. Journal of Pentecostal Theology Supplement Series, v. 11. Sheffield: Sheffield Academic, 1997.

———. "'The Lord's Pentecostal Missionary Movement': The Restorationist Impulse of a Modern Mission Movement." *Asian Journal of Pentecostal Studies* 8.1 (January 1, 2005) 49–65.

McGee, G.B., and S.M. Burgess. "India." In *The New International Dictionary of Pentecostal and Charismatic Movements*, edited by Stanley M. Burgess and Eduard M. Van Der Mass, 118–1 26. Grand Rapids, MI: Zondervan, 2003.

McIntyre, Joe. *E. W. Kenyon and His Message of Faith: The True Story*. Orlando: Charisma House, 1997.

McKenzie, Brian Alexander. *Fundamentalism, Christian Unity, and Premillennialism in the Thought of Rowland Victor Bingham, 1872-1942 a Study of Anti-Modernism in Canada*. Canadian Theses = Thèses Canadiennes. Ottawa: National Library of Canada, 1987.

McMullen, Joshua J. "Maria B Woodworth-Etter: Bridging the Wesleyan-Pentecostal Divide." In *From Aldersgate to Azusa Street*, edited by Henry H. Knight, 185–93. Eugene, OR: Pickwick, 2010.

Melton, J. Gordon. *Melton's Encyclopedia of American Religions*. 8th ed. Detroit: Gale Cengage, 2009.

Menzies, Glen W. "Tongues as 'The Initial Physical Sign' of Spirit Baptism in the Thought of D W Kerr." *Pneuma* 20.2 (September 1, 1998) 175–89.

Menzies, William W. *Anointed to Serve: The Story of the Assemblies of God*. Springfield, MO: Gospel, 1971.

Miskov, Jennifer A. *Life on Wings: The Forgotten Life and Theology of Carrie Judd Montgomery, 1858–1946*. Cleveland, TN: CPT, 2012.

Moon, Tony G. "J. H. King on Initial Evidence: Did He Change?" *Journal of Pentecostal Theology* 14.2 (April 1, 2006) 261–86.

Morton, Barry. "'The Devil Who Heals': Fraud and Falsification in the Evangelical Career of John G. Lake, Missionary to South Africa 1908–1913." *African Historical Review* 44.2 (2012) 98–118.

Mullin, Robert Bruce. *Miracles and the Modern Religious Imagination.* New Haven: Yale University Press, 1996.

Murray, Frank S. *The Sublimity of Faith: The Life and Work of Frank W. Sandford.* Amherst, NH: Kingdom, 1981.

Niklaus, Robert L., John S. Sawin, and Samuel J. Stoesz. *All for Jesus: God at Work in the Christian and Missionary Alliance, 125th Anniversary Edition.* Colorado Springs, CO: Christian & Missionary Alliance, 2013.

Oliverio, Jr., L. William. *Theological Hermeneutics in the Classical Pentecostal Tradition: A Typological Account.* Leiden: Brill, 2012.

Opp, James. "Balm of Gilead: Faith, Healing, and Medicine in the Life of Dr. Lilian B. Yeomans." Memorial University of Newfoundland, 1997.

———. *The Lord for the Body: Religion, Medicine, and Protestant Faith Healing in Canada, 1880–1930.* Montreal: McGill-Queen's University Press, 2005.

Parfitt, Tudor. *The Lost Tribes of Israel: The History of a Myth.* London: Phoenix, 2003.

Patterson, James Oglethorpe, and Church of God in Christ. *History and Formative Years of the Church of God in Christ; with Excerpts from the Life and Works of Its Founder, Bishop C.H. Mason.* Memphis, TN: Church of God in Christ, 1969.

Peters, John Leland. *Christian Perfection and American Methodism.* New York; Nashville: Abingdon, 1956.

Pierard, Richard V. "The Contribution of British-Israelism to Antisemitism within Conservative Protestantism." In *Holocaust and Church Struggle: Religion, Power and the Politics of Resistance*, edited by Hubert G. Locke and Marcia Sachs Littell, 45–68. Studies in the Shoah. Lanham, MD: University Press of America, 1996.

Poloma, Margaret M. "Old Wine, New Wineskins: The Rise of Healing Rooms in Revival Pentecostalism." *Pneuma* 28.1 (March 1, 2006) 59–71.

Raser, Harold E. *Phoebe Palmer: Her Life and Thought.* Studies in Women and Religion, v. 22. Lewiston, NY: Mellen, 1987.

Reed, David A. *"In Jesus' Name": The History and Beliefs of Oneness Pentecostals.* Journal of Pentecostal Theology Supplement Series no. 31. Dorset, UK: Deo, 2008.

Reynolds, Lindsay. *Rebirth: The Redevelopment of the Christian and Missionary Alliance in Canada.* Willowdale, Ontario: Christian and Missionary Alliance in Canada, 1992.

Richmann, Christopher. "Blaspheming in Tongues: Demons, Glossolalia, and the Christian and Missionary Alliance." *Wesleyan Theological Journal* 49.1 (Spring 2014) 139–55.

———. "Evangelical Unity in the Pentecostal Theology of Alexander A. Boddy." Springfield, MO, 2014.

———. "Prophecy and Politics: British-Israelism in American Pentecostalism." *Cyberjournal for Pentecostal-Charismatic Research* 22 (January 2013).

Robeck, Cecil M. "An Emerging Magisterium? The Case of the Assemblies of God." *Pneuma* 25.2 (September 1, 2003) 164–215.

———. "McDonnell, Kilian." In *The New International Dictionary of Pentecostal and Charismatic Movements*, edited by Stanley M. Burgess and Van der Maas, 853. Grand Rapids, MI: Zondervan, 2002.

———. "The Assemblies of God and Ecumenical Cooperation: 1920–1965." In *Pentecostalism in Context: Essays in Honor of William W. Menzies*, edited by Wonsuk Ma and Robert P. Menzies, 107–50. Eugene, OR: Wipf and Stock, 2008.

———. *The Azusa Street Mission and Revival: The Birth of the Global Pentecostal Movement*. Nashville: Nelson, 2006.

———. "William J. Seymour and the 'Bible Evidence.'" In *Initial Evidence: Historical and Biblical Perspectives on the Pentecostal Doctrine of Spirit Baptism*, edited by Gary B. McGee, 72–95. Peabody, MA: Hendrickson, 1991.

Robinson, James. *Divine Healing: The Formative Years, 1830–1890: Theological Roots in the Transatlantic World*. Eugene, OR: Pickwick, 2011.

———. *Divine Healing: The Holiness-Pentecostal Transition Years, 1890–1906: Theological Transpositions in the Transatlantic World*. Eugene, OR: Pickwick, 2013.

———. *Divine Healing: The Years of Expansion, 1906–1930—Theological Variation in the Transatlantic World*. Eugene, OR: Pickwick, 2014.

———. *Pentecostal Origins: Early Pentecostalism in Ireland in the Context of the British Isles*. Studies in Evangelical History and Thought. Milton Keynes, UK: Paternoster, 2005.

Robins, R. G. *A. J. Tomlinson: Plainfolk Modernist*. New York: Oxford University Press, 2004.

Rodgers, Darrin J. "The Assemblies of God and the Long Journey toward Racial Reconciliation." *Assemblies of God Heritage* 28 (January 1, 2008) 50–61.

Sandeen, Ernest Robert. *The Roots of Fundamentalism: British and American Millenarianism, 1800–1930*. Chicago: University of Chicago Press, 1970.

Schmidgall, Paul. *European Pentecostalism: Its Origins, Development, and Future*. CPT Press, 2013.

Sepulveda, Juan. "Another Way of Being Pentecostal." In *Pentecostal Power: Expressions, Impact and Faith of Latin American Pentecostalism*, edited by Calvin Smith, 37–62. Leiden: Brill, 2010.

Sheppard, Gerald T. "Pentecostals and the Hermeneutics of Dispensationalism : The Anatomy of an Uneasy Relationship." *Pneuma* 6.2 (September 1, 1984) 5–33.

Simmons, Dale H. *E. W. Kenyon and the Postbellum Pursuit of Peace, Power and Plenty*. Studies in Evangelicalism no. 13. Lanham, MD: Scarecrow, 1997.

Simpson, Carl. "Jonathan Paul and the German Pentecostal Movement: The First Seven Years, 1907–1914." *Journal of the European Pentecostal Theological Association* 28.2 (January 1, 2008) 169–82.

Smith, C. Calvin. "The Houston Riot of 1917, Revisited." *Houston Review* 13 (1991) 85–102.

Smith, Timothy L. "Doctrine of the Sanctifying Spirit : Charles G. Finney's Synthesis of Wesleyan and Covenant Theology." *Wesleyan Theological Journal* 13 (March 1, 1978) 92–113.

Smith, Timothy Lawrence. *Called Unto Holiness; the Story of the Nazarenes: The Formative Years*. Kansas City, MO: Nazarene, 1962.

———. *Revivalism and Social Reform: American Protestantism on the Eve of the Civil War*. Baltimore: Johns Hopkins University Press, 1980.

Starr, Paul. *The Social Transformation of American Medicine*. New York: Basic, 1982.

Stephens, Michael S. "'Who Healeth All Thy Diseases': Health, Healing, and Holiness in the Church of God Reformation Movement, 1880–1925." PhD diss., Vanderbilt University, 2004.

Stephens, Randall J. *The Fire Spreads: Holiness and Pentecostalism in the American South*. Cambridge, MA: Harvard University Press, 2008.

Stewart, Adam. "A Canadian Azusa? The Implications of the Hebden Mission for Pentecostal Historiography." In *Winds from the North*, edited by Michael Wilkinson and Peter Althouse, 17–37. Leiden: Brill, 2010.

Sumrall, Lester. *Pioneers of Faith*. Tulsa: Harrison House, 1995.

Sutton, Matthew Avery. *Aimee Semple McPherson and the Resurrection of Christian America*. Cambridge, MA: Harvard University Press, 2007.

———. "'Between the Refrigerator and the Wildfire': Aimee Semple McPherson, Pentecostalism, and the Fundamentalist-Modernist Controversy." *Church History* 72.1 (March 1, 2003) 159–88.

Synan, Vinson. *The Holiness-Pentecostal Tradition: Charismatic Movements in the Twentieth Century*. Grand Rapids, MI: W.B. Eerdmans, 1997.

———. "The Role of Tongues as Initial Evidence." In *Spirit and Renewal: Essays in Honor of J. Rodman Williams*, edited by Mark W. Wilson, 67–82. Sheffield: Sheffield Academic, 1994.

Tallman, Matthew W. "Demos Shakarian: The Life, Legacy, and Vision of a Full Gospel Business Man." PhD diss., Regent University, 2009.

Tan, May Ling. "A Response to Frank Macchia's 'Groans Too Deep for Words: Towards a Theology of Tongues as Initial Evidence.'" *Asian Journal of Pentecostal Studies* 1.2 (July 1, 1998) 175–83.

Taves, Ann. *Fits, Trances, & Visions: Experiencing Religion and Explaining Experience from Wesley to James*. Princeton, NJ: Princeton University Press, 1999.

Thompson, Matthew K. *Kingdom Come: Revisioning Pentecostal Eschatology*. Journal of Pentecostal Theology Supplement Series, 37. Blandford Forum, Dorset, U.K.: Deo, 2010.

Trimble, Michael R. "Functional Diseases." *British Medical Journal (Clinical Research Edition)* 285.6357 (December 18, 1982) 1768–70.

Turner, William Clair. *The United Holy Church of America: A Study in Black Holiness-Pentecostalism*. Piscataway, NJ: Gorgias, 2006.

Van De Walle, Bernie A. *The Heart of the Gospel: A. B. Simpson, the Fourfold Gospel, and Late Nineteenth-Century Evangelical Theology*. Princeton Theological Monograph Series, 106. Eugene, OR: Pickwick, 2009.

Wacker, Grant. "Are the Golden Oldies Still Worth Playing : Reflections on History Writing among Early Pentecostals." *Pneuma* 8.2 (September 1, 1986) 81–100.

———. *Heaven Below: Early Pentecostals and American Culture*. Cambridge, MA: Harvard University Press, 2001.

———. "Marching to Zion: Religion in a Modern Utopian Community." *Church History* 54.4 (December 1, 1985) 496–511.

———. "The Pentecostal Tradition." In *Caring and Curing: Health and Medicine in the Western Religious Traditions*, edited by Ronald L. Numbers and Darrel W. Amundsen, 514–38. Baltimore, MD: Johns Hopkins University Press, 1998.

———. "Travail of a Broken Family: Radical Evangelical Responses to the Emergence of Pentecostalism in America, 1906–1 6." In *Pentecostal Currents in American Protestantism*, edited by Edith L. Blumhofer, Russell P. Spittler, and Grant Wacker, 23–49. Urbana: University of Illinois Press, 1999.

Wacker, Grant, Chris R. Armstrong, and Jay S.F. Blossom. "John Alexander Dowie: Harbinger of Pentecostal Power." In *Portraits of a Generation: Early Pentecostal Leaders*, edited by Grant Wacker and James R. Goff, 3–19. Fayetteville: University of Arkansas Press, 2002.

Wakefield, Gavin. *Alexander Boddy: Pentecostal Anglican Pioneer*. Colorado Springs: Authentic Paternoster, 2007.
Waldvogel, Edith Lydia. "The 'Overcoming Life': A Study in the Reformed Evangelical Origins of Pentecostalism." PhD diss., Harvard University, 1977.
Walters, Orville S. "Concept of Attainment in John Wesley's Christian Perfection." *Methodist History* 10.3 (April 1, 1972) 12–29.
Ware, Steven L. *Restorationism in the Holiness Movement in the Late Nineteenth and Early Twentieth Centuries*. Lewiston, NY: Mellen, 2004.
Warner, Wayne. *For Such a Time As This: Maria Woodworth-Etter Her Healing and Evangelizing Ministry*. Gainsville: Bridge Logos, 2005.
———. *The Woman Evangelist: The Life and Times of Charismatic Evangelist Maria B. Woodworth-Etter*. Studies in Evangelicalism No. 8. Metuchen, NJ: Scarecrow, 1986.
Weaver, C. Douglas. *The Healer-Prophet, William Marrion Branham: A Study of the Prophetic in American Pentecostalism*. Macon, GA: Mercer University Press, 2000.
———. "Baptists and Holiness in the Nineteenth Century: A Story Rarely Told." *Wesleyan Theological Journal* 49.1 (Spring 2014) 156–74.
Weber, Timothy P. *Living in the Shadow of the Second Coming: American Premillennialism, 1875–1982*. Chicago: University of Chicago Press, 1987.
———. "The Two-Edged Sword: The Fundamentalist Use of the Bible." In *The Bible in America: Essays in Cultural History*, edited by Nathan O. Hatch and Mark A. Noll, 101–20. New York: Oxford University Press, 1982.
White, Charles Edward. *The Beauty of Holiness: Phoebe Palmer as Theologian, Revivalist, Feminist, and Humanitarian*. Grand Rapids, MI: Francis Asbury, 1986.
———. "The Beauty of Holiness : The Career of Phoebe Palmer." *Fides et Historia* 19.1 (February 1, 1987) 22–34.
———. "What the Holy Spirit Can and Cannot Do: The Ambiguities of Phoebe Palmer's Theology of Experience." *Wesleyan Theological Journal* 20.1 (March 1, 1985) 108–21.
Whorton, James C. *Nature Cures: The History of Alternative Medicine in America*. New York; Oxford: Oxford University Press, 2004.
Williams, Joseph W. *Spirit Cure: A History of Pentecostal Healing*. New York: Oxford University Press, 2013.
Wilson, Bryan R. *Sects and Society*. Berkeley: University of California Press, 1961.
Wilson, Ernest Gerald. "The Christian and Missionary Alliance: Developments and Modifications of Its Original Objectives." PhD diss., New York University, 1984.
Wood, Laurence W. "The Origin, Development, and Consistency of John Wesley's Theology of Holiness." *Wesleyan Theological Journal* 43.2 (September 1, 2008) 33–55.
Ziefle, Joshua R. *David Du Plessis and the Assemblies of God: The Struggle for the Soul of a Movement*. Leiden: Brill, 2013.

Index

Allen, A. A., 213, 217
Allen, Ethan O., 30
Allen, J. H., 174–76, 179, 182–84
Anglo-Israelism. *See* British-Israelism
Assemblies of God, 3, 5, 8, 45, 52, 57, 61, 64–65, 68, 84–87, 91, 93–96, 100–5, 108, 111–12, 115–19, 122–23, 126–30, 132–33, 166, 187, 216, 244
Azusa Street Revival, 4–5, 8, 33, 37, 40–41, 54, 57–59, 65–66, 71–73, 84, 91, 107, 110, 113, 243–44

Baptism with the Holy Spirit, 2–4, 8, 18–21, 33, 36–37, 40–42, 45–46, 53–56, 59–63, 65–66, 67–69, 71–73, 76, 79, 81–86, 91, 93, 97, 100–101, 103–30, 153, 166–68, 204, 221–23, 228–29, 235, 238, 243, 245
Barratt, T. B., 114, 121–22, 124, 164
Boardman, William, 13–14, 32
Booth-Clibborn, A. S., 34, 155–56
Beecher, Lyman, 22–23
Bell, E. N., 87, 94–95, 106, 116, 123, 127
Bellin, Ruth, 161–62
Benham, Charles O., 99, 168, 170, 177, 180, 184–85, 199, 205
Bingham, Roland V., 139, 141–43, 146, 163, 168
Boddy, A. A., 93, 113–14
Bosworth, Burt, 81, 99, 101, 123, 155
Bradway, Dorothea Ann, 153, 158
Branham, William, 3, 6, 180, 193–220, 239, 241, 243–44

British-Israelism, 3, 9, 170–92, 199, 208, 221, 229–30, 240–41, 245
Bryant, Daniel, 29, 60, 71, 107, 176
Burgess, Marie, 8, 62–64, 66, 71, 73, 95, 110

Carothers, Warren F., 56, 74–75, 105–6, 117, 129, 166
Christian and Missionary Alliance, 2–3, 14, 36, 39, 44, 115, 128, 133–44, 149–52, 156, 159–61, 163–64, 166–68, 187–88, 190–91, 217
Christian Science, 7, 28–30, 62, 162, 224, 228
Church of God in Christ, 16, 94, 113, 129
Church of God (Cleveland, Tennessee), 45, 94
Cody, Sadie, 47, 71, 97
Copley, A. S., 85, 109–10
Cullis, Charles, 31–32, 34, 142, 238

Dallas Revival, 8, 68, 75–78, 81–88, 90–91, 96–100, 199, 243
Darby, John Nelson, 22, 240
Demons, 6, 30, 60, 74, 106, 159, 207, 226–7, 233, 235
Dispensationalism, 3, 9, 22, 142–43, 146, 163, 173, 176–78, 180, 183–85, 188, 190–92, 241
Doctors. *See* Medicine
Dowie, John Alexander, 3, 27, 29, 32–35, 39–41, 47–66, 71–72, 80, 120–21, 142, 159, 162, 176, 198, 205, 215–16, 226, 238, 243
Du Plessis, David J., 2–3, 202, 217

Durham, William H., 37, 76, 84–86, 93, 108–9, 125–26, 128, 234–36

Eddy, Mary Baker, 7, 27–28, 90
Eschatology. *See* British-Israelism, Dispensationalism, Premillennialism
Exploits of Faith, 152, 161, 170, 172, 176, 210, 232

Finney, Charles, 12–13, 18, 20, 28, 117, 224–25
Fitch, May Wyburn, 149–50
Flower, J. Roswell, 52, 57, 109, 111–12
Fletcher, John, 18
Fockler, Cyrus, 55–56, 61, 65, 70, 72–73, 77, 87, 90, 98–99, 224
Frodsham, Stanley, 83–85, 166, 196
Full Gospel Business Men's Fellowship International, 203, 217
Fundamentalism, 9, 132–33, 139–41, 147–48, 151, 155, 162, 171, 173, 181, 184–85, 187–88, 192

Gaebelein, Arno Clemens, 143, 145, 150–51, 166, 176, 185–86, 188–89, 228
Garr, A.G., 66, 97, 99, 102, 105, 115
Gee, Donald, 187, 215–16, 244
Glossolalia. *See* Tongues
Gordon, Adoniram Judson, 7, 142
Goss, Howard A., 85, 87, 94–95, 106–7

Hagin, Kenneth E. 213, 233, 237
Hagin, Kenneth (Jr.) W., 214
Haldeman, I.M., 139, 144–48, 150, 166, 176
Healing *en masse*, 210–12
Hezmalhalch, Tom, 59–60, 65, 70–71, 73
Hickson, James Moore, 135, 163
Holiness Movement, 3–4, 6–8, 10–38, 40–41, 43–45, 54–56, 58, 64, 66, 67–68, 79, 81, 93–94, 98, 100, 104, 120, 124–27, 130–31, 152, 154, 174, 181, 216, 240, 243

Irwin, B. H., 16, 20

Jamieson, S. A., 85–86

Jeffreys, George, 183
Jennings, F. C., 143–44

Kenyon, Essek W., 9, 62, 90, 134, 115, 214, 231–33, 235, 237
Kerr, D. W., 122, 127–29
King, J. H., 126–27
Kinne, Seeley D., 119–22, 128
Knapp, Martin Wells, 16, 21, 33, 35, 45

Lake, John G., 4, 8, 37, 53, 56, 58–62, 64–66, 70–73, 90, 110, 182, 202, 216, 224, 238
Leatherman, Lucy, 65–66
Lee, Bernice C., 39, 41, 55, 61, 63, 69, 73, 88
Lindsay, Gordon, 47, 58, 61, 182, 193, 195–98, 200, 205, 215–16, 218, 240–41

MacKenzie, Kenneth, 144, 146–48, 163–64
MacMillan, John A., 188–90
Mahan, Asa, 12–14, 19
Mason, Charles H., 16, 113
McPherson, Aimee Semple, 5–6, 37, 135, 140–41, 143, 156, 163, 166, 193, 215–16, 245
McWhirter, James, 183–84
Medicine, 2–3, 7–8, 25–32, 35, 37, 42–43, 47–48, 59, 66, 72, 133, 139–40, 145, 159–62, 207, 218, 225, 237
Methodism, 8, 11–13, 16, 18, 25, 32, 42–44, 59, 66, 101, 125, 153, 165, 171
Montgomery, Carrie Judd, 4, 30–32, 36, 80, 83–84, 99, 114, 168, 234–36, 243
Moody, Dwight L., 14, 22, 35
Moorhead, Max Wood, 67

National Labor Tribune, 134, 140, 143, 146–47, 152, 154, 157, 161, 167
Nazarene, Church of the, 16, 35–36

Oberlin Theology, 12–13, 23
Oneness Pentecostalism, 86, 100, 118, 127, 130, 195

INDEX   291

Opperman, Daniel C. O., 54–55, 74–76, 107
Osborn, T. L., 199, 210–12, 218–20
Ozman, Agnes, 109

Palmer, Phoebe, 11, 13, 18, 20, 31, 55, 236
Parham, Charles F., 3–4, 20–21, 24, 33, 39–41, 53–59, 61, 63, 65–66, 67, 69–71, 74, 94, 106–7, 115, 117, 120, 181–84, 216, 238, 243
Paul, Jonathan, 114
Perkins, Eunice May, 40, 46, 50–51, 115–16, 137, 146, 152
Perkins, Jonathan Ellsworth, 167
Perry, Mattie E., 3, 43–46, 114, 198, 243
Piper, William H., 56–57, 64, 70–72, 87, 107–9, 135
Physicians. *See* Medicine
Premillennialism, 7, 9, 15–17, 21–25, 30, 33–35, 125, 172, 240, 245
Price, Charles, 141, 193, 209, 215–16
Prophecy, 2, 6, 9, 17, 80–81, 124, 126–27, 172–75, 178–84, 187, 192, 215, 240–41
Prosperity Gospel. *See* Word of Faith Movement
Putnam, C. E., 145–46, 162

Rader, Luke, 152, 176–77, 188, 192
Rader, Paul, 134, 152, 167
Radio, 138, 152, 155, 170–72, 177–78, 180, 191, 244
Rand, Howard B., 175–77
Richey, Raymond T., 101–2, 135, 153, 193, 200, 207, 209, 216, 232, 245
Riley, William B., 150–51
Roberts, Oral, 198, 213, 215, 220, 236, 245

Salvation Army, 34, 52, 141, 166
Sanctification, 10–14, 16–21, 24, 31, 33, 36, 43, 53, 55–56, 60–61, 85–86, 92, 100, 113, 124–25, 234–38
Sandford, Frank, 181, 238
Scofield Reference Bible, 141, 143, 148
Seymour, William J., 4, 40–41, 54, 65, 71, 109
Shakarian, Demos, 203

Simpson, A. B., 14, 20, 22, 25, 31–32, 34, 36, 121, 142, 162
Smith, Amanda Berry, 16
Smith, Hannah Whitall, 14
Smith, Oswald J., 149, 167, 187–89, 192
South Africa, 52, 60–61, 71, 180, 201–3, 206–9, 218
Spiritual Gifts, 6, 30, 32, 57–58, 106, 113, 117–18, 206, 222–23, 240
Sproul, John, 137–38, 204
Stadsklev, Carl Oliver, 180
Stadsklev, Julius W., 180
Stone Church (Chicago), 57, 63, 71, 78, 87–90, 93–94, 96–97, 99, 103, 186

Thomas, W. H. Griffith, 144
Tomlinson, A. J., 181–82
Torrey, R. A., 33, 35, 147–48, 228
Trance Evangelism, 79
Tongues, 3–6, 8, 33–38, 40–41, 45, 53–60, 63–64, 66, 68, 71–72, 74, 76, 80–83, 91, 93, 98, 100, 102–131, 163–64, 166, 168, 191, 206, 216, 221–23, 229, 232, 240, 245

Voliva, Wilbur, 49, 55, 69–70, 107, 151
Voice of Healing, 197–200, 202–3, 213, 216, 240

Walthall, W. Jethro, 126
Warner, Daniel S., 15, 32
Wesley, John, 10–12, 17–20, 125
Woodworth-Etter, Maria B., 4, 6, 8, 32, 36, 68, 78–91, 94, 97–99, 114–15, 131, 216, 238–39, 245
Word of Faith Movement, 194, 209, 213–14, 219, 231, 233, 237
Wigglesworth, Smith, 97, 215–16, 238

Yeomans, Lilian B., 66
Yoakum, F. E., 115

Zion City, 3, 29, 32–33, 37, 40–41, 47–66, 67–75, 81–82, 90–91, 99, 101, 107, 110, 151, 176, 182, 195, 198–99
Zion City Band, 49, 51–53, 58

www.ingramcontent.com/pod-product-compliance
Lightning Source LLC
Chambersburg PA
CBHW061434300426
44114CB00014B/1676